Software Technology and Theoretical Computer Science

Software Technology and Theoretical Computer Science

Edited by
Lara Briggs

Willford Press
www.willfordpress.com

Published by Willford Press,
118-35 Queens Blvd., Suite 400,
Forest Hills, NY 11375, USA

ISBN: 978-1-64728-445-9

Cataloging-in-publication Data

Software technology and theoretical computer science / edited by Lara Briggs.
p. cm.
Includes bibliographical references and index.
ISBN 978-1-64728-445-9
1. Computer software. 2. Systems software. 3. Software engineering.
4. Computer science. I. Briggs, Lara.
QA76.754 .S64 2023
005.3--dc23

For information on all Willford Press publications
visit our website at www.willfordpress.com

Willford Press

Contents

Preface

Software refers to the complete set of processes, programs and routines linked with the operation of a computer system. It is utilized to develop non-physical tools to solve information-based issues. Software technology encompasses the programming languages, methods and tools that may be used in the development of software. Some examples of software are Google Docs, Directory Opus, MySQL, BIOS, MS Access, WinZip, etc. Theoretical computer science (TCS) is a branch of general computer science and mathematics that focuses on the mathematical aspects of computer science including the type theory, theory of computation and lambda calculus. It covers a wide range of topics such as parallel and distributed computation, automata theory, algorithms, information theory, data structures, quantum computation, computational complexity, and probabilistic computation. This book explores all the important aspects of software technology and theoretical computer science in the present day scenario. It elucidates new techniques and their applications in a multidisciplinary manner. This book is a resource guide for experts as well as students.

This book is the end result of constructive efforts and intensive research done by experts in this field. The aim of this book is to enlighten the readers with recent information in this area of research. The information provided in this profound book would serve as a valuable reference to students and researchers in this field.

At the end, I would like to thank all the authors for devoting their precious time and providing their valuable contribution to this book. I would also like to express my gratitude to my fellow colleagues who encouraged me throughout the process.

Editor

1

Identifiers in Registers
Describing Network Algorithms with Logic

Benedikt Bollig, Patricia Bouyer, and Fabian Reiter(✉)

LSV, CNRS, ENS Paris-Saclay, Université Paris-Saclay, Cachan, France
{bollig,bouyer}@lsv.fr, fabian.reiter@gmail.com

Abstract. We propose a formal model of distributed computing based on register automata that captures a broad class of synchronous network algorithms. The local memory of each process is represented by a finite-state controller and a fixed number of registers, each of which can store the unique identifier of some process in the network. To underline the naturalness of our model, we show that it has the same expressive power as a certain extension of first-order logic on graphs whose nodes are equipped with a total order. Said extension lets us define new functions on the set of nodes by means of a so-called partial fixpoint operator. In spirit, our result bears close resemblance to a classical theorem of descriptive complexity theory that characterizes the complexity class PSPACE in terms of partial fixpoint logic (a proper superclass of the logic we consider here).

1 Introduction

This paper is part of an ongoing research project aiming to develop a *descriptive complexity* theory for *distributed computing.*

In classical sequential computing, descriptive complexity is a well-established field that connects computational complexity classes to equi-expressive classes of logical formulas. It began in the 1970s, when Fagin showed in [6] that the graph properties decidable by nondeterministic Turing machines in polynomial time are exactly those definable in existential second-order logic. This provided a logical—and thus machine-independent—characterization of the complexity class NP. Subsequently, many other popular classes, such as P, PSPACE, and EXPTIME were characterized in a similar manner (see for instance the textbooks [8,12,15]).

Of particular interest to us is a result due to Abiteboul, Vianu [1], and Vardi [19], which states that on structures equipped with a total order relation, the properties decidable in PSPACE coincide with those definable in *partial fixpoint logic.* The latter is an extension of first-order logic with an operator that allows us to inductively define new relations of arbitrary arity. Basically, this means that new relations can occur as free (second-order) variables in the logical formulas that define them. Those variables are initially interpreted as empty relations and then iteratively updated, using the defining formulas as update rules. If the sequence of updates converges to a fixpoint, then the ultimate interpretations are the relations reached in the limit. Otherwise, the variables are simply interpreted as empty relations. Hence the term "partial fixpoint".

While well-developed in the classical case, descriptive complexity has so far not received much attention in the setting of distributed network computing. As far as the authors are aware, the first step in this direction was taken by Hella et al. in [10,11], where they showed that basic *modal logic* evaluated on finite graphs has the same expressive power as a particular class of *distributed automata* operating in constant time. Those automata constitute a weak model of distributed computing in arbitrary network topologies, where all nodes synchronously execute the same finite-state machine and communicate with each other by broadcasting messages to their neighbors. Motivated by this result, several variants of distributed automata were investigated by Kuusisto and Reiter in [14,18] and [17] to establish similar connections with standard logics such as the *modal μ-calculus* and *monadic second-order logic*. However, since the models of computation investigated in those works are based on anonymous finite-state machines, they are much too weak to solve many of the problems typically considered in distributed computing, such as leader election or constructing a spanning tree. It would thus be desirable to also characterize stronger models.

A common assumption underlying many distributed algorithms is that each node of the considered network is given a unique identifier. This allows us, for instance, to elect a leader by making the nodes broadcast their identifiers and then choose the one with the smallest identifier as the leader. To formalize such algorithms, we need to go beyond finite-state machines because the number of bits required to encode a unique identifier grows logarithmically with the number of nodes in the network. Recently, in [2,3], Aiswarya, Bollig and Gastin introduced a synchronous model where, in addition to a finite-state controller, nodes also have a fixed number of registers in which they can store the identifiers of other nodes. Access to those registers is rather limited in the sense that their contents can be compared with respect to a total order, but their numeric values are unknown to the nodes. (This restriction corresponds precisely to the notion of *order-invariant* distributed algorithms, which was introduced by Naor and Stockmeyer in [16].) Similarly, register contents can be copied, but no new values can be generated. Since the original motivation for the model was to automatically verify certain distributed algorithms running on ring networks, its formal definition is tailored to that particular setting. However, the underlying principle can be generalized to arbitrary networks of unbounded maximum degree, which was the starting point for the present work.

Contributions. While on an intuitive level, the idea of finite-state machines equipped with additional registers might seem very natural, it does not immediately yield a formal model for distributed algorithms in arbitrary networks. In particular, it is not clear what would be the canonical way for nodes to communicate with a non-constant number of peers, if we require that they all follow the same, finitely representable set of rules.

The model we propose here, dubbed *distributed register automata*, is an attempt at a solution. As in [2,3], nodes proceed in synchronous rounds and have a fixed number of registers, which they can compare and update without having access to numeric values. The new key ingredient that allows us to formalize communication between nodes of unbounded degree is a local computing device we call *transition maker*. This is a special kind of register machine that the nodes can use to scan the states and register values of their entire neighborhood in a sequential manner. In every round, each node runs the transition maker to update its own local configuration (i.e., its state and register valuation) based on a snapshot of the local configurations of its neighbors in the previous round. A way of interpreting this is that the nodes communicate by broadcasting their local configurations as messages to their neighbors. Although the resulting model of computation is by no means universal, it allows formalizing algorithms for a wide range of problems, such as constructing a spanning tree (see Example 5) or testing whether a graph is Hamiltonian (see Example 6).

Nevertheless, our model is somewhat arbitrary, since it could be just one particular choice among many other similar definitions capturing different classes of distributed algorithms. What justifies our choice? This is where descriptive complexity comes into play. By identifying a logical formalism that has the same expressive power as distributed register automata, we provide substantial evidence for the naturalness of that model. Our formalism, referred to as *functional fixpoint logic*, is a fragment of the above-mentioned partial fixpoint logic. Like the latter, it also extends first-order logic with a partial fixpoint operator, but a weaker one that can only define unary functions instead of arbitrary relations. We show that on totally ordered graphs, this logic allows one to express precisely the properties that can be decided by distributed register automata. The connection is strongly reminiscent of Abiteboul, Vianu and Vardi's characterization of PSPACE, and thus contributes to the broader objective of extending classical descriptive complexity to the setting of distributed computing. Moreover, given that logical formulas are often more compact and easier to understand than abstract machines (compare Examples 6 and 8), logic could also become a useful tool in the formal specification of distributed algorithms.

The remainder of this paper is structured around our main result:

Theorem 1. *When restricted to finite graphs whose nodes are equipped with a total order, distributed register automata are effectively equivalent to functional fixpoint logic.*

After giving some preliminary definitions in Sect. 2, we formally introduce distributed register automata in Sect. 3 and functional fixpoint logic in Sect. 4. We then sketch the proof of Theorem 1 in Sect. 5, and conclude in Sect. 6.

2 Preliminaries

We denote the empty set by $\emptyset$, the set of nonnegative integers by $\mathbb{N} = \{0, 1, 2, \dots\}$, and the set of integers by $\mathbb{Z} = \{\dots, -1, 0, 1, \dots\}$. The cardinality of any set S is written as $|S|$ and the power set as 2^S.

In analogy to the commonly used notation for real intervals, we define the notation $[m:n] := \{i \in \mathbb{Z} \mid m \leq i \leq n\}$ for any $m, n \in \mathbb{Z}$ such that $m \leq n$. To indicate that an endpoint is excluded, we replace the corresponding square bracket with a parenthesis, e.g., $(m:n] := [m:n] \setminus \{m\}$. Furthermore, if we omit the first endpoint, it defaults to 0. This gives us shorthand notations such as $[n] := [0:n]$ and $[n) := [0:n) = [0:n-1]$.

All graphs we consider are finite, simple, undirected, and connected. For notational convenience, we identify their nodes with nonnegative integers, which also serve as unique identifiers. That is, when we talk about the *identifier* of a node, we mean its numerical representation. A *graph* is formally represented as a pair $G = (V, E)$, where the set V of *nodes* is equal to $[n)$, for some integer $n \geq 2$, and the set E consists of undirected *edges* of the form $e = \{u, v\} \subseteq V$ such that $u \neq v$. Additionally, E must satisfy that every pair of nodes is connected by a sequence of edges. The restriction to graphs of size at least two is for technical reasons; it ensures that we can always encode Boolean values as nodes.

We refer the reader to [5] for standard graph theoretic terms such as *neighbor*, *degree*, *maximum degree*, *distance*, and *spanning tree*.

Graphs are used to model computer networks, where nodes correspond to processes and edges to communication links. To represent the current configuration of a system as a graph, we equip each node with some additional information: the current state of the corresponding process, taken from a nonempty finite set Q, and some pointers to other processes, modeled by a finite set R of registers.

We call $\Sigma = (Q, R)$ a *signature* and define a *Σ-configuration* as a tuple $C = (G, \mathfrak{q}, \mathfrak{r})$, where $G = (V, E)$ is a graph, called the *underlying* graph of C, $\mathfrak{q}\colon V \to Q$ is a *state function* that assigns to each node a state $q \in Q$, and $\mathfrak{r}\colon V \to V^R$ is a *register valuation function* that associates with each node a *register valuation* $\rho \in V^R$. The set of all Σ-configurations is denoted by $\mathbb{C}(\Sigma)$. Figure 1 on page 6 illustrates part of a $(\{q_1, q_2, q_3\}, \{r_1, r_2, r_3\})$-configuration.

If $R = \emptyset$, then we are actually dealing with a tuple $(G, \mathfrak{q})$, which we call a *Q-labeled graph*. Accordingly, the elements of Q may also be called *labels*. A set P of labeled graphs will be referred to as a *graph property*. Moreover, if the labels are irrelevant, we set Q equal to the singleton $\mathbb{1} := \{\varepsilon\}$, where ε is our dummy label. In this case, we identify $(G, \mathfrak{q})$ with G and call it an *unlabeled* graph.

3 Distributed Register Automata

Many distributed algorithms can be seen as *transducers*. A leader-election algorithm, for instance, takes as input a network and outputs the same network, but with every process storing the identifier of the unique leader in some dedicated register r. Thus, the algorithm transforms a $(\mathbb{1}, \emptyset)$-configuration into a $(\mathbb{1}, \{r\})$-configuration. We say that it defines a $(\mathbb{1}, \emptyset)$-$(\mathbb{1}, \{r\})$-transduction. By the same token, if we consider distributed algorithms that *decide* graph properties (e.g., whether a graph is Hamiltonian), then we are dealing with a $(I, \emptyset)$-$(\{\text{YES}, \text{NO}\}, \emptyset)$-transduction, where I is some set of labels. The idea is that a graph will be accepted if and only if every process eventually outputs YES.

Let us now formalize the notion of transduction. For any two signatures $\Sigma^{in} = (I, R^{in})$ and $\Sigma^{out} = (O, R^{out})$, a Σ^{in}-Σ^{out}-*transduction* is a *partial* mapping $T\colon \mathbb{C}(\Sigma^{in}) \to \mathbb{C}(\Sigma^{out})$ such that, if defined, $T(G, \mathfrak{q}, \mathfrak{r}) = (G, \mathfrak{q}', \mathfrak{r}')$ for some $\mathfrak{q}'$ and $\mathfrak{r}'$. That is, a transduction does not modify the underlying graph but only the states and register valuations. We denote the set of all Σ^{in}-Σ^{out}-transductions by $\mathbb{T}(\Sigma^{in}, \Sigma^{out})$ and refer to Σ^{in} and Σ^{out} as the *input* and *output signatures* of T. By extension, I and O are called the sets of *input* and *output labels*, and R^{in} and R^{out} the sets of *input* and *output registers*. Similarly, any Σ^{in}-configuration C can be referred to as an *input configuration* of T and $T(C)$ as an *output configuration*.

Next, we introduce our formal model of distributed algorithms.

Definition 2 (Distributed register automaton). *Let $\Sigma^{in} = (I, R^{in})$ and $\Sigma^{out} = (O, R^{out})$ be two signatures. A* distributed register automaton *(or simply* automaton*) with input signature Σ^{in} and output signature Σ^{out} is a tuple $A = (Q, R, \iota, \Delta, H, o)$ consisting of a nonempty finite set Q of* states*, a finite set R of* registers *that includes both R^{in} and R^{out}, an* input function *$\iota\colon I \to Q$, a transition maker Δ whose specification will be given in Definition 3 below, a set $H \subseteq Q$ of* halting states*, and an* output function *$o\colon H \to O$. The registers in $R \setminus (R^{in} \cup R^{out})$ are called* auxiliary registers.

Automaton A computes a transduction $T_A \in \mathbb{T}(\Sigma^{in}, \Sigma^{out})$. To do so, it runs in a sequence of synchronous rounds on the input configuration's underlying graph $G = (V, E)$. After each round, the automaton's global configuration is a (Q, R)-configuration $C = (G, \mathfrak{q}, \mathfrak{r})$, i.e., the underlying graph is always G. As mentioned before, for a node $v \in V$, we interpret $\mathfrak{q}(v) \in Q$ as the current state of v and $\mathfrak{r}(v) \in V^R$ as the current register valuation of v. Abusing notation, we let $C(v) := (\mathfrak{q}(v), \mathfrak{r}(v))$ and say that $C(v)$ is the *local configuration* of v. In Fig. 1, the local configuration node 17 is $(q_1, \{r_1, r_2, r_3 \mapsto 17, 34, 98\})$.

For a given input configuration $C = (G, \mathfrak{q}, \mathfrak{r}) \in \mathbb{C}(\Sigma^{in})$, the automaton's *initial configuration* is $C' = (G, \iota \circ \mathfrak{q}, \mathfrak{r}')$, where for all $v \in V$, we have $\mathfrak{r}'(v)(r) = \mathfrak{r}(v)(r)$ if $r \in R^{in}$, and $\mathfrak{r}'(v)(r) = v$ if $r \in R \setminus R^{in}$. This means that every node v is initialized to state $\iota(\mathfrak{q}(v))$, and v's initial register valuation $\mathfrak{r}'(v)$ assigns v's own identifier (provided by G) to all non-input registers while keeping the given values assigned by $\mathfrak{r}(v)$ to the input registers.

Each subsequent configuration is obtained by running the transition maker Δ synchronously on all nodes. As we will see, Δ computes a function

$$[\![\Delta]\!]\colon (Q \times V^R)^+ \to Q \times V^R$$

that maps from nonempty sequences of local configurations to local configurations. This allows the automaton A to transition from a given configuration C to the next configuration C' as follows. For every node $u \in V$ of degree d, we consider the list $v_1, \ldots v_d$ of u's neighbors sorted in ascending (identifier) order, i.e., $v_i < v_{i+1}$ for $i \in [1:d)$. (See Fig. 1 for an example, where u corresponds to node 17.) If u is already in a halting state, i.e., if $C(u) = (q, \rho) \in H \times V^R$,

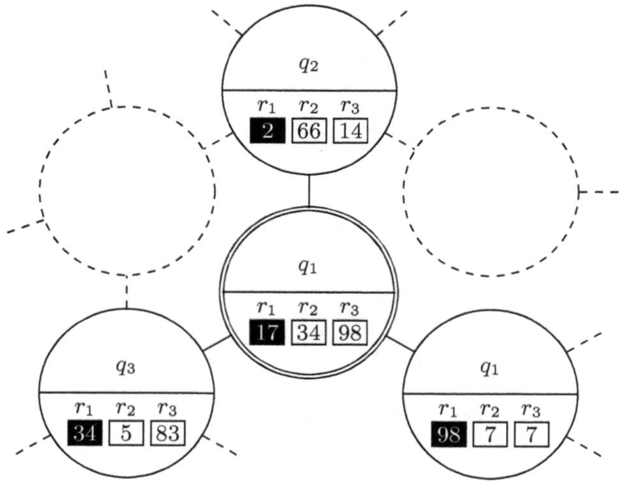

Fig. 1. Part of a configuration, as seen by a single node. Assuming the identifiers of the nodes are the values represented in black boxes (i.e., those stored in register r_1), the automaton at node 17 will update its own local configuration (q_1, $\{r_1, r_2, r_3 \mapsto 17, 34, 98\}$) by running the transition maker on the sequence consisting of the local configurations of nodes 17, 2, 34, and 98 (in that exact order).

then its local configuration does not change anymore, i.e., $C'(u) = C(u)$. Otherwise, we define $C'(u) = [\![\Delta]\!]\big(C(u), C(v_1), \dots, C(v_d)\big)$, which we may write more suggestively as

$$[\![\Delta]\!]\colon C(u) \xmapsto{C(v_1),\dots,C(v_d)} C'(u).$$

Intuitively, node u updates its own local configuration by using Δ to scan a snapshot of its neighbors' local configurations. As the system is synchronous, this update procedure is performed simultaneously by all nodes.

A configuration $C = (G, \mathfrak{q}, \mathfrak{r})$ is called a *halting configuration* if all nodes are in a halting state, i.e., if $\mathfrak{q}(v) \in H$ for all $v \in V$. We say that A *halts* if it reaches a halting configuration.

The output configuration produced by a halting configuration $C = (G, \mathfrak{q}, \mathfrak{r})$ is the Σ^{out}-configuration $C' = (G, o \circ \mathfrak{q}, \mathfrak{r}')$, where for all $v \in V$ and $r \in R^{out}$, we have $\mathfrak{r}'(v)(r) = \mathfrak{r}(v)(r)$. In other words, each node v outputs the state $o(\mathfrak{q}(v))$ and keeps in its output registers the values assigned by $\mathfrak{r}(v)$.

It is now obvious that A defines a transduction $T_A\colon \mathbb{C}(\Sigma^{in}) \to \mathbb{C}(\Sigma^{out})$. If A receives the input configuration $C \in \mathbb{C}(\Sigma^{in})$ and eventually halts and produces the output configuration $C' \in \mathbb{C}(\Sigma^{out})$, then $T_A(C) = C'$. Otherwise (if A does not halt), $T_A(C)$ is undefined.

Deciding graph properties. Our primary objective is to use distributed register automata as decision procedures for graph properties. Therefore, we will focus on automata A that halt in a finite number of rounds on *every* input configuration, and we often restrict to input signatures of the form $(I, \emptyset)$ and the output signature $(\{\text{YES}, \text{NO}\}, \emptyset)$. For example, for $I = \{a, b\}$, we may be interested in the set of I-labeled graphs that have exactly one a-labeled node v (the "leader"). We stipulate that A *accepts* an input configuration C with underlying graph $G = (V, E)$ if $T_A(C) = (G, \mathfrak{q}, \mathfrak{r})$ such that $\mathfrak{q}(v) = \text{YES}$ for *all* $v \in V$. Conversely, A *rejects* C if $T_A(C) = (G, \mathfrak{q}, \mathfrak{r})$ such that $\mathfrak{q}(v) = \text{NO}$ for *some* $v \in V$. This corresponds to the usual definition chosen in the emerging field of *distributed decision* [7]. Accordingly, a graph property P is *decided* by A if the automaton accepts all input configurations that satisfy P and rejects all the others.

It remains to explain how the transition maker Δ works internally.

Definition 3 (Transition maker). *Suppose that $A = (Q, R, \iota, \Delta, H, o)$ is a distributed register automaton. Then its* transition maker $\Delta = (\tilde{Q}, \tilde{R}, \tilde{\iota}, \tilde{\delta}, \tilde{o})$ *consists of a nonempty finite set $\tilde{Q}$ of* inner states, *a finite set $\tilde{R}$ of* inner registers *that is disjoint from R, an* inner initial state $\tilde{\iota} \in \tilde{Q}$, *an* inner transition function $\tilde{\delta}\colon \tilde{Q} \times Q \times 2^{(\tilde{R} \cup R)^2} \to \tilde{Q} \times (\tilde{R} \cup R)^{\tilde{R}}$, *and an* inner output function $\tilde{o}\colon \tilde{Q} \to Q \times \tilde{R}^R$.

Basically, a transition maker $\Delta = (\tilde{Q}, \tilde{R}, \tilde{\iota}, \tilde{\delta}, \tilde{o})$ is a sequential register automaton (in the spirit of [13]) that reads a nonempty sequence $(q_0, \rho_0), \ldots, (q_d, \rho_d) \in (Q \times V^R)^+$ of local configurations of A in order to produce a new local configuration (q', ρ'). While reading this sequence, it traverses itself a sequence $(\tilde{q}_0, \tilde{\rho}_0), \ldots, (\tilde{q}_{d+1}, \tilde{\rho}_{d+1})$ of *inner configurations*, which each consist of an inner state $\tilde{q}_i \in \tilde{Q}$ and an *inner register valuation* $\tilde{\rho}_i \in (V \cup \{\bot\})^{\tilde{R}}$, where the symbol $\bot$ represents an undefined value. For the initial inner configuration, we set $\tilde{q}_0 = \tilde{\iota}$ and $\tilde{\rho}_0(\tilde{r}) = \bot$ for all $\tilde{r} \in \tilde{R}$. Now for $i \in [d]$, when Δ is in the inner configuration $(\tilde{q}_i, \tilde{\rho}_i)$ and reads the local configuration (q_i, ρ_i), it can compare all values assigned to the inner registers and registers by $\tilde{\rho}_i$ and ρ_i (with respect to the order relation on V). In other words, it has access to the binary relation $\prec_i \subseteq (\tilde{R} \cup R)^2$ such that for $\tilde{r}, \tilde{s} \in \tilde{R}$ and $r, s \in R$, we have $\tilde{r} \prec_i r$ if and only if $\tilde{\rho}_i(\tilde{r}) < \rho_i(r)$, and analogously for $r \prec_i \tilde{r}$, $\tilde{r} \prec_i \tilde{s}$, and $r \prec_i s$. In particular, if $\tilde{\rho}_i(\tilde{r}) = \bot$, then $\tilde{r}$ is incomparable with respect to $\prec_i$. Equipped with this relation, Δ transitions to $(\tilde{q}_{i+1}, \tilde{\rho}_{i+1})$ by evaluating $\tilde{\delta}(\tilde{q}_i, q_i, \prec_i) = (\tilde{q}_{i+1}, \tilde{\alpha})$ and computing $\tilde{\rho}_{i+1}$ such that $\tilde{\rho}_{i+1}(\tilde{r}) = \tilde{\rho}_i(\tilde{s})$ if $\tilde{\alpha}(\tilde{r}) = \tilde{s}$, and $\tilde{\rho}_{i+1}(\tilde{r}) = \rho_i(s)$ if $\tilde{\alpha}(\tilde{r}) = s$, where $\tilde{r}, \tilde{s} \in \tilde{R}$ and $s \in R$. Finally, after having read the entire input sequence and reached the inner configuration $(\tilde{q}_{d+1}, \tilde{\rho}_{d+1})$, the transition maker outputs the local configuration (q', ρ') such that $\tilde{o}(\tilde{q}_{d+1}) = (q', \tilde{\beta})$ and $\tilde{\beta}(r) = \tilde{r}$ implies $\rho'(r) = \tilde{\rho}_{d+1}(\tilde{r})$. Here we assume without loss of generality that Δ guarantees that $\rho'(r) \neq \bot$ for all $r \in R$.

Remark 4. Recall that $V = [n]$ for any graph $G = (V, E)$ with n nodes. However, as registers cannot be compared with constants, this actually represents an arbitrary assignment of unique, totally ordered identifiers. To determine the smallest identifier (i.e., 0), the nodes can run an algorithm such as the following.

Example 5 (Spanning tree). We present a simple automaton $A = (Q, R, \iota, \Delta, H, o)$ with input signature $\Sigma^{in} = (\mathbb{1}, \emptyset)$ and output signature $\Sigma^{out} = (\mathbb{1}, \{\mathit{parent}, \mathit{root}\})$ that computes a (breadth-first) spanning tree of its input

Algorithm 1. Transition maker of the automaton from Example 5

```
if ∃ neighbor nb (nb.root < my.root):                                              } Rule 1
    my.state ← 1;   my.parent ← nb.self;   my.root ← nb.root

else if my.state = 1
        ∧ ∀ neighbor nb [ nb.root = my.root ∧                                       } Rule 2
                          (nb.parent ≠ my.self ∨ nb.state = 2) ]:
    my.state ← 2

else if (my.state = 2 ∧ my.root = my.self) ∨ (my.parent.state = 3):                } Rule 3
    my.state ← 3

else do nothing
```

graph $G = (V, E)$, rooted at the node with the smallest identifier. More precisely, in the computed output configuration $C = (G, \mathfrak{q}, \mathfrak{r})$, every node will store the identifier of its tree parent in register *parent* and the identifier of the root (i.e., the smallest identifier) in register *root*. Thus, as a side effect, A also solves the leader election problem by electing the root as the leader.

The automaton operates in three phases, which are represented by the set of states $Q = \{1, 2, 3\}$. A node terminates as soon as it reaches the third phase, i.e., we set $H = \{3\}$. Accordingly, the (trivial) input and output functions are $\iota\colon \varepsilon \mapsto 1$ and $o\colon 3 \mapsto \varepsilon$. In addition to the output registers, each node has an auxiliary register *self* that will always store its own identifier. Thus, we choose $R = \{\mathit{self}, \mathit{parent}, \mathit{root}\}$. For the sake of simplicity, we describe the transition maker Δ in Algorithm 1 using pseudocode rules. However, it should be clear that these rules could be relatively easily implemented according to Definition 3.

All nodes start in state 1, which represents the tree-construction phase. By Rule 1, whenever an active node (i.e., a node in state 1 or 2) sees a neighbor whose *root* register contains a smaller identifier than the node's own *root* register, it updates its *parent* and *root* registers accordingly and switches to state 1. To resolve the nondeterminism in Rule 1, we stipulate that *nb* is chosen to be the neighbor with the smallest identifier among those whose *root* register contains the smallest value seen so far.

As can be easily shown by induction on the number of communication rounds, the nodes have to apply Rule 1 no more than diameter(G) times in order for the pointers in register *parent* to represent a valid spanning tree (where the root points to itself). However, since the nodes do not know when diameter(G) rounds have elapsed, they must also check that the current configuration does indeed represent a single tree, as opposed to a forest. They do so by propagating a signal, in form of state 2, from the leaves up to the root.

By Rule 2, if an active node whose neighbors all agree on the same root realizes that it is a leaf or that all of its children are in state 2, then it switches to state 2 itself. Assuming the *parent* pointers in the current configuration already represent a single tree, Rule 2 ensures that the root will eventually be notified of this fact (when all of its children are in state 2). Otherwise, the *parent* pointers represent a forest, and every tree contains at least one node that has a neighbor outside of the tree (as we assume the underlying graph is connected).

Depending on the input graph, a node can switch arbitrarily often between states 1 and 2. Once the spanning tree has been constructed and every node is in state 2, the only node that knows this is the root. In order for the algorithm to terminate, Rule 3 then makes the root broadcast an acknowledgment message down the tree, which causes all nodes to switch to the halting state 3. □

Building on the automaton from Example 5, we now give an example of a graph property that can be decided in our model of distributed computing. The following automaton should be compared to the logical formula presented later in Example 8, which is much more compact and much easier to specify.

Example 6 (Hamiltonian cycle). We describe an automaton with input signature $\Sigma^{in} = (\mathbb{1}, \{parent, root\})$ and output signature $\Sigma^{out} = (\{\text{YES}, \text{NO}\}, \emptyset)$ that decides if the underlying graph $G = (V, E)$ of its input configuration $C = (G, \mathfrak{q}, \mathfrak{r})$ is Hamiltonian, i.e., whether G contains a cycle that goes through each node exactly once. The automaton works under the assumption that $\mathfrak{r}$ encodes a valid spanning tree of G in the registers *parent* and *root*, as constructed by the automaton from Example 5. Hence, by combining the two automata, we could easily construct a third one that decides the graph property of Hamiltonicity.

The automaton $A = (Q, R, \iota, \Delta, H, o)$ presented here implements a simple backtracking algorithm that tries to traverse G along a Hamiltonian cycle. Its set of states is $Q = \big(\{unvisited, visited, backtrack\} \times \{idle, request, good, bad\}\big) \cup H$, with the set of halting states $H = \{\text{YES}, \text{NO}\}$. Each non-halting state consists of two components, the first one serving for the backtracking procedure and the second one for communicating in the spanning tree. The input function ι initializes every node to the state $(unvisited, idle)$, while the output function simply returns the answers chosen by the nodes, i.e., $o\colon \text{YES} \mapsto \text{YES},\ \text{NO} \mapsto \text{NO}$. In addition to the input registers, each node has a register *self* storing its own identifier and a register *successor* to point to its successor in a (partially constructed) Hamiltonian path. That is, $R = \{self, parent, root, successor\}$. We now describe the algorithm in an informal way. It is, in principle, easy to implement in the transition maker Δ, but a thorough formalization would be rather cumbersome.

In the first round, the root marks itself as *visited* and updates its *successor* register to point towards its smallest neighbor (the one with the smallest identifier). Similarly, in each subsequent round, any *unvisited* node that is pointed to by one of its neighbors marks itself as *visited* and points towards its smallest *unvisited* neighbor. However, if all neighbors are already *visited*, the node instead sends the *backtrack* signal to its predecessor and switches back to *unvisited* (in the following round). Whenever a *visited* node receives the *backtrack* signal from its *successor*, it tries to update its *successor* to the next-smallest *unvisited* neighbor. If no such neighbor exists, it resets its *successor* pointer to itself, propagates the *backtrack* signal to its predecessor, and becomes *unvisited* in the following round.

There is only one exception to the above rules: if a node that is adjacent to the root cannot find any *unvisited* neighbor, it chooses the root as its *successor*.

This way, the constructed path becomes a cycle. In order to check whether that cycle is Hamiltonian, the root now broadcast a *request* down the spanning tree. If the *request* reaches an *unvisited* node, that node replies by sending the message *bad* towards the root. On the other hand, every *visited* leaf replies with the message *good*. While *bad* is always forwarded up to the root, *good* is only forwarded by nodes that receive this message from all of their children. If the root receives only *good*, then it knows that the current cycle is Hamiltonian and it switches to the halting state YES. The information is then broadcast through the entire graph, so that all nodes eventually accept. Otherwise, the root sends the *backtrack* signal to its predecessor, and the search for a Hamiltonian cycle continues. In case there is none (in particular, if there is not even an arbitrary cycle), the root will eventually receive the *backtrack* signal from its greatest neighbor, which indicates that all possibilities have been exhausted. If this happens, the root switches to the halting state NO, and all other nodes eventually do the same. □

4 Functional Fixpoint Logic

In order to introduce functional fixpoint logic, we first give a definition of first-order logic that suits our needs. Formulas will always be evaluated on *ordered*, undirected, connected, I-labeled graphs, where I is a fixed finite set of labels.

Throughout this paper, let $\mathcal{N}$ be an infinite supply of *node variables* and $\mathcal{F}$ be an infinite supply of *function variables*; we refer to them collectively as *variables*. The corresponding set of *terms* is generated by the grammar $t ::= x \mid f(t)$, where $x \in \mathcal{N}$ and $f \in \mathcal{F}$. With this, the set of *formulas* of *first-order logic* over I is given by the grammar

$$\varphi ::= \langle a \rangle\, t \mid s < t \mid s \leftrightarrow t \mid \neg\varphi \mid \varphi \vee \varphi \mid \exists x\, \varphi,$$

where s and t are terms, $a \in I$, and $x \in \mathcal{N}$. As usual, we may also use the additional operators $\wedge$, $\Rightarrow$, $\Leftrightarrow$, $\forall$ to make our formulas more readable, and we define the notations $s \leq t$, $s = t$, and $s \neq t$ as abbreviations for $\neg(t < s)$, $(s \leq t) \wedge (t \leq s)$, and $\neg(s = t)$, respectively.

The sets of *free variables* of a term t and a formula φ are denoted by $\mathrm{free}(t)$ and $\mathrm{free}(\varphi)$, respectively. While node variables can be bound by the usual quantifiers $\exists$ and $\forall$, function variables can be bound by a partial fixpoint operator that we will introduce below.

To interpret a formula φ on an I-labeled graph $(G, \mathfrak{q})$ with $G = (V, E)$, we are given a *variable assignment* σ for the variables that occur freely in φ. This is a partial function $\sigma \colon \mathcal{N} \cup \mathcal{F} \to V \cup V^V$ such that $\sigma(x) \in V$ if x is a free node variable and $\sigma(f) \in V^V$ if f is a free function variable. We call $\sigma(x)$ and $\sigma(f)$ the *interpretations* of x and f under σ, and denote them by x^σ and f^σ, respectively. For a composite term t, the corresponding interpretation t^σ under σ is defined in the obvious way.

We write $(G, \mathfrak{q}), \sigma \models \varphi$ to denote that $(G, \mathfrak{q})$ *satisfies* φ under assignment σ. If φ does not contain any free variables, we simply write $(G, \mathfrak{q}) \models \varphi$ and refer to the set P of I-labeled graphs that satisfy φ as the graph property *defined* by φ. Naturally enough, we say that two devices (i.e., automata or formulas) are *equivalent* if they specify (i.e., decide or define) the same graph property and that two classes of devices are equivalent if their members specify the same class of graph properties.

As we assume that the reader is familiar with first-order logic, we only define the semantics of the atomic formulas (whose syntax is not completely standard):

$$\begin{array}{llll}
(G,\mathfrak{q}),\sigma \models \langle a\rangle\, t & \text{iff} & \mathfrak{q}(t^\sigma) = a & (\text{“}t \text{ has label } a\text{”}),\\
(G,\mathfrak{q}),\sigma \models s < t & \text{iff} & s^\sigma < t^\sigma & (\text{“}s \text{ is smaller than } t\text{”}),\\
(G,\mathfrak{q}),\sigma \models s \leftrightarrow t & \text{iff} & \{s^\sigma, t^\sigma\} \in E & (\text{“}s \text{ and } t \text{ are adjacent”}).
\end{array}$$

We now turn to *functional fixpoint logic*. Syntactically, it is defined as the extension of first-order logic that allows us to write formulas of the form

$$\operatorname{pfp}\begin{bmatrix} f_1\colon\ \varphi_1(f_1,\dots,f_\ell,\textsc{in},\textsc{out}) \\ \vdots \\ f_\ell\colon\ \varphi_\ell(f_1,\dots,f_\ell,\textsc{in},\textsc{out}) \end{bmatrix}\psi, \qquad (*)$$

where $f_1,\dots,f_\ell \in \mathcal{F}$, $\textsc{in},\textsc{out} \in \mathcal{N}$, and $\varphi_1,\dots,\varphi_\ell,\psi$ are formulas. We use the notation “$\varphi_i(f_1,\dots,f_\ell,\textsc{in},\textsc{out})$” to emphasize that $f_1,\dots,f_\ell,\textsc{in},\textsc{out}$ may occur freely in φ_i (possibly among other variables). The free variables of formula $(*)$ are given by $\bigcup_{i\in(\ell]}\big[\mathrm{free}(\varphi_i)\setminus\{f_1,\dots,f_\ell,\textsc{in},\textsc{out}\}\big] \cup \big[\mathrm{free}(\psi)\setminus\{f_1,\dots,f_\ell\}\big]$.

The idea is that the *partial fixpoint operator* pfp binds the function variables $f_1,\dots,f_\ell$. The ℓ lines in square brackets constitute a system of function definitions that provide an interpretation of $f_1,\dots,f_\ell$, using the special node variables IN and OUT as helpers to represent input and output values. This is why pfp also binds any free occurrences of IN and OUT in $\varphi_1,\dots,\varphi_\ell$, but not in ψ.

To specify the semantics of $(*)$, we first need to make some preliminary observations. As before, we consider a fixed I-labeled graph $(G,\mathfrak{q})$ with $G=(V,E)$ and assume that we are given a variable assignment σ for the free variables of $(*)$. With respect to $(G,\mathfrak{q})$ and σ, each formula φ_i induces an operator $F_{\varphi_i}\colon (V^V)^\ell \to V^V$ that takes some interpretation of the function variables $f_1,\dots,f_\ell$ and outputs a new interpretation of f_i, corresponding to the function graph defined by φ_i via the node variables IN and OUT. For inputs on which φ_i does not define a functional relationship, the new interpretation of f_i behaves like the identity function. More formally, given a variable assignment $\hat{\sigma}$ that extends σ with interpretations of $f_1,\dots,f_\ell$, the operator F_{φ_i} maps $f_1^{\hat{\sigma}},\dots,f_\ell^{\hat{\sigma}}$ to the function f_i^{new} such that for all $u \in V$,

$$f_i^{\text{new}}(u) = \begin{cases} v & \text{if } v \text{ is the unique node in } V \textit{ s.t. } (G,\mathfrak{q}),\hat{\sigma}[\textsc{in},\textsc{out} \mapsto u,v] \models \varphi_i,\\ u & \text{otherwise.}\end{cases}$$

Here, $\hat{\sigma}[\text{IN}, \text{OUT} \mapsto u, v]$ is the extension of $\hat{\sigma}$ interpreting IN as u and OUT as v.

In this way, the operators $F_{\varphi_1}, \dots, F_{\varphi_\ell}$ give rise to an infinite sequence $(f_1^k, \dots, f_\ell^k)_{k \geq 0}$ of tuples of functions, called *stages*, where the initial stage contains solely the identity function id_V and each subsequent stage is obtained from its predecessor by componentwise application of the operators. More formally,

$$f_i^0 = \text{id}_V = \{u \mapsto u \mid u \in V\} \qquad \text{and} \qquad f_i^{k+1} = F_{\varphi_i}(f_1^k, \dots, f_\ell^k),$$

for $i \in (\ell]$ and $k \geq 0$. Now, since we have not imposed any restrictions on the formulas φ_i, this sequence might never stabilize, i.e, it is possible that $(f_1^k, \dots, f_\ell^k) \neq (f_1^{k+1}, \dots, f_\ell^{k+1})$ for all $k \geq 0$. Otherwise, the sequence reaches a (simultaneous) fixpoint at some position k no greater than $|V|^{|V| \cdot \ell}$ (the number of ℓ-tuples of functions on V).

We define the *partial fixpoint* $(f_1^\infty, \dots, f_\ell^\infty)$ of the operators $F_{\varphi_1}, \dots, F_{\varphi_\ell}$ to be the reached fixpoint if it exists, and the tuple of identity functions otherwise. That is, for $i \in (\ell]$,

$$f_i^\infty = \begin{cases} f_i^k & \text{if there exists } k \geq 0 \text{ such that } f_j^k = f_j^{k+1} \text{ for all } j \in (\ell], \\ \text{id}_V & \text{otherwise.} \end{cases}$$

Having introduced the necessary background, we can finally provide the semantics of the formula $\text{pfp}[f_i \colon \varphi_i]_{i \in (\ell]}\, \psi$ presented in $(*)$:

$$(G, \mathfrak{q}), \sigma \models \text{pfp}[f_i \colon \varphi_i]_{i \in (\ell]}\, \psi \qquad \text{iff} \qquad (G, \mathfrak{q}), \sigma[f_i \mapsto f_i^\infty]_{i \in (\ell]} \models \psi,$$

where $\sigma[f_i \mapsto f_i^\infty]_{i \in (\ell]}$ is the extension of σ that interprets f_i as f_i^∞, for $i \in (\ell]$. In other words, the formula $\text{pfp}[f_i \colon \varphi_i]_{i \in (\ell]}\, \psi$ can intuitively be read as

"if $f_1, \dots, f_\ell$ are interpreted as the partial fixpoint of $\varphi_1, \dots, \varphi_\ell$, then ψ holds".

Syntactic Sugar

Before we consider a concrete formula (in Example 8), we first introduce some "syntactic sugar" to make using functional fixpoint logic more pleasant.

Set variables. According to our definition of functional fixpoint logic, the operator pfp can bind only function variables. However, functions can be used to encode sets of nodes in a straightforward manner: any set U may be represented by a function that maps nodes outside of U to themselves and nodes inside U to nodes distinct from themselves. Therefore, we may fix an infinite supply $\mathcal{S}$ of *set variables*, and extend the syntax of first-order logic to allow atomic formulas of the form $t \in X$, where t is a term and X is a set variable in $\mathcal{S}$. Naturally, the semantics is that "t is an element of X". To bind set variables, we can then write partial fixpoint formulas of the form $\text{pfp}\big[(f_i \colon \varphi_i)_{i \in (\ell]}, (X_i \colon \vartheta_i)_{i \in (m]}\big]\, \psi$, where $f_1, \dots, f_\ell \in \mathcal{F}$, $X_1, \dots, X_m \in \mathcal{S}$, and $\varphi_1, \dots, \varphi_\ell, \vartheta_1, \dots, \vartheta_m, \psi$ are formulas. The stages of the partial fixpoint induction are computed as before, but each set variable X_i is initialized to $\emptyset$, and falls back to $\emptyset$ in case the sequence of stages does not converge to a fixpoint.

Quantifiers over functions and sets. Partial fixpoint inductions allow us to iterate over various interpretations of function and set variables and thus provide a way of expressing (second-order) quantification over functions and sets. Since we restrict ourselves to graphs whose nodes are totally ordered, we can easily define a suitable order of iteration and a corresponding partial fixpoint induction that traverses all possible interpretations of a given function or set variable. To make this more convenient, we enrich the language of functional fixpoint logic with second-order quantifiers, allowing us to write formulas of the form $\exists f\, \varphi$ and $\exists X\, \varphi$, where $f \in \mathcal{F}$, $X \in \mathcal{S}$, and φ is a formula. Obviously, the semantics is that "there exists a function f, or a set X, respectively, such that φ holds".

As a consequence, it is possible to express any graph property definable in *monadic second-order logic*, the extension of first-order logic with set quantifiers.

Corollary 7. *When restricted to finite graphs equipped with a total order, functional fixpoint logic is strictly more expressive than monadic second-order logic.*

The strictness of the inclusion in the above corollary follows from the fact that even on totally ordered graphs, Hamiltonicity cannot be defined in monadic second-order logic (see, e.g., the proof in [4, Prp. 5.13]). As the following example shows, this property is easy to express in functional fixpoint logic.

Example 8 (Hamiltonian cycle). The following formula of functional fixpoint logic defines the graph property of Hamiltonicity. That is, an unlabeled graph G satisfies this formula if and only if there exists a cycle in G that goes through each node exactly once.

$$\exists f \left[\begin{array}{l} \forall x\big(f(x) \leftrightarrow x\big) \;\wedge\; \forall x\, \exists y\big[f(y) = x \;\wedge\; \forall z\big(f(z) = x \;\Rightarrow\; z = y\big)\big] \;\wedge \\ \forall X\Big(\big[\exists x(x \in X) \;\wedge\; \forall y\big(y \in X \Rightarrow f(y) \in X\big)\big] \;\Rightarrow\; \forall y(y \in X)\Big) \end{array} \right]$$

Here, $x, y, z \in \mathcal{N}$, $X \in \mathcal{S}$, and $f \in \mathcal{F}$. Intuitively, we represent a given Hamiltonian cycle by a function f that tells us for each node x, which of x's neighbors we should visit next in order to traverse the entire cycle. Thus, f actually represents a directed version of the cycle.

To ensure the existence of a Hamiltonian cycle, our formula states that there is a function f satisfying the following two conditions. By the first line, each node x must have exactly one f-predecessor and one f-successor, both of which must be neighbors of x. By the second line, if we start at any node x and collect into a set X all the nodes reachable from x (by following the path specified by f), then X must contain all nodes. □

5 Translating Between Automata and Logic

Having introduced both automata and logic, we can proceed to explain the first part of Theorem 1 (stated in Sect. 1), i.e., how distributed register automata can be translated into functional fixpoint logic.

Proposition 9. *For every distributed register automaton that decides a graph property, we can construct an equivalent formula of functional fixpoint logic.*

Proof (sketch). Given a distributed register automaton $A = (Q, R, \iota, \Delta, H, o)$ deciding a graph property P over label set I, we can construct a formula φ_A of functional fixpoint logic that defines P. For each state $q \in Q$, our formula uses a set variable X_q to represent the set of nodes of the input graph that are in state q. Also, for each register $r \in R$, it uses a function variable f_r to represent the function that maps each node u to the node v whose identifier is stored in u's register r. By means of a partial fixpoint operator, we enforce that on any I-labeled graph $(G, \mathfrak{q})$, the final interpretations of $(X_q)_{q \in Q}$ and $(f_r)_{r \in R}$ represent the halting configuration reached by A on $(G, \mathfrak{q})$. The main formula is simply

$$\varphi_A := \operatorname{pfp}\begin{bmatrix}(X_q \colon \varphi_q)_{q \in Q} \\ (f_r \colon \varphi_r)_{r \in R}\end{bmatrix} \forall x \Big(\bigvee_{p \in H \colon o(p) = \text{YES}} x \in X_p \Big),$$

which states that all nodes end up in a halting state that outputs YES.

Basically, the subformulas $(\varphi_q)_{q \in Q}$ and $(\varphi_r)_{r \in R}$ can be constructed in such a way that for all $i \in \mathbb{N}$, the $(i+1)$-th stage of the partial fixpoint induction represents the configuration reached by A in the i-th round. To achieve this, each of the subformulas contains a nested partial fixpoint formula describing the result computed by the transition maker Δ between two consecutive synchronous rounds, using additional set and function variables to encode the inner configurations of Δ at each node. Thus, each stage of the nested partial fixpoint induction corresponds to a single step in the transition maker's sequential scanning process. □

Let us now consider the opposite direction and sketch how to go from functional fixpoint logic to distributed register automata.

Proposition 10. *For every formula of functional fixpoint logic that defines a graph property, we can construct an equivalent distributed register automaton.*

Proof (sketch). We proceed by structural induction: each subformula φ will be evaluated by a dedicated automaton A_φ, and several such automata can then be combined to build an automaton for a composite formula. For this purpose, it is convenient to design *centralized* automata, which operate on a givenspanning tree (as computed in Example 5) and are coordinated by the root in a fairly sequential manner. In A_φ, each free node variable x of φ is represented by a corresponding input register x whose value at the root is the current interpretation x^σ of x. Similarly, to represent a function variable f, every node v has a register f storing $f^\sigma(v)$. The nodes also possess some auxiliary registers whose purpose will be explained below. In the end, for any formula φ (potentially with free variables), we will have an automaton A_φ computing a transduction $T_{A_\varphi} \colon \mathbb{C}(I, \{\mathit{parent}, \mathit{root}\} \cup \operatorname{free}(\varphi)) \to \mathbb{C}(\{\text{YES}, \text{NO}\}, \emptyset)$, where *parent* and *root* are supposed to constitute a spanning tree. The computation is triggered by the root, which means that the other nodes are waiting for a signal to wake up.

Algorithm 2. A_φ for $\varphi = \mathrm{pfp}[f_i\colon \varphi_i]_{i\in[1:\ell]}\,\psi$, as controlled by the root

1 **init**(A_{inc})
2 **repeat**
3   **@every node do for** $i \in [1:\ell]$ **do** $f_i \leftarrow f_i^{\mathrm{new}}$
4   **for** $i \in [1:\ell]$ **do** *update*(f_i^{new})
5   **if @every node** ($\forall i \in [1:\ell] : f_i^{\mathrm{new}} = f_i$) **then goto** 8
6 **until execute**(A_{inc}) **returns** NO /* until global counter at maximum */
7 **@every node do for** $i \in [1:\ell]$ **do** $f_i \leftarrow$ *self*
8 **execute**(A_ψ)

Essentially, the nodes involved in the evaluation of φ collect some information, send it towards the root, and go back to sleep. The root then returns YES or NO, depending on whether or not φ holds in the input graph under the variable assignment provided by the input registers. Centralizing A_φ in that way makes it very convenient (albeit not efficient) to evaluate composite formulas. For example, in $A_{\varphi\vee\psi}$, the root will first run A_φ, and then A_ψ in case A_φ returns NO.

The evaluation of atomic formulas is straightforward. So let us focus on the most interesting case, namely when $\varphi = \mathrm{pfp}[f_i\colon \varphi_i]_{i\in(\ell]}\,\psi$. The root's program is outlined in Algorithm 2. Line 1 initializes a counter that ranges from 0 to $n^{\ell n}-1$, where n is the number of nodes in the input graph. This counter is distributed in the sense that every node has some dedicated registers that together store the current counter value. Every execution of A_{inc} will increment the counter by 1, or return NO if its maximum value has been exceeded. Now, in each iteration of the loop starting at Line 2, all registers f_i and f_i^{new} are updated in such a way that they represent the current and next stage, respectively, of the partial fixpoint induction. For the former, it suffices that every node copies, for all i, the contents of f_i^{new} to f_i (Line 3). To update f_i^{new}, Line 4 calls a subroutine *update*(f_i^{new}) whose effect is that $f_i^{\mathrm{new}} = F_{\varphi_i}((f_i)_{i\in(\ell]})$ for all i, where $F_{\varphi_i}\colon (V^V)^\ell \to V^V$ is the operator defined in Sect. 4. Line 5 checks whether we have reached a fixpoint: The root asks every node to compare, for all i, its registers f_i^{new} and f_i. The corresponding truth value is propagated back to the root, where *false* is given preference over *true*. If the result is *true*, we exit the loop and proceed with calling A_ψ to evaluate ψ (Line 8). Otherwise, we try to increment the global counter by executing A_{inc} (Line 6). If the latter returns NO, the fixpoint computation is aborted because we know that it has reached a cycle. In accordance with the partial fixpoint semantics, all nodes then write their own identifier to every register f_i (Line 7) before ψ is evaluated (Line 8). □

6 Conclusion

This paper makes some progress in the development of a descriptive distributed complexity theory by establishing a logical characterization of a wide class of network algorithms, modeled as distributed register automata.

In our translation from logic to automata, we did not pay much attention to algorithmic efficiency. In particular, we made extensive use of centralized subroutines that are triggered and controlled by a leader process. A natural question for future research is to identify cases where we can understand a distributed architecture as an opportunity that allows us to evaluate formulas faster. In other words, is there an expressive fragment of functional fixpoint logic that gives rise to efficient distributed algorithms in terms of running time? What about the required number of messages? We are then entering the field of automatic *synthesis of practical distributed algorithms* from logical specifications. This is a worthwhile task, as it is often much easier to declare what should be done than how it should be done (cf. Examples 6 and 8).

As far as the authors are aware, this area is still relatively unexplored. However, one noteworthy advance was made by Grumbach and Wu in [9], where they investigated distributed evaluation of first-order formulas on bounded-degree graphs and planar graphs. We hope to follow up on this in future work.

Acknowledgments. We thank Matthias Függer for helpful discussions. Work supported by ERC *EQualIS* (FP7-308087) (http://www.lsv.fr/~bouyer/equalis) and ANR *FREDDA* (17-CE40-0013) (https://www.irif.fr/anr/fredda/index).

References

1. Abiteboul, S., Vianu, V.: Fixpoint extensions of first-order logic and datalog-like languages. In: Proceedings of the Fourth Annual Symposium on Logic in Computer Science (LICS 1989), Pacific Grove, California, USA, 5–8 June 1989, pp. 71–79. IEEE Computer Society (1989). https://doi.org/10.1109/LICS.1989.39160
2. Aiswarya, C., Bollig, B., Gastin, P.: An automata-theoretic approach to the verification of distributed algorithms. In: Aceto, L., de Frutos-Escrig, D. (eds.) 26th International Conference on Concurrency Theory, CONCUR 2015, Madrid, Spain, 14 September 2015. LIPIcs, vol. 42, pp. 340–353. Schloss Dagstuhl - Leibniz-Zentrum fuer Informatik (2015). https://doi.org/10.4230/LIPIcs.CONCUR.2015.340
3. Aiswarya, C., Bollig, B., Gastin, P.: An automata-theoretic approach to the verification of distributed algorithms. Inf. Comput. **259**(Part 3), 305–327 (2018). https://doi.org/10.1016/j.ic.2017.05.006
4. Courcelle, B., Engelfriet, J.: Graph Structure and Monadic Second-Order Logic: A Language-Theoretic Approach. Encyclopedia of Mathematics and Its Applications, vol. 138. Cambridge University Press, Cambridge (2012). https://hal.archives-ouvertes.fr/hal-00646514. https://doi.org/10.1017/CBO9780511977619
5. Diestel, R.: Graph Theory. GTM, vol. 173. Springer, Heidelberg (2017). https://doi.org/10.1007/978-3-662-53622-3
6. Fagin, R.: Generalized first-order spectra and polynomial-time recognizable sets. In: Karp, R.M. (ed.) Complexity of Computation. SIAM-AMS Proceedings, vol. 7, pp. 43–73 (1974). http://www.almaden.ibm.com/cs/people/fagin/genspec.pdf
7. Feuilloley, L., Fraigniaud, P.: Survey of distributed decision. Bull. EATCS **119** (2016). http://eatcs.org/beatcs/index.php/beatcs/article/view/411
8. Grädel, E., et al.: Finite Model Theory and Its Applications. Texts in Theoretical Computer Science. An EATCS Series, 1st edn. Springer, Heidelberg (2007). https://doi.org/10.1007/3-540-68804-8

9. Grumbach, S., Wu, Z.: Logical locality entails frugal distributed computation over graphs (extended abstract). In: Paul, C., Habib, M. (eds.) WG 2009. LNCS, vol. 5911, pp. 154–165. Springer, Heidelberg (2010). https://doi.org/10.1007/978-3-642-11409-0_14
10. Hella, L., et al.: Weak models of distributed computing, with connections to modal logic. In: Kowalski, D., Panconesi, A. (eds.) ACM Symposium on Principles of Distributed Computing, PODC 2012, Funchal, Madeira, Portugal, 16–18 July 2012, pp. 185–194. ACM (2012). https://doi.org/10.1145/2332432.2332466
11. Hella, L., et al.: Weak models of distributed computing, with connections to modallogic. Distrib. Comput. **28**(1), 31–53 (2015). https://arxiv.org/abs/1205.2051. http://dx.doi.org/10.1007/s00446-013-0202-3
12. Immerman, N.: Descriptive Complexity. Texts in Computer Science. Springer, New York (1999). https://doi.org/10.1007/978-1-4612-0539-5
13. Kaminski, M., Francez, N.: Finite-memory automata. Theor. Comput. Sci. **134**(2), 329–363 (1994). https://doi.org/10.1016/0304-3975(94)90242-9
14. Kuusisto, A.: Modal logic and distributed message passing automata. In: Rocca, S.R.D. (eds.) Computer Science Logic 2013 (CSL 2013), Torino, Italy, 2–5 September 2013, LIPIcs, vol. 23, pp. 452–468. Schloss Dagstuhl - Leibniz-Zentrum fuer Informatik (2013). https://doi.org/10.4230/LIPIcs.CSL.2013.452
15. Libkin, L., et al.: Elements of Finite Model Theory. Texts in Theoretical Computer Science. An EATCS Series, 1st edn. Springer, Heidelberg (2004). https://doi.org/10.1007/978-3-662-07003-1
16. Naor, M., Stockmeyer, L.J.: What can be computed locally? SIAM J. Comput. **24**(6), 1259–1277 (1995). https://doi.org/10.1137/S0097539793254571
17. Reiter, F.: Distributed graph automata. In: 30th Annual ACM/IEEE Symposium on Logic in Computer Science, LICS 2015, Kyoto, Japan, 6–10 July 2015, pp. 192–201. IEEE Computer Society (2015). https://arxiv.org/abs/1408.3030. https://doi.org/10.1109/LICS.2015.27
18. Reiter, F.: Asynchronous distributed automata: a characterization of the modal MU-fragment. In: Chatzigiannakis, I., Indyk, P., Kuhn, F., Muscholl, A. (eds.) 44th International Colloquium on Automata, Languages, and Programming, ICALP 2017, Warsaw, Poland, 10–14 July 2017. LIPIcs, vol. 80, pp. 100:1–100:14. Schloss Dagstuhl - Leibniz-Zentrum fuer Informatik (2017). http://arxiv.org/abs/1611.08554. https://doi.org/10.4230/LIPIcs.ICALP.2017.100
19. Vardi, M.Y.: The complexity of relational query languages (extended abstract). In: Lewis, H.R., Simons, B.B., Burkhard, W.A., Landweber, L.H. (eds.) Proceedings of the 14th Annual ACM Symposium on Theory of Computing, San Francisco, California, USA, 5–7 May 1982, pp. 137–146. ACM (1982). https://doi.org/10.1145/800070.802186

2

Two-Way Parikh Automata with a Visibly Pushdown Stack

Luc Dartois[1(✉)], Emmanuel Filiot[2], and Jean-Marc Talbot[3]

[1] LACL-Université Paris-Est Créteil, Créteil, France
ldartois@lacl.fr
[2] Université Libre de Bruxelles, Brussels, Belgium
[3] LIM-Aix-Marseille Université, Marseille, France

Abstract. In this paper, we investigate the complexity of the emptiness problem for Parikh automata equipped with a pushdown stack. Pushdown Parikh automata extend pushdown automata with counters which can only be incremented and an acceptance condition given as a semi-linear set, which we represent as an existential Presburger formula over the final values of the counters. We show that the non-emptiness problem both in the deterministic and non-deterministic cases is NP-c. If the input head can move in a two-way fashion, emptiness gets undecidable, even if the pushdown stack is visibly and the automaton deterministic. We define a restriction, called the single-use restriction, to recover decidability in the presence of two-wayness, when the stack is visibly. This syntactic restriction enforces that any transition which increments at least one dimension is triggered only a bounded number of times per input position. Our main contribution is to show that non-emptiness of two-way visibly Parikh automata which are single-use is NExpTime-c. We finally give applications to decision problems for expressive transducer models from nested words to words, including the equivalence problem.

1 Introduction

Parikh automata. Since the classical automata-based approach to model-checking [28], finite automata have been extended in many ways to tackle the automatic verification of more realistic and powerful systems against more expressive specifications. For instance, they have been extended to pushdown systems [3,26,30], concurrent systems [5], and systems with counters or specifications with arithmetic constraints have been the focus of many works in verification [7,11,15–18,23].

Along this line of work, Parikh automata (or PA), introduced in [22], are an important instance of automata extension with arithmetic constraints. They are automata on finite words whose transitions are equipped with counter operations. The counters can only be incremented, and do not influence the run (enabling a transition requires no test on counter values), but the acceptance of a run is defined by the membership of the final counter valuations to some semi-linear set S. Expressivity of PAs goes beyond regularity, as the language

$L = \{w \mid |w|_a = |w|_b\}$ of words having the same numbers of as and bs is realised by a simple automaton counting the numbers of as and bs in counters x_1 and x_2 respectively, and the accepting condition is given by the linear-set $\{(i, i) \mid i \in \mathbb{N}\}$. Semi-linear sets can be defined by formulas in existential Presburger arithmetic, ie first-order formulas with equality and sum predicates over integers, whose free variables are evaluated by the counter values calculated by the run.

A central problem in automata theory is the non-emptiness problem: does the automaton accepts at least one input. Although PAs go beyond regular languages, they retain relatively good algorithmic properties. The emptiness problem is decidable, and it is NP-c [12]. The hardness holds even if the semi-linear set is represented as a set of generator vectors. Motivated by applications in transducer theory for well-nested words, we investigate in this article extensions of Parikh automata with a pushdown stack.

First contribution: pushdown Parikh automata. As a first contribution, we study the complexity of the emptiness problem for Parikh automata with a pushdown store. Parikh automata extend finite automata with counter operations and an acceptance condition given as a semi-linear set, *pushdown Parikh automata* extend pushdown automata in the same way. We show that adding a stack can be done for free with respect to the emptiness problem, which remains, as for stack-free Parikh automata, NP-c. However in this case, we are able to strengthen the lower bound: it remains NP-hard even if there are only two counters, the automaton is deterministic, and the Presburger formula only tests for equality of these two counters. In the stack-free setting, it is necessary to have an unfixed number of counters to get such a lower bound.

Contribution 1. The emptiness problem for pushdown Parikh automata (PPA) is NP-c. The lower bound holds even if the automaton is deterministic, has only two counters whose operations are encoded in unary, and they are eventually tested for equality.

Second contribution: adding two-wayness. We investigate the complexity of pushdown Parikh automata when the input head is allowed to move in two directions. It is not difficult to see that in that case emptiness gets undecidable, since, already without counters, one can simulate the intersection of two deterministic pushdown automata, by performing two passes over the input (visiting each input position at most three times). We consider a first restriction on the stack behaviour, which is required to be *visibly*.

A pushdown stack is called visibly if it is driven by the type of letters it reads, which can be either call symbols, return symbols or internal symbols. Words formed over such a structured alphabet are called nested words, and well-nested words if additionally the call/return structure of the word is well-balanced, such as in the following example:

Automata for nested words, called *visibly pushdown automata* (or VPA), have been introduced in [2]. They are pushdown automata whose stack behaviour is constrained by the input in the following way. Upon reading a call symbol, exactly one symbol is pushed onto the stack. Upon reading a return symbol, exactly one symbol is popped from it. Upon reading an internal symbol, the stack is left unchanged. Hence, the symbol that is pushed while reading a given call symbol is popped while reading its matching return symbol. Consequently, visibly pushdown automata enjoy nice properties, such as closure under Boolean operations and determinisation.

VPA have been extended to two-way VPA (2VPA) [8] with the following stack constraints: in a backward reading mode, the role of the return and call symbols regarding the stack are inverted: when reading a call, exactly one symbol is popped from the stack and when reading a return, one symbol is pushed. It was shown in [8] that adding this visibly condition to two-way pushdown automata allows one to recover decidability for the emptiness problem. However, for Parikh acceptance, this restriction is not sufficient. Indeed, by encoding diophantine equations, we show the following undecidability result:

Contribution 2. The emptiness problem for two-way visibly pushdown Parikh automata (2VPPA) is undecidable.

Single-use property. The problem is that by using the combination of two-wayness and a pushdown stack, it is possible to encode polynomially, and even exponentially large counter values, with respect to the length of the input word. We consider therefore the single-use restriction, which appears in several transducer models [6,8,10], by which it is possible to keep a linear behaviour for the counters. Informally, a *single-use* two-way machine bounds the size of the production per input positions. It is syntactically enforced by asking that transitions which strictly increment at least one counter are triggered at most once per input position. Our main result is the decidability of 2VPPA emptiness under the single-use restriction, with tight complexity.

Contribution 3 (Main). The emptiness problem for two-way single-use visibly pushdown Parikh automata ($\mathsf{2VPPA_{su}}$) is NExpTime-c. The hardness holds even if the automaton is deterministic, has only two counters whose operations are encoded in unary, and they are eventually tested for equality.

To prove the upper-bound, we show that two-wayness can be removed from single-use 2VPPA, at the price of one exponential. In other words, single-use 2VPPA and VPPA have the same expressive power, although it can be shown that the former model is exponentially more succinct. The lower bound is obtained by encoding the succinct variant of the subset sum problem, based on a reduction which uses the fact that, by combining the pushdown and two-way features, single-use 2VPPA can encode doubly-exponential values 2^{2^n} with a polynomial number of states (in n).

	Visibly Pushdown	Pushdown
one-way	NP-complete	NP-complete
2-way Single-use	NExptime-complete	Undecidable
2-way	Undecidable	Undecidable

Fig. 1. Complexity of the emptiness of different Pushdown Parikh Automata. All results hold for deterministic and non-deterministic machines.

Contribution 4 (Applications). As an application, we give an elementary upper-bound (NExpTime) for the equivalence problem of functional single-use two-way visibly pushdown transducers [8], while an ExpTime lower bound was known. This transducer model defines transductions from well-nested words to words and, as shown in [8], they are well-suited to define XML transformations, have the same expressive power as Courcelle's MSO-transducers [6] (casted to well-nested words), and admit a memory-efficient evaluation algorithm. We also provide two other new results on single-use 2VPT (not necessarily functional). First, we show that given a positive integer k, it is decidable whether a single-use 2VPT produces at most k different output words per input (k-valuedness problem). Then, we show the decidability of a typechecking problem: given a single-use 2VPT T and a finite (stack-free) Parikh automaton P, it is decidable whether the codomain of T has a non-empty intersection with P. This allows for instance to decide whether a single-use 2VPT produces only well-nested words and thus describes a well-nested words to well-nested words transformation, since the property of a word to be non well-nested is definable, as we show, by a Parikh automaton.

Finite-visit vs single-useness. The single-use property is more general than the more classical *finite-visit* restriction, used for instance in [9,19]: it requires to visit any input position a (machine-dependent) constant number of times, while single-useness only bounds the number of visits by producing transitions. Although, consequently to our results, 2VPPA single-use and finite-visit have the same expressive power, this extra modelling feature is desirable, for instance when using 2VPPA to test properties of 2VPT: single-use 2VPT are strictly more expressive than finite-visit ones, and this relaxation is crucial to capture MSO transductions [8]. Moreover, we somehow get it for free: we show that the NExpTime lower bound also holds for finite-visit 2VPPA. Finally, we note that as we deal with single-use machines rather than finite-visit ones, the usual ingredient for going from two-way to one-way consisting of memorizing simply crossing sections of states, is not sufficient to get the result here, since we cannot bound the size of these crossing sections.

Related work. Parikh automata are closely related to reversal-bounded counter machines [18]. In fact, both models have equivalent expressiveness in the non-deterministic case [22]. The difference of expressive power in the deterministic case is due to the fact that counter machines can perform tests on its counters that can influence the run, while counters in Parikh automata only matter at the end of the run. Several extensions of reversal-bounded counter machines were studied, whether they are two-way or equipped with a (visibly) pushdown stack. However, to the best of our knowledge, the combination of the two features has never been studied (see [19] for a survey). It is possible to define a model of single-use reversal-bounded two-way visibly pushdown counter machines, where the single-useness is put on transitions that modify the counters. This model is expressively equivalent to $\mathsf{2VPPA_{su}}$ in the non-determinstic case, and thanks to our result, has a decidable emptiness problem. The non-emptiness problem for reversal-bounded (one-way) pushdown counter machines for fixed numbers of counters and reversals is known to be in NP [13] and NP-hard [16]. Converting PPA into reversal-bounded counter machines would yield an unfixed number of counters. Our NP lower-bound for PPA however follows ideas of [16] about encoding, using the stack, integers n with $O(log(n))$ states and stack symbols.

Two-way (stack-free) reversal-bounded counter machines, even deterministic, are known to have undecidable emptiness problem [19]. Decidability is recovered by taking the finite-visit restriction [19]. Our result on $\mathsf{2VPPA_{su}}$ entails the decidability of emptiness of two-way reversal-bounded counter machines which are single-use.

Finally, all the decidability results we prove on two-way visibly pushdown transducers were already known in the one-way case [13]. Two-way visibly pushdown transducers, which are strictly more expressive, can also be seen as a model of unranked tree-to-word transducers, modulo tree linearisation. To the best of our knowledge, this is the first model of unranked tree-to-word transducers for which k-valuedness and codomain well-nestedness is shown to be decidable. Another model, introduced in [1], is known to be expressively equivalent to $\mathsf{2VPT_{su}}$ [8], and in the functional case, has decidable equivalence problem in NExpTime. However, translating $\mathsf{2VPT_{su}}$ to this model requires an exponential blow-up, yielding a worst complexity for equivalence testing.

Structure. Section 2 introduces the computing models used, the proof of the lower bound for $\mathsf{2VPPA_{su}}$ is given in Sect. 3 and the upper bound in Sect. 4. Finally, some applications to the main theorem to transducers are given in Sect. 5.

2 Two-Way Visibly Pushdown (Parikh) Automata

In this section, we first recall the definition of two-way visibly pushdown automata and later on extend them to two-way visibly pushdown Parikh automata.

We consider a structured alphabet Σ defined as the disjoint union of call symbols Σ_c, return symbols Σ_r and internal symbols Σ_i. The set of words over Σ is Σ^*. As usual, ϵ denotes the empty word. Amongst nested words, the set of well-nested words Σ^*_{wn} is defined as the least set such that $\Sigma_i \cup \{\epsilon\}$ is included into Σ^*_{wn} and if $w_1, w_2 \in \Sigma^*_{\mathsf{wn}}$ then both w_1w_2 and cw_1r (for all $c \in \Sigma_c$ and $r \in \Sigma_r$) belong to Σ^*_{wn}.

When dealing with two-way machines, we assume the structured alphabet Σ to be extended to $\overline{\Sigma}$ by adding a left and right marker symbols $\triangleright, \triangleleft$ in $\overline{\Sigma}_c$ and $\overline{\Sigma}_r$ respectively, and we consider words in the language $\triangleright\Sigma^*\triangleleft$.

Definition 1. *A two way visibly pushdown automaton (*2VPA *for short) A over $\overline{\Sigma}$ is given by $(Q, q_I, F, \Gamma, \delta)$ where Q is a finite set of states, $q_I \in Q$ is the initial state, $F \subseteq Q$ is a set of final states and Γ is a finite stack alphabet. Given the set $\mathbb{D} = \{\leftarrow, \rightarrow\}$ of directions, the transition relation δ is defined by $\delta^{push} \cup \delta^{pop} \cup \delta^{int}$ where*

- $\delta^{push} \subseteq ((Q \times \{\rightarrow\} \times \Sigma_c) \cup (Q \times \{\leftarrow\} \times \Sigma_r)) \times ((Q \times \mathbb{D}) \times \Gamma)$
- $\delta^{pop} \subseteq ((Q \times \{\leftarrow\} \times \Sigma_c \times \Gamma) \cup (Q \times \{\rightarrow\} \times \Sigma_r \times \Gamma)) \times (Q \times \mathbb{D})$
- $\delta^{int} \subseteq ((Q \times \mathbb{D} \times \Sigma_i) \times (Q \times \mathbb{D})$

Additionally, we require that for any states q, q' and any stack symbol γ, if $(q, \leftarrow, \triangleright, \gamma, q', d) \in \delta^{pop}$ then $d = \rightarrow$ and if $(q, \rightarrow, \triangleleft, \gamma, q', d) \in \delta^{pop}$ then $d = \leftarrow$ ensuring that the reading head stays within the bounds of the input word.

Informally, a 2VPA has a reading head pointing between symbols (and possibly on the left of $\triangleright$ or the right of $\triangleleft$). A configuration of the machine is given by a state, a direction d and a stack content. The next symbol to be read is on the right of the head if $d = \rightarrow$ and on the left if $d = \leftarrow$. Note that when reading the left marker from right to left $\leftarrow$ (resp. the right marker from left to right $\rightarrow$), the next direction can only be $\rightarrow$ (resp. $\leftarrow$). The structure of the alphabet induces the behavior of the machine regarding the stack when reading the input word: when reading on the right, a call symbol leads to push one symbol onto the stack while a return symbol pops one symbol from the stack. When reading on the left, a dual behaviour holds. In any direction internal transitions from δ^{int} read internal symbols and do not affect the stack; hence, at a given position in the input word, the height of the stack is always constant at each visit of that position in the run of the machine. The triggering of a transition leads to the update of the state of the machine, the future direction as well as the stack content. For a direction d, a natural i $(0 \leq i \leq |w|)$ and a word w, we denote by

- $\text{move}(d, i)$ the integer $i - 1$ if $d = \leftarrow$ and $i + 1$ if $d = \rightarrow$.
- $\text{read}(w, d, i)$ the symbol $w(i)$ if $d = \leftarrow$ and $w(i + 1)$ if $d = \rightarrow$.

Note that when switching directions (i.e. when the direction of the first part of the transition is different from the second part), we read twice the same letter. This ensures the good behavior of the stack, as reading a call letter from left to right pushes a stack symbol, we need to pop it if we start moving from right to left.

Formally, a stack σ is a finite word over Γ. The empty stack/word over Γ is denoted $\perp$. For a word w from $\overline{\Sigma}$ and a 2VPA $A = (Q, q_I, F, \Gamma, \delta)$, a *configuration* κ of A is a tuple (q, i, d, σ) where $q \in Q$, $0 \leq i \leq |w|$, $d \in \mathbb{D}$ and σ is a stack. A *run* of A on a word w is a finite sequence ρ from $K(\delta K)^*$, where K is the set of all configurations κ (that is a sequence starting and ending with a configuration and alternating between configurations and transitions); a run ρ is of the form

$(q_0, i_0, d_0, \sigma_0)\tau_1(q_1, i_1, d_1, \sigma_1)\tau_2 \ldots \tau_\ell(q_\ell, i_\ell, d_\ell, \sigma_\ell)$ where for all $0 \leq j < \ell$, we have:

- either $d_j =\rightarrow$ and $\text{read}(w, d_j, i_j) \in \Sigma_c$ or $d_j =\leftarrow$ and $\text{read}(w, d_j, i_j) \in \Sigma_r$, $\tau_{j+1} = (q_j, d_j, \text{read}(w, d_j, i_j), q_{j+1}, d_{j+1}, \gamma) \in \delta^{\text{push}}$, $i_{j+1} = \text{move}(i_j, d_j)$ and $\sigma_{j+1} = \sigma_j\gamma$
- either $d_j =\leftarrow$ and $\text{read}(w, d_j, i_j) \in \Sigma_c$ or $d_j =\rightarrow$ and $\text{read}(w, d_j, i_j) \in \Sigma_r$, $\tau_{j+1} = (q_j, d_j, \text{read}(w, d_j, i_j), \gamma, q_{j+1}, d_{j+1}) \in \delta^{\text{pop}}$, $i_{j+1} = \text{move}(i_j, d_j)$ and $\sigma_{j+1}\gamma = \sigma_j$
- $\text{read}(w, d_j, i_j) \in \Sigma_i$, $\tau_{j+1} = (q_j, d_j, \text{read}(w, d_j, i_j), q_{j+1}, d_{j+1}) \in \delta^{\text{int}}$, $i_{j+1} = i_j$ and $\sigma_{j+1} = \sigma_j$.

Note that any configuration is actually a run on the empty word ϵ. The initial configuration is $(q_I, 0, \rightarrow, \perp)$. A configuration $(q, i, d, \perp)$ is *final* if $q \in F$ and i is the last position. A run for the word w is accepting if its first configuration is initial and its last configuration is final. A two-way visibly pushdown automaton A is:

- *deterministic* (denoted D2VPA) if δ^{push} (resp. δ^{pop}, δ^{int}) is a function from $Q \times \mathbb{D} \times \Sigma$ (resp. $Q \times \mathbb{D} \times \Sigma \times \Gamma$, $Q \times \mathbb{D} \times \Sigma$) to $Q \times \mathbb{D} \times \Gamma$ (resp. $Q \times \mathbb{D}$, $Q \times \mathbb{D}$).
- *one-way* (denoted VPA) if all transitions in A have $\rightarrow$ for direction.
- *finite-visit* if for some $k \geq 0$, any run visits at most k times the same input position.

The size of a 2VPA is the number of states times the size of the stack alphabet. For A an automaton, we denote by $L(A)$ the language recognized by A.

Lemma 1 ([8]). *Given a* 2VPA *A, deciding if $L(A)$ is empty is* ExpTime-complete.

Parikh automata. Parikh automata were introduced in [22]. Informally, they are automata with counters that can only be incremented, and do not act on the transition relation. Acceptance of runs is done by evaluating a Presburger formula whose free variables are set to the counter values. In our setting, a *Presburger formula* is a positive formula $\psi(x_1, \ldots, x_n) = \exists y_1 \ldots y_m \varphi(x_1, \ldots, x_n, y_1, \ldots, y_m)$ such that φ is a boolean combination of atoms $s + s' \leq t + t'$, for $s, s', t, t' \in \{0, 1, x_1, \ldots, x_n, y_1, \ldots, y_m\}$. For a set S and some positive number m, we denote by S^m the set of all mappings from $[1 \ldots m]$ to S. If $(s_1, \ldots, s_m)$ and $(t_1, \ldots, t_m)$ are two tuples of S^m and $+$ is an binary operation on S, we extend $+$ to S^m by considering the operation element-wise, i.e. $(s_1, \ldots, s_m) + (t_1, \ldots, t_m) = (s_1 + t_1, \ldots, s_m + t_m)$.

Definition 2. *A two-way visibly pushdown Parikh automaton (*2VPPA *for short) is a tuple $P = (A, \lambda, \phi)$ where A is a* 2VPA *and for some natural dim, λ is a mapping from δ to $\mathbb{N}^{dim}$, the set of vectors of length dim of naturals and $\phi(x_1, \ldots, x_{dim})$ is a Presburger formula with dim free variables.*

When clear from context, we may omit the free variables from the Presburger formula, and simply note ϕ. A run of a 2VPPA is a run of its underlying 2VPA. We extend canonically the mapping λ to runs. For a run ρ of the form $(q_0, i_0, d_0, \sigma_0)\tau_1(q_1, i_1, d_1, \sigma_1)\tau_2 \ldots \tau_\ell(q_\ell, i_\ell, d_\ell, \sigma_\ell)$, we set

$$\lambda(\rho) = \lambda(\tau_1) + \lambda(\tau_2) + \ldots + \lambda(\tau_\ell)$$

We recall that a single configuration c is a run over the empty word ϵ. For such a run c, we set $\lambda(c) = 0^{dim}$. A run $(q_0, i_0, d_0, \sigma_0)\tau_1(q_1, i_1, d_1, \sigma_1)$ $\tau_2 \ldots \tau_\ell(q_\ell, i_\ell, d_\ell, \sigma_\ell)$ is accepted if $(q_0, i_0, d_0, \sigma_0)$, $(q_\ell, i_\ell, d_\ell, \sigma_\ell)$ are respectively an initial and a final configuration of the underlying automaton and for $\lambda(\rho) = (n_1, \ldots, n_{dim})$, $[x_1 \leftarrow n_1, \ldots, x_\ell \leftarrow n_{dim}] \models \phi(x_1, \ldots, x_{dim})$. The language $L(P)$ is the set of words which admit an accepting run. We define the set of values computed by P as $Val(P) = \{\lambda(\rho) \mid \rho \text{ a valid run of the underlying automaton of } P\}$. We define the size of P as the size of A plus the number of symbols in ϕ and $|\delta| \cdot dim \cdot log(W)$ where W is the maximal value occurring in the codomain of λ.

It is deterministic (resp. one-way), denoted D2VPPA (resp. VPPA) if its underlying automaton is deterministic (resp. one-way). It is known from [4] that DPA (i.e. deterministic one-way and stack-free Parikh automata in our setting) are strictly less expressive than their nondeterministic counterpart. As a counter example, they exhibit the language $L = \{w \mid w_{\#_a(w)} = b\}$, ie all words w such that if n is the number of a in w, the letter at the nth position is a b. Note that even in the two-way case, a deterministic machine recognizing L needs to either have access, during the computation, to the number of a's, or be able to store, in counters, the position of each b. As the first solution cannot be done since Parikh automata only access their counters at the end of the run, and the second is also impossible since there are only a finite number of counters, this language is also non definable by a D2VPPA, furthering the separation between deterministic and nondeterministic Parikh automata.

Example 1. As an example, we give a deterministic 2VPPA P that, given an input $i^n c^k i^\ell r^k$ with c, i, r in Σ_c, Σ_i and Σ_r respectively, accepts if $k = \ell$ and $n = k^2$. The 2VPPA P uses 4 variables x_n, x_k, x_ℓ and y. The first 3 variables are used to count the number of the first block of is, the number of calls and the second block of is respectively. The handling of these 3 variables is straightforward and can be done in a single pass over the input. The fourth variables y counts the multiplication $k \cdot \ell$ and doing so is more involved. The part of the underlying 2VPA of P handling y is given in Fig. 2. On this part, the mapping λ simply increments the counter on transitions going to state 2 (i.e. on reading the letters i from left to right). It makes as many passes on the set of internal symbols in state 2 as there are call symbols, and the state of the stack upon reading i^ℓ for the jth time is $1^j 0^{k-j}$. Finally, the accepting formula ϕ of P is defined by $x_n = y \wedge x_k = x_\ell$. Note that this widget allows us to compute the set $\{(k^2, k, k, k^2) \mid k \in \mathbb{N}\}$ which is not semilinear.

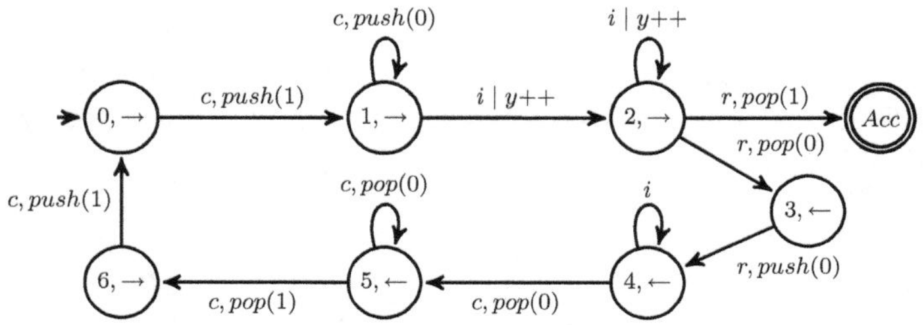

Fig. 2. A 2VPPA reading words $c^k i^\ell r^k$ and making k passes on i^ℓ, adding $k \cdot \ell$ to the variable y. The transitions have two components, the first being the letter read, and the second being the stack operation. There is no stack operation upon reading internal symbols. The variable y is incremented in transitions going to state 2 only.

As we have seen in the previous example, the set $Val(P)$ is not necessarily semi-linear, even with P a D2VPPA. We use this fact to encode diophantine equations, and get the following undecidability result:

Theorem 1. *The emptiness problem of* D2VPPA *is undecidable.*

Single-useness. In order to recover decidability, we adapt to Parikh Automata the notion of single-useness introduced in [8]. Simply put, a 2VPPA is *single-use* (denoted $\mathsf{2VPPA_{su}}$) if the transitions that affect the variables can only be taken once on any given input position, thus effectively bounding the size of variables linearly with respect to the size of the input. Formally, a state p of a 2VPPA P is *producing* if there exists a transition t from p on some symbol and $\lambda(t) \neq 0^{dim}$. A 2VPPA is single-use if for every input w and every accepting run ρ over w, there do not exist two different configurations (p, i, d, σ) and (p, i, d, σ') with p a producing state, meaning that ρ does not reach any position in the same direction twice in any given state of P. This property is a syntaxic restriction of the model. However, since this property is regular, it can equivalently be seen as a semantic one. Moreover, deciding the single-useness of a 2VPPA is ExpTime-c (see [8] for the same result but on transducers). Note that the Parikh automaton given in Example 1 is not single-use, since it passes over the second subword of internal letters i in state 2 as many times as there are call symbols. In the following, we prove that $\mathsf{2VPPA_{su}}$ have the same expressiveness as VPPA, while being exponentially more succinct. In particular, this equivalence implies by Parikh's Theorem [24], semi-linearity of $Val(P)$ for any $\mathsf{2VPPA_{su}}$ P.

3 Emptiness Complexity

We show that the non-emptiness problem for VPPA is NP-complete. We actually show the upper-bound for the strictly more expressive *Pushdown Parikh Automata* (PPA), i.e. VPPA without the visibly restriction. While decidability was known [20, 21], the precise complexity was, to the best of our knowledge, unknown. Let us also remark that the model and the proof are similar to the proof of NP-completeness of k-reversal pushdown systems from [16]. However, it is adapted here to Parikh automata as well as deterministic machines, which was not the case in [16].

Theorem 2. *The non-emptiness problem for* VPPA *and* PPA *is* NP-complete. *The complexity bounds hold even if the automata are deterministic, with a fixed dimension 2, tuples of values in* $\{0,1\}^2$ *and with a fixed Presburger formula* $\phi(x_1, x_2) \equiv x_1 = x_2$.

From $\mathsf{2VPPA_{su}}$ *to* VPPA From a two-way visibly pushdown Parikh automaton satisfying the single-useness restriction, one can build an equivalent one-way visibly pushdown Parikh automaton. The construction induces an exponential blow-up, which cannot be avoided, as with most constructions from two-way to one-way machines.

Theorem 3. *For any* $\mathsf{2VPPA_{su}}$ A*, one can construct a* VPPA B *whose size is at most exponential in the size of* A *and such that* $L(A)=L(B)$*. Moreover, the procedure can be done in exponential time.*

Proof (Sketch). The goal is to be able to correctly guess all the transitions exactly taken by a run of the two-way machine at once. More precisely, the one-way machine guesses the behavior of the two-way machine on each well-nested subword of the input, i.e. a set of partial runs over a subword. A partial run is a pair from $Q \times \{\leftarrow, \rightarrow\}$. Informally, they describe a maximal subrun over a subword of the input. We call these sets of partial runs *profiles*, and we define relations C and $N_{c,r}$ to describe compatible profiles. Formally, the relation $C \subseteq \mathcal{P}^3$ is the *concatenation* relation, defined as set of triples (P, P', P'') such that there exists a word $u = u_1vv'u_2$ where v and v' are well-nested subwords of u, and a run r on u such that P (resp. P') is the profile of v in r (resp. of v') and P'' is the profile of vv' in r. Similarly, the relation $N_{c,r} \subseteq \mathcal{P}^2$ for c, r call and return letters respectively, is the *cr-nesting* relation, and defined as the set of pairs (P, P') such that there exists a word $u = u_1cvru_2$ where v is well-nested, and a run r of A on u such that P is the profile of v in r and P' is the profile of cvr in r. We prove that these relations are computable in exponential time.

Given these relations, we can compute a VPPA B whose runs are bijective to the runs of A. Moreover, we can recover from a run of B which transitions are effectively taken at each positions by its bijective run of A. Then, the increment function simply does all the increments done by the run at a given position at once. Since the operation is the addition on integers, it is commutative and the variables are updated in the same way they were by the run of A. Note that we only recover which transitions are taken, and not how many times they are taken, which can depend on the size of the input. However, since A is single-use, we only have to add each non zero transition once, which gives the result.

As a direct corollary of Theorems 3 and 2, we get the following.

Corollary 1. *The emptiness of* $\mathsf{2VPPA_{su}}$ *can be decided in* NExpTime.

4 NExpTime-Hardness

In this section, we show that the problem of deciding whether the language of a $2VPPA_{su}$ is non-empty is hard for NExpTime. Moreover, we show that this hardness does not depend on the fact that we have taken existential Presburger formulas, nor on the vector dimensions, and nor on the fact that the values in the tuples are encoded in binary.

Theorem 4. *The non-emptiness problem for* $2VPPA_{su}$ *is NExpTime-hard. The result holds even if the automaton is deterministic, of dimension 2, with counter updates in* $\{0,1\}$, *the Presburger formula is* $\phi(x_1, x_2) \equiv x_1 = x_2$, *and it is finite-visit.*

Succinct Subset Sum Problem. We reduce to the succinct subset sum problem (SSSP), which is NExpTime-hard [16]. Let us define SSSP. Let $m, k \geq 1$, $X = \{x_1, \ldots, x_k\}$ and $Y = \{y_1, \ldots, y_m\}$ be sets of Boolean variables. Let θ be a Boolean formula over $X \cup Y$. Any word $v \in \{0,1\}^{k+m}$ naturally defines a valuation of $X \cup Y$ (the first bit of v is the value of x_1, etc.). We denote by $\theta[v] \in \{0,1\}$ the truth value of θ under the valuation v. The formula θ defines 2^k non-negative integers $a_1, \ldots, a_{2^k}$ each with 2^m bits, as follows:

$$a_i = \theta[b_i d_1].2^{2^m-1} + \theta[b_i d_2].2^{2^m-2} + \cdots + \theta[b_i d_{2^m}].2^0$$

where b_i is the binary encoding over k bits of i, and $d_1, \ldots, d_{2^m}$ is the lexicographic enumeration of $\{0,1\}^m$, starting from 0^m. Note that for all $i \in \{1, \ldots, 2^k\}$, $a_i \in \{0, \ldots, 2^{2^m} - 1\}$. The *Succinct Subset Sum Problem* asks, given X, Y and θ, whether there exists $J \subseteq \{1, \ldots, 2^k - 1\}$ such that $\sum_{j \in J} a_j = a_{2^k}$.

Overview of the construction and encoding the values a_i. Given an instance of SSSP $\mathcal{I}$, our goal is to construct a $D2VPPA_{su}$ $\mathcal{P} = (C, \rho, \phi)$ of dimension 2 such that $|\mathcal{P}|$ is polynomial in $|\theta| + k + m$ and $\mathcal{L}(\mathcal{P}) \neq \varnothing$ iff $\mathcal{I}$ has a solution.

The main idea is to ensure that $\mathcal{L}(C) = \{X_1 e_1 \ldots X_{2^k-1} e_{2^k-1} \# e_{2^k} \mid X_i \in \{0,1\}\}$ where the X_i are internal symbols which are used to encode a subset $J \subseteq \{1, \ldots, 2^k - 1\}$, and each e_i is an encoding of a_i, defined later, over some alphabet containing the symbol $\mathbb{1}$, and such that the number of occurrences of $\mathbb{1}$ in e_i is a_i. In other words, e_i somehow encodes a_i in unary. For the vector part, the machine $\mathcal{P}$, when running over $X_i e_i$, updates its dimensions depending on two cases: (1) if $X_i = 1$ ("put value a_i in J"), then any transition reading $\mathbb{1}$ has weight $(1,0)$ and any other transition has weight $(0,0)$, (2) if $X_i = 0$, then every transition has weight $(0,0)$. So, if $X_i = 1$, the value in the first dimension after processing $X_i e_i$ has been incremented by a_i. Similarly, when processing $\# e_{2^k}$, any transition reading $\mathbb{1}$ increments the 2nd dimension by 1, so that after processing $\# e_{2^k}$, this dimension has value a_{2^k}. The formula $\phi(x_1, x_2)$ then only requires equality of x_1 and x_2, i.e. $\phi(x_1, x_2) \equiv x_1 = x_2$.

We now explain how to encode a_i by a well-nested word e_i. Due to the finite-visit restriction, every incremental transition can be triggered at most once for each input position. Since the value a_i is possibly doubly exponential in m and

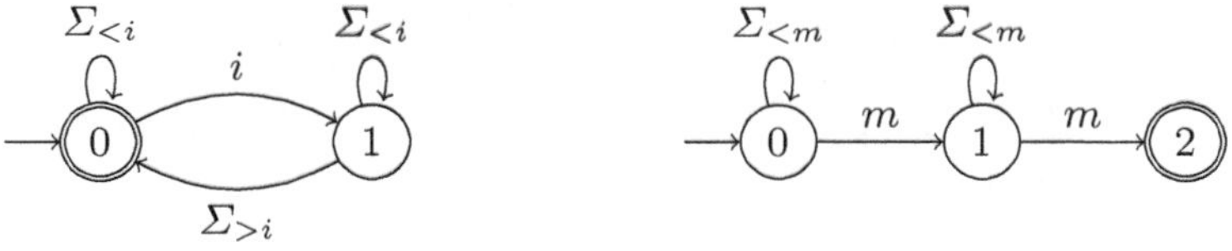

Fig. 3. On the left, the automaton A_i, for $i < m$. On the right, the automaton A_m.

we are allowed to have a polynomial number of transitions (in $|\theta| + k + m$), necessarily e_i must be of doubly exponential length. The main idea is to use the stack and the two-wayness to recognise with a polynomial number of states well-nested words which are of doubly exponential length. We need a series of intermediate lemmas to achieve this idea. We start with a useful result about intersection of finite automata, here *reversible* finite automata (deterministic and backward deterministic). Let $\Sigma = \{1, \ldots, m\}$ and let us define recursively the sequence of words $(u_i)_{0 \leq i \leq m} \in \Sigma^*$ as follows: $u_0 = 1$, $u_i = u_{i-1} i u_{i-1}$ for $1 \leq i < m$ and $u_m = u_{m-1} m u_{m-1} m$.

Lemma 2. *The word u_m has length 2^m, and there exist m reversible finite automata $A_0, \ldots, A_m$ (Fig. 3) such that (i) each A_i has $O(1)$ states, and (ii) $\bigcap_{i=1}^{m} L(A_i) = \{u_m\}$.*

Encoding of the values a_i. The idea is to define a well-nested word e_i over an alphabet of call symbols $\Sigma_c = \{c_1, \ldots, c_m\}$, an alphabet of return symbols $\Sigma_r = \{r_1, \ldots, r_m\}$ and an alphabet of internal symbols $\Sigma_\iota = \{0, 1, \mathbb{1}, \mathbb{0}\}$. The number of occurrences of $\mathbb{1}$ in e_i will be exactly a_i, i.e. $\#_{\mathbb{1}}(e_i) = a_i$ and hence, the Parikh automaton will just have to count the number of $\mathbb{1}$ occurrences. Let us remind the reader that a_i is actually given by θ, and therefore, the automaton $\mathcal{P}$ will somehow have to evaluate θ for valuations of its variables that will be contained in e_i. Let us now define the words e_i. For that, we call a *binary tree* either an internal symbol $\mathbb{1}, \mathbb{0}$, or a well-nested word of the form $c_j t_1 t_2 r_j$ where t_1, t_2 are themselves binary trees. For a well-nested word of the form cwr, a root-to-leaf branch π is a sequence of calls $x_1 \ldots x_n$ such that $cwr = x_1 w_1 x_2 w_2 \ldots x_n w_n r_n w'_n r_{n-1} w'_{n-1} \ldots r_2 w'_2 r_1$ where $x_1 = c$, $r_1 = r$ and for some w_i, w'_i well-nested words such that w_n contains only internal symbols. The *height* of a binary tree t is the maximal length of a root-to-leaf branch, and it is *complete* if all root-to-leaf branches have the same length. Note that the number of internal symbols of a complete binary tree of height n is 2^n.

Then, e_i is the well-nested word defined by $e_i = c_{j_1} b_i d_1 t_1 c_{j_2} b_i d_2 t_2 \ldots c_{j_{2^m}} b_i d_{2^m} t_{2^m} r_{j_{2^m}} \ldots r_{j_1}$ where

1. the words t_i are binary trees
2. every root-to-leaf branch $\pi = c_{i_1} \ldots c_{i_\ell}$ of e_i satisfies $i_1 \ldots i_\ell = u_m$
3. $b_i \in \{0,1\}^k$ and $d_1, \ldots, d_{2^m}$ is a lexicographic enumeration of $\{0,1\}^m$ (starting from 0^m)
4. for all j, all internal symbols occurring in t_j are $\mathbb{1}$ if $\theta[b_i d_j] = 1$, $\mathbb{0}$ otherwise.

Our goal is now to prove that e_i is a correct encoding of a_i.

Lemma 3. *For all $i \in \{1, \ldots, 2^k\}$, $\#_{\mathbb{1}}(e_i) = a_i$, where $\#_{\mathbb{1}}(e_i)$ denotes the number of occurrences of $\mathbb{1}$ in e_i.*

Proof. By Condition 2, every root-to-leaf branch of e_i has length 2^m. Therefore, for all $j \in \{1, \ldots, 2^m\}$, every root-to-leaf branch in t_j has length $2^m - j$. In particular, t_{2^m} does not contain any call symbol. Hence all the trees t_j are complete binary trees of height $2^m - j$. So, every t_j has 2^{2^m-j} internal symbols and by Condition 4, we get $\#_{\mathbb{1}}(t_j) = \theta[b_i d_j].2^{2^m-j}$. Therefore, $\#_{\mathbb{1}}(e_i) = \sum_{j=1}^{2^m} \#_{\mathbb{1}}(t_j) = \sum_{j=1}^{2^m} \theta[b_i d_j].2^{2^m-j} = a_i$.

Note that Condition 3 was not used in the previous proof, but it will be useful to define a succinct D2VPA recognising e_i. The key result is the following. It states the existence of a succinct D2VPA which recognises exactly the candidate solutions to SSSP.

Lemma 4. *One can construct a* D2VPA *$\mathcal{B}$ such that $\mathcal{B}$ has polynomially many states in $|\theta| + k + m$ and $L(\mathcal{B}) = \{X_1 e_1 \ldots X_{2^k-1} e_{2^k-1} \# e_{2^k} \mid X_i \in \{0, 1\}\}$.*

Proof (Sketch). First, we show the existence of a D2VPA $\mathcal{A}$ with polynomially many states in $|\theta|+k+m$ such that $L(\mathcal{A}) = \{e_i \mid i \in \{1, \ldots, 2^k\}\}$ (Proposition ?? in Appendix). The main idea is to construct succinct D2VPA which check each of the conditions 1 to 4 of the definition of the encoding independently, and then to take their intersection (by running the first, then the second, etc.). Condition 1 is easy to check. For condition 2, we rely on Lemma 2, and run sequentially the automata A_i (in m passes) to check independently that for all i, each root-to-leaf branch has a sequence of indices that belongs to A_i. Thanks to the reversibility of A_i, it is possible when going upward in the tree, to recover the previous state of A_i. For condition 3, we rely on the two-wayness to check that a sequence of m bits is a successor of another sequence succinctly, by doing $O(m)$ passes over the two successor vectors. The stack is not necessary there. For condition 4, we rely on the existence of a succinct 2DFA which accepts all the valuations that satisfy a given Boolean formula.

We can finally construct the D2VPPA$_{\text{su}}$ $\mathcal{P} = (\mathcal{C}, \rho, \phi)$ of dimension 2 whose language is non-empty iff the SSSP instance $\mathcal{I}$ has a solution. The automaton $\mathcal{C}$ performs a first pass on the whole word by running the automaton $\mathcal{B}$ of Lemma 4, to check that the input is of the form $X_1 e_1 \ldots X_{2^k-1} e_{2^k-1} \# e_{2^k}$. During this pass, no vector dimension is incremented. During a second pass, $\mathcal{C}$, when reading some $X_i = 1$, it goes to some state q_1 from which it increments the 1st dimension whenever $\mathbb{1}$ is read (all other transitions have value $(0, 0)$). When reading some X_{i+1}, it stays in q_1 if $X_{i+1} = 1$ or to q_0 otherwise, from which no transition touches the counters. When reading $\#$, it goes to a state from which it increments only the 2nd dimension on reading $\mathbb{1}$. Note that this automaton is *single-use*: any symbol $\mathbb{1}$ occurring in the whole input word is counted at most once. It is even finite-visit (each position is visited $O(m + k + |\theta|)$ times). Finally, one only needs to check whether the first dimension equals the second one, using a formula $\phi(x_1, x_2) \equiv x_1 = x_2$. Note that the following lemma proves Theorem 4, since SSSP is NExpTime-c.

Lemma 5. *Given an instance X, Y, θ of SSSP, one can construct a* $\mathsf{D2VPPA_{su}}$ *$\mathcal{P}$ of polynomial size in $|\theta| + |X| + |Y|$ such that $L(\mathcal{P}) \neq \varnothing$ iff SSSP has a solution.*

5 Applications to Decision Problems for Nested Word Transducers

In this section, we give two applications of 2VPPA, namely on decision problems for two-way visibly pushdown transducers (2VPT). 2VPT were introduced in [8] as a model to define transductions from well-nested words to words, or, modulo tree linearisation, from tree to words. It was shown that they can express, even in their deterministic and single-use version, all functions from well-nested words to words definable in MSOT, in the sense of Courcelle [6], while having decidable equivalence problem. No upper bound was provided however. Using 2VPPA, we show that the equivalence of $\mathsf{2VPT_{su}}$ defining functions can be tested in NExpTime. We also consider other standard problems from transducer theory and show, again using 2VPPA, their decidability. First, let us define formally 2VPT.

A *two-way visibly pushdown transducer* (2VPT for short) is a pair (A, μ) where A is a 2VPA and μ is a morphism from the sequences of transitions δ^* to some output alphabet Γ^*. A run of a 2VPT is a run of its underlying 2VPA. The *output* of a run ρ of the form $(q_0, i_0, d_0, \sigma_0)\tau_1(q_1, i_1, d_1, \sigma_1)\tau_2 \dots \tau_\ell(q_\ell, i_\ell, d_\ell, \sigma_\ell)$ is $\mu(\tau_1 ... \tau_\ell)$. A run is accepted if it is accepted by its underlying automaton. The transduction defined by a 2VPT is the set of pairs (u, v) such that v is the output of some accepting run on u. A state p of a 2VPT is *producing* if there exists a transition τ such that p is the first component of τ and $\mu(\tau) \neq \epsilon$. Similarly to Parikh automata, a 2VPT T is single-use (denoted $\mathsf{2VPT_{su}}$) if for any valid run of T, we do not reach the same position twice in the same producing state. It is deterministic, denoted D2VPT, if its underlying automaton is deterministic.

Deciding the k-valuedness and equivalence problems. For any positive integer k, we say that a transducer is *k-valued* if all input word have at most k different outputs. In particular, it is 1-valued if it defines a (partial) function, and also called *functional* in that case.

Theorem 5. *Let T be a* $\mathsf{2VPT_{su}}$*, and k an integer. Then the k-valuedness of T can be decided in* NExpTime*. It is also* ExpTime-hard.

The theorem is proved by reducing the k-valuedness of T to the emptiness of a $\mathsf{2VPPA_{su}}$ $\mathcal{P}$ that guesses $k+1$ runs of T that produce $k+1$ different outputs. To ensure that the output are different, during each run $\mathcal{P}$ guesses, and stores in counters, k output positions and the letters produced at these positions. The formula of $\mathcal{P}$ at the end simply checks, for each pairs of runs, that the same positions were guessed by both runs, and that the letters were different, ensuring that the guessed runs have different output pairwise. As two functional transducers are equivalent if they have the same domain and their union is 1-valued, we get the following corollary.

Corollary 2. *The equivalence of two functional* $\mathsf{2VPT_{su}}$ T *and* T' *can be decided in* NExpTime. *It is also* ExpTime-hard.

The NexpTime complexity of equivalence of tree to string transducers was already established for *Streaming Tree to string transducers* (STST), introduced in [1]. However, the conversion between the $\mathsf{2VPT_{su}}$ and STST yields an exponential blow-up.

We can generalize Corollary 2 to *strictly* k-valued transducers. We say that a transducer T is strictly k-valued if each input word in the domain of T has *exactly* k different images. Then similarly to the previous corollary, two strictly k-valued transducers are equivalent if, and only if, they have same domain and their union is k-valued.

Corollary 3. *The equivalence of two strictly* k*-valued* $\mathsf{2VPT_{su}}$ T *and* T' *can be decided in* NExpTime. *It is also* ExpTime-hard.

Strict k-valuedness is however an undecidable property (this can be shown by using the Post correspondence problem), even for $k = 2$. Deciding the equivalence problem for k-valued $\mathsf{2VPT_{su}}$ (which are not necessarily strictly k-valued) is open already in the stack-less case, and a (very) particular case has been solved in [14].

Type-checking against Parikh properties. Given a 2VPT T, it might be desirable to check some properties of the output words it produces, i.e., for a language L, whether the codomain of T is included in L. Formally, the *type-checking problem* asks, given a transducer T and a language L, whether $T(\Sigma^*) \subseteq L$. Unfortunately, this problem is undecidable when L is given by a visibly pushdown automaton (and T is a VPT) [13]. Nevertheless, we show that the type-checking problem is decidable when T is a $\mathsf{2VPT_{su}}$ and L is the complement of the language given by a (stack-less) Parikh Automaton. As a consequence, we are able to decide whether a $\mathsf{2VPT_{su}}$ T produces only well-nested words, i.e. if the output alphabet of T is structured and for every input word u and any $v \in T(u)$, v is a well-nested word.

Theorem 6. *Let* T *be a* $\mathsf{2VPT_{su}}$ *and* P *be a (stack-free) Parikh Automaton over the output alphabet of* T. *Then we can decide whether* $T(\Sigma^*) \cap L(P) = \emptyset$ *in* NExpTime. *It is also* ExpTime-hard.

This is done by constructing a $\mathsf{2VPPA_{su}}$ P' which simulates T, and instead of producing letters, simulates P on the output of T. A word w on a structured alphabet Σ is not well-nested if either $|w|_c \neq |w|_r$, i.e. the number of call letters is not equal to the number of return letters, or if there exists a prefix u of w such that $|u|_c < |u|_r$. As this can be checked by a (non-deterministic) Parikh automata, we get the following corollary.

Corollary 4. *Let T be a* $2\mathsf{VPT}_{\mathsf{su}}$ *whose output alphabet is structured. It can be decided in* CoNExpTime *whether T only produces well-nested words.*

Acknowledgements. This work was supported by the Belgian FNRS CDR project Flare (J013116), the ARC project Transform (Fédération Wallonie Bruxelles) and by the ANR Project *DELTA*, ANR-16-CE40-0007. Emmanuel Filiot is an FNRS research associate (Chercheur Qualifié).

References

1. Alur, R., D'Antoni, L.: Streaming tree transducers. In: Czumaj, A., Mehlhorn, K., Pitts, A., Wattenhofer, R. (eds.) ICALP 2012. LNCS, vol. 7392, pp. 42–53. Springer, Heidelberg (2012). https://doi.org/10.1007/978-3-642-31585-5_8
2. Alur, R., Madhusudan, P.: Adding nesting structure to words. J. ACM **56**(3), 16:1–16:43 (2009)
3. Burkart, O., Steffen, B.: Model checking the full modal mu-calculus for infinite sequential processes. In: Degano, P., Gorrieri, R., Marchetti-Spaccamela, A. (eds.) ICALP 1997. LNCS, vol. 1256, pp. 419–429. Springer, Heidelberg (1997). https://doi.org/10.1007/3-540-63165-8_198
4. Cadilhac, M., Finkel, A., McKenzie, P.: On the expressiveness of Parikh automata and related models. In: Proceedings of the Third Workshop on Non-Classical Models for Automata and Applications - NCMA 2011, Milan, Italy, 18 July–19 July 2011, pp. 103–119 (2011)
5. Clarke, E.M., Emerson, E.A., Sistla, A.P.: Automatic verification of finite state concurrent systems using temporal logic specifications. In: Conference Record of the Tenth Annual ACM Symposium on Principles of Programming Languages, pp. 117–126. ACM, January 1983
6. Courcelle, B., Engelfriet, J.: Graph Structure and Monadic Second-Order Logic - A Language-Theoretic Approach. Encyclopedia of Mathematics and its Applications, vol. 138. Cambridge University Press (2012). http://www.cambridge.org/fr/knowledge/isbn/item5758776/?site_locale=fr_FR
7. Dang, Z., Ibarra, O.H., Bultan, T., Kemmerer, R.A., Su, J.: Binary reachability analysis of discrete pushdown timed automata. In: Emerson, E.A., Sistla, A.P. (eds.) CAV 2000. LNCS, vol. 1855, pp. 69–84. Springer, Heidelberg (2000). https://doi.org/10.1007/10722167_9
8. Dartois, L., Filiot, E., Reynier, P.-A., Talbot, J.-M.: Two-way visibly pushdown automata and transducers. In: Proceedings of the 31st Annual ACM/IEEE Symposium on Logic in Computer Science, LICS 2016, New York, NY, USA, 5–8 July 2016, pp. 217–226 (2016). https://doi.org/10.1145/2933575.2935315
9. Engelfriet, J., Hoogeboom, H.J.: MSO definable string transductions and two-way finite-state transducers. ACM Trans. Comput. Logic **2**(2), 216–254 (2001)
10. Engelfriet, J., Maneth, S.: Macro tree transducers, attribute grammars, and MSO definable tree translations. Inf. Comput. **154**(1), 34–91 (1999). https://doi.org/10.1006/inco.1999.2807. http://www.sciencedirect.com/science/article/pii/S0890540199928079
11. Esparza, J., Ganty, P.: Complexity of pattern-based verification for multithreaded programs. ACM SIGPLAN Not. - POPL 2011 **46**(1), 499–510 (2011). https://doi.org/10.1145/1925844.1926443

12. Figueira, D., Libkin, L.: Path logics for querying graphs: combining expressiveness and efficiency. In: 30th Annual ACM/IEEE Symposium on Logic in Computer Science, LICS 2015, Kyoto, Japan, 6–10 July 2015, pp. 329–340 (2015). https://doi.org/10.1109/LICS.2015.39
13. Filiot, E., Raskin, J.-F., Reynier, P.-A., Servais, F., Talbot, J.-M.: Properties of visibly pushdown transducers. In: Hliněný, P., Kučera, A. (eds.) MFCS 2010. LNCS, vol. 6281, pp. 355–367. Springer, Heidelberg (2010). https://doi.org/10.1007/978-3-642-15155-2_32
14. Gallot, P., Muscholl, A., Puppis, G., Salvati, S.: On the decomposition of finite-valued streaming string transducers. In: STACS 2017. LIPIcs, vol. 66, pp. 34:1–34:14 (2017). https://doi.org/10.4230/LIPIcs.STACS.2017.34. http://drops.dagstuhl.de/opus/volltexte/2017/6999
15. Haase, C.: On the complexity of model checking counter automata. Ph.D. thesis, University of Oxford, UK (2012). http://ora.ox.ac.uk/objects/uuid:f43bf043-de93-4b5c-826f-88f1bd4c191d
16. Hague, M., Lin, A.W.: Model checking recursive programs with numeric data types. In: Gopalakrishnan, G., Qadeer, S. (eds.) CAV 2011. LNCS, vol. 6806, pp. 743–759. Springer, Heidelberg (2011). https://doi.org/10.1007/978-3-642-22110-1_60
17. Hague, M., Lin, A.W.: Synchronisation- and reversal-bounded analysis of multithreaded programs with counters. In: Madhusudan, P., Seshia, S.A. (eds.) CAV 2012. LNCS, vol. 7358, pp. 260–276. Springer, Heidelberg (2012). https://doi.org/10.1007/978-3-642-31424-7_22
18. Ibarra, O.H.: Reversal-bounded multicounter machines and their decision problems. J. ACM **25**(1), 116–133 (1978). http://doi.acm.org/10.1145/322047.322058
19. Ibarra, O.H.: Automata with reversal-bounded counters: a survey. In: Jürgensen, H., Karhumäki, J., Okhotin, A. (eds.) DCFS 2014. LNCS, vol. 8614, pp. 5–22. Springer, Cham (2014). https://doi.org/10.1007/978-3-319-09704-6_2
20. Karianto, W.: Parikh automata with pushdown stack. Technical report (2004)
21. Klaedtke, F.: Parikh automata and monadic second-order logics with linear cardinality constraints. Technical report, 30 July 2002
22. Klaedtke, F., Rueß, H.: Monadic second-order logics with cardinalities. In: Baeten, J.C.M., Lenstra, J.K., Parrow, J., Woeginger, G.J. (eds.) ICALP 2003. LNCS, vol. 2719, pp. 681–696. Springer, Heidelberg (2003). https://doi.org/10.1007/3-540-45061-0_54. http://dl.acm.org/citation.cfm?id=1759210.1759277
23. König, B., Esparza, J.: Verification of graph transformation systems with context-free specifications. In: Ehrig, H., Rensink, A., Rozenberg, G., Schürr, A. (eds.) ICGT 2010. LNCS, vol. 6372, pp. 107–122. Springer, Heidelberg (2010). https://doi.org/10.1007/978-3-642-15928-2_8
24. Parikh, R.J.: On context-free languages. J. ACM **13**(4), 570–581 (1966). https://doi.org/10.1145/321356.321364
25. Scarpellini, B.: Complexity of subcases of Presburger arithmetic. Trans. Am. Math. Soc. **284**(1), 203–218 (1984)
26. Schwoon, S.: Model checking pushdown systems. Ph.D. thesis, Technical University Munich, Germany (2002). http://tumb1.biblio.tu-muenchen.de/publ/diss/in/2002/schwoon.html
27. Shepherdson, J.C.: The reduction of two-way automata to one-way automata. IBM J. Res. Dev. **3**(2), 198–200 (1959)
28. Vardi, M.Y., Wolper, P.: An automata-theoretic approach to automatic program verification (preliminary report). In: LICS, pp. 332–344. IEEE Computer Society (1986)

29. Verma, K.N., Seidl, H., Schwentick, T.: On the complexity of equational horn clauses. In: Nieuwenhuis, R. (ed.) CADE 2005. LNCS (LNAI), vol. 3632, pp. 337–352. Springer, Heidelberg (2005). https://doi.org/10.1007/11532231_25
30. Walukiewicz, I.: Pushdown processes: games and model-checking. Inf. Comput. **164**(2), 234–263 (2001). https://doi.org/10.1006/inco.2000.2894. http://www.sciencedirect.com/science/article/pii/S0890540100928943

3

Equational Axiomatization of Algebras with Structure

Stefan Milius and Henning Urbat(✉)

Friedrich-Alexander-Universität Erlangen-Nürnberg, Erlangen, Germany
henning.urbat@fau.de

Abstract. This paper proposes a new category theoretic account of equationally axiomatizable classes of algebras. Our approach is well-suited for the treatment of algebras equipped with additional computationally relevant structure, such as ordered algebras, continuous algebras, quantitative algebras, nominal algebras, or profinite algebras. Our main contributions are a generic HSP theorem and a sound and complete equational logic, which are shown to encompass numerous flavors of equational axiomizations studied in the literature.

1 Introduction

A key tool in the algebraic theory of data structures is their specification by operations (constructors) and equations that they ought to satisfy. Hence, the study of models of equational specifications has been of long standing interest both in mathematics and computer science. The seminal result in this field is Birkhoff's celebrated HSP theorem [7]. It states that a class of algebras over a signature Σ is a *variety* (i.e. closed under homomorphic images, subalgebras, and products) iff it is axiomatizable by equations $s = t$ between Σ-terms. Birkhoff also introduced a complete deduction system for reasoning about equations.

In algebraic approaches to the semantics of programming languages and computational effects, it is often natural to study algebras whose underlying sets are equipped with additional computationally relevant structure and whose operations preserve that structure. An important line of research thus concerns extensions of Birkhoff's theory of equational axiomatization beyond ordinary Σ-algebras. On the syntactic level, this requires to enrich Birkhoff's notion of an equation in ways that reflect the extra structure. Let us mention a few examples:

(1) *Ordered algebras* (given by a poset and monotone operations) and *continuous algebras* (given by a complete partial order and continuous operations) were identified by the ADJ group [14] as an important tool in denotational semantics. Subsequently, Bloom [8] and Adámek, Nelson, and Reiterman [2,3]

established ordered versions of the HSP theorem along with complete deduction systems. Here, the role of equations $s = t$ is taken over by inequations $s \leq t$.

(2) *Quantitative algebras* (given by an extended metric space and nonexpansive operations) naturally arise as semantic domains in the theory of probabilistic computation. In recent work, Mardare, Panangaden, and Plotkin [18, 19] presented an HSP theorem for quantitative algebras and a complete deduction system. In the quantitative setting, equations $s =_\varepsilon t$ are equipped with a non-negative real number ε, interpreted as "s and t have distance at most ε".

(3) *Nominal algebras* (given by a nominal set and equivariant operations) are used in the theory of name binding [24] and have proven useful for characterizing logics for data languages [9, 11]. Varieties of nominal algebras were studied by Gabbay [13] and Kurz and Petrişan [16]. Here, the appropriate syntactic concept involves equations $s = t$ with constraints on the support of their variables.

(4) *Profinite algebras* (given by a profinite topological space and continuous operations) play a central role in the algebraic theory of formal languages [22]. They serve as a technical tool in the investigation of *pseudovarieties* (i.e. classes of finite algebras closed under homomorphic images, subalgebras, and finite products). As shown by Reiterman [25] and Eilenberg and Schützenberger [12], pseudovarieties can be axiomatized by *profinite equations* (formed over free profinite algebras) or, equivalently, by sequences of ordinary equations $(s_i = t_i)_{i<\omega}$, interpreted as "all but finitely many of the equations $s_i = t_i$ hold".

The present paper proposes a general category theoretic framework that allows to study classes of algebras with extra structure in a systematic way. Our overall goal is to isolate the domain-specific part of any theory of equational axiomatization from its generic core. Our framework is parametric in the following data:

- a category $\mathscr{A}$ with a factorization system $(\mathcal{E}, \mathcal{M})$;
- a full subcategory $\mathscr{A}_0 \subseteq \mathscr{A}$;
- a class Λ of cardinal numbers;
- a class $\mathscr{X} \subseteq \mathscr{A}$ of objects.

Here, $\mathscr{A}$ is the category of algebras under consideration (e.g. ordered algebras, quantitative algebras, nominal algebras). Varieties are formed within $\mathscr{A}_0$, and the cardinal numbers in Λ determine the arities of products under which the varieties are closed. Thus, the choice $\mathscr{A}_0$ = finite algebras and Λ = finite cardinals corresponds to pseudovarieties, and $\mathscr{A}_0 = \mathscr{A}$ and Λ = all cardinals to varieties. The crucial ingredient of our setting is the parameter $\mathscr{X}$, which is the class of objects over which equations are formed; thus, typically, $\mathscr{X}$ is chosen to be some class of freely generated algebras in $\mathscr{A}$. Equations are modeled as $\mathcal{E}$-quotients $e\colon X \twoheadrightarrow E$ (more generally, filters of such quotients) with domain $X \in \mathscr{X}$.

The choice of $\mathscr{X}$ reflects the desired expressivity of equations in a given setting. Furthermore, it determines the type of quotients under which equationally axiomatizable classes are closed. More precisely, in our general framework a *variety* is defined to be a subclass of $\mathscr{A}_0$ closed under $\mathcal{E}_{\mathscr{X}}$-quotients, $\mathcal{M}$-subobjects, and Λ-products, where $\mathcal{E}_{\mathscr{X}}$ is a subclass of $\mathcal{E}$ derived from $\mathscr{X}$. Due to its parametric nature, this concept of a variety is widely applicable and turns out to specialize to many interesting cases. The main result of our paper is the

General HSP Theorem. *A subclass of $\mathscr{A}_0$ forms a variety if and only if it is axiomatizable by equations.*

In addition, we introduce a generic deduction system for equations, based on two simple proof rules (see Sect. 4), and establish a

General Completeness Theorem. *The generic deduction system for equations is sound and complete.*

The above two theorems can be seen as the generic building blocks of the model theory of algebras with structure. They form the common core of numerous Birkhoff-type results and give rise to a systematic recipe for deriving concrete HSP and completeness theorems in settings such as (1)–(4). In fact, all that needs to be done is to translate our abstract notion of equation and equational deduction, which involves (filters of) quotients, into an appropriate syntactic concept. This is the domain-specific task to fulfill, and usually amounts to identifying an "exactness" property for the category $\mathscr{A}$. Subsequently, one can apply our general results to obtain HSP and completeness theorems for the type of algebras under consideration. Several instances of this approach are shown in Sect. 5. Omitted proofs and details for the examples can be found in [20].

Related work. Generic approaches to universal algebra have a long tradition in category theory. They aim to replace syntactic notions like terms and equations by suitable categorical abstractions, most prominently Lawvere theories and monads [4,17]. Our present work draws much of its inspiration from the classical paper of Banaschewski and Herrlich [6] on HSP classes in $(\mathcal{E}, \mathcal{M})$-structured categories. These authors were the first to model equations as quotients $e\colon X \twoheadrightarrow E$. However, their approach does not feature the parameter $\mathscr{X}$ and assumes that equations are formed over $\mathcal{E}$-projective objects X. This limits the scope of their results to categories with enough projectives, a property that typically fails in categories of algebras with structure (including continuous, quantitative or nominal algebras). The identification of the parameter $\mathscr{X}$ and of the derived parameter $\mathcal{E}_{\mathscr{X}}$ as a key concept is thus a crucial step towards a categorical view of such structures.

Equational logics on the level of abstraction of Banaschewski and Herrlich's work were studied by Roşu [26,27] and Adámek, Hébert, and Sousa [1]. These authors work under assumptions on the category $\mathscr{A}$ different from our framework, e.g. they require existence of pushouts. Hence, the proof rules and completeness results in *loc. cit.* are not directly comparable to our approach in Sect. 4.

In the present paper, we model equations as filters of quotients rather than single quotients, which allows us to encompass several HSP theorems for finite algebras [12,23,25]. The first categorical generalization of such results was given by Adámek, Chen, Milius, and Urbat [10,29] who considered algebras for a monad $\mathbb{T}$ on an algebraic category and modeled equations as filters of finite quotients of free $\mathbb{T}$-algebras (equivalently, as profinite quotients of free profinite $\mathbb{T}$-algebras). This idea was generalized by Salamánca [28] to monads on concrete categories. However, again, this work only applies to categories with enough projectives.

2 Preliminaries

We start by recalling some notions from category theory. A *factorization system* $(\mathcal{E}, \mathcal{M})$ in a category $\mathscr{A}$ consists of two classes $\mathcal{E}, \mathcal{M}$ of morphisms in $\mathscr{A}$ such that (1) both $\mathcal{E}$ and $\mathcal{M}$ contain all isomorphisms and are closed under composition, (2) every morphism f has a factorization $f = m \cdot e$ with $e \in \mathcal{E}$ and $m \in \mathcal{M}$, and (3) the *diagonal fill-in* property holds: for every commutative square $g \cdot e = m \cdot f$ with $e \in \mathcal{E}$ and $m \in \mathcal{M}$, there exists a unique d with $m \cdot d = g$ and $d \cdot e = f$. The morphisms m and e in (2) are unique up to isomorphism and are called the *image* and *coimage* of f, resp. The factorization system is *proper* if all morphisms in $\mathcal{E}$ are epic and all morphisms in $\mathcal{M}$ are monic. From now on, we will assume that $\mathscr{A}$ is a category equipped with a proper factorization system $(\mathcal{E}, \mathcal{M})$. Quotients and subobjects in $\mathscr{A}$ are taken with respect to $\mathcal{E}$ and $\mathcal{M}$. That is, a *quotient* of an object X is represented by a morphism $e\colon X \twoheadrightarrow E$ in $\mathcal{E}$ and a *subobject* by a morphism $m\colon M \rightarrowtail X$ in $\mathcal{M}$. The quotients of X are ordered by $e \leq e'$ iff e' factorizes through e, i.e. there exists a morphism h with $e' = h \cdot e$. Identifying quotients e and e' which are isomorphic (i.e. $e \leq e'$ and $e' \leq e$), this makes the quotients of X a partially ordered class. Given a full subcategory $\mathscr{A}_0 \subseteq \mathscr{A}$ we denote by $X{\downarrow}\mathscr{A}_0$ the class of all quotients of X represented by $\mathcal{E}$-morphisms with codomain in $\mathscr{A}_0$. The category $\mathscr{A}$ is *$\mathcal{E}$-co-wellpowered* if for every object $X \in \mathscr{A}$ there is only a set of quotients with domain X. In particular, $X{\downarrow}\mathscr{A}_0$ is then a poset. Finally, an object $X \in \mathscr{A}$ is called *projective* w.r.t. a morphism $e\colon A \to B$ if for every $h\colon X \to B$, there exists a morphism $g\colon X \to A$ with $h = e \cdot g$.

3 The Generalized Variety Theorem

In this section, we introduce our categorical notions of equation and variety, and derive the HSP theorem. Fix a category $\mathscr{A}$ with a proper factorization system $(\mathcal{E}, \mathcal{M})$, a full subcategory $\mathscr{A}_0 \subseteq \mathscr{A}$, a class Λ of cardinal numbers, and a class $\mathscr{X} \subseteq \mathscr{A}$ of objects. An object of $\mathscr{A}$ is called *$\mathscr{X}$-generated* if it is a quotient of some object in $\mathscr{X}$. A key role will be played by the subclass $\mathcal{E}_{\mathscr{X}} \subseteq \mathcal{E}$ defined by

$$\mathcal{E}_{\mathscr{X}} = \{e \in \mathcal{E} \ : \ \text{every } X \in \mathscr{X} \text{ is projective w.r.t. } e\}.$$

Note that $\mathscr{X} \subseteq \mathscr{X}'$ implies $\mathcal{E}_{\mathscr{X}'} \subseteq \mathcal{E}_{\mathscr{X}}$. The choice of $\mathscr{X}$ is a trade-off between "having enough equations" (that is, $\mathscr{X}$ needs to be rich enough to make equations sufficiently expressive) and "having enough projectives" (cf. (3) below).

Assumptions 3.1. Our data is required to satisfy the following properties:

(1) $\mathscr{A}$ has Λ-products, i.e. for every $\lambda \in \Lambda$ and every family $(A_i)_{i<\lambda}$ of objects in $\mathscr{A}$, the product $\prod_{i<\lambda} A_i$ exists.
(2) $\mathscr{A}_0$ is closed under isomorphisms, Λ-products and $\mathscr{X}$-generated subobjects. The last statement means that for every subobject $m: A \rightarrowtail B$ in $\mathcal{M}$ where $B \in \mathscr{A}_0$ and A is $\mathscr{X}$-generated, one has $A \in \mathscr{A}_0$.
(3) Every object of $\mathscr{A}_0$ is an $\mathcal{E}_{\mathscr{X}}$-quotient of some object of $\mathscr{X}$, that is, for every object $A \in \mathscr{A}_0$ there exists some $e: X \twoheadrightarrow A$ in $\mathcal{E}_{\mathscr{X}}$ with domain $X \in \mathscr{X}$.

Example 3.2. Throughout this section, we will use the following three running examples to illustrate our concepts. For further applications, see Sect. 5.

(1) *Classical Σ-algebras.* The setting of Birkhoff's seminal work [7] in general algebra is that of algebras for a signature. Recall that a *(finitary) signature* is a set Σ of operation symbols each with a prescribed finite arity, and a *Σ-algebra* is a set A equipped with operations $\sigma: A^n \to A$ for each n-ary $\sigma \in \Sigma$. A *morphism* of Σ-algebras (or a *Σ-homomorphism*) is a map preserving all Σ-operations. The forgetful functor from the category $\mathbf{Alg}(\Sigma)$ of Σ-algebras and Σ-homomorphisms to $\mathbf{Set}$ has a left adjoint assigning to each set X the *free Σ-algebra* $T_\Sigma X$, carried by the set of all Σ-terms in variables from X. To treat Birkhoff's results in our categorical setting, we choose the following parameters:
   - $\mathscr{A} = \mathscr{A}_0 = \mathbf{Alg}(\Sigma)$;
   - $(\mathcal{E}, \mathcal{M}) =$ (surjective morphisms, injective morphisms);
   - $\Lambda =$ all cardinal numbers;
   - $\mathscr{X} =$ all free Σ-algebras $T_\Sigma X$ with $X \in \mathbf{Set}$.

   One easily verifies that $\mathcal{E}_{\mathscr{X}}$ consists of all surjective morphisms, that is, $\mathcal{E}_{\mathscr{X}} = \mathcal{E}$.
(2) *Finite Σ-algebras.* Eilenberg and Schützenberger [12] considered classes of finite Σ-algebras, where Σ is assumed to be a signature with only finitely many operation symbols. In our framework, this amounts to choosing
   - $\mathscr{A} = \mathbf{Alg}(\Sigma)$ and $\mathscr{A}_0 = \mathbf{Alg}_{\mathsf{f}}(\Sigma)$, the full subcategory of finite Σ-algebras;
   - $(\mathcal{E}, \mathcal{M}) =$ (surjective morphisms, injective morphisms);
   - $\Lambda =$ all finite cardinal numbers;
   - $\mathscr{X} =$ all free Σ-algebras $T_\Sigma X$ with $X \in \mathbf{Set}_{\mathsf{f}}$.

   As in (1), the class $\mathcal{E}_{\mathscr{X}}$ consists of all surjective morphisms.
(3) *Quantitative Σ-algebras.* In recent work, Mardare, Panangaden, and Plotkin [18,19] extended Birkhoff's theory to algebras endowed with a metric. Recall that an *extended metric space* is a set A with a map $d_A: A \times A \to [0, \infty]$ (assigning to any two points a possibly infinite distance), subject to the axioms (i) $d_A(a, b) = 0$ iff $a = b$, (ii) $d_A(a, b) = d_A(b, a)$, and (iii) $d_A(a, c) \leq d_A(a, b) + d_A(b, c)$ for all $a, b, c \in A$. A map $h: A \to B$ between extended metric spaces is *nonexpansive* if $d_B(h(a), h(a')) \leq d_A(a, a')$ for $a, a' \in A$. Let $\mathbf{Met}_\infty$ denote the category of extended metric spaces and nonexpansive maps. Fix a, not necessarily finitary, signature Σ, that is, the arity of an operation symbol $\sigma \in \Sigma$ is any cardinal number. A *quantitative Σ-algebra*

is a Σ-algebra A endowed with an extended metric d_A such that all Σ-operations $\sigma\colon A^n \to A$ are nonexpansive. Here, the product A^n is equipped with the sup-metric $d_{A^n}((a_i)_{i<n},(b_i)_{i<n}) = \sup_{i<n} d_A(a_i,b_i)$. The forgetful functor from the category $\mathbf{QAlg}(\Sigma)$ of quantitative Σ-algebras and nonexpansive Σ-homomorphisms to $\mathbf{Met}_\infty$ has a left adjoint assigning to each space X the free quantitative Σ-algebra $T_\Sigma X$. The latter is carried by the set of all Σ-terms (equivalently, well-founded Σ-trees) over X, with metric inherited from X as follows: if s and t are Σ-terms of the same shape, i.e. they differ only in the variables, their distance is the supremum of the distances of the variables in corresponding positions of s and t; otherwise, it is ∞.

We aim to derive the HSP theorem for quantitative algebras proved by Mardare et al. as an instance of our general results. The theorem is parametric in a regular cardinal number $c > 1$. In the following, an extended metric space is called *c-clustered* if it is a coproduct of spaces of size $< c$. Note that coproducts in $\mathbf{Met}_\infty$ are formed on the level of underlying sets. Choose the parameters

- $\mathscr{A} = \mathscr{A}_0 = \mathbf{QAlg}(\Sigma)$;
- $(\mathcal{E}, \mathcal{M})$ given by morphisms carried by surjections and subspaces, resp.;
- $\Lambda =$ all cardinal numbers;
- $\mathscr{X} =$ all free algebras $T_\Sigma X$ with $X \in \mathbf{Met}_\infty$ a c-clustered space.

One can verify that a quotient $e\colon A \twoheadrightarrow B$ belongs to $\mathcal{E}_\mathscr{X}$ if and only if for each subset $B_0 \subseteq B$ of cardinality $< c$ there exists a subset $A_0 \subseteq A$ such that $e[A_0] = B_0$ and the restriction $e\colon A_0 \to B_0$ is isometric (that is, $d_B(e(a), e(a')) = d_A(a, a')$ for $a, a' \in A_0$). Following the terminology of Mardare et al., such a quotient is called *c-reflexive*. Note that for $c = 2$ every quotient is c-reflexive, so $\mathcal{E}_\mathscr{X} = \mathcal{E}$. If c is infinite, $\mathcal{E}_\mathscr{X}$ is a proper subclass of $\mathcal{E}$.

Definition 3.3. An *equation over* $X \in \mathscr{X}$ is a class $\mathscr{T}_X \subseteq X{\downarrow}\mathscr{A}_0$ that is

(1) *Λ-codirected:* every subset $F \subseteq \mathscr{T}_X$ with $|F| \in \Lambda$ has a lower bound in F;
(2) *closed under $\mathcal{E}_\mathscr{X}$-quotients:* for every $e\colon X \twoheadrightarrow E$ in $\mathscr{T}_X$ and $q\colon E \twoheadrightarrow E'$ in $\mathcal{E}_\mathscr{X}$ with $E' \in \mathscr{A}_0$, one has $q \cdot e \in \mathscr{T}_X$.

An object $A \in \mathscr{A}$ *satisfies* the equation $\mathscr{T}_X$ if every morphism $h\colon X \to A$ factorizes through some $e \in \mathscr{T}_X$. In this case, we write

$$A \models \mathscr{T}_X.$$

Remark 3.4. In many of our applications, one can simplify the above definition and replace classes of quotients by single quotients. Specifically, if $\mathscr{A}$ is $\mathcal{E}$-cowellpowered (so that every equation is a set, not a class) and $\Lambda =$ all cardinal numbers, then every equation $\mathscr{T}_X \subseteq X{\downarrow}\mathscr{A}_0$ contains a least element $e_X\colon X \twoheadrightarrow E_X$, viz. the lower bound of all elements in $\mathscr{T}_X$. Then an object A satisfies $\mathscr{T}_X$ iff it satisfies e_X, in the sense that every morphism $h\colon X \to A$ factorizes through e_X. Therefore, in this case, one may equivalently define an equation to be a morphism $e_X\colon X \twoheadrightarrow E_X$ with $X \in \mathscr{X}$. This is the concept of equation investigated by Banaschewski and Herrlich [6].

Example 3.5. In our running examples, we obtain the following concepts:

(1) *Classical Σ-algebras.* By Remark 3.4, an equation corresponds to a quotient $e_X: T_\Sigma X \twoheadrightarrow E_X$ in $\mathbf{Alg}(\Sigma)$, where X is a set of variables.
(2) *Finite Σ-algebras.* An equation $\mathscr{T}_X$ over a finite set X is precisely a filter (i.e. a codirected and upwards closed subset) in the poset $T_\Sigma X{\downarrow}\mathbf{Alg}_\mathsf{f}(\Sigma)$.
(3) *Quantitative Σ-algebras.* By Remark 3.4, an equation can be presented as a quotient $e_X: T_\Sigma X \twoheadrightarrow E_X$ in $\mathbf{QAlg}(\Sigma)$, where X is a c-clustered space.

We shall demonstrate in Sect. 5 how to interpret the above abstract notions of equations, i.e. (filters of) quotients of free algebras, in terms of concrete syntax.

Definition 3.6. A *variety* is a full subcategory $\mathcal{V} \subseteq \mathscr{A}_0$ closed under $\mathcal{E}_\mathscr{X}$-quotients, subobjects, and Λ-products. More precisely,

(1) for every $\mathcal{E}_\mathscr{X}$-quotient $e: A \twoheadrightarrow B$ in $\mathscr{A}_0$ with $A \in \mathcal{V}$ one has $B \in \mathcal{V}$,
(2) for every $\mathcal{M}$-morphism $m: A \rightarrowtail B$ in $\mathscr{A}_0$ with $B \in \mathcal{V}$ one has $A \in \mathcal{V}$, and
(3) for every family of objects A_i $(i < \lambda)$ in $\mathcal{V}$ with $\lambda \in \Lambda$ one has $\prod_{i<\lambda} A_i \in \mathcal{V}$.

Example 3.7. In our examples, we obtain the following notions of varieties:

(1) *Classical Σ-algebras.* A *variety of Σ-algebras* is a class of Σ-algebras closed under quotient algebras, subalgebras, and products. This is Birkhoff's original concept [7].
(2) *Finite Σ-algebras.* A *pseudovariety of Σ-algebras* is a class of finite Σ-algebras closed under quotient algebras, subalgebras, and finite products. This concept was studied by Eilenberg and Schützenberger [12].
(3) *Quantitative Σ-algebras.* For any regular cardinal number $c > 1$, a *c-variety of quantitative Σ-algebras* is a class of quantitative Σ-algebras closed under c-reflexive quotients, subalgebras, and products. This notion of a variety was introduced by Mardare et al. [19].

Construction 3.8. Given a class $\mathbb{E}$ of equations, put

$$\mathcal{V}(\mathbb{E}) = \{A \in \mathscr{A}_0 : A \models \mathscr{T}_X \text{ for each } \mathscr{T}_X \in \mathbb{E}\}.$$

A subclass $\mathcal{V} \subseteq \mathscr{A}_0$ is called *equationally presentable* if $\mathcal{V} = \mathcal{V}(\mathbb{E})$ for some $\mathbb{E}$.

We aim to show that varieties coincide with the equationally presentable classes (see Theorem 3.16 below). The "easy" part of the correspondence is established by the following lemma, which is proved by a straightforward verification.

Lemma 3.9. *For every class $\mathbb{E}$ of equations, $\mathcal{V}(\mathbb{E})$ is a variety.*

As a technical tool for establishing the general HSP theorem and the corresponding sound and complete equational logic, we introduce the following concept:

Definition 3.10. An *equational theory* is a family of equations

$$\mathscr{T} = (\mathscr{T}_X \subseteq X{\downarrow}\mathscr{A}_0)_{X\in\mathscr{X}}$$

with the following two properties (illustrated by the diagrams below):

(1) *Substitution invariance.* For every morphism $h\colon X \to Y$ with $X, Y \in \mathscr{X}$ and every $e_Y : Y \twoheadrightarrow E_Y$ in $\mathscr{T}_Y$, the coimage $e_X : X \twoheadrightarrow E_X$ of $e_Y \cdot h$ lies in $\mathscr{T}_X$.

(2) $\mathcal{E}_{\mathscr{X}}$*-completeness.* For every $Y \in \mathscr{X}$ and every quotient $e\colon Y \twoheadrightarrow E_Y$ in $\mathscr{T}_Y$, there exists an $X \in \mathscr{X}$ and a quotient $e_X : X \twoheadrightarrow E_X$ in $\mathscr{T}_X \cap \mathcal{E}_{\mathscr{X}}$ with $E_X = E_Y$.

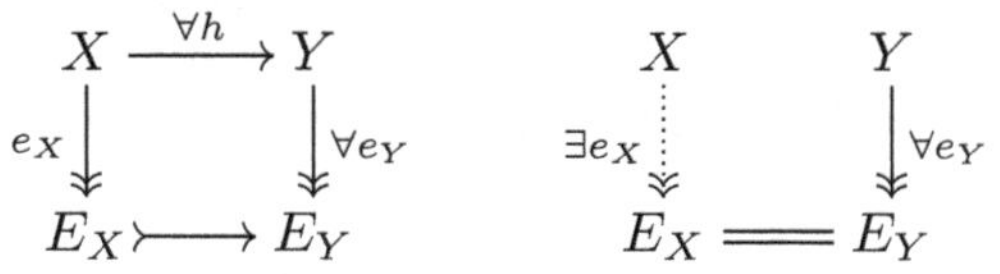

Remark 3.11. In many settings, the slightly technical concept of an equational theory can be simplified. First, note that $\mathcal{E}_{\mathscr{X}}$-completeness is trivially satisfied whenever $\mathcal{E}_{\mathscr{X}} = \mathcal{E}$. If, additionally, every equation contains a least element (e.g. in the setting of Remark 3.4), an equational theory corresponds exactly to a family of quotients $(e_X : X \twoheadrightarrow E_X)_{X\in\mathscr{X}}$ such that $E_X \in \mathscr{A}_0$ for all $X \in \mathscr{X}$, and for every $h\colon X \to Y$ with $X, Y \in \mathscr{X}$ the morphism $e_Y \cdot h$ factorizes through e_X.

Example 3.12 (Classical Σ-algebras). Recall that a *congruence* on a Σ-algebra A is an equivalence relation $\equiv\, \subseteq A \times A$ that forms a subalgebra of $A \times A$. It is well-known that there is an isomorphism of complete lattices

$$\text{quotient algebras of } A \quad \cong \quad \text{congruences on } A \tag{3.1}$$

assigning to a quotient $e\colon A \twoheadrightarrow B$ its *kernel*, given by $a \equiv_e a'$ iff $e(a) = e(a')$. Consequently, in the setting of Example 3.2(1), an equational theory – presented as a family of single quotients as in Remark 3.11 – corresponds precisely to a family of congruences $(\equiv_X\, \subseteq T_\Sigma X \times T_\Sigma X)_{X\in\mathbf{Set}}$ closed under substitution, that is, for every $s, t \in T_\Sigma X$ and every morphism $h\colon T_\Sigma X \to T_\Sigma Y$ in $\mathbf{Alg}(\Sigma)$,

$$s \equiv_X t \quad \text{implies} \quad h(s) \equiv_Y h(t).$$

We saw in Lemma 3.9 that every class of equations, so in particular every equational theory $\mathscr{T}$, yields a variety $\mathcal{V}(\mathscr{T})$ consisting of all objects of $\mathscr{A}_0$ that satisfy every equation in $\mathscr{T}$. Conversely, to every variety one can associate an equational theory as follows:

Construction 3.13. Given a variety $\mathcal{V}$, form the family of equations

$$\mathscr{T}(\mathcal{V}) = (\mathscr{T}_X \subseteq X{\downarrow}\mathscr{A}_0)_{X\in\mathscr{X}},$$

where $\mathscr{T}_X$ consists of all quotients $e_X : X \twoheadrightarrow E_X$ with codomain $E_X \in \mathcal{V}$.

Lemma 3.14. *For every variety $\mathcal{V}$, the family $\mathscr{T}(\mathcal{V})$ is an equational theory.*

We are ready to state the first main result of our paper, the HSP Theorem. Given two equations $\mathscr{T}_X$ and $\mathscr{T}'_X$ over $X \in \mathscr{X}$, we put $\mathscr{T}_X \leq \mathscr{T}'_X$ if every quotient in $\mathscr{T}'_X$ factorizes through some quotient in $\mathscr{T}_X$. Theories form a poset with respect to the order $\mathscr{T} \leq \mathscr{T}'$ iff $\mathscr{T}_X \leq \mathscr{T}'_X$ for all $X \in \mathscr{X}$. Similarly, varieties form a poset (in fact, a complete lattice) ordered by inclusion.

Theorem 3.15 (HSP Theorem). *The complete lattices of equational theories and varieties are dually isomorphic. The isomorphism is given by*

$$\mathcal{V} \mapsto \mathscr{T}(\mathcal{V}) \quad \textit{and} \quad \mathscr{T} \mapsto \mathcal{V}(\mathscr{T}).$$

One can recast the HSP Theorem into a more familiar form, using equations in lieu of equational theories:

Theorem 3.16 (HSP Theorem, equational version). *A class $\mathcal{V} \subseteq \mathscr{A}_0$ is equationally presentable if and only if it forms a variety.*

Proof. By Lemma 3.9, every equationally presentable class $\mathcal{V}(\mathbb{E})$ is a variety. Conversely, for every variety $\mathcal{V}$ one has $\mathcal{V} = \mathcal{V}(\mathscr{T}(\mathcal{V}))$ by Theorem 3.15, so $\mathcal{V}$ is presented by the equations $\mathbb{E} = \{\mathscr{T}_X : X \in \mathscr{X}\}$ where $\mathscr{T} = \mathscr{T}(\mathcal{V})$. □

4 Equational Logic

The correspondence between theories and varieties gives rise to the second main result of our paper, a generic sound and complete deduction system for reasoning about equations. The corresponding semantic concept is the following:

Definition 4.1. An equation $\mathscr{T}_X \subseteq X{\downarrow}\mathscr{A}_0$ *semantically entails* the equation $\mathscr{T}'_Y \subseteq Y{\downarrow}\mathscr{A}_0$ if every $\mathscr{A}_0$-object satisfying $\mathscr{T}_X$ also satisfies $\mathscr{T}'_Y$ (that is, if $\mathcal{V}(\mathscr{T}_X) \subseteq \mathcal{V}(\mathscr{T}'_Y)$). In this case, we write $\mathscr{T}_X \models \mathscr{T}'_Y$.

The key to our proof system is a categorical formulation of term substitution:

Definition 4.2. Let $\mathscr{T}_X \subseteq X{\downarrow}\mathscr{A}_0$ be an equation over $X \in \mathscr{X}$. The *substitution closure* of $\mathscr{T}_X$ is the smallest theory $\overline{\mathscr{T}} = (\overline{\mathscr{T}}_Y)_{Y \in \mathscr{X}}$ such that $\mathscr{T}_X \leq \overline{\mathscr{T}}_X$.

The substitution closure of an equation can be computed as follows:

Lemma 4.3. *For every equation $\mathscr{T}_X \subseteq X{\downarrow}\mathscr{A}_0$ one has $\overline{\mathscr{T}} = \mathscr{T}(\mathcal{V}(\mathscr{T}_X))$.*

The deduction system for semantic entailment consists of two proof rules:

(Weakening) $\mathscr{T}_X \vdash \mathscr{T}'_X$ for all equations $\mathscr{T}'_X \leq \mathscr{T}_X$ over $X \in \mathscr{X}$.
(Substitution) $\mathscr{T}_X \vdash \overline{\mathscr{T}}_Y$ for all equations $\mathscr{T}_X$ over $X \in \mathscr{X}$ and all $Y \in \mathscr{X}$.

Given equations $\mathscr{T}_X$ and $\mathscr{T}'_Y$ over X and Y, respectively, we write $\mathscr{T}_X \vdash \mathscr{T}'_Y$ if $\mathscr{T}'_Y$ arises from $\mathscr{T}_X$ by a finite chain of applications of the above rules.

Theorem 4.4 (Completeness Theorem). *The deduction system for semantic entailment is sound and complete: for every pair of equations $\mathscr{T}_X$ and $\mathscr{T}'_Y$,*

$$\mathscr{T}_X \models \mathscr{T}'_Y \quad \textit{iff} \quad \mathscr{T}_X \vdash \mathscr{T}'_Y.$$

5 Applications

In this section, we present some of the applications of our categorical results (see [20] for full details). Transferring the general HSP theorem of Sect. 3 into a concrete setting requires to perform the following four-step procedure:

Step 1. Instantiate the parameters $\mathscr{A}$, $(\mathcal{E}, \mathcal{M})$, $\mathscr{A}_0$, Λ and $\mathscr{X}$ of our categorical framework, and characterize the quotients in $\mathcal{E}_{\mathscr{X}}$.
Step 2. Establish an *exactness property* for the category $\mathscr{A}$, i.e. a correspondence between quotients $e\colon A \twoheadrightarrow B$ in $\mathscr{A}$ and suitable relations between elements of A.
Step 3. Infer a suitable syntactic notion of equation, and prove it to be expressively equivalent to the categorical notion of equation given by Definition 3.3.
Step 4. Invoke Theorem 3.15 to deduce an HSP theorem.

The details of Steps 2 and 3 are application-specific, but typically straightforward. In each case, the bulk of the usual work required for establishing the HSP theorem is moved to our general categorical results and thus comes for free.

Similarly, to obtain a complete deduction system in a concrete application, it suffices to phrase the two proof rules of our generic equational logic in syntactic terms, using the correspondence of quotients and relations from Step 2; then Theorem 4.4 gives the completeness result.

5.1 Classical Σ-Algebras

The classical Birkhoff theorem emerges from our general results as follows.

Step 1. Choose the parameters of Example 3.2(1), and recall that $\mathcal{E}_{\mathscr{X}} = \mathcal{E}$.
Step 2. The exactness property of $\mathbf{Alg}(\Sigma)$ is given by the correspondence (3.1).
Step 3. Recall from Example 3.5(1) that equations can be presented as single quotients $e\colon T_\Sigma X \twoheadrightarrow E_X$. The exactness property (3.1) leads to the following classical syntactic concept: a *term equation* over a set X of variables is a pair $(s,t) \in T_\Sigma X \times T_\Sigma X$, denoted as $s = t$. It is *satisfied* by a Σ-algebra A if for every map $h\colon X \to A$ we have $h^\sharp(s) = h^\sharp(t)$. Here, $h^\sharp\colon T_\Sigma X \to A$ denotes the unique extension of h to a Σ-homomorphism. Equations and term equations are expressively equivalent in the following sense:

(1) For every equation $e\colon T_\Sigma X \twoheadrightarrow E_X$, the kernel $\equiv_e \subseteq T_\Sigma X \times T_\Sigma X$ is a set of term equations equivalent to e, that is, a Σ-algebra satisfies the equation e iff it satisfies all term equations in $\equiv_e$. This follows immediately from (3.1).
(2) Conversely, given a term equation $(s,t) \in T_\Sigma X \times T_\Sigma X$, form the smallest congruence $\equiv$ on $T_\Sigma X$ with $s \equiv t$ (viz. the intersection of all such congruences) and let $e\colon T_\Sigma X \twoheadrightarrow E_X$ be the corresponding quotient. Then a Σ-algebra satisfies $s = t$ iff it satisfies e. Again, this is a consequence of (3.1).

Step 4. From Theorem 3.16 and Example 3.7(1), we deduce the classical

Theorem 5.1 (Birkhoff [7]). *A class of Σ-algebras is a variety (i.e. closed under quotients, subalgebras, products) iff it is axiomatizable by term equations.*

Similarly, one can obtain Birkhoff's complete deduction system for term equations as an instance of Theorem 4.4; see [20, Section B.1] for details.

5.2 Finite Σ-Algebras

Next, we derive Eilenberg and Schützenberger's equational characterization of pseudovarieties of algebras over a finite signature Σ using our four-step plan:

Step 1. Choose the parameters of Example 3.2(2), and recall that $\mathcal{E}_{\mathscr{X}} = \mathcal{E}$.
Step 2. The exactness property of $\mathbf{Alg}(\Sigma)$ is given by (3.1).
Step 3. By Example 3.2(2), an equational theory is given by a family of filters $\mathscr{T}_n \subseteq T_\Sigma n{\downarrow}\mathbf{Alg}_\mathsf{f}(\Sigma)$ $(n < \omega)$. The corresponding syntactic concept involves sequences $(s_i = t_i)_{i<\omega}$ of term equations. We say that a finite Σ-algebra A *eventually satisfies* such a sequence if there exists $i_0 < \omega$ such that A satisfies all equations $s_i = t_i$ with $i \geq i_0$. Equational theories and sequences of term equations are expressively equivalent:

(1) Let $\mathscr{T} = (\mathscr{T}_n)_{n<\omega}$ be a theory. Since Σ is a finite signature, for each finite quotient $e\colon T_\Sigma n \twoheadrightarrow E$ the kernel $\equiv_e$ is a finitely generated congruence [12, Prop. 2]. Consequently, for each $n < \omega$ the algebra $T_\Sigma n$ has only countably many finite quotients. In particular, the codirected poset $\mathscr{T}_n$ is countable, so it contains an ω^{op}-chain $e_0^n \geq e_1^n \geq e_2^n \geq \cdots$ that is *cofinal*, i.e., each $e \in \mathscr{T}_n$ is above some e_i^n. The e_i^n can be chosen in such a way that, for each $m > n$ and $q\colon m \to n$, the morphism $e_i^n \cdot T_\Sigma q$ factorizes through e_i^m. For each $n < \omega$, choose a finite subset $W_n \subseteq T_\Sigma n \times T_\Sigma n$ generating the kernel of e_n^n. Let $(s_i = t_i)_{i<\omega}$ be a sequence of term equations where (s_i, t_i) ranges over $\bigcup_{n<\omega} W_n$. One can verify that a finite Σ-algebra lies in $\mathcal{V}(\mathscr{T})$ iff it eventually satisfies $(s_i = t_i)_{i<\omega}$.

(2) Conversely, given a sequence of term equations $(s_i = t_i)_{i<\omega}$ with $(s_i, t_i) \in T_\Sigma m_i \times T_\Sigma m_i$, form the theory $\mathscr{T} = (\mathscr{T}_n)_{n<\omega}$ where $\mathscr{T}_n$ consists of all finite quotients $e\colon T_\Sigma n \twoheadrightarrow E$ with the following property:

$$\exists i_0 < \omega : \forall i \geq i_0 : \forall (g\colon T_\Sigma m_i \to T_\Sigma n) : e \cdot g(s_i) = e \cdot g(t_i).$$

Then a finite Σ-algebra eventually satisfies $(s_i = t_i)_{i<\omega}$ iff it lies in $\mathcal{V}(\mathscr{T})$.

Step 4. The theory version of our HSP theorem (Theorem 3.16) now implies:

Theorem 5.2 (Eilenberg-Schützenberger [12]). *A class of finite Σ-algebras is a pseudovariety (i.e. closed under quotients, subalgebras, and finite products) iff it is axiomatizable by a sequence of term equations.*

In an alternative characterization of pseudovarieties due to Reiterman [25], where the restriction to finite signatures Σ can be dropped, sequences of term equations are replaced by the topological concept of a *profinite equation*. This result can also be derived from our general HSP theorem, see [20, Section B.4].

5.3 Quantitative Algebras

In this section, we derive an HSP theorem for quantitative algebras.

Step 1. Choose the parameters of Example 3.2(3). Recall that we work with fixed regular cardinal $c > 1$ and that $\mathcal{E}_{\mathscr{X}}$ consists of all c-reflexive quotients.
Step 2. To state the exactness property of $\mathbf{QAlg}(\Sigma)$, recall that an *(extended) pseudometric* on a set A is a map $p\colon A \times A \to [0, \infty]$ satisfying all axioms of an extended metric except possibly the implication $p(a, b) = 0 \Rightarrow a = b$. Given a quantitative Σ-algebra A, a pseudometric p on A is called a *congruence* if (i) $p(a, a') \le d_A(a, a')$ for all $a, a' \in A$, and (ii) every Σ-operation $\sigma\colon A^n \to A$ ($\sigma \in \Sigma$) is nonexpansive w.r.t. p. Congruences are ordered by $p \le q$ iff $p(a, a') \le q(a, a')$ for all $a, a' \in A$. There is a dual isomorphism of complete lattices

$$\text{quotient algebras of } A \quad \cong \quad \text{congruences on } A \tag{5.1}$$

mapping $e\colon A \twoheadrightarrow B$ to the congruence p_e on A given by $p_e(a, b) = d_B(e(a), e(b))$.
Step 3. By Example 3.5(3), equations can be presented as single quotients $e\colon T_\Sigma X \twoheadrightarrow E$, where X is a c-clustered space. The exactness property (5.1) suggests to replace equations by the following syntactic concept. A *c-clustered equation* over the set X of variables is an expression

$$x_i =_{\varepsilon_i} y_i \ (i \in I) \ \vdash \ s =_\varepsilon t \tag{5.2}$$

where (i) I is a set, (ii) $x_i, y_i \in X$ for all $i \in I$, (iii) s and t are Σ-terms over X, (iv) $\varepsilon_i, \varepsilon \in [0, \infty]$, and (v) the equivalence relation on X generated by the pairs (x_i, y_i) $(i \in I)$ has all equivalence classes of cardinality $< c$. In other words, the set of variables can be partitioned into subsets of size $< c$ such that only relations between variables in the same subset appear on the left-hand side of (5.2). A quantitative Σ-algebra A *satisfies* (5.2) if for every map $h\colon X \to A$ with $d_A(h(x_i), h(y_i)) \le \varepsilon_i$ for all $i \in I$, one has $d_A(h^\sharp(s), h^\sharp(t)) \le \varepsilon$. Here $h^\sharp\colon T_\Sigma X \to A$ denotes the unique Σ-homomorphism extending h.

Equations and c-clustered equations are expressively equivalent:
(1) Let X be a c-clustered space, i.e. $X = \coprod_{j \in J} X_j$ with $|X_j| < c$. Every equation $e\colon T_\Sigma X \twoheadrightarrow E$ induces a set of c-clustered equations over X given by

$$x =_{\varepsilon_{x,y}} y \ (j \in J,\ x, y \in X_j) \ \vdash \ s =_{\varepsilon_{s,t}} t \quad (s, t \in T_\Sigma X), \tag{5.3}$$

with $\varepsilon_{x,y} = d_X(x, y)$ and $\varepsilon_{s,t} = d_E(e(s), e(t))$. It is not difficult to show that e and (5.3) are equivalent: an algebra satisfies e iff it satisfies all equations (5.3).
(2) Conversely, to every c-clustered equation (5.2) over a set X of variables, we associate an equation in two steps:
- Let p the largest pseudometric on X with $p(x_i, y_i) \le \varepsilon_i$ for all i (that is, the pointwise supremum of all such pseudometrics). Form the corresponding quotient $e_p\colon X \twoheadrightarrow X_p$, see (5.1). It is easy to see that X_p is c-clustered.

- Let q be the largest congruence on $T_\Sigma(X_p)$ with $q(T_\Sigma e_p(s), T_\Sigma e_p(t)) \leq \varepsilon$ (that is, the pointwise supremum of all such congruences). Form the corresponding quotient $e_q : T_\Sigma(X_p) \twoheadrightarrow E_q$.

A routine verification shows that (5.2) and e_q are expressively equivalent, i.e. satisfied by the same quantitative Σ-algebras.

Step 4. From Theorem 3.16 and Example 3.7(3), we deduce the following

Theorem 5.3 (Quantitative HSP Theorem). *A class of quantitative Σ-algebras is a c-variety (i.e. closed under c-reflexive quotients, subalgebras, and products) iff it is axiomatizable by c-clustered equations.*

The above theorem generalizes a recent result of Mardare, Panangaden, and Plotkin [19] who considered only signatures Σ with operations of finite or countably infinite arity and cardinal numbers $c \leq \aleph_1$. Theorem 5.3 holds without any restrictions on Σ and c. In addition to the quantitative HSP theorem, one can also derive the completeness of quantitative equational logic [18] from our general completeness theorem, see [20, Section B.5] for details.

5.4 Nominal Algebras

In this section, we derive an HSP theorem for algebras in the category **Nom** of nominal sets and equivariant maps; see Pitts [24] for the required terminology. We denote by $\mathbb{A}$ the countably infinite set of atoms, by $\mathrm{Perm}(\mathbb{A})$ the group of finite permutations of $\mathbb{A}$, and by $\mathsf{supp}_X(x)$ the least support of an element x of a nominal set X. Recall that X is *strong* if, for all $x \in X$ and $\pi \in \mathrm{Perm}(\mathbb{A})$,

$$[\forall a \in \mathsf{supp}_X(x) : \pi(a) = a] \quad \iff \quad \pi \cdot x = x.$$

A *supported set* is a set X equipped with a map $\mathsf{supp}_X : X \to \mathcal{P}_f(\mathbb{A})$. A *morphism* $f : X \to Y$ of supported sets is a function with $\mathsf{supp}_Y(f(x)) \subseteq \mathsf{supp}_X(x)$ for all $x \in X$. Every nominal set X is a supported set w.r.t. its least-support map supp_X. The following lemma, whose first part is a reformulation of [21, Prop. 5.10], gives a useful description of strong nominal sets in terms of supported sets.

Lemma 5.4. *The forgetful functor from* **Nom** *to* **SuppSet** *has a left adjoint* $F : \mathbf{SuppSet} \to \mathbf{Nom}$. *The nominal sets of the form FY ($Y \in$ **SuppSet**) are up to isomorphism exactly the strong nominal sets.*

Fix a finitary signature Σ. A *nominal Σ-algebra* is a Σ-algebra A carrying the structure of a nominal set such that all Σ-operations $\sigma : A^n \to A$ are equivariant. The forgetful functor from the category $\mathbf{NomAlg}(\Sigma)$ of nominal Σ-algebras and equivariant Σ-homomorphisms to **Nom** has a left adjoint assigning to each nominal set X the *free nominal Σ-algebra $T_\Sigma X$*, carried by the set of Σ-terms and with group action inherited from X. To derive a nominal HSP theorem from our general categorical results, we proceed as follows.

Step 1. Choose the parameters of our setting as follows:

- $\mathscr{A} = \mathscr{A}_0 = \mathbf{NomAlg}(\Sigma)$;
- $(\mathcal{E}, \mathcal{M}) =$ (surjective morphisms, injective morphisms);
- $\Lambda =$ all cardinal numbers;
- $\mathscr{X} = \{T_\Sigma X \ : \ X \text{ is a strong nominal set}\}$.

One can show that a quotient $e\colon A \twoheadrightarrow B$ belongs to $\mathcal{E}_{\mathscr{X}}$ iff it is *support-reflecting*: for every $b \in B$ there exists $a \in A$ with $e(a) = b$ and $\mathsf{supp}_A(a) = \mathsf{supp}_B(b)$.

Step 2. A *nominal congruence* on a nominal Σ-algebra A is a Σ-algebra congruence $\equiv\ \subseteq A \times A$ that forms an equivariant subset of $A \times A$. In analogy to (3.1), there is an isomorphism of complete lattices

$$\text{quotient algebras of } A \quad \cong \quad \text{nominal congruences on } A. \tag{5.4}$$

Step 3. By Remark 3.4, an equation can be presented as a single quotient $e\colon T_\Sigma X \twoheadrightarrow E$, where X is a strong nominal set. Equations can be described by syntactic means as follows. A *nominal Σ-term* over a set Y of variables is an element of $T_\Sigma(\mathrm{Perm}(\mathbb{A}) \times Y)$. Every map $h\colon Y \to A$ into a nominal Σ-algebra A extends to the Σ-homomorphism

$$\hat{h} = (T_\Sigma(\mathrm{Perm}(\mathbb{A}) \times Y) \xrightarrow{T_\Sigma(\mathrm{Perm}(\mathbb{A})\times h)} T_\Sigma(\mathrm{Perm}(\mathbb{A}) \times A) \xrightarrow{T_\Sigma(-\cdot-)} T_\Sigma A \xrightarrow{id^\sharp} A)$$

where $id^\sharp$ is the unique Σ-homomorphism extending the identity map $id\colon A \to A$. A *nominal equation* over Y is an expression of the form

$$\mathsf{supp}_Y \vdash s = t, \tag{5.5}$$

where $\mathsf{supp}_Y : Y \to \mathcal{P}_f(\mathbb{A})$ is a function and s and t are nominal Σ-terms over Y. A nominal Σ-algebra A *satisfies* the equation $\mathsf{supp}_Y \vdash s = t$ if for every map $h\colon Y \to A$ with $\mathsf{supp}_A(h(y)) \subseteq \mathsf{supp}_Y(y)$ for all $y \in Y$ one has $\hat{h}(s) = \hat{h}(t)$. Equations and nominal equations are expressively equivalent:

(1) Given an equation $e\colon T_\Sigma X \twoheadrightarrow E$ with X a strong nominal set, choose a supported set Y with $X = FY$, and denote by $\eta_Y : Y \to FY$ the universal map (see Lemma 5.4). Form the nominal equations over Y given by

$$\mathsf{supp}_Y \vdash s = t \quad (s, t \in T_\Sigma(\mathrm{Perm}(\mathbb{A}) \times Y) \text{ and } e \cdot T_\Sigma m(s) = e \cdot T_\Sigma m(t)) \tag{5.6}$$

where m is the composite $\mathrm{Perm}(\mathbb{A}) \times Y \xrightarrow{\mathrm{Perm}(\mathbb{A})\times\eta_Y} \mathrm{Perm}(\mathbb{A}) \times X \xrightarrow{-\cdot-} X$. It is not difficult to see that a nominal Σ-algebra satisfies e iff it satisfies (5.6).

(2) Conversely, given a nominal equation (5.5) over the set Y, let $X = FY$ and form the nominal congruence on $T_\Sigma X$ generated by the pair $(T_\Sigma m(s), T_\Sigma m(t))$, with m defined as above. Let $e\colon T_\Sigma X \twoheadrightarrow E$ be the corresponding quotient, see (5.4). One can show that a nominal Σ-algebra satisfies e iff it satisfies (5.5).

Step 4. We thus deduce the following result as an instance of Theorem 3.16:

Theorem 5.5 (Kurz and Petrişan [16]). *A class of nominal Σ-algebras is a variety (i.e. closed under support-reflecting quotients, subalgebras, and products) iff it is axiomatizable by nominal equations.*

For brevity and simplicity, in this section we restricted ourselves to algebras for a signature. Kurz and Petrişan proved a more general HSP theorem for algebras over an endofunctor on **Nom** with a suitable finitary presentation. This extra generality allows to incorporate, for instance, algebras for binding signatures.

5.5 Further Applications

Let us briefly mention some additional instances of our framework, all of which are given a detailed treatment in the full arXiv paper [20].

Ordered Algebras. Bloom [8] proved an HSP theorem for Σ-algebras in the category of posets: a class of such algebras is closed under homomorphic images, subalgebras, and products, iff it is axiomatizable by inequations $s \leq t$ between Σ-terms. This result can be derived much like the unordered case in Sect. 5.1.

Continuous Algebras. A more intricate ordered version of Birkhoff's theorem concerns *continuous algebras*, i.e. Σ-algebras with an ω-cpo structure on their underlying set and continuous Σ-operations. Adámek, Nelson, and Reiterman [3] proved that a class of continuous algebras is closed under homomorphic images, subalgebras, and products, iff it axiomatizable by inequations between terms with formal suprema (e.g. $\sigma(x) \leq \vee_{i<\omega} c_i$). This result again emerges as an instance of our general HSP theorem. A somewhat curious feature of this application is that the appropriate factorization system $(\mathcal{E}, \mathcal{M})$ takes as $\mathcal{E}$ the class of dense morphisms, i.e. morphisms of $\mathcal{E}$ are not necessarily surjective. However, one has $\mathcal{E}_{\mathscr{X}}$ = surjections, so homomorphic images are formed in the usual sense.

Abstract HSP Theorems. Our results subsume several existing categorical generalizations of Birkhoff's theorem. For instance, Theorem 3.15 yields Manes' [17] correspondence between quotient monads $\mathbb{T} \twoheadrightarrow \mathbb{T}'$ and varieties of $\mathbb{T}$-algebras for any monad $\mathbb{T}$ on **Set**. Similarly, Banaschewski and Herrlich's [6] HSP theorem for objects in categories with enough projectives is a special case of Theorem 3.16.

6 Conclusions and Future Work

We have presented a categorical approach to the model theory of algebras with additional structure. Our framework applies to a broad range of different settings and greatly simplifies the derivation of HSP-type theorems and completeness results for equational deduction systems, as the generic part of such derivations now comes for free using our Theorems 3.15, 3.16 and 4.4. There remain a number of interesting directions and open questions for future work.

As shown in Sect. 5, the key to arrive at a syntactic notion of equation lies in identifying a correspondence between quotients and suitable relations, which we informally coined "exactness". The similarity of these correspondences in our applications suggests that there should be a (possibly enriched) notion of *exact category* that covers our examples; cf. Kurz and Velebil's [15] 2-categorical view of ordered algebras. This would allow to move more work to the generic theory.

Theorem 4.4 can be used to recover several known sound and complete equational logics, but it also applies to settings where no such logic is known, for instance, a logic of profinite equations (however, cf. recent work of Almeida and Klíma [5]). In each case, the challenge is to translate our two abstract proof rules into concrete syntax, which requires the identification of a syntactic equivalent of the two properties of an equational theory. While substitution invariance always translates into a syntactic substitution rule in a straightforward manner, $\mathcal{E}_{\mathscr{X}}$-completeness does not appear to have an obvious syntactic counterpart. In most of the cases where a concrete equational logic is known, this issue is obfuscated by the fact that one has $\mathcal{E}_{\mathscr{X}} = \mathcal{E}$, so $\mathcal{E}_{\mathscr{X}}$-completeness becomes a trivial property. Finding a syntactic account of $\mathcal{E}_{\mathscr{X}}$-completeness remains an open problem. One notable case where $\mathcal{E}_{\mathscr{X}} \neq \mathcal{E}$ is the one of nominal algebras. Gabbay's work [13] does provide an HSP theorem and a sound and complete equational logic in a setting slightly different from Sect. 5.4, and it should be interesting to see whether this can be obtained as an instance of our framework.

Finally, in previous work [29] we have introduced the notion of a *profinite theory* (a special case of the equational theories in the present paper) and shown how the dual concept can be used to derive Eilenberg-type correspondences between varieties of languages and pseudovarieties of finite algebras. Our present results pave the way to an extension of this method to new settings, such as nominal sets. Indeed, a simple modification of the parameters in Sect. 5.4 yields a new HSP theorem for *orbit-finite* nominal Σ-algebras. We expect that a dualization of this result in the spirit of *loc. cit.* leads to a correspondence between varieties of data languages and varieties of orbit-finite nominal monoids, an important step towards an algebraic theory of data languages.

Acknowledgement. The authors would like to thank Thorsten Wißmann for insightful discussions on nominal sets.

References

1. Adámek, J., Hébert, M., Sousa, L.: A logic of injectivity. J. Homotopy Relat. Struct. **2**(2), 13–47 (2007)
2. Adámek, J., Mekler, A.H., Nelson, E., Reiterman, J.: On the logic of continuous algebras. Notre Dame J. Formal Logic **29**(3), 365–380 (1988)
3. Adámek, J., Nelson, E., Reiterman, J.: The Birkhoff variety theorem for continuous algebras. Algebra Univers. **20**(3), 328–350 (1985)
4. Adámek, J., Rosický, J., Vitale, E.M.: Algebraic Theories: A Categorical Introduction to General Algebra. Cambridge Tracts in Mathematics. Cambridge University Press, Cambridge (2010)

5. Almeida, J., Klíma, O.: Towards a pseudoequational proof theory. arXiv preprint arXiv:1708.09681 (2017)
6. Banaschewski, B., Herrlich, H.: Subcategories defined by implications. Houston J. Math. **2**(2), 149–171 (1976)
7. Birkhoff, G.: On the structure of abstract algebras. Proc. Camb. Philos. Soc. **10**, 433–454 (1935)
8. Bloom, S.L.: Varieties of ordered algebras. J. Comput. Syst. Sci. **2**(13), 200–212 (1976)
9. Bojańczyk, M.: Nominal monoids. Theory Comput. Syst. **53**(2), 194–222 (2013)
10. Chen, L.-T., Adámek, J., Milius, S., Urbat, H.: Profinite monads, profinite equations, and Reiterman's theorem. In: Jacobs, B., Löding, C. (eds.) FoSSaCS 2016. LNCS, vol. 9634, pp. 531–547. Springer, Heidelberg (2016). https://doi.org/10.1007/978-3-662-49630-5_31
11. Colcombet, T., Ley, C., Puppis, G.: Logics with rigidly guarded data tests. Log. Methods Comput. Sci. **11**(3) (2015)
12. Eilenberg, S., Schützenberger, M.P.: On pseudovarieties. Adv. Math. **10**, 413–418 (1976)
13. Gabbay, M.J.: Nominal algebra and the HSP theorem. J. Logic Comput. **19**, 341–367 (2009)
14. Goguen, J.A., Thatcher, J.W., Wagner, E.G., Wright, J.B.: Initial algebra semantics and continuous algebras. J. ACM **24**(1), 68–95 (1977)
15. Kurz, A., Velebil, J.: Quasivarieties and varieties of ordered algebras: regularity and exactness. Math. Struct. Comput. Sci. **27**, 1153–1194 (2017)
16. Kurz, A., Petrisan, D.: On universal algebra over nominal sets. Math. Struct. Comput. Sci. **20**(2), 285–318 (2010)
17. Manes, E.G.: Algebraic Theories. Graduate Texts in Mathematics, vol. 26. Springer, New York (1976). https://doi.org/10.1007/978-1-4612-9860-1
18. Mardare, R., Panangaden, P., Plotkin, G.: Quantitative algebraic reasoning. In: Proceedings of the 31st Annual ACM/IEEE Symposium on Logic in Computer Science, LICS 2016, pp. 700–709. ACM (2016)
19. Mardare, R., Panangaden, P., Plotkin, G.: On the axiomatizability of quantitative algebras. In: 32nd Annual ACM/IEEE Symposium on Logic in Computer Science, LICS 2017, Reykjavik, Iceland, 20–23 June 2017, pp. 1–12. IEEE Computer Society (2017). https://doi.org/10.1109/LICS.2017.8005102
20. Milius, S., Urbat, H.: Equational axiomatization of algebras with structure. CoRR abs/1812.02016 (2018). http://arxiv.org/abs/1812.02016
21. Milius, S., Schröder, L., Wißmann, T.: Regular behaviours with names. Appl. Categorical Struct. **24**(5), 663–701 (2016)
22. Pin, J.É.: Profinite methods in automata theory. In: Albers, S., Marion, J.Y. (eds.) 26th International Symposium on Theoretical Aspects of Computer Science STACS 2009, pp. 31–50. IBFI Schloss Dagstuhl (2009)
23. Pin, J.É., Weil, P.: A Reiterman theorem for pseudovarieties of finite first-order structures. Algebra Univers. **35**, 577–595 (1996)
24. Pitts, A.M.: Nominal Sets: Names and Symmetry in Computer Science. Cambridge University Press, Cambridge (2013)
25. Reiterman, J.: The Birkhoff theorem for finite algebras. Algebra Univers. **14**(1), 1–10 (1982)
26. Roşu, G.: Complete categorical equational deduction. In: Fribourg, L. (ed.) CSL 2001. LNCS, vol. 2142, pp. 528–538. Springer, Heidelberg (2001). https://doi.org/10.1007/3-540-44802-0_37

27. Roşu, G.: Complete categorical deduction for satisfaction as injectivity. In: Futatsugi, K., Jouannaud, J.-P., Meseguer, J. (eds.) Algebra, Meaning, and Computation. LNCS, vol. 4060, pp. 157–172. Springer, Heidelberg (2006). https://doi.org/10.1007/11780274_9
28. Salamánca, J.: Unveiling Eilenberg-type Correspondences: Birkhoff's Theorem for (finite) Algebras + Duality (2017). https://arxiv.org/abs/1702.02822
29. Urbat, H., Adámek, J., Chen, L., Milius, S.: Eilenberg theorems for free. CoRR abs/1602.05831 (2017). http://arxiv.org/abs/1602.05831

4

Justness: A Completeness Criterion for Capturing Liveness Properties (Extended Abstract)

Rob van Glabbeek[1,2](✉)

[1] Data61, CSIRO, Sydney, Australia
[2] Computer Science and Engineering, University of New South Wales, Sydney, Australia
rvg@cs.stanford.edu

Abstract. This paper poses that transition systems constitute a good model of distributed systems only in combination with a criterion telling which paths model complete runs of the represented systems. Among such criteria, progress is too weak to capture relevant liveness properties, and fairness is often too strong; for typical applications we advocate the intermediate criterion of justness. Previously, we proposed a definition of justness in terms of an asymmetric concurrency relation between transitions. Here we define such a concurrency relation for the transition systems associated to the process algebra CCS as well as its extensions with broadcast communication and signals, thereby making these process algebras suitable for capturing liveness properties requiring justness.

1 Introduction

Transition systems are a common model for distributed systems. They consist of sets of states, also called *processes*, and transitions—each transition going from a source state to a target state. A given distributed system $\mathcal{D}$ corresponds to a state P in a transition system $\mathbb{T}$—the initial state of $\mathcal{D}$. The other states of $\mathcal{D}$ are the processes in $\mathbb{T}$ that are reachable from P by following the transitions. A run of $\mathcal{D}$ corresponds with a *path* in $\mathbb{T}$: a finite or infinite alternating sequence of states and transitions, starting with P, such that each transition goes from the state before to the state after it. Whereas each finite path in $\mathbb{T}$ starting from P models a *partial run* of $\mathcal{D}$, i.e., an initial segment of a (complete) run, typically not each path models a run. Therefore a transition system constitutes a good model of distributed systems only in combination with what we here call a *completeness criterion*: a selection of a subset of all paths as *complete paths*, modelling runs of the represented system.

A *liveness property* says that "something [good] must happen" eventually [18]. Such a property holds for a distributed system if the [good] thing happens in each of its possible runs. One of the ways to formalise this in terms of transition systems is to postulate a set of good states $\mathscr{G}$, and say that the liveness property $\mathscr{G}$ holds for the process P if all complete paths starting in P pass through a state of $\mathscr{G}$ [16]. Without a completeness criterion the concept of a liveness property appears to be meaningless.

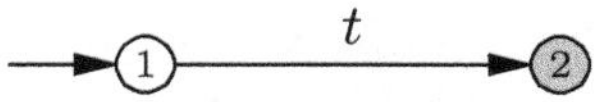

Example 1. The transition system on the right models Cataline eating a croissant in Paris. It abstracts from all activity in the world except the eating of that croissant, and thus has two states only—the states of the world before and after this event—and one transition t. We depict states by circles and transitions by arrows between them. An initial state is indicated by a short arrow without a source state. A possible liveness property says that the croissant will be eaten. It corresponds with the set of states $\mathscr{G}$ consisting of state 2 only. The states of $\mathscr{G}$ are indicated by shading.

The depicted transition system has three paths starting with state 1: 1, $1\,t$ and $1\,t\,2$. The path $1\,t\,2$ models the run in which Cataline finishes the croissant. The path 1 models a run in which Cataline never starts eating the croissant, and the path $1\,t$ models a run in which Cataline starts eating it, but never finishes. The liveness property $\mathscr{G}$ holds only when using a completeness criterion that rules out the paths 1 and $1\,t$ as modelling actual runs of the system, leaving $1\,t\,2$ as the sole complete path.

The transitions of transition systems can be understood to model atomic actions that can be performed by the represented systems. Although we allow these actions to be instantaneous or durational, in the remainder of this paper we adopt the assumption that "atomic actions always terminate" [23]. This is a partial completeness criterion. It rules out the path $1\,t$ in Example 1. We build in this assumption in the definition of a path by henceforth requiring that finite paths should end with a state.

Progress. The most widely employed completeness criterion is *progress.*[1] In the context of *closed systems*, having no run-time interactions with the environment, it is the assumption that a run will never get stuck in a state with outgoing transitions. This rules out the path 1 in Example 1, as t is outgoing. When adopting progress as completeness criterion, the liveness property $\mathscr{G}$ holds for the system modelled in Example 1.

Progress is assumed in almost all work on process algebra that deals with liveness properties, mostly implicitly. Milner makes an explicit progress assumption for the process algebra CCS in [20]. A progress assumption is built into the temporal logics LTL [24], CTL [7] and CTL* [8], namely by disallowing states without outgoing transitions and evaluating temporal formulas by quantifying over infinite paths only.[2] In [17] the 'multiprogramming axiom' is a progress assumption, whereas in [1] progress is assumed as a 'fundamental liveness property'.

[1] Misra [21,22] calls this the 'minimal progress assumption'. In [22] he uses 'progress' as a synonym for 'liveness'. In session types, 'progress' and 'global progress' are used as names of particular liveness properties [4]; this use has no relation with ours.

[2] Exceptionally, states without outgoing transitions are allowed, and then quantification is over all *maximal* paths, i.e. paths that are infinite or end in a state without outgoing transitions [5].

As we argued in [10,15,16], a progress assumption as above is too strong in the context of reactive systems, meaning that it rules out as incomplete too many paths. There, a transition typically represents an interaction between the distributed system being modelled and its environment. In many cases a transition can occur only if both the modelled system *and* the environment are ready to engage in it. We therefore distinguish *blocking* and *non-blocking* transitions. A transition is non-blocking if the environment cannot or will not block it, so that its execution is entirely under the control of the system under consideration. A blocking transition on the other hand may fail to occur because the environment is not ready for it. The same was done earlier in the setting of Petri nets [26], where blocking and non-blocking transitions are called *cold* and *hot*, respectively.

In [10,15,16] we worked with transition systems that are equipped with a partitioning of the transitions into blocking and non-blocking ones, and reformulated the progress assumption as follows:

> *a (transition) system in a state that admits a non-blocking transition will eventually progress, i.e., perform a transition.*

In other words, a run will never get stuck in a state with outgoing non-blocking transitions. In Example 1, when adopting progress as our completeness criterion, we assume that Cataline actually wants to eat the croissant, and does not willingly remain in State 1 forever. When that assumption is unwarranted, one would model her behaviour by a transition system different from that of Example 1. However, she may still be stuck in State 1 by lack of any croissant to eat. If we want to model the capability of the environment to withhold a croissant, we classify t as a blocking transition, and the liveness property $\mathcal{G}$ does not hold. If we abstract from a possible shortage of croissants, t is deemed a non-blocking transition, and, when assuming progress, $\mathcal{G}$ holds.

As an alternative approach to a dogmatic division of transitions in a transition system, we could shift the status of transitions to the progress property, and speak of B-progress when B is the set of blocking transitions. In that approach, $\mathcal{G}$ holds for State 1 of Example 1 under the assumption of B-progress when $t \notin B$, but not when $t \in B$.

Justness. Justness is a completeness criterion proposed in [10,15,16]. It strengthens progress. It can be argued that once one adopts progress it makes sense to go a step further and adopt even justness.

Example 2. The transition system on the top right models Alice making an unending sequence of phone calls in London. There is no interaction of any kind between Alice and Cataline. Yet, we may chose to abstracts from all activity in the world except the eating of the croissant by Cataline, and the making of calls by Alice. This yields the combined transition system on the bottom right. Even when taking the transition t to be non-blocking, progress is not a strong enough completeness criterion to ensure that Cataline will ever eat the croissant. For the infinite path

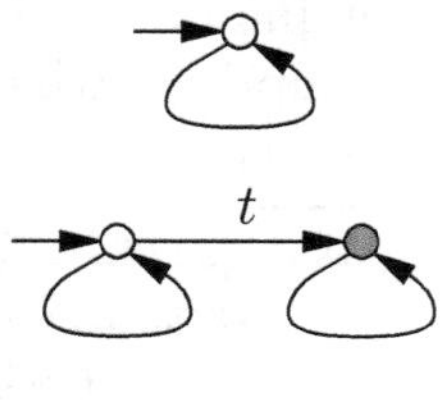

that loops in the first state is complete. Nevertheless, as nothing stops Cataline from making progress, in reality t will occur [16].

This example is not a contrived corner case, but a rather typical illustration of an issue that is central to the study of distributed systems. Other illustrations of this phenomena occur in [10, Section 9.1], [14, Section 10], [11, Section 1.4], [12] and [6, Section 4]. The criterion of justness aims to ensure the liveness property occurring in these examples. In [16] it is formulated as follows:

> *Once a non-blocking transition is enabled that stems from a set of parallel components, one (or more) of these components will eventually partake in a transition.*

In Example 2, t is a non-blocking transition enabled in the initial state. It stems from the single parallel component Cataline of the distributed system under consideration. Justness therefore requires that Cataline must partake in a transition. This can only be t, as all other transitions involve component Alice only. Hence justness says that t must occur. The infinite path starting in the initial state and not containing t is ruled out as unjust, and thereby incomplete.

In [13,16] we explain how justness is fundamentally different from fairness, and why fairness is too strong a completeness criterion for many applications.

Unlike progress, the concept of justness as formulated above is in need of some formalisation, i.e., to formally define a component, to make precise for concrete transition systems what it means for a transition to stem from a set of components, and to define when a component partakes in a transition.

A formalisation of justness for the transition system generated by the process algebra AWN, the *Algebra for Wireless Networks* [9], was provided in [10]. In the same vain, [15] offered a formalisation for the transition systems generated by CCS [20], and its extension ABC, the *Algebra of Broadcast Communication* [15], a variant of CBS, the *Calculus of Broadcasting Systems* [25]. The same was done for CCS extended with *signals* in [6]. These formalisations coinductively define *B-justness*, where B ranges over sets of transitions deemed to be blocking, as a family of predicates on paths, and proceed by a case distinction on the operators in the language. Although these definitions *do* capture the concept of justness formulated above, it is not easy to see why.

A more syntax-independent formalisation of justness occurs in [16]. There it is defined directly on transition systems equipped with a, possibly asymmetric, concurrency relation between transitions. However, the concurrency relation itself is defined only for the transition system generated by a fragment of CCS, and the generalisation to full CCS, and other process algebras, is non-trivial.

It is the purpose of this paper to make the definition of justness from [16] available to a large range of process algebras by defining the concurrency relation for CCS, for ABC, and for the extension of CCS with signals used in [6]. We do this in a precise as well as in an approximate way, and show that both approaches lead to the same concept of justness. Moreover, in all cases we establish a closure property on the concurrency relation ensuring that justness is a meaningful notion. We show that for all these algebras justness is *feasible*. Here feasibility is a requirement on completeness criteria advocated in [1, 16, 19]. Finally, we establish agreement between the formalisation of justness from [16] and the present paper, and the original coinductive ones from [15] and [6].

2 Labelled Transition Systems with Concurrency

We start with the formal definitions of a labelled transition system, a path, and the completeness criterion *progress*, which is parametrised by the choice of a collection B of blocking actions. Then we define the completeness criterion *justness* on labelled transition system upgraded with a concurrency relation.

Definition 1. A *labelled transition system* (LTS) is a tuple $(S, \mathit{Tr}, \mathit{src}, \mathit{target}, \ell)$ with S and Tr sets (of *states* and *transitions*), $\mathit{src}, \mathit{target} : \mathit{Tr} \to S$ and $\ell : \mathit{Tr} \to \mathscr{L}$, for some set of transition labels $\mathscr{L}$.

Here we work with LTSs labelled over a structured set of labels $(\mathscr{L}, \mathit{Act}, \mathit{Rec})$, where $\mathit{Rec} \subseteq \mathit{Act} \subseteq \mathscr{L}$. Labels in Act are *actions*; the ones in $\mathscr{L} \setminus \mathit{Act}$ are *signals*. Transitions labelled with actions model a state chance in the represented system; signal transitions do not—they satisfy $\mathit{src}(t) = \mathit{target}(t)$ and merely convey a property of a state. $\mathit{Rec} \subseteq \mathit{Act}$ is the set of *receptive* actions; sets $B \subseteq \mathit{Act}$ of blocking actions must always contain Rec. In CCS and most other process algebras $\mathit{Rec} = \emptyset$ and $\mathit{Act} = \mathscr{L}$. Let $\mathit{Tr}^\bullet = \{t \in \mathit{Tr} \mid \ell(t) \in \mathit{Act} \setminus \mathit{Rec}\}$ be the set of transitions that are neither signals nor receptive.

Definition 2. A *path* in a transition system $(S, \mathit{Tr}, \mathit{src}, \mathit{target})$ is an alternating sequence $s_0\, t_1\, s_1\, t_2\, s_2 \cdots$ of states and non-signal transitions, starting with a state and either being infinite or ending with a state, such that $\mathit{src}(t_i) = s_{i-1}$ and $\mathit{target}(t_i) = s_i$ for all relevant i.

A *completeness criterion* is a unary predicate on the paths in a transition system.

Definition 3. Let $B \subseteq \mathit{Act}$ be a set of actions with $\mathit{Rec} \subseteq B$—the *blocking* ones. Then $\mathit{Tr}^\bullet_{\neg B} := \{t \in \mathit{Tr}^\bullet \mid \ell(t) \notin B\}$ is the set of *non-blocking* transitions. A path in $\mathbb{T}$ is *B-progressing* if either it is infinite or its last state is the source of no non-blocking transition $t \in \mathit{Tr}^\bullet_{\neg B}$.

B-progress is a completeness criterion for any choice of $B \subseteq \mathit{Act}$ with $\mathit{Rec} \subseteq B$.

Definition 4. A *labelled transition system with concurrency* (LTSC) is a tuple $(S, \mathit{Tr}, \mathit{src}, \mathit{target}, \ell, \smile^\bullet)$ consisting of a LTS $(S, \mathit{Tr}, \mathit{src}, \mathit{target}, \ell)$ and a *concurrency relation* $\smile^\bullet \subseteq \mathit{Tr}^\bullet \times \mathit{Tr}$, such that:

$$t \not\smile^\bullet t \text{ for all } t \in \mathit{Tr}^\bullet, \tag{1}$$

if $t \in \mathit{Tr}^\bullet$ and π is a path from $\mathit{src}(t)$ to $s \in S$ such that $t \smile^\bullet v$ for all transitions v occurring in π, then there is a $u \in \mathit{Tr}^\bullet$ such that $\mathit{src}(u) = s$, $\ell(u) = \ell(t)$ and $t \not\smile^\bullet u$. (2)

Informally, $t \smile^{\bullet} v$ means that the transition v does not interfere with t, in the sense that it does not affect any resources that are needed by t, so that in a state where t and v are both possible, after doing v one can still do (a future variant u of) t. In many transition systems $\smile^{\bullet}$ is a symmetric relation, denoted $\smile$.

The transition relation in a labelled transition system is often defined as a relation $Tr \subseteq S \times \mathscr{L} \times S$. This approach is not suitable here, as we will encounter multiple transitions with the same source, target and label that ought to be distinguished based on their concurrency relations with other transitions.

Definition 5. A path π in an LTSC is *B-just*, for $Rec \subseteq B \subseteq Act$, if for each transition $t \in Tr^{\bullet}_{\neg B}$ with $s := src(t) \in \pi$, a transition u occurs in the suffix of π starting at s, such that $t \not\smile^{\bullet} u$.

Informally, justness requires that once a non-blocking non-signal transition t is enabled, sooner or later a transition u will occur that interferes with it, possibly t itself. Note that, for any $Rec \subseteq B \subseteq Act$, B-justness is a completeness criterion stronger than B-progress.

Components. Instead of introducing $\smile^{\bullet}$ as a primitive, it is possible to obtain it as a notion derived from two functions $npc, afc : Tr \rightarrow \mathscr{P}(\mathscr{C})$, for a given set of *components* $\mathscr{C}$. These functions could then be added as primitives to the definition of an LTS. They are based on the idea that a process represents a system built from parallel components. Each transition is obtained as a synchronisation of activities from some of these components. Now $npc(t)$ describes the (nonempty) set of components that are *necessary participants* in the execution of t, whereas $afc(t)$ describes the components that are *affected* by the execution of t. The concurrency relation is then defined by

$$t \smile^{\bullet} u \quad \Leftrightarrow \quad npc(t) \cap afc(u) = \emptyset$$

saying that u interferes with t iff a necessary participant in t is affected by u.

Most material above stems from [16]. However, there $Tr^{\bullet} = Tr$, so that $\smile^{\bullet}$ is irreflexive, i.e., $npc(t) \cap afc(t) \neq \emptyset$ for all $t \in Tr$. Moreover, a fixed set B is postulated, so that the notions of progress and justness are not explicitly parametrised with the choice of B. Furthermore, property (2) is new here; it is the weakest closure property that supports Theorem 1 below. In [16] only the model in which $\smile^{\bullet}$ is derived from npc and afc comes with a closure property:

$$\begin{array}{l}\text{If } t, v \in Tr^{\bullet} \text{ with } src(t) = src(v) \text{ and } npc(t) \cap afc(v) = \emptyset, \text{ then} \\ \exists u \in Tr^{\bullet} \text{ with } src(u) = target(v),\ \ell(u) = \ell(t) \text{ and } npc(u) = npc(t).\end{array} \tag{3}$$

Trivially (3) implies (2).

An important requirement on completeness criteria is that any finite path can be extended into a complete path. This requirement was proposed by Apt, Francez and Katz in [1] and called *feasibility*. It also appears in Lamport [19] under the name *machine closure*. The theorem below list conditions under which B-justness is feasible. Its proof is a variant of a similar theorem from [16] showing conditions under which notions of strong and weak fairness are feasible.

Table 1. Structural operational semantics of CCS

$\alpha.P \stackrel{\alpha}{\longrightarrow} P$ (Act)	$\dfrac{P \stackrel{\alpha}{\longrightarrow} P'}{P+Q \stackrel{\alpha}{\longrightarrow} P'}$ (Sum-l)	$\dfrac{Q \stackrel{\alpha}{\longrightarrow} Q'}{P+Q \stackrel{\alpha}{\longrightarrow} Q'}$ (Sum-r)
$\dfrac{P \stackrel{\eta}{\longrightarrow} P'}{P\|Q \stackrel{\eta}{\longrightarrow} P'\|Q}$ (Par-l)	$\dfrac{P \stackrel{c}{\longrightarrow} P',\ Q \stackrel{\bar{c}}{\longrightarrow} Q'}{P\|Q \stackrel{\tau}{\longrightarrow} P'\|Q'}$ (Comm)	$\dfrac{Q \stackrel{\eta}{\longrightarrow} Q'}{P\|Q \stackrel{\eta}{\longrightarrow} P\|Q'}$ (Par-r)
$\dfrac{P \stackrel{\ell}{\longrightarrow} P'}{P\backslash L \stackrel{\ell}{\longrightarrow} P'\backslash L}$ $(\ell, \bar{\ell} \notin L)$ (Res)	$\dfrac{P \stackrel{\ell}{\longrightarrow} P'}{P[f] \stackrel{f(\ell)}{\longrightarrow} P'[f]}$ (Rel)	$\dfrac{P \stackrel{\alpha}{\longrightarrow} P'}{A \stackrel{\alpha}{\longrightarrow} P'}$ $(A \stackrel{def}{=} P)$ (Rec)

Theorem 1. If, in an LTSC with set of blocking actions B, only countably many transitions from $Tr^{\bullet}_{\neg B}$ are enabled in each state, then B-justness is feasible.

All proofs can found in the full version of this paper [13].

3 CCS and Its Extensions with Broadcast and Signals

This section presents four process algebras: Milner's *Calculus of Communicating Systems* (CCS) [20], its extensions with broadcast communication ABC [15] and signals CCSS [6], and an alternative presentation of ABC that avoids negative premises in favour of *discard* transitions.

3.1 CCS

CCS [20] is parametrised with sets $\mathscr{A}$ of *agent identifiers* and $\mathscr{C}_h$ of *(handshake communication) names*; each $A \in \mathscr{A}$ comes with a defining equation $A \stackrel{def}{=} P$ with P being a CCS expression as defined below. $\bar{\mathscr{C}}_h := \{\bar{c} \mid c \in \mathscr{C}_h\}$ is the set of *co-names*. Complementation is extended to $\bar{\mathscr{C}}_h$ by setting $\bar{\bar{c}} = c$. $Act := \mathscr{C}_h \dot{\cup} \bar{\mathscr{C}}_h \dot{\cup} \{\tau\}$ is the set of *actions*, where τ is a special *internal action*. Below, c ranges over $\mathscr{C}_h \cup \bar{\mathscr{C}}_h$, η, α, ℓ over Act, and A, B over $\mathscr{A}$. A *relabelling* is a function $f : \mathscr{C}_h \rightarrow \mathscr{C}_h$; it extends to Act by $f(\bar{c}) = \overline{f(c)}$ and $f(\tau) := \tau$. The set $\mathbb{P}_{\text{CCS}}$ of CCS expressions or *processes* is the smallest set including:

$\mathbf{0}$		*inaction*
$\alpha.P$	for $\alpha \in Act$ and $P \in \mathbb{P}_{\text{CCS}}$	*action prefixing*
$P + Q$	for $P, Q \in \mathbb{P}_{\text{CCS}}$	*choice*
$P\|Q$	for $P, Q \in \mathbb{P}_{\text{CCS}}$	*parallel composition*
$P\backslash L$	for $L \subseteq \mathscr{C}_h$ and $P \in \mathbb{P}_{\text{CCS}}$	*restriction*
$P[f]$	for f a relabelling and $P \in \mathbb{P}_{\text{CCS}}$	*relabelling*
A	for $A \in \mathscr{A}$	*agent identifier*

One often abbreviates $\alpha.\mathbf{0}$ by α, and $P\backslash\{c\}$ by $P\backslash c$. The traditional semantics of CCS is given by the labelled transition relation $\rightarrow \subseteq \mathbb{P}_{\text{CCS}} \times Act \times \mathbb{P}_{\text{CCS}}$, where transitions $P \stackrel{\ell}{\longrightarrow} Q$ are derived from the rules of Table 1.

Table 2. Structural operational semantics of ABC broadcast communication

$$\text{(Bro-l)}\ \frac{P \xrightarrow{b\sharp_1} P',\ Q \stackrel{b?}{\not\rightarrow}}{P|Q \xrightarrow{b\sharp_1} P'|Q} \qquad \text{(Bro-c)}\ \frac{P \xrightarrow{b\sharp_1} P',\ Q \xrightarrow{b\sharp_2} Q'}{P|Q \xrightarrow{b\sharp} P'|Q'}\ \sharp_1 \circ \sharp_2 = \sharp \neq \_ \ \text{ with } \begin{array}{c|cc} \circ & ! & ? \\ \hline ! & \_ & ! \\ ? & ! & ? \end{array} \qquad \text{(Bro-r)}\ \frac{P \stackrel{b?}{\not\rightarrow},\ Q \xrightarrow{b\sharp_2} Q'}{P|Q \xrightarrow{b\sharp_2} P|Q'}$$

3.2 ABC—The Algebra of Broadcast Communication

The Algebra of Broadcast Communication (ABC) [15] is parametrised with sets $\mathscr{A}$ of *agent identifiers*, $\mathscr{B}$ of *broadcast names* and $\mathscr{C}_h$ of *handshake communication names*; each $A \in \mathscr{A}$ comes with a defining equation $A \stackrel{def}{=} P$ with P being a guarded ABC expression as defined below.

The collections $\mathscr{B}!$ and $\mathscr{B}?$ of *broadcast* and *receive* actions are given by $\mathscr{B}\sharp := \{b\sharp \mid b \in \mathscr{B}\}$ for $\sharp \in \{!, ?\}$. $Act := \mathscr{B}! \stackrel{\bullet}{\cup} \mathscr{B}? \stackrel{\bullet}{\cup} \mathscr{C}_h \stackrel{\bullet}{\cup} \bar{\mathscr{C}}_h \stackrel{\bullet}{\cup} \{\tau\}$ is the set of *actions*. Below, A ranges over $\mathscr{A}$, b over $\mathscr{B}$, c over $\mathscr{C}_h \cup \bar{\mathscr{C}}_h$, η over $\mathscr{C}_h \cup \bar{\mathscr{C}}_h \cup \{\tau\}$ and α, ℓ over Act. A *relabelling* is a function $f : (\mathscr{B} \rightarrow \mathscr{B}) \cup (\mathscr{C}_h \rightarrow \mathscr{C}_h)$. It extends to Act by $f(\bar{c}) = \overline{f(c)}$, $f(b\sharp) = f(b)\sharp$ and $f(\tau) := \tau$. The set $\mathbb{P}_{\text{ABC}}$ of ABC expressions is defined exactly as $\mathbb{P}_{\text{CCS}}$. An expression is guarded if each agent identifier occurs within the scope of a prefixing operator. The structural operational semantics of ABC is the same as the one for CCS (see Table 1) but augmented with the rules for broadcast communication in Table 2.

ABC is CCS augmented with a formalism for broadcast communication taken from the Calculus of Broadcasting Systems (CBS) [25]. The syntax without the broadcast and receive actions and all rules except (Bro-l), (Bro-c) and (Bro-r) are taken verbatim from CCS. However, the rules now cover the different name spaces; (Act) for example allows labels of broadcast and receive actions. The rule (Bro-c)—without rules like (Par-l) and (Par-r) with label $b!$—implements a form of broadcast communication where any broadcast $b!$ performed by a component in a parallel composition is guaranteed to be received by any other component that is ready to do so, i.e., in a state that admits a $b?$-transition. In order to ensure associativity of the parallel composition, one also needs this rule for components receiving at the same time ($\sharp_1 = \sharp_2 = ?$). The rules (Bro-l) and (Bro-r) are added to make broadcast communication *non-blocking*: without them a component could be delayed in performing a broadcast simply because one of the other components is not ready to receive it.

3.3 CCS with Signals

CCS with signals (CCSS) [6] is CCS extended with a signalling operator $P\hat{\ }s$. Informally, $P\hat{\ }s$ emits the signal s to be read by another process. $P\hat{\ }s$ could for instance be a traffic light emitting the signal *red*. The reading of the signal emitted by $P\hat{\ }s$ does not interfere with any transition of P, such as jumping to *green*. Formally, CCS is extended with a set $\mathscr{S}$ of *signals*, ranged over by s and r. In CCSS the set of actions is defined as $Act := \mathscr{S} \stackrel{\bullet}{\cup} \mathscr{C}_h \cup \bar{\mathscr{C}}_h \stackrel{\bullet}{\cup} \{\tau\}$, and the set

Table 3. Structural operational semantics for signals of CCSS

$P\hat{\ }s \xrightarrow{\bar{s}} P\hat{\ }s$	$\dfrac{P \xrightarrow{\bar{s}} P'}{P+Q \xrightarrow{\bar{s}} P'+Q}$	$\dfrac{Q \xrightarrow{\bar{s}} Q'}{P+Q \xrightarrow{\bar{s}} P+Q'}$
$\dfrac{P \xrightarrow{\alpha} P'}{P\hat{\ }r \xrightarrow{\alpha} P'}$	$\dfrac{P \xrightarrow{\bar{s}} P'}{P\hat{\ }r \xrightarrow{\bar{s}} P'\hat{\ }r}$	$\dfrac{P \xrightarrow{\bar{s}} P'}{A \xrightarrow{\bar{s}} A}\ (A \stackrel{def}{=} P)$

of labels by $\mathscr{L} := Act \,\dot{\cup}\, \bar{\mathscr{S}}$, where $\bar{\mathscr{S}} := \{\bar{s} \mid s \in \mathscr{S}\}$. A relabelling is a function $f : (\mathscr{S} \to \mathscr{S}) \cup (\mathscr{C}_h \to \mathscr{C}_h)$. It extends to $\mathscr{L}$ by $f(\bar{c}) = \overline{f(c)}$ for $c \in \mathscr{C}_h \cup \mathscr{S}$ and $f(\tau) := \tau$. The set $\mathbb{P}_{\text{CCSS}}$ of CCSS expressions is defined just as $\mathbb{P}_{\text{CCS}}$, but now also $P\hat{\ }s$ is a process for $P \in \mathbb{P}_{\text{CCSS}}$ and $s \in \mathscr{S}$, and restriction also covers signals.

The semantics of CCSS is given by the labelled transition relation $\to\ \subseteq \mathbb{P}_{\text{CCSS}} \times \mathscr{L} \times \mathbb{P}_{\text{CCSS}}$ derived from the rules of CCS (Table 1), where now η, ℓ range over $\mathscr{L}$, α over Act, c over $\mathscr{C}_h \cup \mathscr{S}$ and $L \subseteq \mathscr{C}_h \cup \mathscr{S}$, augmented with the rules of Table 3. The first rule is the base case showing that a process $P\hat{\ }s$ emits the signal s. The rule below models the fact that signalling cannot prevent a process from making progress.

The original semantics of CCSS [6] featured unary predicates $P^{\curvearrowright s}$ on processes to model that P emits the signal s; here, inspired by [3], these predicates are represented as transitions $P \xrightarrow{\bar{s}} P$. Whereas this leads to a simpler operational semantics, the price paid is that these new *signal transitions* need special treatment in the definition of justness—cf. Definitions 2 and 5.

3.4 Using Signals to Avoid Negative Premises in ABC

Finally, we present an alternative operational semantics ABCd of ABC that avoids negative premises. The price to be paid is the introduction of signals that indicate when a state does not admit a receive action.[3] To this end, let $\mathscr{B}{:} := \{b{:} \mid b \in \mathscr{B}\}$ be the set of *broadcast discards*, and $\mathscr{L} := \mathscr{B}{:} \,\dot{\cup}\, Act$ the set of *transition labels*, with Act as in Sect. 3.2. The semantics is given by the labelled transition relation $\to\ \subseteq \mathbb{P}_{\text{ABC}} \times \mathscr{L} \times \mathbb{P}_{\text{ABC}}$ derived from the rules of CCS (Table 1), where now c ranges over $\mathscr{C}_h \cup \bar{\mathscr{C}}_h$, η over $\mathscr{C}_h \cup \bar{\mathscr{C}}_h \cup \{\tau\}$, α over Act and ℓ over $\mathscr{L}$, augmented with the rules of Table 4.

Lemma 1. [25] $P \xrightarrow{b:} Q$ iff $Q = P \wedge P \stackrel{b?}{\not\longrightarrow}$, for $P, Q \in \mathbb{P}_{\text{ABC}}$ and $b \in \mathscr{B}$.

So the structural operational semantics of ABC from Sects. 3.2 and 3.4 yield the same labelled transition relation $\longrightarrow$ when transitions labelled $b{:}$ are ignored. This approach stems from the Calculus of Broadcasting Systems (CBS) [25].

[3] A state P admits an action $\alpha \in Act$ if there exists a transition $P \xrightarrow{\alpha} Q$.

Table 4. SOS of ABC broadcast communication with discard transitions

$$\mathbf{0} \xrightarrow{b:} \mathbf{0} \qquad \alpha.P \xrightarrow{b:} \alpha.P \quad (\alpha{\neq}b?) \qquad \frac{P \xrightarrow{b:} P',\ Q \xrightarrow{b:} Q'}{P+Q \xrightarrow{b:} P'+Q'}$$

$$\frac{P \xrightarrow{b\sharp_1} P',\ Q \xrightarrow{b\sharp_2} Q'}{P|Q \xrightarrow{b\sharp} P'|Q'}\ \sharp_1\circ\sharp_2{=}\sharp{\neq}\_\ \text{ with} \qquad \frac{P \xrightarrow{b:} P'}{A \xrightarrow{b:} A}\ (A \stackrel{def}{=} P)$$

$\circ$	!	?	:
!	_	!	!
?	!	?	?
:	!	?	:

4 An LTS with Concurrency for CCS and Its Extensions

The forthcoming material applies to each of the process algebras from Sect. 3, or combinations thereof. Let $\mathbb{P}$ be the set of processes in the language.

We allocate an LTS as in Definition 1 to these languages by taking S to be the set $\mathbb{P}$ of processes, and Tr the set of *derivations* t of transitions $P \xrightarrow{\ell} Q$ with $P, Q \in \mathbb{P}$. Of course $src(t) = P$, $target(t) = Q$ and $\ell(t) = \ell$. Here a *derivation* of a transition $P \xrightarrow{\ell} Q$ is a well-founded tree with the nodes labelled by transitions, such that the root has label $P \xrightarrow{\ell} Q$, and if μ is the label of a node and K is the set of labels of the children of this node then $\frac{K}{\mu}$ is an instance of a rule of Tables 1, 2, 3 and 4.

We take $Rec := \mathscr{B}?$ in ABC and ABCd: broadcast receipts can always be blocked by the environment, namely by not broadcasting the requested message. For CCS and CCSS we take $Rec := \emptyset$, thus allowing environments that can always participate in certain handshakes, and/or always emit certain signals.

Following [15], we give a name to any derivation of a transition: The unique derivation of the transition $\alpha.P \xrightarrow{\alpha} P$ using the rule (Act) is called $\xrightarrow{\alpha}P$. The unique derivation of the transition $P\hat{\ }s \xrightarrow{\bar{s}} P\hat{\ }s$ is called $P^{\rightarrow s}$. The derivation obtained by application of (Comm) or (Bro-c) on the derivations t and u of the premises of that rule is called $t|u$. The derivation obtained by application of (Par-l) or (Bro-l) on the derivation t of the (positive) premise of that rule, and using process Q at the right of $|$, is $t|Q$. In the same way, (Par-r) and (Bro-r) yield $P|u$, whereas (Sum-l), (Sum-r), (Res), (Rel) and (Rec) yield $t{+}Q$, $P{+}t$, $t\backslash L$, $t[f]$ and $A{:}t$. These names reflect syntactic structure: $t|P \neq P|t$ and $(t|u)|v \neq t|(u|v)$.

Table 3, moreover, contributes derivations $t\hat{\ }r$. The derivations obtained by application of the rules of Table 4 are called $b{:}\mathbf{0}$, $b{:}\alpha.P$, $t+u$, $t|u$ and $A{:}t$, where t and u are the derivations of the premises.

Synchrons. Let $Arg := \{+_{\text{L}}, +_{\text{R}}, |_{\text{L}}, |_{\text{R}}, \backslash L, [f], A{:}, \hat{\ }r \mid L \subseteq \mathscr{C}h \wedge f \text{ a relabelling} \wedge A \in \mathscr{A} \wedge r \in \mathscr{S}\}$. A *synchron* is an expression $\sigma(\xrightarrow{\alpha}P)$ or $\sigma(P^{\rightarrow s})$ or $\sigma(b{:})$ with $\sigma \in Arg^*$, $\alpha \in Act$, $s \in \mathscr{S}$, $P \in \mathbb{P}$ and $b \in \mathscr{B}$. An *argument* $\iota \in Arg$ is applied componentwise to a set Σ of synchrons: $\iota(\Sigma) := \{\iota\varsigma \mid \varsigma \in \Sigma\}$.

The set of synchrons $\varsigma(t)$ of a derivation t of a transition is defined by

$$
\begin{array}{lll}
\varsigma(\xrightarrow{\alpha}P) = \{(\xrightarrow{\alpha}P)\} & \varsigma(t+Q) = +_L\varsigma(t) & \varsigma(P+t) = +_R\varsigma(t) \\
\varsigma(t|Q) = |_L\varsigma(t) & \varsigma(t|u) = |_L\varsigma(t) \cup |_R\varsigma(u) & \varsigma(P|u) = |_R\varsigma(u) \\
\varsigma(t\backslash L) = \backslash L\,\varsigma(t) & \varsigma(t[f]) = [f]\varsigma(t) & \varsigma(A{:}t) = A{:}\varsigma(t) \\
\varsigma(P^{\rightarrow s}) = \{(P^{\rightarrow s})\} & \varsigma(t\hat{\ }r) = \hat{\ }r\,\varsigma(t) & \\
\varsigma(b{:}\mathbf{0}) = \{(b{:})\} & \varsigma(b{:}\alpha.P) = \{(b{:})\} & \varsigma(t+v) = +_L\varsigma(t) \cup +_R\varsigma(v)
\end{array}
$$

Thus, a synchron of t represents a path in the proof-tree t from its root to a leaf. Each transition derivation can be seen as the synchronisation of one or more synchrons. Note that we use the symbol ς as a variable ranging over synchrons, and as the name of a function—context disambiguates.

Example 3. The CCS process $P = \big((c.Q + (d.R|e.S))|\bar{c}.T\big)\backslash c$ has 3 outgoing transitions: $P \xrightarrow{\tau} (Q|T)\backslash c$, $P \xrightarrow{d} ((R|e.S)|\bar{c}.T)\backslash c$ and $P \xrightarrow{e} ((d.R|S)|\bar{c}.T)\backslash c$. Let t_τ, t_d and $t_e \in \mathit{Tr}$ be the unique derivations of these transitions. Then t_τ is a synchronisation of two synchrons, whereas t_d and $t_e \in \mathit{Tr}$ have only one each: $\varsigma(t_\tau) = \{\backslash c\,|_L +_L(\xrightarrow{c}Q), \backslash c\,|_R(\xrightarrow{\bar{c}}T)\}$, $\varsigma(t_d) = \{\backslash c\,|_L +_R\,|_L(\xrightarrow{d}R)\}$ and $\varsigma(t_e) = \{\backslash c\,|_L +_R\,|_R(\xrightarrow{e}S)\}$. The derivations t_d and $t_e \in \mathit{Tr}$ can be seen as *concurrent*, because their synchrons come from opposite sides of the same parallel composition; one would expect that after one of them occurs, a variant of the other is still possible. Indeed, there is a transition $((d.R|S)|\bar{c}.T)\backslash c \xrightarrow{d} ((R|S)|\bar{c}.T)\backslash c$. Let t'_d be its unique derivation. The derivation t_d and t'_d are surely different, for they have a different source state. Even their synchrons are different: $\varsigma(t'_d) = \{\backslash c\,|_L\,|_L(\xrightarrow{d}R)\}$. Nevertheless, t'_d can be recognised as a future variant of t_d: its only synchron has merely lost an argument $+_R$. This choice got resolved when taking the transition t_e.

We proceed to formalise the concepts "future variant" and "concurrent" that occur above, by defining two binary relations $\leadsto \subseteq \mathit{Tr}^\bullet \times \mathit{Tr}^\bullet$ and $\smile^\bullet \subseteq \mathit{Tr}^\bullet \times \mathit{Tr}$ such that the following properties hold:

The relation $\leadsto$ is reflexive and transitive. (4)

If $t \leadsto t'$ and $t \smile^\bullet v$, then $t' \smile^\bullet v$. (5)

If $t \smile^\bullet v$ with $\mathit{src}(t) = \mathit{src}(v)$ then $\exists t'$ with $\mathit{src}(t') = \mathit{target}(v)$ and $t \leadsto t'$. (6)

If $t \leadsto t'$ then $\ell(t') = \ell(t)$ and $t \not\smile^\bullet t'$. (7)

With $t \smile^\bullet v$ we mean that the possible occurrence of t is unaffected by the occurrence of v. Although for CCS the relation $\smile^\bullet$ is symmetric (and $\mathit{Tr}^\bullet = \mathit{Tr}$), for ABC and CCSS it is not:

Example 4 ([15])**.** Let P be the process $b!|(b? + c)$, and let t and v be the derivations of the $b!$- and c-transitions of P. The broadcast $b!$ is in our view completely under the control of the left component; it will occur regardless of whether the right component listens to it or not. It so happens that if $b!$ occurs in state P, the right component will listen to it, thereby disabling the possible occurrence of c. For this reason we have $t \smile^\bullet v$ but $v \not\smile^\bullet t$.

Example 5. Let P be the process $a\hat{}s|s$, and let t and υ be the derivations of the a- and τ-transitions of P. The occurrence of a disrupts the emission of the signal s, thereby disabling the τ-transition. However, reading the signal does not affect the possible occurrence of a. For this reason we have $t \smile^\bullet \upsilon$ but $\upsilon \not\smile^\bullet t$.

Proposition 1. Assume (4)–(7). Then the LTS $(\mathbb{P}, \mathit{Tr}, \mathit{src}, \mathit{target}, \ell)$, augmented with the concurrency relation $\smile^\bullet$, is an LTSC in the sense of Definition 4.

We now proceed to define the relations $\leadsto$ and $\smile^\bullet$ on synchrons, and then lift them to derivations. Subsequently, we establish (4)–(7).

The elements $+_L$, $+_R$, A: and $\hat{}r$ of Arg are called *dynamic* [20]; the others are *static*. (Static operators stay around when their arguments perform transitions.) For $\sigma \in \mathit{Arg}^*$ let $\mathit{static}(\sigma)$ be the result of removing all dynamic elements from σ. For $\varsigma = \sigma\upsilon$ with $\upsilon \in \{(\stackrel{\alpha}{\rightarrow}P), (P^{\rightarrow s}), (b{:})\}$ let $\mathit{static}(\varsigma) := \mathit{static}(\sigma)\upsilon$.

Definition 6. A synchron ς' is a *possible successor* of a synchron ς, notation $\varsigma \leadsto \varsigma'$, if either $\varsigma' = \varsigma$, or ς has the form $\sigma_1|_D\varsigma_2$ for some $\sigma_1 \in \mathit{Arg}^*$, $D \in \{L, R\}$ and ς_2 a synchron, and $\varsigma' = \mathit{static}(\sigma_1)|_D\varsigma_2$.

Definition 7. Two synchrons ς and υ are *directly concurrent*, notation $\varsigma \smile_d \upsilon$, if ς has the form $\sigma_1|_D\varsigma_2$ and $\upsilon = \sigma_1|_E\upsilon_2$ with $\{D, E\} = \{L, R\}$. Two synchrons ς' and υ' are *concurrent*, notation $\varsigma' \smile \upsilon'$, if $\exists\varsigma,\upsilon.\, \varsigma' \leftsquigarrow \varsigma \smile_d \upsilon \leadsto \upsilon'$.

Necessary and Active Synchrons. All synchrons of the form $\sigma(\stackrel{\alpha}{\rightarrow}P)$ are *active*; their execution causes a transition $\alpha.P \xrightarrow{\alpha} P$ in the relevant component of the represented system. Synchrons $\sigma(P^{\rightarrow s})$ and $\sigma(b{:})$ are passive; they are not affecting any state change. Let $a\varsigma(t)$ denote the set of active synchrons of a derivation t. So a transition t is labelled by a signal, i.e. $\ell(t) \notin \mathit{Act}$, iff $a\varsigma(t) = \emptyset$.

Whether a synchron $\varsigma \in \varsigma(t)$ is *necessary* for t to occur is defined only for $t \in \mathit{Tr}^\bullet$. If t is the derivation of a broadcast transition, i.e., $\ell(t) = b!$ for some $b \in \mathscr{B}$, then exactly one synchron $\upsilon \in \varsigma(t)$ is of the form $\sigma(\stackrel{b!}{\rightarrow}P)$, while all the other $\varsigma \in \varsigma(t)$ are of the form $\sigma'(\stackrel{b?}{\rightarrow}Q)$ (or possibly $\sigma'(b{:})$ in ABCd). Only the synchron υ is necessary for the broadcast to occur, as a broadcast is unaffected by whether or not someone listens to it. Hence we define $n\varsigma(t) := \{\upsilon\}$. For all $t \in \mathit{Tr}^\bullet$ with $\ell(t) \notin \mathscr{B}!$ (i.e. $\ell(t) \in \mathscr{S} \cup \mathscr{C}_h \cup \bar{\mathscr{C}}_h \cup \{\tau\}$) we set $n\varsigma(t) := \varsigma(t)$, thereby declaring all synchrons of the derivation necessary.

Definition 8. A derivation $t' \in \mathit{Tr}^\bullet$ is a *possible successor* of a derivation $t \in \mathit{Tr}^\bullet$, notation $t \leadsto t'$, if t and t' have equally many necessary synchrons and each necessary synchron of t' is a possible successor of one of t; i.e., if $|n\varsigma(t)| = |n\varsigma(t')|$ and $\forall\varsigma' \in n\varsigma(t').\, \exists\varsigma \in n\varsigma(t).\, \varsigma \leadsto \varsigma'$.

This implies that the relation $\leadsto$ between $n\varsigma(t)$ and $n\varsigma(u)$ is a bijection.

Definition 9. Derivation $t \in \mathit{Tr}^\bullet$ is *unaffected by* u, notation $t \smile^\bullet u$, if $\forall\varsigma \in n\varsigma(t).\, \forall\upsilon \in a\varsigma(u).\, \varsigma \smile \upsilon$.

So t is unaffected by u if no active synchron of u interferes with a necessary synchron of t. Passive synchrons do not interfere at all.

In Example 3 one has $t_d \smile t_e$, $t_d \leadsto t'_d$ and $t'_d \smile t_e$. Here $t \smile u$ denotes $t \smile^{\bullet} u \wedge u \smile^{\bullet} t$.

Proposition 2. The relations $\leadsto$ and $\smile^{\bullet}$ satisfy the properties (4)–(7).

5 Components

This section proposes a concept of system components associated to a transition, with a classification of components as necessary and/or affected. We then define a concurrency relation $\smile^{\bullet}_s$ in terms of these components closely mirroring Definition 9 in Sect. 4 of the concurrency relation $\smile^{\bullet}$ in terms of synchrons. We show that $\smile^{\bullet}$ and $\smile^{\bullet}_s$, as well as the concurrency relation defined in terms of components in Sect. 2, give rise to the same concept of justness.

A *static component* is a string $\sigma \in Arg^*$ of static arguments. Let $\mathscr{C}$ be the set of static components. The *static component* $c(\varsigma)$ of a synchron ς is defined to be the largest prefix γ of ς that is a static component.

Let $comp(t) := \{c(\varsigma) \mid \varsigma \in \varsigma(t)\}$ be the set of *static components* of t. Moreover, $npc(t) := \{c(\varsigma) \mid \varsigma \in n\varsigma(t)\}$ and $afc(t) := \{c(\varsigma) \mid \varsigma \in a\varsigma(t)\}$ are the *necessary* and *affected* static components of $t \in Tr$. Since $n\varsigma(t) \subseteq \varsigma(t)$ and $a\varsigma(t) \subseteq \varsigma(t)$, we have $npc(t) \subseteq comp(t)$ and $afc(t) \subseteq comp(t)$.

Two static components γ and δ are *concurrent*, notation $\gamma \smile \delta$, if $\gamma = \sigma_1|_D\gamma_2$ and $\delta = \sigma_1|_E\delta_2$ with $\{D, E\} = \{L, R\}$.

Definition 10. Derivation $t \in Tr^{\bullet}$ is *statically unaffected by* u, $t \smile^{\bullet}_s u$, iff $\forall\gamma \in npc(t).\, \forall\delta \in afc(u).\, \gamma \smile \delta$.

Proposition 3. If $t \smile^{\bullet}_s u$ then $t \smile^{\bullet} u$.

In Example 3 we have $t_d \smile t_e$ but $t_d \not\smile_s t_e$, for $npc(t_e) = comp(t_e) = comp(t_d) = afc(t_d) = \{\backslash c|_L\}$. Here $t \smile_s u$ denotes $t \smile^{\bullet}_s u \wedge u \smile^{\bullet}_s t$. Hence the implication of Proposition 3 is strict.

Proposition 4. The functions npc and $afc : Tr \rightarrow \mathscr{P}(\mathscr{C})$ satisfy closure property (3) of Sect. 2.

The concurrency relation $\smile^{\bullet}_c$ defined in terms of static components according to the template in [16], recalled in Sect. 2, is not identical to $\smile^{\bullet}_s$:

Definition 11. Let t, u be derivations. Write $t \smile^{\bullet}_c u$ iff $npc(t) \cap afc(u) = \emptyset$.

Nevertheless, we show that for the study of justness it makes no difference whether justness is defined using the concurrency relation $\smile^{\bullet}$, $\smile^{\bullet}_s$ or $\smile^{\bullet}_c$.

Theorem 2. A path is $\smile^{\bullet}$-B-just iff it is $\smile^{\bullet}_c$-B-just iff it is $\smile^{\bullet}_s$-B-just.

6 A Coinductive Characterisation of Justness

In this section we show that the $\smile\!\!\bullet$-based concept of justness defined in this paper coincides with a coinductively defined concept of justness, for CCS and ABC originating from [15]. To state the coinductive definition of justness, we need to define the notion of the decomposition of a path starting from a process with a leading static operator.

Any derivation $t \in \mathit{Tr}$ of a transition with $\mathit{src}(t) = P|Q$ has the shape

- $u|Q$, with $\mathit{target}(t) = \mathit{target}(u)|Q$,
- $u|v$, with $\mathit{target}(t) = \mathit{target}(u)|\mathit{target}(v)$,
- or $P|v$, with $\mathit{target}(t) = P|\mathit{target}(v)$.

Let a path *of* a process P be a path as in Definition 2 starting with P. Now the *decomposition* of a path π of $P|Q$ into paths π_1 and π_2 of P and Q, respectively, is obtained by concatenating all left-projections of the states and transitions of π into a path of P and all right-projections into a path of Q—notation $\pi \Rrightarrow \pi_1|\pi_2$. Here it could be that π is infinite, yet either π_1 or π_2 (but not both) are finite.

Likewise, $t \in \mathit{Tr}$ with $\mathit{src}(t) = P[f]$ has the shape $u[f]$ with $\mathit{target}(t) = \mathit{target}(u)[f]$. The *decomposition* π' of a path π of $P[f]$ is the path obtained by leaving out the outermost $[f]$ of all states and transitions in π, notation $\pi \Rrightarrow \pi'[f]$. In the same way one defines the decomposition of a path of $P\backslash c$.

The following co-inductive definition of the family B-justness of predicates on paths, with one family member of each choice of a set B of blocking actions, stems from [15, Appendix E]—here $\bar{D} := \{\bar{c} \mid c \in D\}$.

Definition 12. *B-justness*, for $\mathscr{B}? \subseteq B \subseteq \mathit{Act}$, is the largest family of predicates on the paths in the LTS of ABC such that

- a finite B-just path ends in a state that admits actions from B only;
- a B-just path of a process $P|Q$ can be decomposed into a C-just path of P and a D-just path of Q, for some $C, D \subseteq B$ such that $\tau \in B \vee C \cap \bar{D} = \emptyset$;
- a B-just path of $P\backslash L$ can be decomposed into a $B \cup L \cup \bar{L}$-just path of P;
- a B-just path of $P[f]$ can be decomposed into an $f^{-1}(B)$-just path of P;
- and each suffix of a B-just path is B-just.

Intuitively, justness is a completeness criterion, telling which paths can actually occur as runs of the represented system. A path is B-just if it can occur in an environment that may block the actions in B. In this light, the first, third, fourth and fifth requirements above are intuitively plausible. The second requirement first of all says that if $\pi \Rrightarrow \pi_1|\pi_2$ and π can occur in the environment that may block the actions in B, then π_1 and π_2 must be able to occur in such an environment as well, or in environments blocking less. The last clause in this requirement prevents a C-just path of P and a D-just path of Q to compose into a B-just path of $P|Q$ when C contains an action c and D the complementary action $\bar{c}$ (except when $\tau \in B$). The reason is that no environment (except one that can block τ-actions) can block both actions for their respective components, as nothing can prevent them from synchronising with each other.

The fifth requirement helps characterising processes of the form $b+(A|b)$ and $a.(A|b)$, with $A \stackrel{def}{=} a.A$. Here, the first transition 'gets rid of' the choice and of the leading action a, respectively, and this requirement reduces the justness of paths of such processes to their suffixes.

Example 6. To illustrate Definition 12 consider the unique infinite path of the process Alice|Cataline of Example 2 in which the transition t does not occur. Taking the empty set of blocking actions, we ask whether this path is $\emptyset$-just. If it were, then by the second requirement of Definition 12 the projection of this path on the process Cataline would need to be $\emptyset$-just as well. This is the path 1 (without any transitions) in Example 1. It is not $\emptyset$-just by the first requirement of Definition 12, because its last state 1 admits a transition.

We now establish that the concept of justness from Definition 12 agrees with the concept of justness defined earlier in this paper.

Theorem 3. *A path is $\smile\!\!\bullet_s$-B-just iff it is B-just in the sense of Definition 12.*

If a path π is B-just then it is C-just for any $C \supseteq B$. Moreover, the collection of sets B such that a given path π is B-just is closed under arbitrary intersection, and thus there is a least set B_π such that π is B-just. Actions $\alpha \in \mathscr{B}_\pi$ are called *π-enabled* [14]. A path is called *just* (without a predicate B) iff it is B-just for some $\mathscr{B}? \subseteq B \subseteq \mathscr{B}? \mathbin{\dot\cup} \mathscr{C}_h \mathbin{\dot\cup} \bar{\mathscr{C}}_h \mathbin{\dot\cup} \mathscr{S}$ [3,6,14,15], which is the case iff it is $\mathscr{B}? \mathbin{\dot\cup} \mathscr{C}_h \mathbin{\dot\cup} \bar{\mathscr{C}}_h \mathbin{\dot\cup} \mathscr{S}$-just.

In [3] a definition of justness for CCS with signal transition appears, very similar to Definition 12; it also applies to CCSS as presented here. Generalising Theorem 3, one can show that a path is ($\smile\!\!\bullet_s$ or $\smile\!\!\bullet_c$ or) $\smile\!\!\bullet$-just iff it is just in this sense. The same holds for the coinductive definition of justness from [6].

7 Conclusion

We advocate justness as a reasonable completeness criterion for formalising liveness properties when modelling distributed systems by means of transition systems. In [16] we proposed a definition of justness in terms of a, possibly asymmetric, concurrency relation between transitions. The current paper defined such a concurrency relation for the transition systems associated to CCS, as well as its extensions with broadcast communication and signals, thereby making the definition of justness from [16] available to these languages. In fact, we provided three versions of the concurrency relation, and showed that they all give rise to the same concept of justness. We expect that this style of definition will carry over to many other process algebras. We showed that justness satisfies the criterion of feasibility, and proved that our formalisation agrees with previous coinductive formalisations of justness for these languages.

Concurrency relations between transitions in transition systems have been studied in [28]. Our concurrency relation $\smile\!\!\bullet$ follows the same computational intuition. However, in [28] transitions are classified as concurrent or not only when they have the same source, whereas as a basis for the definition of justness here we need to compare transitions with different sources. Apart from that, our concurrency relation is more general in that it satisfies fewer closure properties, and moreover is allowed to be asymmetric.

Concurrency is represented explicitly in models like Petri nets [26], event structures [29], or asynchronous transition systems [2, 27, 30]. We believe that the semantics of CCS in terms of such models agrees with its semantics in terms of labelled transition systems with a concurrency relation as given here. However, formalising such a claim requires a choice of an adequate justness-preserving semantic equivalence defined on the compared models. Development of such semantic equivalences is a topic for future research.

Acknowledgement. I am grateful to Peter Höfner, Victor Dyseryn and Filippo de Bortoli for valuable feedback.

References

1. Apt, K.R., Francez, N., Katz, S.: Appraising fairness in languages for distributed programming. Distrib. Comput. **2**(4), 226–241 (1988). https://doi.org/10.1007/BF01872848
2. Bednarczyk, M.: Categories of asynchronous systems. Ph.D. thesis, Computer Science, University of Sussex, Brighton (1987)
3. Bouwman, M.S.: Liveness analysis in process algebra: simpler techniques to model mutex algorithms. Technical report, Eindhoven University of Technology (2018). http://www.win.tue.nl/~timw/downloads/bouwman_seminar.pdf
4. Coppo, M., Dezani-Ciancaglini, M., Padovani, L., Yoshida, N.: Inference of global progress properties for dynamically interleaved multiparty sessions. In: De Nicola, R., Julien, C. (eds.) COORDINATION 2013. LNCS, vol. 7890, pp. 45–59. Springer, Heidelberg (2013). https://doi.org/10.1007/978-3-642-38493-6_4
5. De Nicola, R., Vaandrager, F.W.: Three logics for branching bisimulation. J. ACM **42**(2), 458–487 (1995). https://doi.org/10.1145/201019.201032
6. Dyseryn, V., van Glabbeek, R.J., Höfner, P.: Analysing mutual exclusion using process algebra with signals. In: Peters, K., Tini, S. (eds.) Proceedings of the Combined 24th International Workshop on Expressiveness in Concurrency and 14th Workshop on Structural Operational Semantics, Electronic Proceedings in Theoretical Computer Science 255. Open Publishing Association, pp. 18–34 (2017). https://doi.org/10.4204/EPTCS.255.2
7. Emerson, E.A., Clarke, E.M.: Using branching time temporal logic to synthesize synchronization skeletons. Sci. Comput. Program. **2**(3), 241–266 (1982). https://doi.org/10.1016/0167-6423(83)90017-5
8. Emerson, E.A., Halpern, J.Y.: 'Sometimes' and 'Not Never' revisited: on branching time versus linear time temporal logic. J. ACM **33**(1), 151–178 (1986). https://doi.org/10.1145/4904.4999
9. Fehnker, A., van Glabbeek, R.J., Höfner, P., McIver, A., Portmann, M., Tan, W.L.: A process algebra for wireless mesh networks. In: Seidl, H. (ed.) ESOP 2012. LNCS, vol. 7211, pp. 295–315. Springer, Heidelberg (2012). https://doi.org/10.1007/978-3-642-28869-2_15

10. Fehnker, A., van Glabbeek, R.J., Höfner, P., McIver, A.K., Portmann, M., Tan, W.L.: A process algebra for wireless mesh networks used for modelling, verifying and analysing AODV. Technical report 5513, NICTA (2013). http://arxiv.org/abs/1312.7645
11. van Glabbeek, R.J.: Structure preserving bisimilarity, supporting an operational petri net semantics of CCSP. In: Meyer, R., Platzer, A., Wehrheim, H. (eds.) Correct System Design. LNCS, vol. 9360, pp. 99–130. Springer, Cham (2015). https://doi.org/10.1007/978-3-319-23506-6_9. http://arxiv.org/abs/1509.05842
12. van Glabbeek, R.J.: Ensuring Liveness Properties of Distributed Systems (A Research Agenda). Position paper (2016). http://arxiv.org/abs/org/abs/1711.04240
13. van Glabbeek, R.J.: Justness: a completeness criterion for capturing liveness properties. Technical report, Data61, CSIRO (2018). http://www.cse.unsw.edu.au/~rvg/synchrons.pdf. Full version of the present paper
14. van Glabbeek, R.J., Höfner, P.: CCS: It's not fair! Acta Inform. **52**(2–3), 175–205 (2015). https://doi.org/10.1007/s00236-015-0221-6
15. van Glabbeek, R.J., Höfner, P.: Progress, fairness and justness in process algebra. Technical report 8501, NICTA (2015). http://arxiv.org/abs/1501.03268
16. van Glabbeek, R.J., Höfner, P.: Progress, justness and fairness. Survey paper, Data61, CSIRO, Sydney, Australia (2018). https://arxiv.org/abs/1810.07414
17. Kuiper, R., de Roever, W.-P.: Fairness assumptions for CSP in a temporal logic framework. In: Bjørner, D. (ed.) Formal Description of Programming Concepts II, North-Holland, pp. 159–170 (1983)
18. Lamport, L.: Proving the correctness of multiprocess programs. IEEE Trans. Softw. Eng. **3**(2), 125–143 (1977). https://doi.org/10.1109/TSE.1977.229904
19. Lamport, L.: Fairness and hyperfairness. Distrib. Comput. **13**(4), 239–245 (2000). https://doi.org/10.1007/PL00008921
20. Milner, R. (ed.): A Calculus of Communicating Systems. LNCS, vol. 92. Springer, Heidelberg (1980). https://doi.org/10.1007/3-540-10235-3
21. Misra, J.: A Rebuttal of Dijkstra's position on fairness (1988). http://www.cs.utexas.edu/users/misra/Notes.dir/fairness.pdf
22. Misra, J.: A Discipline of Multiprogramming—Programming Theory for Distributed Applications. Springer, New York (2001). https://doi.org/10.1007/978-1-4419-8528-6
23. Owicki, S.S., Lamport, L.: Proving liveness properties of concurrent programs. ACM TOPLAS **4**(3), 455–495 (1982). https://doi.org/10.1145/357172.357178
24. Pnueli, A.: The temporal logic of programs. In: Proceedings of the 18th Annual Symposium on Foundations of Computer Science (FOCS 1977), pp. 46–57. IEEE (1977). https://doi.org/10.1109/SFCS.1977.32
25. Prasad, K.V.S.: A calculus of broadcasting systems. In: Abramsky, S., Maibaum, T.S.E. (eds.) CAAP 1991. LNCS, vol. 493, pp. 338–358. Springer, Heidelberg (1991). https://doi.org/10.1007/3-540-53982-4_19
26. Reisig, W.: Understanding Petri Nets—Modeling Techniques, Analysis Methods, Case Studies. Springer, Heidelberg (2013). https://doi.org/10.1007/978-3-642-33278-4
27. Shields, M.W.: Concurrent machines. Comput. J. **28**(5), 449–465 (1985). https://doi.org/10.1093/comjnl/28.5.449
28. Stark, E.W.: Concurrent transition systems. Theor. Comput. Sci. **64**(3), 221–269 (1989). https://doi.org/10.1016/0304-3975(89)90050-9

29. Winskel, G.: Event structures. In: Brauer, W., Reisig, W., Rozenberg, G. (eds.) ACPN 1986, Part II. LNCS, vol. 255, pp. 325–392. Springer, Heidelberg (1987). https://doi.org/10.1007/3-540-17906-2_31
30. Winskel, G., Nielsen, M.: Models for concurrency. In: Abramsky, S., Gabbay, D., Maibaum, T. (eds.) Handbook of Logic in Computer Science, Chap. 1, 4: Semantic Modelling, pp. 1–148. Oxford University Press, Oxford (1995)

5

Change Actions: Models of Generalised Differentiation

Mario Alvarez-Picallo(✉) and C.-H. Luke Ong(✉)

University of Oxford, Oxford, UK
{mario.alvarez-picallo,luke.ong}@cs.ox.ac.uk

Abstract. Change structures, introduced by Cai et al., have recently been proposed as a semantic framework for incremental computation. We generalise change actions, an alternative to change structures, to arbitrary cartesian categories and propose the notion of *change action model* as a categorical model for (higher-order) generalised differentiation. Change action models naturally arise from many geometric and computational settings, such as (generalised) cartesian differential categories, group models of discrete calculus, and Kleene algebra of regular expressions. We show how to build canonical change action models on arbitrary cartesian categories, reminiscent of the Fàa di Bruno construction.

1 Introduction

Incremental computation is the process of incrementally updating the output of some given function as the input is gradually changed, without recomputing the entire function from scratch. Recently, Cai et al. [6] introduced the notion of change structure to give a semantic account of incremental computation. Change structures have subsequently been generalised to *change actions* [2], and proposed as a model for automatic differentiation [16]. These developments raise a number of questions about the structure of change actions themselves and how they relate to more traditional notions of differentiation.

A *change action* $A = (|A|, \Delta A, \oplus_A, +_A, 0)$ is a set $|A|$ equipped with a monoid $(\Delta A, +_A, 0_A)$ acting on it, via action $\oplus_A : |A| \times \Delta A \to |A|$. For example, every monoid $(S, +, 0)$ gives rise to a (so-called *monoidal*) change action $(S, S, +, +, 0)$. Given change actions A and B, consider functions $f : |A| \to |B|$. A *derivative* of f is a function $\partial f : |A| \times \Delta A \to \Delta B$ such that for all $a \in |A|, \delta a \in \Delta A$, $f(a \oplus_A \delta a) = f(a) \oplus_B \partial f(a, \delta a)$. Change actions and differentiable functions (i.e. functions that have a regular derivative) organise themselves into categories (and indeed 2-categories) with finite (co)products, whereby morphisms are composed via the chain rule.

The definition of change actions (and derivatives of functions) makes no use of properties of **Set** beyond the existence of products. We develop the theory of change actions on arbitrary cartesian categories and study their properties.

A first contribution is the notion of a *change action model*, which is defined to be a coalgebra for a certain (copointed) endofunctor CAct on the category $\mathbf{Cat}_{\times}$ of (small) cartesian categories. The functor CAct sends a category $\mathbf{C}$ to the category $\mathrm{CAct}(\mathbf{C})$ of (internal) change actions and differential maps on $\mathbf{C}$.

There is a natural, extrinsic, notion of higher-order derivative in change action models. In such a model $\alpha : \mathbf{C} \to \mathrm{CAct}(\mathbf{C})$, a $\mathbf{C}$-object A is associated (via α) with a change action, the carrier object of whose monoid is in turn associated with a change action, and so on *ad infinitum.* We construct a "canonical" change action model, $\mathrm{CAct}_{\omega}(\mathbf{C})$, that internalises such ω-sequences that exhibit higher-order differentiation. Objects of $\mathrm{CAct}_{\omega}(\mathbf{C})$ are ω-sequences of "contiguously compatible" change actions; and morphisms are corresponding ω-sequences of differential maps, each map being the canonical (via α) derivative of the preceding in the ω-sequence. We show that $\mathrm{CAct}_{\omega}(\mathbf{C})$ is the final CAct-coalgebra (relativised to change action models on $\mathbf{C}$). The category $\mathrm{CAct}_{\omega}(\mathbf{C})$ may be viewed as a kind of Faà di Bruno construction [8, 10] in the more general setting of change action models.

Change action models capture many versions of differentiation that arise in mathematics and computer science. We illustrate their generality via three examples. The first, *(generalised) cartesian differential categories* (GCDC) [4, 10], are themselves an axiomatisation of the essential properties of the derivative. We show that a GCDC $\mathbf{C}$—which by definition associates every object A with a monoid $L(A) = (L_0(A), +_A, 0_A)$—gives rise to change action models in various non-trivial ways.

Secondly we show how discrete differentiation in both the *calculus of finite differences* [15] and *Boolean differential calculus* [22, 23] can be modelled using the full subcategory $\mathbf{Grp}_{\mathbf{Set}}$ of $\mathbf{Set}$ whose objects are groups. Our unifying formulation generalises these discrete calculi to arbitrary groups, and gives an account of the chain rule in these settings.

Our third example is differentiation of regular expressions. Recall that Kleene algebra $\mathbb{K}$ is the algebra of regular expressions. We show that the algebra of polynomials over a commutative Kleene algebra is a change action model.

Outline. In Sect. 2 we present the basic definitions of change actions and differential maps, and show how they can be organised into categories. The theory of change action is extended to arbitrary cartesian categories $\mathbf{C}$ in Sect. 3: we introduce the category $\mathrm{CAct}(\mathbf{C})$ of internal change actions on $\mathbf{C}$. In Sect. 4 we present change action models, and properties of the tangent bundle functors. In Sect. 5 we illustrate the unifying power of change action models via three examples. In Sect. 6, we study the category $\mathrm{CAct}_{\omega}(\mathbf{C})$ of ω-change actions and ω-differential maps. Missing proofs are provided in an extended version of the present paper [1].

2 Change Actions

A *change action* is a tuple $A = (|A|, \Delta A, \oplus_A, +_A, 0_A)$ where $|A|$ and ΔA are sets, $(\Delta A, +_A, 0_A)$ is a monoid, and $\oplus_A : |A| \times \Delta A \to |A|$ is an action of the monoid on $|A|$.[1] We omit the subscript from $\oplus_A, +_A$ and 0_A whenever we can.

Definition 1 (Derivative condition). Let A and B be change actions. A function $f : |A| \to |B|$ is *differentiable* if there is a function $\partial f : |A| \times \Delta A \to \Delta B$ satisfying $f(a \oplus_A \delta a) = f(a) \oplus_B \partial f(a, \delta a)$, for all $a \in |A|, \delta a \in \Delta A$. We call ∂f a *derivative* for f, and write $f : A \to B$ whenever f is differentiable.

Lemma 1 (Chain rule). *Given $f : A \to B$ and $g : B \to C$ with derivatives ∂f and ∂g respectively, the function $\partial(g \circ f) : |A| \times \Delta A \to \Delta C$ defined by $\partial(g \circ f)(a, \delta a) := \partial g(f(a), \partial f(a, \delta a))$ is a derivative for $g \circ f : |A| \to |C|$.*

Proof. Unpacking the definition, we have $(g \circ f)(a) \oplus_C \partial(g \circ f)(a, \delta a) = g(f(a)) \oplus_C \partial g(f(a), \partial f(a, \delta a)) = g(f(a) \oplus_B \partial f(a, \delta a)) = g(f(a \oplus_A \delta a))$, as desired. □

Example 1 (Some useful change actions).

1. If $(A, +, 0)$ is a monoid, $(A, A, +, +, 0)$ is a change action (called *monoidal*).
2. For any set A, $A_\star := (A, \{\star\}, \pi_1, \pi_1, \star)$ is a (trivial) change action.
3. Let $A \Rightarrow B$ be the set of functions from A from B, and $\mathrm{ev}_{A,B} : A \times (A \Rightarrow B) \to B$ be the usual evaluation map. Then $(A, A \Rightarrow A, \mathrm{ev}_{A,A}, \circ, \mathrm{Id}_A)$ is a change action. If $U \subseteq (A \Rightarrow A)$ contains the identity map and is closed under composition, $(A, U, \mathrm{ev}_{A,A} \restriction_{A \times U}, \circ \restriction_{U \times U}, \mathrm{Id}_U)$ is a change action.

Regular Derivatives. The preceding definitions neither assume nor guarantee a derivative to be additive (i.e. they may not satisfy $\partial f(x, \Delta a + \Delta b) = \partial f(x, \Delta a) + \partial f(x, \Delta b)$), as they are in standard differential calculus. A strictly weaker condition that we will now require is *regularity*: if a derivative is additive in its second argument then it is regular, but not vice versa. Under some conditions, the converse is also true.

Definition 2. Given a differentiable map $f : A \to B$, a derivative ∂f for f is *regular* if, for all $a \in |A|$ and $\delta a, \delta b \in \Delta A$, we have $f(a, 0_A) = 0_B$ and $\partial f(a, \delta a +_A \delta b) = \partial f(a, \delta a) +_B \partial f(a \oplus_A \delta a, \delta b)$.

Proposition 1. *Whenever $f : A \to B$ is differentiable and has a unique derivative ∂f, this derivative is regular.*

Proposition 2. *Given $f : A \to B$ and $g : B \to C$ with regular derivatives ∂f and ∂g respectively, the derivative $\partial(g \circ f) = \partial g \circ \langle f \circ \pi_1, \partial f \rangle$ is regular.*

[1] Change actions are closely related to the notion of *change structures* introduced in [6] but differ from the latter in not being dependently typed or assuming the existence of an $\ominus$ operator, and requiring ΔA to have a monoid structure compatible with the map $\oplus$.

Two Categories of Change Actions. The study of change actions can be undertaken in two ways: one can consider functions that are differentiable (without choosing a derivative); alternatively, the derivative itself can be considered part of the morphism. The former leads to the category $\mathbf{CAct}^-$, whose objects are change actions and morphisms are the differentiable maps.

The category $\mathbf{CAct}^-$ was the category we originally proposed [2]. It is well-behaved, possessing limits, colimits, and exponentials, which is a trivial corollary of the following result:

Theorem 1. *The category* $\mathbf{CAct}^-$ *of change actions and differentiable morphisms is equivalent to* **PreOrd***, the category of preorders and monotone maps.*

The actual structure of the limits and colimits in $\mathbf{CAct}^-$ is, however, not so satisfactory. One can, for example, obtain the product of two change actions A and B by taking their product in **PreOrd** and turning it into a change action, but the corresponding monoid action map $\oplus$ is not, in general, easily expressible, even if those for A and B are. Derivatives of morphisms in $\mathbf{CAct}^-$ can also be hard to obtain, as exhibiting f as a morphism in $\mathbf{CAct}^-$ merely proves it is differentiable but gives no clue as to how a derivative might be constructed.

A more constructive approach is to consider morphism as a function together with a choice of a derivative for it.

Definition 3. Given change actions A and B, a *differential map* $f : A \to B$ is a pair $(|f|, \partial f)$ where $|f| : |A| \to |B|$ is a function, and $\partial f : |A| \times \Delta A \to \Delta B$ is a regular derivative for $|f|$.

The category **CAct** has change actions as objects and differential maps as morphisms. The identity morphisms are (Id_A, π_1); given morphisms $f : A \to B$ and $g : B \to C$, define the composite $g \circ f := (|g| \circ |f|, \partial g \circ \langle |f| \circ \pi_1, \partial f \rangle) : A \to C$.

Finite products and coproducts exist in **CAct** (see Theorems 2 and 4 for a more general statement). Whether limits and colimits exist in **CAct** beyond products and coproducts is open.

Remark 1. If one thinks of changes (i.e. elements of ΔA) as morphisms between elements of $|A|$, then regularity resembles functoriality. This intuition is explored in [1, Appendix F], where we show that categories of change actions organise themselves into 2-categories.

3 Change Actions on Arbitrary Categories

The definition of change actions makes no use of any properties of **Set** beyond the existence of products. Indeed, change actions can be characterised as just a kind of multi-sorted algebra, which is definable in any category with products.

The Category CAct(C). Consider the category $\mathbf{Cat}_\times$ of (small) cartesian categories (i.e. categories with chosen finite products) and product-preserving functors. We can define an endofunctor $\mathrm{CAct} : \mathbf{Cat}_\times \to \mathbf{Cat}_\times$ sending a category $\mathbf{C}$ to the category of (internal) change actions on $\mathbf{C}$.

The objects of $\mathrm{CAct}(\mathbf{C})$ are tuples $A = (|A|, \Delta A, \oplus_A, +_A, 0_A)$ where $|A|$ and ΔA are (arbitrary) objects in $\mathbf{C}$, $(\Delta A, +_A, 0_A)$ is a monoid object in $\mathbf{C}$, and $\oplus_A : |A| \times \Delta A \to |A|$ is a monoid action in $\mathbf{C}$, i.e. a $\mathbf{C}$-morphism satisfying, for all $a : C \to |A|, \delta_1 a, \delta_2 a : C \to \Delta A$:

$$\oplus_A \circ \langle a, 0_A \circ ! \rangle = a$$
$$\oplus_A \circ \langle a, +_A \circ \langle \delta_1 a, \delta_2 a \rangle \rangle = \oplus_A \circ \langle \oplus_A \circ \langle a, \delta_1 a \rangle, \delta_2 a \rangle$$

Given objects A, B in $\mathrm{CAct}(\mathbf{C})$, the morphisms of $\mathrm{CAct}(A, B)$ are pairs $f = (|f|, \partial f)$ where $|f| : |A| \to |B|$ and $\partial f : |A| \times \Delta A \to \Delta B$ are morphisms in $\mathbf{C}$, satisfying a diagrammatic version of the derivative condition:

$$\begin{tikzcd} |A| \times \Delta A \arrow[r, "\langle |f| \circ \pi_1, \partial f \rangle"] \arrow[d, "\oplus_A"'] & |B| \times \Delta B \arrow[d, "\oplus_B"] \\ |A| \arrow[r, "|f|"'] & |B| \end{tikzcd}$$

Additionally, we require our derivatives to be regular, as in Definition 2, i.e. for all morphisms $a : C \to |A|, \delta_1 a, \delta_2 a : C \to \Delta A$, the following equations hold:

$$\partial f \circ \langle a, 0_A \circ ! \rangle = 0_B$$
$$\partial f \circ \langle a, +_A \circ \langle \delta_1 a, \delta_2 a \rangle \rangle = +_A \circ \langle \partial f \circ \langle a, \delta_1 a \rangle, \partial f \circ \langle +_A \circ \langle a, \delta_1 a \rangle, \delta_2 a \rangle \rangle$$

The chain rule can then be expressed naturally by pasting two instances of the previous diagram together:

$$\begin{tikzcd} |A| \times \Delta A \arrow[r, "\langle |f| \circ \pi_1, \partial f \rangle"] \arrow[d, "\oplus_A"'] \arrow[rr, bend left, "\langle (|g| \circ |f|) \circ \pi_1, \partial g \circ \langle |f| \circ \pi_1, \partial f \rangle \rangle"] & |B| \times \Delta B \arrow[r, "\langle |g| \circ \pi_1, \partial |g| \rangle"] \arrow[d, "\oplus_B"] & |C| \times \Delta C \arrow[d, "\oplus_C"] \\ |A| \arrow[r, "|f|"] \arrow[rr, bend right, "|g| \circ |f|"'] & |B| \arrow[r, "|g|"] & |C| \end{tikzcd}$$

Hence $f \circ g = \langle (|g| \circ |f|) \circ \pi_1, \partial g \circ \langle |f| \circ \pi_1, \partial f \rangle \rangle$.

Now, given a product-preserving functor $\mathrm{F} : \mathbf{C} \to \mathbf{D}$, there is a corresponding functor $\mathrm{CAct}(\mathrm{F}) : \mathrm{CAct}(\mathbf{C}) \to \mathrm{CAct}(\mathbf{D})$ given by:

$$\mathrm{CAct}(\mathrm{F})(|A|, \Delta A, \oplus_A, +_A, 0_A) := (\mathrm{F}(|A|), \mathrm{F}(\Delta A), \mathrm{F}(\oplus_A), \mathrm{F}(+_A), \mathrm{F}(0_A))$$
$$\mathrm{CAct}(\mathrm{F})(|f|, \partial f) := (\mathrm{F}(|f|), \mathrm{F}(\partial f))$$

We can embed $\mathbf{C}$ fully and faithfully into $\mathrm{CAct}(\mathbf{C})$ via the functor $\eta_{\mathbf{C}}$ which sends an object A of $\mathbf{C}$ to the "trivial" change action $A_\star = (A, \top, \pi_1, !, !)$ and every morphism $f : A \to B$ of $\mathbf{C}$ to the morphism $(f, !)$. As before, this functor extends to a natural transformation from the identity functor to CAct.

Additionally, there is an obvious forgetful functor $\varepsilon_{\mathbf{C}} : \mathrm{CAct}(\mathbf{C}) \to \mathbf{C}$, which defines the components of a natural transformation ε from the functor CAct to the identity endofunctor Id.

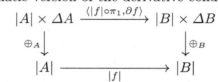

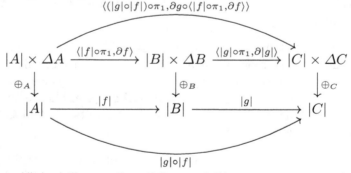

Given $\mathbf{C}$, we write $\xi_{\mathbf{C}}$ for the functor $\mathrm{CAct}(\varepsilon_{\mathbf{C}}) : \mathrm{CAct}(\mathrm{CAct}(\mathbf{C})) \to \mathrm{CAct}(\mathbf{C})$.[2] Explicitly, this functor maps an object $(A, B, \oplus, +, 0)$ in $\mathrm{CAct}(\mathrm{CAct}(\mathbf{C}))$ to the object $(|A|, |B|, |\oplus|, |+|, |0|)$. Intuitively, $\varepsilon_{\mathrm{CAct}(\mathbf{C})}$ prefers the "original" structure on objects, whereas $\xi_{\mathbf{C}}$ prefers the "higher" structure. The equaliser of these two functors is precisely the category of change actions whose higher structure is the original structure.

Products and Coproducts in CAct(C). We have defined CAct as an endofunctor on cartesian categories. This is well-defined: if $\mathbf{C}$ has all finite (co)products, so does $\mathrm{CAct}(\mathbf{C})$. Let $A = (|A|, \Delta A, \oplus_A, +_A, 0_A)$ and $B = (|B|, \Delta B, \oplus_B, +_B, 0_B)$ be change actions on $\mathbf{C}$. We present their product and coproducts as follows.

Theorem 2. *The following change action is the product of A and B in* $\mathrm{CAct}(\mathbf{C})$

$$A \times B := (|A| \times |B|, \Delta A \times \Delta B, \oplus_{A\times B}, +_{A\times B}, \langle 0_A, 0_B \rangle)$$

where $\oplus_{A\times B} := \langle \oplus_A \circ (\pi_1 \times \pi_1), \oplus_B \circ (\pi_2 \times \pi_2) \rangle$ *and* $+_{A\times B} := \langle +_A \circ (\pi_1 \times \pi_1), +_B \circ (\pi_2 \times \pi_2) \rangle$. *The projections are* $\overline{\pi_1} = (\pi_1, \pi_1 \circ \pi_2)$ *and* $\overline{\pi_2} = (\pi_2, \pi_2 \circ \pi_2)$, *writing* $\overline{f}$ *for maps* f *in* CAct *to distinguish them from* $\mathbf{C}$*-maps.*

Theorem 3. *The change action* $\overline{\top} = (\top, \top, \pi_1, \pi_1, \mathrm{Id}_\top)$ *is the terminal object in* $\mathrm{CAct}(\mathbf{C})$*, where* $\top$ *is the terminal object of* $\mathbf{C}$*. Furthermore, if* A *is a change action every point* $|f| : \top \to |A|$ *in* $\mathbf{C}$ *is differentiable, with (unique) derivative* 0_A.

Whenever we have a differential map $f : A \times B \to C$ between change actions, we can compute its derivative ∂f by adding together its "partial" derivatives:[3].

Lemma 2. *Let* $f : A \times B \to C$ *be a differential map. Then*

$$\partial f((a, b), (\delta a, \delta b)) = +_C \circ \langle \partial f((a, b), (\delta a, 0_B)), \partial f((\oplus_A \circ \langle a, \delta a \rangle, b), (0_A, \delta b)) \rangle$$

(The notational abuse is justified by the internal logic of a cartesian category.)

Theorem 4. *If* $\mathbf{C}$ *is distributive, with law* $\delta_{A,B,C} : (A \sqcup B) \times C \to (A \times C) \sqcup (B \times C)$*, the following change action is the coproduct of* A *and* B *in* $\mathrm{CAct}(\mathbf{C})$

$$A \sqcup B := (|A| \sqcup |B|, \Delta A \times \Delta B, \oplus_{A\sqcup B}, +_{A\sqcup B}, \langle 0_A, 0_B \rangle)$$

where $\oplus_{A\sqcup B} := [\oplus_A \circ (\mathrm{Id}_A \times \pi_1), \oplus_B \circ (\mathrm{Id}_B \times \pi_2)] \circ \delta_{A,B,C}$*, and* $+_{A\sqcup B} := \langle +_A \circ (\pi_1 \times \pi_1), +_B \circ (\pi_2 \times \pi_2) \rangle$*. The injections are* $\overline{\iota_1} = (\iota_1, \langle \pi_2, 0_B \rangle)$ *and* $\overline{\iota_2} = (\iota_2, \langle 0_A, \pi_2 \rangle)$.

[2] One might expect CAct to be a comonad with ε as a counit. But if this were the case, we would have $\xi_{\mathbf{C}} = \varepsilon_{\mathrm{CAct}(\mathbf{C})}$, which is, in general, not true.

[3] Alternatively, one can define the (first) partial derivative of a map $f(x, y)$ as a map $\delta_1 f$ such that $f(x \oplus \delta x, y) = f(x, y) \oplus \delta_1(x, y, \delta x)$. It can be shown that a map is differentiable iff its first and second derivatives exist.

Stable Derivatives and Additivity. We do not require derivatives to be additive in their second argument; indeed in many cases they are not. Under some simple conditions, however, (regular) derivatives can be shown to be additive.

Definition 4. Given a (internal) change action A and objects $|B|, |C|$ in a cartesian category $\mathbf{C}$, a morphism $u : |A| \times |B| \to |C|$ is *stable* whenever the diagram commutes:

$$\begin{array}{ccc} (|A| \times \Delta A) \times |B| & \xrightarrow{\oplus_A \times \mathrm{Id}} & |A| \times |B| \\ {\scriptstyle \pi_1 \times \mathrm{Id}} \downarrow & & \downarrow {\scriptstyle u} \\ |A| \times |B| & \xrightarrow{\quad u \quad} & |C| \end{array}$$

If one thinks of ΔA as the object of "infinitesimal" transformations on $|A|$, then the preceding definition says that a morphism $u : |A| \times |B| \to |C|$ is stable whenever infinitesimal changes on the input A do not affect its output.

Lemma 3. *Let $f = (|f|, \partial f)$ be a differential map in* $\mathrm{CAct}(\mathbf{C})$. *If ∂f is stable, then it is additive in its second argument*[4], *i.e. for all $x, \delta_1 x, \delta_2 x$ we have:*

$$\partial f \circ \langle x, +_A \circ \langle \delta_1 x, \delta_2 x \rangle \rangle = + \circ \langle \partial f \circ \langle x, \delta_1 x \rangle, \partial f \circ \langle x, \delta_2 x \rangle \rangle$$

Lemma 4. *Let $f = (|f|, \partial f)$ and $g = (|g|, \partial g)$ be differential maps, with ∂g stable. Then $\partial(g \circ f)$ is stable.*

It is straightforward to see that the category $\mathrm{Stab}(\mathbf{C})$ of change actions and differential maps with stable derivatives is a subcategory of $\mathrm{CAct}(\mathbf{C})$.

4 Higher-Order Derivatives: The Extrinsic View

In this section we study categories in which every object is equipped with a change action, and every morphism specifies a corresponding differential map. This provides a simple way of characterising categories which are models of higher-order differentiation purely in terms of change actions.

Change Action Models. Recall that a *copointed endofunctor* is a pair (F, σ) where the endofunctor $\mathrm{F} : \mathbf{C} \to \mathbf{C}$ is equipped with a natural transformation $\sigma : \mathrm{F} \xrightarrow{\cdot} \mathrm{Id}$. A *coalgebra of a copointed endofunctor* (F, σ) is an object A of $\mathbf{C}$ together with a morphism $\alpha : A \to \mathrm{F}A$ such that $\sigma_A \circ \alpha = \mathrm{Id}_A$.

Definition 5. We call a coalgebra $\alpha : \mathbf{C} \to \mathrm{CAct}(\mathbf{C})$ of the copointed endofunctor $(\mathrm{CAct}, \varepsilon)$ a *change action model* (on $\mathbf{C}$).

Assumption. Throughout Sect. 4, we fix a change action model $\alpha : \mathbf{C} \to \mathrm{CAct}(\mathbf{C})$.

Given an object A of $\mathbf{C}$, the coalgebra α specifies a (internal) change action $\alpha(A) = (A, \Delta A, \oplus_A, +_A, 0_A)$ in $\mathrm{CAct}(\mathbf{C})$. (We abuse notation and write ΔA for the carrier object of the monoid specified in $\alpha(A)$; similarly for $+_A, \oplus_A$, and 0_A.) Given a morphism $f : A \to B$ in $\mathbf{C}$, there is an associated differential map

[4] Note that the converse is not the case, i.e. a derivative can be additive but not stable.

$\alpha(f) = (f, \partial f) : \alpha(A) \to \alpha(B)$. Since $\partial f : A \times \Delta A \to \Delta B$ is also a $\mathbf{C}$-morphism, there is a corresponding differential map $\alpha(\partial f) = (\partial f, \partial^2 f)$ in $\mathrm{CAct}(\mathbf{C})$, where $\partial^2 f : (A \times \Delta A) \times (\Delta A \times \Delta^2 A) \to \Delta^2 B$ is a second derivative for f. Iterating this process, we obtain an n-th derivative $\partial^n f$ for every $\mathbf{C}$-morphism f. Thus change action models offer a setting for reasoning about higher-order differentiation.

Tangent Bundles in Change Action Models. In differential geometry the tangent bundle functor, which maps every manifold to its tangent bundle, is an important construction. There is an endofunctor on change action models reminiscent of the tangent bundle functor, with analogous properties.

Definition 6. The *tangent bundle functor* $\mathrm{T} : \mathbf{C} \to \mathbf{C}$ is defined as $\mathrm{T}A := A \times \Delta A$ and $\mathrm{T}f := \langle f \circ \pi_1, \partial f \rangle$.

Notation. We use shorthand $\pi_{ij} := \pi_i \circ \pi_j$.

The tangent bundle functor T preserves products up to isomorphism, i.e. for all objects A, B of $\mathbf{C}$, we have $\mathrm{T}(A \times B) \cong \mathrm{T}A \times \mathrm{T}B$ and $\mathrm{T}1 \cong 1$. In particular, $\phi_{A,B} := \langle \langle \pi_{11}, \pi_{12} \rangle, \langle \pi_{21}, \pi_{22} \rangle \rangle : \mathrm{T}A \times \mathrm{T}B \to \mathrm{T}(A \times B)$ is an isomorphism. Consequently, given maps $f : A \to B$ and $g : A \to C$, then, up to the previous isomorphism, $\mathrm{T}\langle f, g \rangle = \langle \mathrm{T}f, \mathrm{T}g \rangle$.

A consequence of the structure of products in $\mathrm{CAct}(\mathbf{C})$ is that the map $\oplus_{A \times B}$ inherits the pointwise structure in the following sense:

Lemma 5. *Let* $\phi_{A,B} : \mathrm{T}A \times \mathrm{T}B \to \mathrm{T}(A \times B)$ *be the canonical isomorphism described above. Then* $\oplus_{A \times B} \circ \phi_{A,B} = \oplus_A \times \oplus_B$.

It will often be convenient to operate directly on the functor T, rather than on the underlying derivatives. For these, the following results are useful:

Lemma 6. *The following families of morphisms are natural transformations:* $\pi_1, \oplus_A : \mathrm{T}(A) \to A$, $\mathrm{z} := \langle \mathrm{Id}, 0 \rangle : A \to \mathrm{T}(A)$ $\mathrm{l} := \langle \langle \pi_1, 0 \rangle, \langle \pi_2, 0 \rangle \rangle : \mathrm{T}(A) \to \mathrm{T}^2(A)$. *Additionally, the triple* $(\mathrm{T}, \mathrm{z}, \mathrm{T}\oplus)$ *defines a monad on* $\mathbf{C}$.

A particularly interesting class of change action models are those that are also cartesian closed. Surprisingly, this has as an immediate consequence that differentiation is itself internal to the category.

Lemma 7 (Internalisation of derivatives). *Whenever* $\mathbf{C}$ *is cartesian closed, there is a morphism* $\mathrm{d}_{A,B} : (A \Rightarrow B) \to (A \times \Delta A) \Rightarrow \Delta B$ *such that, for any morphism* $f : 1 \times A \to B$, $\mathrm{d}_{A,B} \circ \Lambda f = \Lambda(\partial f \circ \langle \langle \pi_1, \pi_{12} \rangle, \langle \pi_1, \pi_{22} \rangle \rangle)$.

Under some conditions, we can classify the structure of the exponentials in $(\mathrm{CAct}, \varepsilon)$-coalgebras. This requires the existence of an infinitesimal object.[5]

[5] The concept of "infinitesimal object" is borrowed from synthetic differential geometry [18]. However, there is nothing intrinsically "infinitesimal" about such objects here.

Definition 7. If $\mathbf{C}$ is cartesian closed, an *infinitesimal object* D is an object of $\mathbf{C}$ such that the tangent bundle functor T is represented by the covariant Hom-functor $D \Rightarrow (\cdot)$, i.e. there is a natural isomorphism $\phi : (D \Rightarrow (\cdot)) \xrightarrow{\cdot} \mathrm{T}$.

Lemma 8. *Whenever there is an infinitesimal object in* $\mathbf{C}$*, the tangent bundle* $\mathrm{T}(A \Rightarrow B)$ *is naturally isomorphic to* $A \Rightarrow \mathrm{T}B$.

We would like the tangent bundle functor to preserve the exponential structure; in particular we would expect a result of the form $\frac{\partial (\lambda y.t)}{\partial x} = \lambda y. \frac{\partial t}{\partial x}$, which is true in differential λ-calculus [11]. Unfortunately it seems impossible to prove in general that this equation holds, although weaker results are available. If the tangent bundle functor is representable, however, additional structure is preserved.

Theorem 5. *The isomorphism between the functors* $\mathrm{T}(A \Rightarrow (\cdot))$ *and* $A \Rightarrow \mathrm{T}(\cdot)$ *respects the structure of* T*, in the sense that the diagram commutes.*

$$\begin{array}{ccc} \mathrm{T}(A \Rightarrow B) & \xrightarrow{\cong} & A \Rightarrow \mathrm{T}(B) \\ {\scriptstyle \oplus_{A \Rightarrow B}} \downarrow & \swarrow {\scriptstyle \mathrm{Id}_A \Rightarrow \oplus_B} & \\ A \Rightarrow B & & \end{array}$$

5 Examples of Change Action Models

Generalised Cartesian Differential Categories. *Generalised cartesian differential categories* (GCDC) [10]—a recent generalisation of cartesian differential categories [4]—are models of differential calculi. We show that change action models generalise GCDC in that GCDCs give rise to change action models in three[6] different (non-trivial) ways. In this subsection let $\mathbf{C}$ be a GCDC (we assume familiarity with the definitions and notations in [10]).

1. The Flat Model. Define the functor $\alpha : \mathbf{C} \to \mathrm{CAct}(\mathbf{C})$ as follows. Let $f : A \to B$ be a $\mathbf{C}$-morphism. Then $\alpha(A) := (A, L_0(A), \pi_1, +_A, 0_A)$ and $\alpha(f) := (f, \mathrm{D}[f])$.

Theorem 6. *The functor* α *is a change action model.*

2. The Kleisli Model. GCDCs admit a tangent bundle functor, defined analogously to the standard notion in differential geometry. Let $f : A \to B$ be a $\mathbf{C}$-morphism. Define the *tangent bundle functor* $\mathrm{T} : \mathbf{C} \to \mathbf{C}$ as: $\mathrm{T}A := A \times L_0(A)$, and $\mathrm{T}f := \langle f \circ \pi_1, \mathrm{D}[f] \rangle$. The functor T is in fact a monad, with unit $\eta = \langle \mathrm{Id}, 0_A \rangle : A \to A \times L_0(A)$ and multiplication $\mu : (A \times L_0(A)) \times L_0(A)^2 \to A \times L_0(A)$ defined by the composite:

$$(A \times L_0(A)) \times L_0(A)^2 \xrightarrow{\langle \pi_1 \circ \pi_1, \langle \pi_2 \circ \pi_1, \pi_1 \circ \pi_2 \rangle \rangle} A \times L_0(A)^2 \xrightarrow{\mathrm{Id} \times +_A} A \times L_0(A)$$

Thus we can define the Kleisli category of this functor by $\mathbf{C}_{\mathrm{T}}$ which has geometric significance as a category of generalised vector fields.

[6] The third, the Eilenberg-Moore model, is presented in [1, Appendix D].

We define the functor $\alpha_{\mathrm{T}} : \mathbf{C}_{\mathrm{T}} \to \mathrm{CAct}(\mathbf{C}_{\mathrm{T}})$: given a $\mathbf{C}_{\mathrm{T}}$-morphism $f : A \to B$, set $\alpha_{\mathrm{T}}(A) := (A, L_0(A), \mathrm{Id}_A \times \mathrm{Id}_{L_0(A)}, \eta \circ +_A, \eta \circ 0_A)$ and $\alpha_{\mathrm{T}}(f) := (f, \mathrm{D}[f])$.

Lemma 9. *α_{T} is a change action model.*

Remark 2. The converse is not true: in general the existence of a change action model on $\mathbf{C}$ does not imply that $\mathbf{C}$ satisfies the GCDC axioms. However, if one requires, additionally, $(\Delta A, +_A, 0_A)$ to be commutative, with $\Delta(\Delta A) = \Delta A$ and $\oplus_{\Delta A} = +_A$ for all objects A, and some technical conditions (stability and uniqueness of derivatives), then it can be shown that $\mathbf{C}$ is indeed a GCDC.

Difference Calculus and Boolean Differential Calculus. Consider the full subcategory $\mathbf{Grp_{Set}}$ of $\mathbf{Set}$ whose objects are all the groups[7]. This is a cartesian closed category which can be endowed with the structure of a $(\mathrm{CAct}, \varepsilon)$-coalgebra α in a straightforward way.

Given a group $A = (A, +, 0, -)$, define change action $\alpha(A) := (A, A, +, +, 0)$ Given a function $f : A \to B$, define differential map $\alpha(f) := (f, \partial f)$ where $\partial f(x, \delta x) := -f(x) + f(x \oplus \delta x)$. Notice $f(x) \oplus \partial f(x, \delta x) = f(x) + (-f(x) + f(x + \delta x)) = f(x + \delta x) = f(x \oplus \delta x)$; hence ∂f is a derivative for f which is regular (but not necessarily additive), and $\alpha(f)$ a map in $\mathrm{CAct}(\mathbf{Grp_{Set}})$. The following result is then immediate.

Lemma 10. *$\alpha : \mathbf{Grp_{Set}} \to \mathrm{CAct}(\mathbf{Grp_{Set}})$ defines a change action model.*

This result is significant: in the calculus of finite differences [15], the *discrete derivative* (or *discrete difference operator*) of a function $f : \mathbb{Z} \to \mathbb{Z}$ is defined as $\delta f(x) := f(x + 1) - f(x)$. In fact the discrete derivative δf is (an instance of) the derivative of f *qua* morphism in $\mathbf{Grp_{Set}}$, i.e. $\delta f(x) = \partial f(x, 1)$.

Finite difference calculus [13,15] has found applications in combinatorics and numerical computation. Our formulation via change action model over $\mathbf{Grp_{Set}}$ has several advantages. First it justifies the chain rule, which seems new. Secondly, it generalises the calculus to arbitrary groups. To illustrate this, consider *Boolean differential calculus* [22,23], a technique that applies methods from calculus to the space $\mathbb{B}^n$ of vectors of elements of some Boolean algebra $\mathbb{B}$.

Definition 8. Given a Boolean algebra $\mathbb{B}$ and function $f : \mathbb{B}^n \to \mathbb{B}^m$, the *i-th Boolean derivative of f at $(u_1, \ldots, u_n) \in \mathbb{B}^n$* is the value $\frac{\partial f}{\partial x_i}(u_1, \ldots, u_n) := f(u_1, \ldots, u_n) \nleftrightarrow f(u_1, \ldots, \neg u_i, \ldots, u_n)$ writing $u \nleftrightarrow v := (u \wedge \neg v) \vee (\neg u \wedge v)$ for exclusive-or.

Now $\mathbb{B}^n$ is a $\mathbf{Grp_{Set}}$-object. Set $\top_i := (\bot, \overset{i-1}{\ldots}, \bot, \top, \bot, \overset{n-i}{\ldots}, \bot) \in \mathbb{B}^n$.

Lemma 11. *The Boolean derivative of $f : \mathbb{B}^n \to \mathbb{B}^m$ coincides with its derivative qua morphism in $\mathbf{Grp_{Set}}$: $\frac{\partial f}{\partial x_i}(u_1, \ldots, u_n) = \partial f((u_1, \ldots, u_n), \top_i)$.*

---

[7] We consider arbitrary functions, rather than group homomorphisms, since, according to this change action structure, every function between groups is differentiable.

Polynomials over Commutative Kleene Algebras. The algebra of polynomials over a commutative Kleene algebra [14, 17] (see [12, 21] for work of a similar vein) is a change action model. Recall that Kleene algebra is the algebra of regular expressions [5, 9]. Formally a *Kleene algebra* $\mathbb{K}$ is a tuple $(K, +, \cdot, ^\star, 0, 1)$ such that $(K, +, \cdot, 0, 1)$ is an idempotent semiring under $+$ satisfying, for all $a, b, c \in K$:

$$1 + a\,a^\star = a^\star \quad 1 + a^\star a = a^\star \quad b + a\,c \leq c \to a^\star\, b \leq c \quad b + c\,a \leq c \to b\,a^\star \leq c$$

where $a \leq b := a + b = b$. A Kleene algebra is *commutative* whenever $\cdot$ is.

Henceforth fix a commutative Kleene algebra $\mathbb{K}$. Define the *algebra of polynomials* $\mathbb{K}[\overline{x}]$ as the free extension of the algebra $\mathbb{K}$ with elements $\overline{x} = x_1, \ldots, x_n$. We write $p(\overline{a})$ for the value of $p(\overline{x})$ evaluated at $\overline{x} \mapsto \overline{a}$. Polynomials, viewed as functions, are closed under composition: when $p \in \mathbb{K}[\overline{x}], q_1, \ldots, q_n \in \mathbb{K}[\overline{y}]$ are polynomials, so is the composite $p(q_1(\overline{y}), \ldots, q_n(\overline{y}))$.

Given a polynomial $p = p(\overline{x})$, we define its *i-th derivative* $\frac{\partial p}{\partial x_i}(\overline{x}) \in \mathbb{K}[\overline{x}]$:

$$\frac{\partial\, a}{\partial x_i}(\overline{x}) = 0 \qquad \frac{\partial\, p^\star}{\partial x_i}(\overline{x}) = p^\star(\overline{x})\,\frac{\partial\, p}{\partial x_i}(\overline{x}) \qquad \frac{\partial\, x_j}{\partial x_i}(\overline{x}) = \begin{cases} 1 \text{ if } i = j \\ 0 \text{ otherwise} \end{cases}$$

$$\frac{\partial\,(p+q)}{\partial x_i}(\overline{x}) = \frac{\partial\, p}{\partial x_i}(\overline{x}) + \frac{\partial\, q}{\partial x_i}(\overline{x}) \qquad \frac{\partial\,(p\,q)}{\partial x_i}(\overline{x}) = p(\overline{x})\frac{\partial\, q}{\partial x_i}(\overline{x}) + q(\overline{x})\frac{\partial\, p}{\partial x_i}(\overline{x})$$

Write $\frac{\partial p}{\partial x_i}(\overline{e})$ to mean the result of evaluating the polynomial $\frac{\partial p}{\partial x_i}(\overline{x})$ at $\overline{x} \mapsto \overline{e}$.

Theorem 7 (Taylor's formula [14]**).** *Let $p(x) \in \mathbb{K}[x]$. For all $a, b \in \mathbb{K}[x]$, we have $p(a + b) = p(a) + b \cdot \frac{\partial p}{\partial x}(a + b)$.*

The category of finite powers of $\mathbb{K}$, $\mathbb{K}_\times$, has all natural numbers n as objects. The morphisms $\mathbb{K}_\times[m, n]$ are n-tuples of polynomials $(p_1, \ldots, p_n)$ where $p_1, \ldots, p_n \in \mathbb{K}[x_1, \ldots, x_m]$. Composition of morphisms is the usual composition of polynomials.

Lemma 12. *The category $\mathbb{K}_\times$ is a cartesian category, endowed with a change action model $\alpha : \mathbb{K}_\times \to \mathrm{CAct}(\mathbb{K}_\times)$ whereby $\alpha(\mathbb{K}) := (\mathbb{K}, \mathbb{K}, +, +, 0)$, $\alpha(\mathbb{K}^i) := \alpha(\mathbb{K})^i$; for $\overline{p} = (p_1(\overline{x}), \ldots, p_n(\overline{x})) : \mathbb{K}^m \to \mathbb{K}^n$, $\alpha(\overline{p}) := (\overline{p}, (p_1', \ldots, p_n'))$, where $(p_i' = p_i'(x_1, \ldots, x_m, y_1, \ldots, y_m) := \sum_{j=1}^n y_j \cdot \frac{\partial p_i}{\partial x_j}(x_1 + y_1, \ldots, x_m + y_m)$.*

Remark 3. Interestingly derivatives are not additive in the second argument. Take $p(x) = x^2$. Then $\partial p(a, b + c) > \partial p(a, b) + \partial p(a, c)$. It follows that $\mathbb{K}[\overline{x}]$ cannot be modelled by GCDC (because of axiom [CD.2]).

6 ω-Change Actions and ω-Differential Maps

A change action model $\alpha : \mathbf{C} \to \mathrm{CAct}(\mathbf{C})$ is a category that supports higher-order differentials: each $\mathbf{C}$-object A is associated with an ω-sequence of change actions—$\alpha(A), \alpha(\Delta A), \alpha(\Delta^2 A), \ldots$—in which every change action is compatible with the neighbouring change actions. We introduce *ω-change actions* as a means of constructing change action models "freely": given a cartesian category $\mathbf{C}$, the objects of the category $\mathrm{CAct}_\omega(\mathbf{C})$ are all ω-sequences of "contiguously compatible" change actions.

We work with ω-sequences $[A_i]_{i\in\omega}$ and $[f_i]_{i\in\omega}$ of objects and morphisms in $\mathbf{C}$. We write $\mathsf{p}_k([A_i]_{i\in\omega}) := A_k$ for the k-th element of the ω-sequence (similarly for $\mathsf{p}_k([f_i]_{i\in\omega})$), and omit the subscript '$i \in \omega$' from $[A_i]_{i\in\omega}$ to reduce clutter. Given ω-sequences $[A_i]$ and $[B_i]$ of objects of a cartesian category $\mathbf{C}$, define ω-sequences, *product* $[A_i] \times [B_i]$, *left shift* $\Pi[A_i]$ and *derivative space* $\mathbf{D}[A_i]$, by:

$$\mathsf{p}_j([A_i] \times [B_i]) := A_j \times B_j \qquad \mathsf{p}_j(\Pi[A_i]) := A_{j+1}$$
$$\mathsf{p}_0(\mathbf{D}[A_i]) := A_0 \qquad \mathsf{p}_{j+1}\mathbf{D}[A_i] := \mathsf{p}_j\mathbf{D}[A_i] \times \mathsf{p}_j\mathbf{D}(\Pi[A_i])$$

Example 2. Given an ω-sequence $[A_i]$, the first few terms of $\mathbf{D}[A_i]$ are:

$$\mathsf{p}_0\mathbf{D}[A_i] = A_0 \quad \mathsf{p}_1\mathbf{D}[A_i] = A_0 \times A_1 \quad \mathsf{p}_2\mathbf{D}[A_i] = (A_0 \times A_1) \times (A_1 \times A_2)$$
$$\mathsf{p}_3\mathbf{D}[A_i] = \big((A_0 \times A_1) \times (A_1 \times A_2)\big) \times \big((A_1 \times A_2) \times (A_2 \times A_3)\big)$$

Definition 9. Given ω-sequences $[A_i]$ and $[B_i]$, a *pre-ω-differential map* between them, written $[f_i] : [A_i] \to [B_i]$, is an ω-sequence $[f_i]$ such that for each j, $f_j : \mathsf{p}_j\mathbf{D}[A_i] \to B_j$ is a $\mathbf{C}$-morphism.

We explain the intuition behind the derivative space $\mathbf{D}[A_i]$. Take a morphism $f : A \to B$, and set $A_i = \Delta^i A$ (where $\Delta^0 := A$ and $\Delta^{n+1}A := \Delta(\Delta^n A)$). Since Δ distributes over product, the domain of the n-th derivative of f is $\mathsf{p}_n\mathbf{D}[A_i]$.
Notation. Define $\pi_1^{\langle 0\rangle} := \pi_1$ and $\pi_1^{\langle j+1\rangle} := \pi_1^{\langle j\rangle} \times \pi_1^{\langle j\rangle}$; and define $\pi_2^{(0)} := \mathrm{Id}$ and $\pi_2^{(j+1)} := \pi_2 \circ \pi_2^{(j)}$.

Definition 10. Let $[f_i] : [A_i] \to [B_i]$ and $[g_i] : [B_i] \to [C_i]$ be pre-ω-differential maps. The *derivative sequence* $\mathbf{D}[f_i]$ is the ω-sequence defined by:

$$\mathsf{p}_j\mathbf{D}[f_i] := \langle f_j \circ \pi_1^{\langle j\rangle}, f_{j+1}\rangle : \mathsf{p}_{j+1}\mathbf{D}[A_i] \to B_j \times B_{j+1}$$

Using the shorthand $\mathbf{D}^n[f_i] := \underbrace{\mathbf{D}(\ldots(\mathbf{D}}_{n \text{ times}}[f_i]))$, the *composite* $[g_i] \circ [f_i] : [A_i] \to [C_i]$ is the pre-ω-differential map given by $\mathsf{p}_j([g_i] \circ [f_i]) = g_j \circ \mathsf{p}_0(\mathbf{D}^j[f_i])$. The *identity* pre-$\omega$-differential map $\mathrm{Id} : [A_i] \to [A_i]$ is defined as: $\mathsf{p}_j\mathrm{Id} := \pi_2^{(j)} : \mathsf{p}_j\mathbf{D}[A_i] \to A_j$.

Example 3. Consider ω-sequences $[f_i]$ and $[g_i]$ as above. Then:

$$\mathsf{p}_0\mathbf{D}[f_i] = \langle f_0 \circ \pi_1^{\langle 0\rangle}, f_1\rangle \qquad \mathsf{p}_1\mathbf{D}[f_i] = \langle f_1 \circ \pi_1^{\langle 1\rangle}, f_2\rangle$$
$$\mathsf{p}_0\mathbf{D}^2[f_i] = \langle\langle f_0 \circ \pi_1^{\langle 0\rangle}, f_1\rangle \circ \pi_1, \langle f_1 \circ \pi_1^{\langle 1\rangle}, f_2\rangle\rangle$$
$$\mathsf{p}_1\mathbf{D}^2[f_i] = \langle\langle f_1 \circ \pi_1^{\langle 1\rangle}, f_2\rangle \circ \pi_1^{\langle 1\rangle}, \langle f_2 \circ \pi_1^{\langle 2\rangle}, f_3\rangle\rangle$$
$$\mathsf{p}_0\mathbf{D}^3[f_i] = \langle \mathsf{p}_0\mathbf{D}^2[f_i] \circ \pi_1^{\langle 0\rangle}, \langle\langle f_1 \circ \pi_1^{\langle 1\rangle}, f_2\rangle \circ \pi_1^{\langle 1\rangle}, \langle f_2 \circ \pi_1^{\langle 2\rangle}, f_3\rangle\rangle\rangle$$

It follows that the first few terms of the composite $[g_i] \circ [f_i]$ are:

$$\mathsf{p}_0([g_i] \circ [f_i]) = g_0 \circ f_0 \qquad \mathsf{p}_1([g_i] \circ [f_i]) = g_1 \circ \langle f_0 \circ \pi_1^{\langle 0 \rangle}, f_1 \rangle$$
$$\mathsf{p}_2([g_i] \circ [f_i]) = g_2 \circ \langle \langle f_0 \circ \pi_1, f_1 \rangle \circ \pi_1^{\langle 0 \rangle}, \langle f_1 \circ \pi_1^{\langle 1 \rangle}, f_2 \rangle \rangle$$

Notice that these correspond to iterations of the chain rule, assuming $f_{i+1} = \partial f_i$ and $g_{i+1} = \partial g_i$.

Proposition 3. *For any pre-ω-differential map $[f_i]$, $\mathrm{Id} \circ [f_i] = [f_i] \circ \mathrm{Id} = [f_i]$.*

Proposition 4. *Composition of pre-ω-differential maps is associative: given pre-ω-differential maps $[f_i] : [A_i] \to [B_i]$, $[g_i] : [B_i] \to [C_i]$ and $[h_i] : [C_i] \to [D_i]$, then for all $n \geq 0$, $h_n \circ \mathsf{p}_0\mathbf{D}^n([g_i] \circ [f_i]) = (h_n \circ \mathsf{p}_0\mathbf{D}^n[g_i]) \circ \mathsf{p}_0\mathbf{D}^n[f_i]$.*

Definition 11. Given pre-ω-differential maps $[f_i] : [A_i] \to [B_i], [g_i] : [A_i] \to [C_i]$, the *pairing* $\langle [f_i], [g_i] \rangle : [A_i] \to [B_i] \times [C_i]$ is the pre-ω-differential map defined by: $\mathsf{p}_j\langle [f_i], [g_i] \rangle = \langle f_j, g_j \rangle$. Define pre-$\omega$-differential maps $\boldsymbol{\pi_1} := [\boldsymbol{\pi_1}_i] : [A_i] \times [B_i] \to [A_i]$ by $\mathsf{p}_j[\boldsymbol{\pi_1}_i] := \pi_1 \circ \pi_2^{(j)}$, and $\boldsymbol{\pi_2} := [\boldsymbol{\pi_2}_i] : [A_i] \times [B_i] \to [B_i]$ by $\mathsf{p}_j[\boldsymbol{\pi_2}_i] := \pi_2 \circ \pi_2^{(j)}$.

Definition 12. A *pre-ω-change action* on a cartesian category $\mathbf{C}$ is a quadruple $\widehat{A} = ([A_i], [\widehat{\oplus^A}_i], [\widehat{+^A}_i], [0_i^A])$ where $[A_i]$ is an ω-sequence of $\mathbf{C}$-objects, and for each $j \geq 0$, $\widehat{\oplus^A}_j$ and $\widehat{+^A}_j$ are ω-sequences, satisfying

1. $\widehat{\oplus^A}_j : \Pi^j[A_i] \times \Pi^{j+1}[A_i] \to \Pi^j[A_i]$ is a pre-ω-differential map.
2. $\widehat{+^A}_j : \Pi^{j+1}[A_i] \times \Pi^{j+1}[A_i] \to \Pi^{j+1}[A_i]$ is a pre-ω-differential map.
3. $0_j^A : \top \to A_{j+1}$ is a $\mathbf{C}$-morphism.
4. $\Delta(\widehat{A}, j) := (A_j, A_{j+1}, \mathsf{p}_0\widehat{\oplus^A}_j, \mathsf{p}_0\widehat{+^A}_j, 0_j^A)$ is a change action in $\mathbf{C}$.

We extend the left-shift operation to pre-ω-change actions by defining $\Pi\widehat{A} := (\Pi[A_i], \Pi[\widehat{\oplus^A}_i], \Pi[\widehat{+^A}_i], [0_i^A])$. Then we define the change actions $\mathbf{D}(\widehat{A}, j)$ inductively by: $\mathbf{D}(\widehat{A}, 0) := \Delta(\widehat{A}, 0)$ and $\mathbf{D}(\widehat{A}, j+1) := \Delta(\widehat{A}, j) \times \Delta(\Pi\widehat{A}, j)$. Notice that the carrier object of $\mathbf{D}(\widehat{A}, j)$ is the j-th element of the ω-sequence $\mathbf{D}[A_i]$.

Definition 13. Given pre-ω-change actions $\widehat{A}$ and $\widehat{B}$ (using the preceding notation), a pre-ω-differential map $[f_i] : [A_i] \to [B_i]$ is *ω-differential* if, for each $j \geq 0$, (f_j, f_{j+1}) is a differential map from the change action $\mathbf{D}(\widehat{A}, j)$ to $\Delta(\widehat{B}, j)$. Whenever $[f_i]$ is an ω-differential map, we write $\widehat{f} : \widehat{A} \to \widehat{B}$.

We say that a pre-ω-change action $\widehat{A}$ is an *ω-change action* if, for each $i \geq 0$, $\widehat{\oplus^A}_i$ and $\widehat{+^A}_i$ are ω-differential maps.[8]

[8] It is important to sequence the definitions appropriately. Notice that we only define ω-differential maps once there is a notion of pre-ω-change action, but pre-ω-change actions need pre-ω-differential maps to make sense of the monoidal sum $\widehat{+}_j$ and action $\widehat{\oplus}_j$.

Remark 4. The reason for requiring each $\widehat{\oplus^A}_i$ and $\widehat{+^A}_i$ in an ω-change object $\widehat{A}$ to be ω-differential is so that $\widehat{A}$ is *internally* a change action in $\mathrm{CAct}_\omega(\mathbf{C})$ (see Definition 15).

Lemma 13. *Let $\widehat{f} : \widehat{A} \to \widehat{B}$ and $\widehat{g} : \widehat{B} \to \widehat{C}$ be ω-differential maps. Qua pre-ω-differential maps, their composite $[g_i] \circ [f_i]$ is ω-differential. Setting $\widehat{g} \circ \widehat{f} := [g_i] \circ [f_i] : \widehat{A} \to \widehat{C}$, it follows that composition of ω-differential maps is associative.*

Lemma 14. *For any ω-change action $\widehat{A}$, the pre-ω-differential map $\mathrm{Id} : [A_i] \to [A_i]$ is ω-differential. Hence $\widehat{\mathrm{Id}} := \mathrm{Id} : \widehat{A} \to \widehat{A}$ satisfies the identity laws.*

Definition 14. Given ω-change actions $\widehat{A}$ and $\widehat{B}$, we define the *product ω-change action* by: $(\widehat{A} \times \widehat{B} := ([A_i \times B_i], [\widehat{\oplus'}_i], [\widehat{+'}_i], [0'_i])$ where

1. $\widehat{\oplus'}_j := \langle \widehat{\oplus^A}_j, \widehat{\oplus^B}_j \rangle \circ \langle \langle \widehat{\pi_{11}}, \widehat{\pi_{12}} \rangle, \langle \widehat{\pi_{21}}, \widehat{\pi_{22}} \rangle \rangle$
2. $\widehat{+'}_j := \langle \widehat{+^A}_j, \widehat{+^B}_j \rangle \circ \langle \langle \widehat{\pi_{11}}, \widehat{\pi_{12}} \rangle, \langle \widehat{\pi_{21}}, \widehat{\pi_{22}} \rangle \rangle$
3. $0'_j := \langle 0^A_j, 0^B_j \rangle$

Notice that $\Delta(\widehat{A} \times \widehat{B}, j) := (A_j \times B_j, A_{j+1} \times B_{j+1}, \mathsf{p}_0 \widehat{\oplus'}_j, \mathsf{p}_0 \widehat{+'}_j, 0'_j)$ is a change action in $\mathbf{C}$ by construction.

Lemma 15. *The pre-ω-differential maps $\boldsymbol{\pi_1}, \boldsymbol{\pi_2}$ are ω-differential. Moreover, for any ω-differential maps $\widehat{f} : \widehat{A} \to \widehat{B}$ and $\widehat{g} : \widehat{A} \to \widehat{C}$, the map $\langle \widehat{f}, \widehat{g} \rangle := \langle [f_i], [g_i] \rangle$ is ω-differential, satisfying $\widehat{\boldsymbol{\pi_1}} \circ \langle \widehat{f}, \widehat{g} \rangle = \widehat{f}$ and $\widehat{\boldsymbol{\pi_2}} \circ \langle \widehat{f}, \widehat{g} \rangle = \widehat{g}$.*

Definition 15. Define the functor $\mathrm{CAct}_\omega : \mathbf{Cat}_\times \to \mathbf{Cat}_\times$ as follows.

- $\mathrm{CAct}_\omega(\mathbf{C})$ is the category whose objects are the ω-change actions over $\mathbf{C}$ and whose morphisms are the ω-differential maps.
- If $\mathrm{F} : \mathbf{C} \to \mathbf{D}$ is a (product-preserving) functor, then $\mathrm{CAct}_\omega(\mathrm{F}) : \mathrm{CAct}_\omega(\mathbf{C}) \to \mathrm{CAct}_\omega(\mathbf{C})$ is the functor mapping the ω-change action $([A_i], [[\oplus_i]_j], [[+_i]_j], [0_j])$ to $([\mathrm{F}A_i], [[\mathrm{F}\oplus_i]_j], [[\mathrm{F}+_i]_j], [\mathrm{F}0_j])$; and the ω-differential map $[f_i]$ to $[\mathrm{F}f_i]$.

Theorem 8. *The category $\mathrm{CAct}_\omega(\mathbf{C})$ is cartesian, with product given in Definition 14. Moreover if $\mathbf{C}$ is closed and has countable limits, $\mathrm{CAct}_\omega(\mathbf{C})$ is cartesian closed.*

Theorem 9. *The category $\mathrm{CAct}_\omega(\mathbf{C})$ is equipped with a canonical change action model: $\gamma : \mathrm{CAct}_\omega(\mathbf{C}) \to \mathrm{CAct}(\mathrm{CAct}_\omega(\mathbf{C}))$.*

Theorem 10 (Relativised final coalgebra). *Let $\mathbf{C}$ be a change action model. The canonical change action model $\gamma : \mathrm{CAct}_\omega(\mathbf{C}) \to \mathrm{CAct}(\mathrm{CAct}_\omega(\mathbf{C}))$ is a relativised[9] final coalgebra of $(\mathrm{CAct}, \varepsilon)$.*
i.e. for all change action models on $\mathbf{C}$, $\alpha : \mathbf{C} \to \mathrm{CAct}(\mathbf{C})$, there is a unique coalgebra homomorphism $\alpha_\omega : \mathbf{C} \to \mathrm{CAct}_\omega(\mathbf{C})$, as witnessed by the commuting diagram:

$$\begin{array}{ccc} \mathbf{C} & \xrightarrow{\quad\alpha\quad} & \mathrm{CAct}(\mathbf{C}) \\ {\scriptstyle \exists!\,\alpha_\omega}\downarrow & & \downarrow{\scriptstyle \mathrm{CAct}(\alpha_\omega)} \\ \mathrm{CAct}_\omega(\mathbf{C}) & \xrightarrow{\quad\gamma\quad} & \mathrm{CAct}(\mathrm{CAct}_\omega(\mathbf{C})) \end{array}$$

[9] Here CAct is restricted to the full subcategory of $\mathbf{Cat}_\times$ with $\mathbf{C}$ as the only object.

Proof. We first exhibit the functor $\alpha_\omega : \mathbf{C} \to \mathrm{CAct}_\omega(\mathbf{C})$.

Take a $\mathbf{C}$-morphism $f : A \to B$. We define the ω-differential map $\alpha_\omega(f) := \widehat{f} : \widehat{A} \to \widehat{B}$, where $\widehat{A} := \big([A_i], [\widehat{\oplus}_i], [\widehat{+}_i], [0_i]\big)$ is the ω-change action determined by A under *iterative actions of* α. I.e. for each $i \geq 0$: $A_i := \Delta^i A$ (by abuse of notation, we write $\Delta A'$ to mean the carrier object of the monoid of the internal change action $\alpha(A')$, for any $\mathbf{C}$-object A'); $\widehat{\oplus}_j : \Pi^j[A_i] \times \Pi^{j+1}[A_i] \to \Pi^j[A_i]$ is specified by: $\mathsf{p}_k \widehat{\oplus}_j$ is the monoid action morphism of $\alpha(A_{j+k})$; $\widehat{+}_j : \Pi^{j+1}[A_i] \times \Pi^{j+1}[A_i] \to \Pi^{j+1}[A_i]$ is specified by: $\mathsf{p}_k \widehat{\oplus}_j$ is the monoid sum morphism of $\alpha(A_{j+k})$; 0_i is the zero object of $\alpha(A_i)$.

The ω-sequence $\widehat{f} := [f_i]$ is defined by induction: $f_0 := f$; assume $f_n : (\mathbf{D}\widehat{A})_n \to B_n$ is defined and suppose $\alpha(f_n) = (f_n, \partial f_n)$ then define $f_{n+1} := \partial f_n$.

To see that the diagram commutes, notice that $\gamma(\widehat{f}) = (\widehat{f}, \Pi \widehat{f})$ and $\mathrm{CAct}(\alpha_\omega)$ maps $\alpha(f) = (f, \partial f)$ to $(\widehat{f}, \widehat{\partial f})$; then observe that $\Pi \widehat{f} = \widehat{\partial f}$ follows from the construction of $\widehat{f}$.

Finally to see that the functor α_ω is unique, consider the $\mathbf{C}$-morphisms $\partial^n f$ $(n = 0, 1, 2, \cdots)$ where $\alpha(\partial^n f) = (\partial^n f, \partial^{n+1} f)$. Suppose $\beta : \mathbf{C} \to \mathrm{CAct}_\omega(\mathbf{C})$ is another homomorphism. Thanks to the commuting diagram, we must have $\Pi^n \beta(f) = \beta(\partial^n f)$, and so, in particular $(\beta(f))_n = (\Pi^n \beta(f))_0 = (\beta(\partial^n f))_0 = \partial^n f$, for each $n \geq 0$. Thus $\widehat{f} = \beta(f)$ as desired. □

Intuitively any change action model on $\mathbf{C}$ is always a "subset" of the change action model on $\mathrm{CAct}_\omega(\mathbf{C})$.

Theorem 11. *The category* $\mathrm{CAct}_\omega(\mathbf{C})$ *is the limit in* $\mathbf{Cat}_\times$ *of the diagram.*

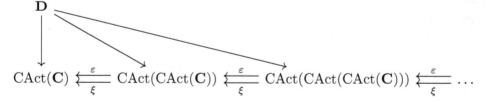

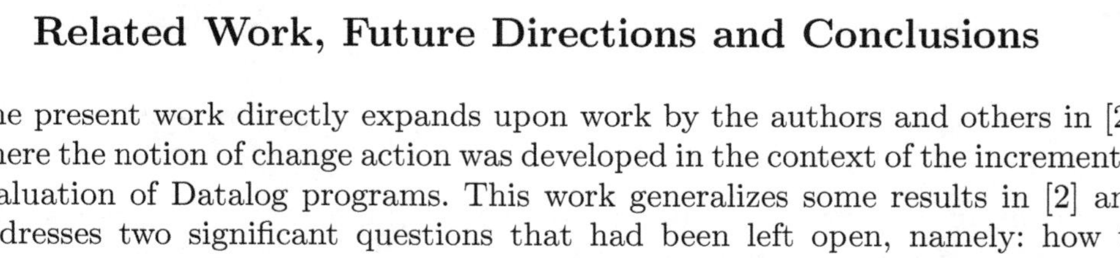

7 Related Work, Future Directions and Conclusions

The present work directly expands upon work by the authors and others in [2], where the notion of change action was developed in the context of the incremental evaluation of Datalog programs. This work generalizes some results in [2] and addresses two significant questions that had been left open, namely: how to construct cartesian closed categories of change actions and how to formalize higher-order derivatives.

Our work is also closely related to Cockett, Seely and Cruttwell's work on cartesian differential categories [3,4,7] and Cruttwell's more recent work on generalised cartesian differential categories [10]. Both cartesian differential categories and change action models aim to provide a setting for differentiation, and the construction of ω-change actions resembles the Faà di Bruno construction

[8,10] (especially its recent reformulation by Lemay [20]) which, given an arbitrary category **C**, builds a cofree cartesian differential category for it. The main difference between these two settings lies in the specific axioms required (change action models are significantly weaker: see Remark 2).

In this sense, the derivative condition is close to the Kock-Lawvere axiom from synthetic differential geometry [18,19], which has provided much of the driving intuition behind this work, and making this connection precise is the subject of ongoing research.

In a different direction, the simplicity of products and exponentials in closed change action models (see Theorem 5) suggests that there should be a reasonable calculus for change action models. Exploring such a calculus and its connections to the differential λ-calculus [11] could lead to practical applications to languages for incremental computation or higher-order automatic differentiation [16].

In conclusion, change actions and change action models constitute a new setting for reasoning about differentiation that is able to unify "discrete" and "continuous" models, as well as higher-order functions. Change actions are remarkably well-behaved and show tantalising connections with geometry and 2-categories. We believe that most ad hoc notions of derivatives found in disparate subjects can be elegantly integrated into the framework of change action models. We therefore expect any further work in this area to have the potential of benefiting these notions of derivatives.

References

1. Alvarez-Picallo, M., Ong, C.H.L.: Change actions: models of generalised differentiation. arXiv preprint arXiv:1902.05465 (2019)
2. Alvarez-Picallo, M., Peyton-Jones, M., Eyers-Taylor, A., Ong, C.H.L.: Fixing incremental computation. In: European Symposium on Programming. Springer (2019, in press)
3. Blute, R., Ehrhard, T., Tasson, C.: A convenient differential category. arXiv preprint arXiv:1006.3140 (2010)
4. Blute, R.F., Cockett, J.R.B., Seely, R.A.: Cartesian differential categories. Theory Appl. Categories **22**(23), 622–672 (2009)
5. Brzozowski, J.A.: Derivatives of regular expressions. J. ACM **11**(4), 481–494 (1964). https://doi.org/10.1145/321239.321249
6. Cai, Y., Giarrusso, P.G., Rendel, T., Ostermann, K.: A theory of changes for higher-order languages: incrementalizing λ-calculi by static differentiation. ACM SIGPLAN Not. **49**, 145–155 (2014)
7. Cockett, J.R.B., Cruttwell, G.S.H.: Differential structure, tangent structure, and SDG. Appl. Categorical Struct. **22**(2), 331–417 (2014)
8. Cockett, J.R.B., Seely, R.A.G.: The Faà di Bruno construction. Theory Appl. Categories **25**, 393–425 (2011)
9. Conway, J.H.: Regular Algebra and Finite Machines. Chapman and Hall, London (1971)
10. Cruttwell, G.S.: Cartesian differential categories revisited. Math. Struct. Comput. Sci. **27**(1), 70–91 (2017)
11. Ehrhard, T., Regnier, L.: The differential lambda-calculus. Theor. Comput. Sci. **309**(1–3), 1–41 (2003). https://doi.org/10.1016/S0304-3975(03)00392-X

12. Esparza, J., Kiefer, S., Luttenberger, M.: Newtonian program analysis. J. ACM **57**(6), 33:1–33:47 (2010). https://doi.org/10.1145/1857914.1857917
13. Gleich, D.: Finite calculus: a tutorial for solving nasty sums. Stanford University (2005)
14. Hopkins, M.W., Kozen, D.: Parikh's theorem in commutative Kleene algebra. In: 14th Annual IEEE Symposium on Logic in Computer Science, Trento, Italy, 2–5 July 1999, pp. 394–401 (1999). https://doi.org/10.1109/LICS.1999.782634
15. Jordan, C.: Calculus of Finite Differences, vol. 33. American Mathematical Society, New York (1965)
16. Kelly, R., Pearlmutter, B.A., Siskind, J.M.: Evolving the incremental lambda-calculus into a model of forward automatic differentiation (ad). arXiv preprint arXiv:1611.03429 (2016)
17. Kleene, S.C.: Representation of events in nerve nets and finite automata. In: Shannon, C.E., McCarthy, J. (eds.) Automata Studies, pp. 3–41. Princeton University Press, Princeton (1956)
18. Kock, A.: Synthetic Differential Geometry, 2nd edn. Cambridge University Press, Cambridge (2006)
19. Lavendhomme, R.: Basic Concepts of Synthetic Differential Geometry, vol. 13. Springer, Boston (2018). https://doi.org/10.1007/978-1-4757-4588-7
20. Lemay, J.S.: A tangent category alternative to the Faà di Bruno construction. arXiv preprint arXiv:1805.01774v1 (2018)
21. Lombardy, S., Sakarovitch, J.: How expressions can code for automata. In: 6th Latin American Symposium on Theoretical Informatics, LATIN 2004, Buenos Aires, Argentina, 5–8 April 2004, Proceedings, pp. 242–251 (2004). https://doi.org/10.1007/978-3-540-24698-5_28
22. Steinbach, B., Posthoff, C.: Boolean differential calculus. Synth. Lect. Digit. Circ. Syst. **12**(1), 1–215 (2017)
23. Thayse, A. (ed.): Boolean Calculus of Differences. LNCS, vol. 101. Springer, Heidelberg (1981). https://doi.org/10.1007/3-540-10286-8

6

Trees in Partial Higher Dimensional Automata

Jérémy Dubut[1,2(✉)]

[1] National Institute of Informatics, Tokyo, Japan
dubut@nii.ac.jp
[2] Japanese-French Laboratory for Informatics, Tokyo, Japan

Abstract. In this paper, we give a new definition of partial Higher Dimension Automata using lax functors. This definition is simpler and more natural from a categorical point of view, but also matches more clearly the intuition that pHDA are Higher Dimensional Automata with some missing faces. We then focus on trees. Originally, for example in transition systems, trees are defined as those systems that have a unique path property. To understand what kind of unique property is needed in pHDA, we start by looking at trees as colimits of paths. This definition tells us that trees are exactly the pHDA with the unique path property modulo a notion of homotopy, and without any shortcuts. This property allows us to prove two interesting characterisations of trees: trees are exactly those pHDA that are an unfolding of another pHDA; and trees are exactly the cofibrant objects, much as in the language of Quillen's model structure. In particular, this last characterisation gives the premisses of a new understanding of concurrency theory using homotopy theory.

Keywords: Higher Dimensional Automata · Trees · Homotopy theories

1 Introduction

Higher Dimensional Automata (HDA, for short), introduced by Pratt in [23], are a geometric model of true concurrency. Geometric, because they are defined very similarly to simplicial sets, and can be interpreted as glueings of geometric objects, here hypercubes of any dimension. Similarly to other models of concurrency much as event structures [21], asynchronous systems [1,25], or transition systems with independence [22], they model true concurrency, in the sense that they distinguish interleaving behaviours from simultaneous behaviours. In [12], van Glabbeek proved that they form the most powerful models of a hierarchy of concurrent models. In [6], Fahrenberg described a notion of bisimilarity of HDA using the general framework of open maps from [17]. If this work is very natural, it is confronted with a design problem: paths (or executions) cannot be nicely encoded as HDA. Indeed, in a HDA, it is impossible to model the fact that two actions *must* be executed at the same time, or that two actions are executed at the same time but one *must* start before the other. From a geometric point of view, those impossibilities are expressed by the fact that we deal with closed cubes, that is, cubes that must contain all of their faces. Motivated by those examples, Fahrenberg, in [7], extended HDA to partial HDA, intuitively, HDA with cubes with some missing faces. If the intuition is clear, the formalisation is still complicated to achieve: the definition from [7] misses the point that faces can be not uniquely defined. This comes from the fact that Fahrenberg wanted to stick to the 'local' definition of precubical sets, that is, that cubes must satisfy some local conditions about faces. As we will show, those local equations are not enough in the partial case. Another missed point is the notion of morphisms of partial HDA: as defined in [7], the natural property that morphisms map executions to executions is not satisfied. In Sect. 2, we address those issues by giving a new definition of partial HDA in terms of lax functors. This definition, similar to the presheaf theoretic definition of HDA, avoid the issues discussed above by considering global inclusions, instead of local equations. This illustrates more clearly the intuition of partial HDA being HDA with missing faces: we coherently replace sets and total functions by sets and partial functions. From this similarity with the original definition of HDA, we can prove that it is possible to complete a partial HDA to turn it into a HDA, by adding the missing faces, and from this completion, it is possible to define a geometric realisation of pHDA (which was impossible with Fahrenberg's definition).

The geometry of Higher Dimensional Automata, and more generally, of true concurrency, has been studied since Goubault's PhD thesis [13]. Since then, numerous pieces of work relating algebraic topology and true concurrency have been achieved (for example, see the textbooks [9,14]). In particular, some attempts of defining nice homotopy theories for true concurrency (or directed topology), through the language of model structures of Quillen [24], have been made by Gaucher [10], and the author [3]. In the second part of this paper (Sects. 3, 4 and 5), we consider another point of view of this relationship between HDA and model structures. The goal is not to understand the true concurrency of HDA, that is, understanding the homotopy theory of HDA as an abstract homotopy theory, but to understand the concurrency theory of HDA. By this we mean to understand how paths (or executions) and extensions of paths can be understood using (co)fibrations (in Quillen's sense). Also, the goal is not to construct a model structure, as Quillen's axioms would fail, but to give intuitions and some preliminary formal statements toward the understanding of concurrency using homotopy theory. Using this point of view, many constructions in concurrency can be understood using the language of model structures:

- Open maps from [17] can be understood as trivial fibrations, namely weak equivalences (here, bisimulations) that have the right lifting properties with respect to some morphisms.

- Those morphisms are precisely extensions of executions, which means that they can be seen as cofibration generators (in the language of cofibrantly generated model structures [15]).
- Cofibrations are then morphisms that have the left lifting property with respect to open maps. In particular, this allows us to define cofibrant objects as those objects whose unique morphisms from the initial object is a cofibration. In a way, cofibrant objects are those objects that are constructed by just using extensions of paths, and should correspond to trees.
- The cofibrant replacement is then given by canonically constructing a cofibrant object, which is weakly equivalent (here, bisimilar) to a given object. That should correspond to the unfolding.

The main ingredient is to understand what trees are in this context. In the case of transition systems for semantics of CCS [19], synchronisation trees are those systems with exactly one path from the initial state to any state. Those trees are then much simpler to reason on, but they are still powerful enough to capture any bisimulation type: by unfolding, it is possible to canonically construct a tree from a system. The goal of Sects. 3 and 4 will be to understand how to generalise this to pHDA. In this context, it is not clear what kind of unique path property should be considered as, in general, in truly concurrent systems, we have to deal with homotopies, namely, equivalences of paths modulo permutation of independent actions. Following [4], we will first consider trees as colimits of paths. This will guide us to determine what kind of unique path property is needed: a tree is a pHDA with exactly one class of paths modulo a notion of homotopy, from the initial state to any state, and without any shortcuts. This will be proved by defining a suitable notion of unfolding of pHDA. Finally, in Sect. 5, we prove that those trees coincide exactly with the cofibrant objects, illustrating the first steps of this new understanding of concurrency, using homotopy theory.

2 Fixing the Definition of pHDA

In this Section, we review the definitions of HDA (Sect. 2.1), the first one using face maps, and the second one using presheaves. In Sect. 2.2, we describe the definition of partial HDA from [7] and explain why it does not give us what we are expecting. We tackle those issues by introducing a new definition in Sect. 2.3, extending the presheaf theoretic definition, using lax functors instead of strict functors. Finally, in Sect. 2.4, we prove that HDA form a reflective subcategory of partial HDA, by constructing a completion of a partial HDA.

2.1 Higher Dimensional Automata

Higher Dimensional Automata are an extension of transition systems: they are labeled graphs, except that, in addition to vertices and edges, the graph structure also has higher dimensional data, expressing the fact that several actions can be made at the same time. Those additional data are intuitively cubes filling up interleaving: if a and b can be made at the same time, instead of having an empty square as on the left figure, with $a.b$ and $b.a$ as only behaviours, we have a full square as on the right figure, with any possible behaviours in-between. This requires to extend the notion of graph to add those higher dimensional cubical data: that is the notion of *precubical sets*.

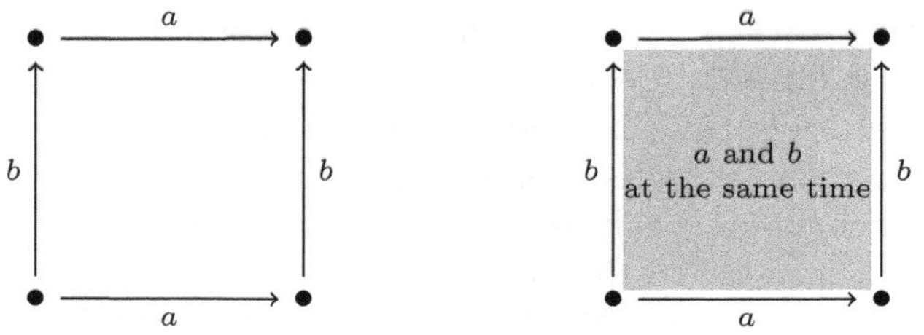

Concrete Definition of Precubical Sets. A **precubical set** X is a collection of sets $(X_n)_{n\in\mathbb{N}}$ together with a collection of functions $(\partial^\alpha_{i,n} : X_n \longrightarrow X_{n-1})_{n>0, 1\leq i\leq n, \alpha\in\{0,1\}}$ satisfying the local equations $\partial^\alpha_{i,n} \circ \partial^\beta_{j,n+1} = \partial^\beta_{j,n} \circ \partial^\alpha_{i+1,n+1}$ for every $\alpha, \beta \in \{0,1\}$, $n > 0$ and $1 \leq j \leq i \leq n$. A **morphism of precubical sets** from X to Y is a collection of functions $(f_n : X_n \longrightarrow Y_n)_{n\in\mathbb{N}}$ satisfying the equations $f_n \circ \partial^\alpha_{i,n} = \partial^\alpha_{i,n} \circ f_{n+1}$ for every $n \in \mathbb{N}$, $1 \leq i \leq n$ and $\alpha \in \{0,1\}$. The elements of X_0 are called **points**, X_1 **segments**, X_2 **squares**, X_n ***n*-cubes**. In the following, we will call **past** (resp. **future**) ***i*-face maps** the $\partial^0_{i,n}$ (resp. $\partial^1_{i,n}$). We denote this category of precubical sets by **pCub**.

Precubical Sets as Presheaves. Equivalently, **pCub** is the category of preshea-ves over the cubical category $\square$. $\square$ is the subcategory of **Set** whose objects are the sets $\{0,1\}^n$ for $n \in \mathbb{N}$ and whose morphisms are generated by the so-called **coface maps**:

$$d^\alpha_{i,n} : \{0,1\}^{n-1} \longrightarrow \{0,1\}^n \quad (\beta_1, \ldots, \beta_{n-1}) \longmapsto (\beta_1, \ldots, \beta_{i-1}, \alpha, \beta_i, \ldots, \beta_{n-1})$$

A precubical set is a functor $X : \square^{op} \longrightarrow$ **Set**, that is, a presheaf over $\square$, and a morphism of precubical sets is a natural transformation.

Higher Dimensional Automata [11]**.** From now on, fix a set L, called the **alphabet**. We can form a precubical set also noted L such that $L_n = L^n$ and the i-face maps are given by $\delta^\alpha_i(a_1 \ldots a_n) = a_1 \ldots a_{i-1}.a_{i+1} \ldots a_n$. We can also form the following precubical set $*$ such that $*_0 = \{*\}$ and $*_n = \varnothing$ for $n > 0$. A **HDA** X on L is a bialgebra $* \to X \to L$ in **pCub**. In other words, a HDA X is a precubical set, also noted X, together with a specified point, the **initial state**, $i \in X_0$ and a **labelling function** $\lambda : X_1 \longrightarrow L$ satisfying the equations $\lambda \circ \partial^0_{i,2} = \lambda \circ \partial^1_{i,2}$ for $i \in \{1,2\}$ (see previous figure, right). A **morphism of HDA** from X to Y is a morphism f of precubical sets from X to Y such that $f_0(i_X) = i_Y$ and $\lambda_X = \lambda_Y \circ f_1$. HDA on L and morphisms of HDA form a category that we denote by $\mathbf{HDA_L}$. This category can also be defined as a the double slice category $*/\mathbf{pCub}/L$. Remark that we are only concerned with labelling-preserving morphisms, not general morphisms as described in [5].

2.2 Original Definition of Partial Higher Dimensional Automata

Originally [7], partial HDA are defined similarly to the concrete definition of HDA, except that the face maps can be partial functions and the local equations hold only when *both* sides are well defined. There are two reasons why it fails to give the good intuition:

– first the 'local' equations are not enough in the partial case. Imagine that we want to model a full cube c without its lower face, that is, $\partial_{3,3}^0$ is not defined on c, and such that $\partial_{1,2}^1$ is undefined on $\partial_{1,3}^1(c)$ and $\partial_{2,3}^1(c)$, that is, we remove an edge. We cannot prove using the local equations that $\partial_1^1 \circ \partial_2^0 \circ \partial_1^1(c) = \partial_1^1 \circ \partial_2^0 \circ \partial_2^1(c)$, that is, that the vertices of the cube are uniquely defined. Indeed, to prove this equality using the local equations, you can only permute two consecutive ∂. From $\partial_1^1 \circ \partial_2^0 \circ \partial_1^1(c)$, you can:

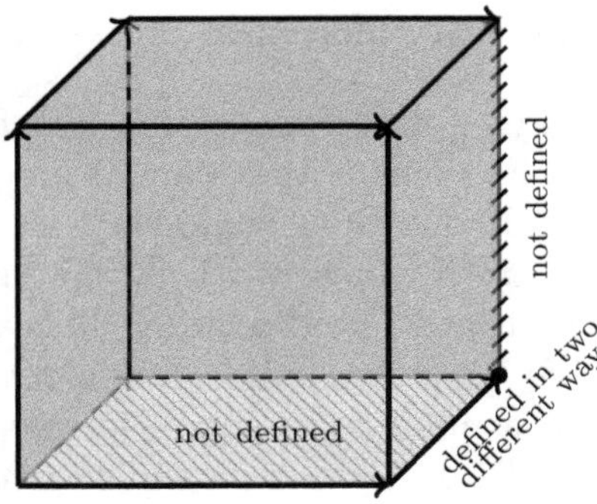

- either permute the first two and you obtain $\partial_1^1 \circ \partial_1^1 \circ \partial_3^0(c)$,
- or permute the last two and you obtain $\partial_1^0 \circ \partial_1^1 \circ \partial_1^1(c)$.

and both faces are not defined. On the other hand, those two should be equal because the comaps $d_1^1 \circ d_2^0 \circ d_1^1$ and $d_2^1 \circ d_2^0 \circ d_1^1$ are equal in $\square$, and $\partial_1^1 \circ \partial_2^0 \circ \partial_1^1$ and $\partial_1^1 \circ \partial_2^0 \circ \partial_2^1$ are both defined on c.

– secondly, the notion of morphism is not good (or at least, ambiguous). The equations $f_n \circ \partial_{i,n,X}^\alpha = \partial_{i,n,Y}^\alpha \circ f_{n+1}$ hold in [7] only when *both* face maps are defined, which authorises many morphisms. For example, consider the segment I, and the 'split' segment I' which is defined as I, except that no face maps are defined (geometrically, this corresponds to two points and an open segment). The identity map from I to I' is a morphism of partial precubical sets in the sense of [7], which is unexpected. A bad consequence of that is that the notion of paths in a partial HDA does not correspond to morphisms from some particular partial HDA, and paths are not preserved by morphisms, as we will see later.

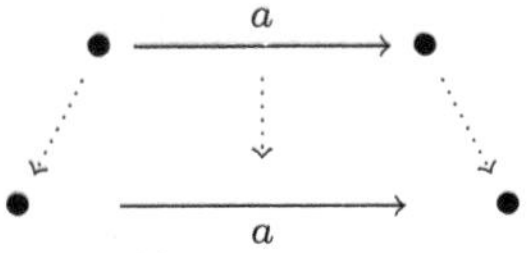

2.3 Partial Higher Dimensional Automata as Lax Functors

The idea is to generalise the 'presheaf' definition of precubical sets. The problem is to deal with partial functions and when two of them should coincide. Let **pSet** be the category of sets and partial functions. A partial function $f : X \longrightarrow Y$ can be either seen as a pair (A, f) of a subset $A \subseteq X$ and a total function $f : A \longrightarrow Y$, or as a functional relation $f \subseteq X \times Y$, that is, a relation such that for every $x \in X$, there is at most one $y \in Y$ with $(x, y) \in f$. We will freely use both views in the following. For two partial maps $f, g : X \longrightarrow Y$, we denote by $f \equiv g$ if and only if for every $x \in X$ such that $f(x)$ and $g(x)$ are defined, then

$f(x) = g(x)$. Note that this is not equality, but equality on the intersection of the domains. We also write $f \subseteq g$ if and only if f is include in g as a relation, that is, if and only if, for every $x \in X$ such that $f(x)$ is defined, then $g(x)$ is defined and $f(x) = g(x)$. By a **lax functor** $F : \mathcal{C} \rightharpoonup \mathbf{pSet}$, we mean the following data [20]:

- for every object c of $\mathcal{C}$, a set Fc,
- for every morphism $i : c \longrightarrow c'$, a partial function $Fi : Fc \longrightarrow Fc'$

satisfying that $F\mathrm{id}_c = \mathrm{id}_{Fc}$ and $Fj \circ Fi \subseteq F(j \circ i)$.

The point is that partial precubical sets as defined in [7] do not satisfy the second condition, while they should. In addition, this definition will authorise a square to have vertices, that is, that some $\partial\partial$ are defined, while having no edge, that is, no ∂ defined. This may be useful to define paths as discrete traces in [8] (that we will call *shortcuts* later), that is, paths that can go directly from a point to a square for example. Observe also that if $j \circ i = j' \circ i'$ then $Fj \circ Fi \equiv Fj' \circ Fi'$, which gives us the local equations from [7]. A **partial precubical set** X is then a lax functor $F : \square^{op} \rightharpoonup \mathbf{pSet}$. It becomes harder to describe explicitly what a partial precubical set is, since we cannot restrict to the ∂_i^α anymore. It is a collection of sets $(X_n)_{n \in \mathbb{N}}$ together with a collection of *partial* functions $(\partial_{i_1<\ldots<i_k}^{\alpha_1,\ldots,\alpha_k} : X_{n+k} \longrightarrow X_n)$ satisfying the inclusions $\partial_{j_1<\ldots<j_m}^{\beta_1,\ldots,\beta_m} \circ \partial_{i_1<\ldots<i_n}^{\alpha_1,\ldots,\alpha_n} \subseteq \partial_{k_1<\ldots<k_{n+m}}^{\gamma_1,\ldots,\gamma_{n+m}}$ where the k_s and γ_s are defined as follows. $(k_1 < \ldots < k_{n+m}; \gamma_1, \ldots, \gamma_{n+m}) = (i_1 < \ldots < i_n; \alpha_1, \ldots, \alpha_n) \star (j_1 < \ldots < j_m; \beta_1, \ldots, \beta_m)$ where $\star$ is defined by induction on $n + m$:

- if $n = 0$, $\epsilon \star (j_1 < \ldots < j_m; \beta_1, \ldots, \beta_m) = (j_1 < \ldots < j_m; \beta_1, \ldots, \beta_m)$,
- if $m = 0$, $(i_1 < \ldots < i_n; \alpha_1, \ldots, \alpha_n) \star \epsilon = (i_1 < \ldots < i_n; \alpha_1, \ldots, \alpha_n)$,
- if $i_1 \leq j_1$, $(i_1 < \ldots < i_n; \alpha_1, \ldots, \alpha_n) \star (j_1 < \ldots < j_m; \beta_1, \ldots, \beta_m) = (i_1; \alpha_1).((i_2 < \ldots < i_n; \alpha_2, \ldots, \alpha_n) \star (j_1 + 1 < \ldots < j_m + 1; \beta_1, \ldots, \beta_m))$,
- if $i_1 > j_1$, $(i_1 < \ldots < i_n; \alpha_1, \ldots, \alpha_n) \star (j_1 < \ldots < j_m; \beta_1, \ldots, \beta_m) = (j_1; \beta_1).((i_1 < \ldots < i_n; \alpha_1, \ldots, \alpha_n) \star (j_2 < \ldots < j_m; \beta_2, \ldots, \beta_m))$.

A **function-valued op-lax transformation** [20] from $F : \mathcal{C} \rightharpoonup \mathbf{pSet}$ to $G : \mathcal{C} \rightharpoonup \mathbf{pSet}$ is a collection $(f_c)_{c \in Ob(\mathcal{C})}$ of *total* functions such that for every $i : c \longrightarrow c'$, $f_{c'} \circ F(i) \subseteq G(i) \circ f_c$. A **morphism of partial precubical sets** from X to Y is then a function-valued op-lax transformation. In other words, this is a collection of *total* functions $(f_n : X_n \longrightarrow Y_n)_{n \in \mathbb{N}}$ satisfying the equations $f_n \circ \partial_{i_1<\ldots<i_k}^{\alpha_1,\ldots,\alpha_k} \subseteq \partial_{i_1<\ldots<i_k}^{\alpha_1,\ldots,\alpha_k} \circ f_{n+k}$. Partial precubical sets and morphisms of partial precubical sets form a category that we denote by **ppCub**. **pCub** is a full subcategory of **ppCub**. In particular, the precubical sets $*$ and L are partial precubical sets. A **partial HDA** X on L is a partial precubical set, also noted X, together with a specified point, the **initial state** $i \in X_0$ and a morphism of ppCub, the **labelling functions**, $(\lambda_n : X_n \longrightarrow L^n)_{n \in \mathbb{N}}$. A **morphism of pHDA** from X to Y is a morphism f of partial precubical sets from X to Y such that $f_0(i_X) = i_Y$ and $\lambda_X = \lambda_Y \circ f$. Partial HDA on L and morphisms of partial HDA form a category that we note $\mathbf{pHDA_L}$. In other words, this is the double slice category $*/\mathbf{ppCub}/L$.

2.4 Completion of a pHDA

Let us describe how it is possible to construct a HDA from a pHDA X, by 'completing' X, that is, by adding the faces that are missing, and by connecting the faces that are not. Let

$$Y_n = \{((i_1 < \ldots < i_k; \alpha_1, \ldots, \alpha_k), x) \mid x \in X_{n+k} \wedge i_k \leq n+k\}$$

$Y = (Y_n)_{n\in\mathbb{N}}$ is intuitively the collection of all abstract faces of all cubes of X, that is, pairs of a cube and all possible ways to define a face from it. Of course, some of those are the same, since there are several ways to describe a cube as the face of some other cube. Define $\sim$ as the smallest equivalence relation such that:

- if $\partial^{\alpha_1,\ldots,\alpha_k}_{i_1<\ldots<i_k}(x)$ is defined, then

$$((i_1 < \ldots < i_k; \alpha_1, \ldots, \alpha_k), x) \sim (\epsilon, \partial^{\alpha_1,\ldots,\alpha_k}_{i_1<\ldots<i_k}(x)).$$

  This means that, if a face of a cube exists in X, this face is identified with both abstract faces $(\epsilon, \partial^{\alpha_1,\ldots,\alpha_k}_{i_1<\ldots<i_k}(x))$ (i.e., the cube $\partial^{\alpha_1,\ldots,\alpha_k}_{i_1<\ldots<i_k}(x)$ itself) and $((i_1 < \ldots < i_k; \alpha_1, \ldots, \alpha_k), x)$ (i.e., the face of x, which consists of taking the (i_k, α_k) face, then the (i_{k-1}, α_{k-1}) face, and so on).
- if $((i_1 < \ldots < i_k; \alpha_1, \ldots, \alpha_k), x) \sim ((j_1 < \ldots < j_l; \beta_1, \ldots, \beta_l), y)$, then $((i_1 < \ldots < i_k; \alpha_1, \ldots, \alpha_k) \star (i, \alpha), x) \sim ((j_1 < \ldots < j_l; \beta_1, \ldots, \beta_l) \star (i, \alpha), y)$. This means that if two abstract faces coincide, then taking both their (i, α) face gives two abstract faces that also coincide.
  Let $\chi(X)_n = Y_n/\sim$ and we denote by $\ll (i_1 < \ldots < i_k; \alpha_1, \ldots, \alpha_k), x \gg$ the equivalence class of $((i_1 < \ldots < i_k; \alpha_1, \ldots, \alpha_k), x)$ modulo $\sim$. We define the i-face map as $\partial^\alpha_i(\ll (i_1 < \ldots < i_k; \alpha_1, \ldots, \alpha_k), x \gg) = \ll (i_1 < \ldots < i_k; \alpha_1, \ldots, \alpha_k) \star (i, \alpha), x \gg$, the initial state as $\ll \epsilon, i \gg$ and the labelling function as $\lambda(\ll (i_1 < \ldots < i_k; \alpha_1, \ldots, \alpha_k), x \gg) = \delta^{\alpha_1}_{i_1} \circ \ldots \circ \delta^{\alpha_k}_{i_k}(\lambda(x))$.

Theorem 1. *χ is a well-defined functor and is the left adjoint of τ, the injection of* ***HDA***$_L$ *into* ***pHDA***$_L$*. Furthermore,* ***HDA***$_L$ *is a reflective subcategory of* ***pHDA***$_L$*.*

Now, we can define the **geometric realisation** of a pHDA X as the subspace of the realisation of $\chi(X)$ consisting of points whose carrier is of the form $\ll \epsilon, x \gg$ for some $x \in X$. This really corresponds to the drawings we have been using to depict pHDA until now.

3 Paths in Partial Higher Dimensional Automata

Executions of HDA are defined using the notion of paths. Those paths describe the succession of starting and finishing of actions in a HDA. For example, a HDA can start an action then start another at the same time, and finish the two actions. This sequence is then not just a sequence of 1-dimensional transitions, since some actions can be made at the same time, but a sequence of hypercubes corresponding to the evolution of the state of the system. We will formalise this idea in Sect. 3.2, and we will see in particular that those paths can be encoded in the category $\mathbf{pHDA_L}$ (while it is not possible in the category $\mathbf{HDA_L}$) as morphisms from particular pHDA, called path shapes. In Sect. 3.1, let us first start by recalling the general framework of [17].

3.1 Path Category, Open Maps, Coverings

In the general framework of [17], we start with a category $\mathcal{M}$ of systems, together with a subcategory $\mathcal{P}$ of execution shapes. For example, keep in mind the case where $\mathcal{M}$ is the category of transition systems and $\mathcal{P}$ is the full subcategory of finite linear systems. One interesting remark about this case is that executions of a given systems are in bijective correspondance with morphisms from a finite linear system to this given system. This means that to reason about behaviours of such systems, it is enough to reason about morphisms and execution shapes.

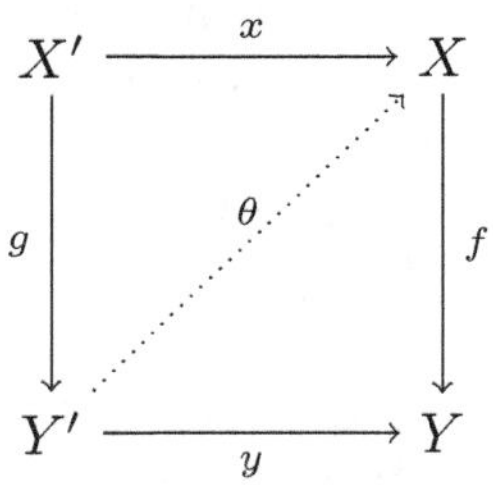

This idea was formalised by describing precisely which morphisms are witnesses for the existence of a bisimulation between systems. This description uses right lifting properties: we say that a morphism $f : X \longrightarrow Y$ has the **right lifting property with respect to** $g : X' \longrightarrow Y'$ if for every $x : X' \longrightarrow X$ and $y : Y' \longrightarrow Y$ such that $f \circ x = y \circ g$, there exists $\theta : Y' \longrightarrow X$ such that $x = \theta \circ g$ and $f \circ \theta = y$. For example, let us assume that f is a morphism of transition systems and that X' and Y' are finite linear systems. Then x (resp. y) is the same as an execution in X (resp. Y), and $f \circ x = y \circ g$ means that the execution y is a extension of the image of the execution x by f. The right lifting property means that the longer execution y of Y can be lifted to a longer execution θ of X, that is, θ is an extension of x and the image of θ by f is y. This property of lifting longer executions is precisely the property needed on a morphism to make its graph relation a bisimulation. They are also very similar to morphisms of coalgebras [16]. We call **$\mathcal{P}$-open** (or simply open when $\mathcal{P}$ is clear), a morphism that has the right lifting property with respect to every morphism in $\mathcal{P}$. From open maps, it is possible to describe similarity and bismilarity as the existence of a span of morphisms/open maps, and many kinds of bisimilarities can be captured in this way [17]. An open map is said to be a **$\mathcal{P}$-covering** (or simply covering) if furthermore the lifts in the right lifting properties are unique. Being a covering is a very strong requirement, as they correspond to partial unfolding of a system.

3.2 Encoding Paths in pHDA

In this section, we describe the classical notion of execution of HDA from [12], extended to partial HDA in [7], defined using the notion of path. We then show that those executions can be encoded as an execution shapes subcategory, as in the general framework of [17], proving in particular that paths are in bijective correspondance with a class of morphisms. A **path** π of a HDA X is a sequence $i = x_0 \xrightarrow{j_1,\alpha_1} x_1 \xrightarrow{j_2,\alpha_2} \ldots \xrightarrow{j_n,\alpha_n} x_n$ where $x_k \in X$, $j_k > 0$ and $\alpha_k \in \{0,1\}$ are such that for every k:

- if $\alpha_k = 0$, then $x_{k-1} = \partial^0_{j_k}(x_k)$,
- if $\alpha_k = 1$, then $x_k = \partial^1_{j_k}(x_{k-1})$.

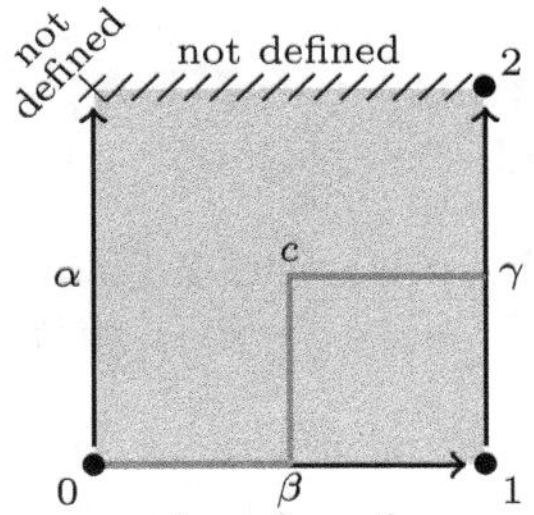

In red: path
$\pi = 0 \xrightarrow{1,0} \beta \xrightarrow{2,0} c \xrightarrow{1,1} \gamma$
in the pHDA X

This definition can easily be extended to pHDA, by requiring that the j_k-face maps are defined on x_k or x_{k-1}. A natural property of executions and morphisms is that morphisms map executions to executions. This is the case here (while it is not for [7], e.g., the split segment):

Proposition 1. *If $f : X \longrightarrow Y$ is a map of pHDA and if $\pi = x_0 \xrightarrow{j_1,\alpha_1} x_1 \xrightarrow{j_2,\alpha_2} \ldots \xrightarrow{j_n,\alpha_n} x_n$ is a path in X, then $\pi' = f(x_0) \xrightarrow{j_1,\alpha_1} f(x_1) \xrightarrow{j_2,\alpha_2} \ldots \xrightarrow{j_n,\alpha_n} f(x_n)$ is a path in Y.*

One advantage of considering pHDA instead of HDA is that paths can be encoded in pHDA, which is not really possible in HDA. It is done as follows. A **spine** σ is a sequence $(0,\epsilon) = (d_0, w_0) \xrightarrow{j_1,\alpha_1} (d_1, w_1) \xrightarrow{j_2,\alpha_2} \ldots \xrightarrow{j_n,\alpha_n} (d_n, w_n)$ where $j_k > 0$, $d_k \in \mathbb{N}$, $w_k \in L^{d_k}$ and $\alpha_k \in \{0,1\}$ are such that:

- if $\alpha_k = 0$, then $d_{k-1} = d_k - 1$, $\delta_{j_k}(w_k) = w_{k-1}$ and $j_k \leq d_k$,
- if $\alpha_k = 1$, then $d_k = d_{k-1} - 1$, $\delta_{j_k}(w_{k-1}) = w_k$ and $j_k \leq d_{k-1}$.

A path π has a underlying spine σ_π by mapping x_k to the pair of its dimension and its label. A spine σ induces a pHDA $B\sigma$ as follows:

- $B\sigma_p = \{k \in \{0,\ldots,n\} \mid d_k = p\}$,
- the partial face maps $\partial^{\alpha_1,\ldots,\alpha_n}_{i_1<\ldots<i_n}$ are the smallest (as relations ordered by inclusion) partial functions such that:
  - if $\alpha_k = 0$, then $\partial^0_{j_k}(k) = k-1$,
  - if $\alpha_k = 1$, then $\partial^1_{j_k}(k-1) = k$,
  - $\partial^{\beta_1,\ldots,\beta_m}_{j_1<\ldots<j_m} \circ \partial^{\alpha_1,\ldots,\alpha_n}_{i_1<\ldots<i_n} \subseteq \partial^{\gamma_1,\ldots,\gamma_{n+m}}_{k_1<\ldots<k_{n+m}}$, for $(k_1,\ldots,k_{n+m};\gamma_1,\ldots,\gamma_{n+m}) = (i_1,\ldots,i_n;\alpha_1,\ldots,\alpha_n) \star (j_1,\ldots,j_m;\beta_1,\ldots,\beta_m)$.

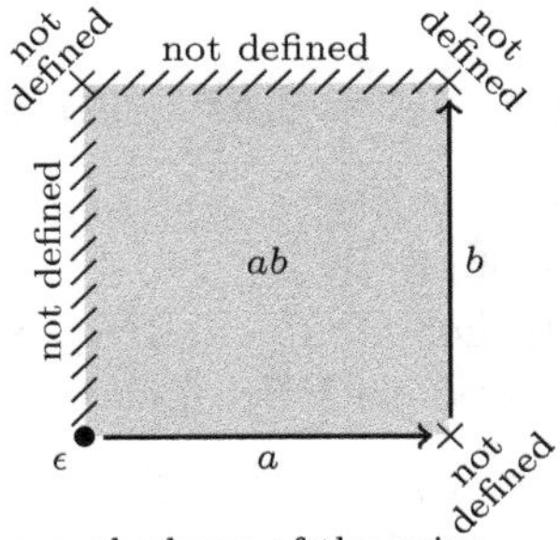

path shape of the spine
$\sigma = (0,\epsilon) \xrightarrow{1,0} (1,a) \xrightarrow{2,0} (2,ab) \xrightarrow{1,1} (1,b)$

- the initial state is 0,
- the labelling functions λ_n map k to w_k.

By a **path shape**, we mean such a pHDA $B\sigma$. The set $\mathbf{Spine_L}$ of spines can be partially ordered by prefix. B can then be extended to an embedding from $\mathbf{Spine_L}$ to $\mathbf{pHDA_L}$. We note $\mathbf{PS_L}$ the image of this embedding, i.e., the full sub-category of path shapes.

Proposition 2. *There is a bijection between paths in a pHDA X and morphisms of pHDA from a path shape to X.*

Again, this is not true with the definition of morphisms from [7] (e.g., the split segment). As an example, the red path π above corresponds to a morphism from the path shape $B\sigma$ to X.

4 Trees and Unfolding in pHDA

In this section, we introduce our notion of trees. Following [4], we consider trees as colimits (or glueings of paths). Section 4.1 is dedicated to proving that those colimits actually exist, by giving an explicit construction of those. From this explicit construction, we will describe the kind of unique path properties that are satisfied by those trees in Sect. 4.2. Starting by showing, that the strict unicity of path fails, we then describe a notion of homotopy, the confluent homotopy, which is weaker than the one from [12], for which every tree has the property that there is exactly one homotopy class of paths form the initial state to any state. We will also see that, because the face maps of trees are defined in a local way, they do not have any shortcuts, that is, paths that 'skip' dimensions, for example, going from a point to a square without going through a segment. Finally, in Sect. 4.3, we will prove that those two properties – the unicity of paths modulo confluent homotopy, and the non-existence of shortcuts – completely characterise trees. This proof will use a suitable notion of unfolding of pHDA, showing furthermore that trees form a coreflective subcategory of pHDA.

4.1 Trees, as Colimits of Paths in pHDA

In this section, we give an explicit construction of colimits of diagrams with values in path shapes. Those will be our first definition of trees in pHDA, following [4]. Let $D : \mathcal{C} \longrightarrow \mathbf{PS_L}$ be a small diagram with values in $\mathbf{PS_L}$, that is, a functor from $\mathcal{C}$ to $\mathbf{PS_L}$. Let us use some notations: for every object u of $\mathcal{C}$, $Du = B\sigma_u$ with $\sigma_u = (d_0^u, w_0^u) \xrightarrow{j_1^u,\alpha_1^u} (d_1^u, w_1^u) \xrightarrow{j_2^u,\alpha_2^u} \ldots \xrightarrow{j_{l_u}^u,\alpha_{l_u}^u} (d_{l_u}^u, w_{l_u}^u)$. The definition of the colimit $\mathrm{col}\, D$ will be in two steps. The first step consists in putting all the paths Du side-by-side, and in glueing them together, along the morphisms Df, for every morphism f of $\mathcal{C}$. This is done as follows. Define $(X_n)_{n\in\mathbb{N}}$ to be:

- $X_0 = \{(u, k) \mid u \in \mathcal{C}, k \leq l_u \wedge d_k^u = 0\} \sqcup \{\epsilon\}$,
- $X_n = \{(u, k) \mid u \in \mathcal{C}, k \leq l_u \wedge d_k^u = n\}$.

We quotient X_n by the smallest equivalence relation $\sim$ (for inclusion) such that:

- for every u, $(u, 0) \sim \epsilon$,
- if $i : u \longrightarrow v \in \mathcal{C}$, and if $k \leq l_u, l_v$, then $(u, k) \sim (v, k)$.

We denote by Y_n the quotient $X_n/\sim$, and by $[u, k]$ the equivalence class of (u, k) modulo $\sim$.

At this stage, we still do not have the colimit because it is not possible to define the face maps. Let us consider the following example.

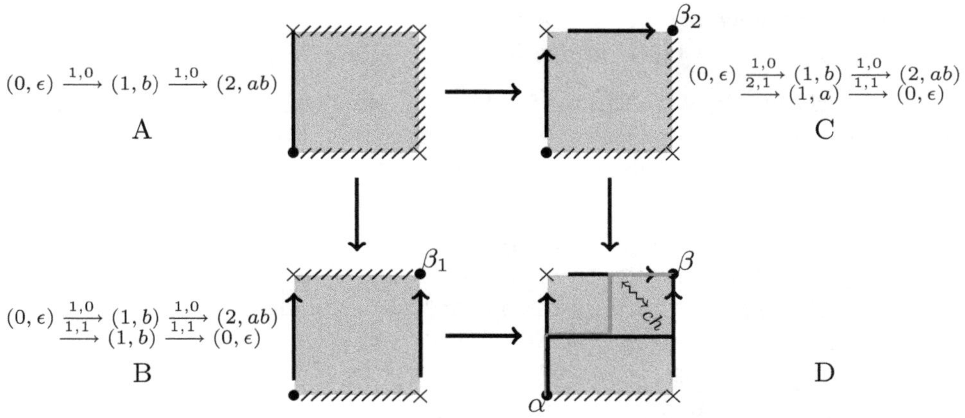

A, B and C are path shapes, and we would like to compute their pushout. The expected outcome is D, since we must identify the three squares by the previous construction. The problem is that the previous construction does not identify β_1 and β_2. Those two must be identified because they are both the top right corner of the same square (after identification). We hence need to quotient a little more to be able to define the face maps, as follows. Define Z_n to be the quotient of Y_n by the smallest equivalence relation $\approx$ such that if there are two sequences $u_0, \ldots, u_l$ and $v_0, \ldots, v_l$ such that:

- $[u_0, k] \approx [v_0, k]$,
- for every $0 \leq s \leq l$, $\alpha^{u_s}_{k+1+s} = \alpha^{v_s}_{k+1+s} = 1$,
- for every $0 \leq s < l$, $[u_s, k+s+1] \approx [u_{s+1}, k+s+1]$ and $[v_s, k+s+1] \approx [v_{s+1}, k+s+1]$,
- $(j^{u_0}_{k+1}; 1) \star \ldots \star (j^{u_l}_{k+l+1}; 1) = (j^{v_0}_{k+1}; 1) \star \ldots \star (j^{v_l}_{k+l+1}; 1)$,
  then, $[u_l, k+l+1] \approx [v_l, k+l+1]$. $\operatorname{col} D$ is the pHDA Z_N with the face maps being the smallest relations for inclusion such that:
- if $\alpha^u_k = 0$, then $\partial^0_{j^u_k}(\langle u, k\rangle)$ is defined and is equal to $\langle u, k-1\rangle$,
- if $\alpha^u_{k+1} = 1$ then $\partial^1_{j^u_k}(\langle u, k\rangle)$ is defined and is equal to $\langle u, k+1\rangle$,
- $\partial^{\beta_1,\ldots,\beta_m}_{j_1<\ldots<j_m} \circ \partial^{\alpha_1,\ldots,\alpha_n}_{i_1<\ldots<i_n} \subseteq \partial^{\gamma_1,\ldots,\gamma_{n+m}}_{k_1<\ldots<k_{n+m}}$, for $(k_1, \ldots, k_{n+m}; \gamma_1, \ldots, \gamma_{n+m}) = (i_1, \ldots, i_n; \alpha_1, \ldots, \alpha_n) \star (j_1, \ldots, j_m; \beta_1, \ldots, \beta_m)$.

The initial state is $\langle \epsilon \rangle$ and the labelling $\lambda : \operatorname{col} D \longrightarrow L$ maps $\langle u, k\rangle$ to w^u_k.

Proposition 3. *$col D$ is the colimit of D in $\mathbf{pHDA_L}$*

By **tree** we mean any pHDA that is the colimit of a diagram with values in path shapes. We denote by $\mathbf{Tr_L}$ the full subcategory of trees.

4.2 The Unique Path Properties of Trees

Failure of the Unicity of Paths. Let us consider the pushout square above again. In particular, the pHDA on the bottom-right corner is a tree, by definition. However, there are two paths from α to β (in red and blue). This actually comes from the fact that we needed to identify β_1 and β_2 to be able to define the face maps. This means that trees do not have the unique path property.

Confluent Homotopy. A careful reader may have observed that the only difference between the two previous paths is that some future faces are swapped. Actually, this is the only obstacle for the unicity of paths for trees: there is a unique path modulo equivalence of paths that permutes arrows of the form $\xrightarrow{-,1}$. That is what we call **confluent homotopy**. This confluent homotopy will be defined by restricting the elementary homotopies of [12] to be of only one type out of the four possible, which means our notion of homotopy makes fewer paths equivalent than the one from [12].

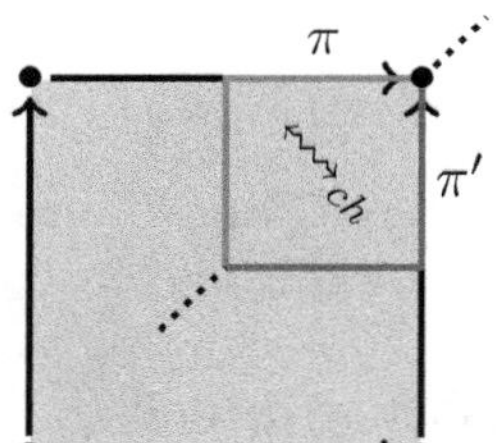

We say that a path $\pi = x_0 \xrightarrow{j_1,\alpha_1} x_1 \xrightarrow{j_2,\alpha_2} \dots \xrightarrow{j_n,\alpha_n} x_n$ is **elementary confluently homotopic** to a path $\pi' = x'_0 \xrightarrow{j'_1,\alpha'_1} x'_1 \xrightarrow{j'_2,\alpha'_2} \dots \xrightarrow{j'_n,\alpha'_n} x'_n$, and denote by $\pi \leftrightsquigarrow_{ch} \pi'$, if and only if there are $0 < s < t \leq n$ such that:

- for all $k < s$ or $k \geq t$, $x_k = x'_k$,
- for all $k < s$ or $k > t$, $j_k = j'_k$ and $\alpha_k = \alpha'_k$,
- for all $s \leq k \leq t$, $\alpha_k = \alpha'_k = 1$,
- $(j_s, \alpha_s) \star \dots \star (j_t, \alpha_t) = (j'_s, \alpha'_s) \star \dots \star (j'_t, \alpha'_t)$.

We denote by $\sim_{ch}$, and call **confluent homotopy**, the reflexive transitive closure of $\leftrightsquigarrow_{ch}$.

Lemma 1. *If X is a tree, then for every element (of any dimension) x of X, there is exactly one path modulo confluent homotopy from the initial state to x.*

Shortcuts. The face maps of path shapes and of the colimits we computed in Sect. 4.1 are of a very particular form: we start by defining the ∂_j^α and we extend this definition to general $\partial_{j_1<\dots<j_n}^{\alpha_1,\dots,\alpha_n}$. In a way, they are locally defined, and then extended to higher face maps. This means in particular that, in addition to having unique paths modulo confluent homotopy, they also do not have any 'shortcut'. A possible shortcut can be defined as a generalisation of paths, in which we allow to make transitions that go, for example, from a point to a square or to a cube, not only to segments, a shortcut being such a possible shortcut which is not confluently homotopic to a path. Those shortcuts may occur in a

pHDA, even if it has the unique path property. Concretely, by **shortcut** we mean the following situation: the face $\partial_{i_1<\ldots<i_n}^{\alpha_1,\ldots,\alpha_n}(x)$ is defined, but there is no sequence $(j_1;\beta_1)\star\ldots\star(j_n;\beta_n)=(i_1<\ldots<i_n;\alpha_1,\ldots,\alpha_n)$ such that $\partial_{j_n}^{\alpha_n}\circ\ldots\circ\partial_{j_1}^{\alpha_1}(x)$ is defined. By local-definedness of the face maps:

Lemma 2. *Trees do not have any shortcuts.*

Trees. We say that a pHDA **has the unique path property modulo confluent homotopy** if it has no shortcut, and there is exactly one class of paths modulo confluent homotopy from the initial state to any state. Given such a pHDA X and an element x of X, by **depth of** x we mean the length of a path from the initial state to x in X. Since homotopic paths have the same length, this is uniquely defined. We deduce from the previous discussions that:

Proposition 4. *Trees have unique path property modulo confluent homotopy.*

In the following, we will prove the converse: trees, defined as colimits of path shapes are exactly those pHDA that have the unique path property modulo confluent homotopy. This will be done by proving that such a pHDA X is isomorphic to its unfolding. A question that occurs now is the following. Much as the general framework of [4], trees are colimits of paths. Everything tends to work well when those trees have a nice property, which we called **accessibility**, intuitively, that the colimit process do not 'create' paths. This property is actually deeply related to the unicity of paths. Since this unicity fails in the case of pHDA, accessibility fails too. However, an accessibility modulo confluent homotopy holds: the colimit process in pHDA do not create confluent homotopy classes of paths.

4.3 Trees Are Unfoldings

We are now constructing our unfolding $U(X)$ of a pHDA X by giving an explicit definition, similar to [6,11], and proving that this is a tree. We will prove that there is a covering $\mathrm{unf}_X : U(X) \longrightarrow X$, which in particular means that the unfolding $U(X)$ is $\mathbf{PS_L}$-bisimilar (in the general sense of [17]) to X, and that this covering is actually an isomorphism when X has the unique path property modulo confluent homotopy.

Unfolding of a pHDA. Let us start with a few notations. Given a path $\pi = x_0 \xrightarrow{j_1,\alpha_1} x_1 \xrightarrow{j_2,\alpha_2} \ldots \xrightarrow{j_n,\alpha_n} x_n$ we note $e(\pi)=x_n$, $l(\pi)=n$ and $\pi_{-k} = x_0 \xrightarrow{j_1,\alpha_1} x_1 \xrightarrow{j_2,\alpha_2} \ldots \xrightarrow{j_{n-k},\alpha_{n-k}} x_{n-k}$. Given a pHDA X, its **unfolding** is the following pHDA:

- $U(X)_n$ is the set of equivalence classes $[\pi]$ of paths modulo confluent homotopy, such that $e(\pi)$ is of dimension n,
- the face maps are the smallest relations for inclusion such that:
  - $\partial_i^1(\alpha)=[\pi \xrightarrow{i,1} \partial_i^1(e(\pi))]$, for any $\pi\in\alpha$ such that $\partial_i^1(e(\pi))$ is defined,
  - $\partial_i^0(\alpha)=[\pi_{-1}]$ for any $\pi\in\alpha$ such that $\pi=\pi_{-1}\xrightarrow{i,0} e(\pi)$,

- $\partial^{\beta_1,\ldots,\beta_m}_{j_1<\ldots<j_m} \circ \partial^{\alpha_1,\ldots,\alpha_n}_{i_1<\ldots<i_n} \subseteq \partial^{\gamma_1,\ldots,\gamma_{n+m}}_{k_1<\ldots<k_{n+m}}$, for $(k_1,\ldots,k_{n+m};\gamma_1,\ldots,\gamma_{n+m}) = (i_1,\ldots,i_n;\alpha_1,\ldots,\alpha_n) \star (j_1,\ldots,j_m;\beta_1,\ldots,\beta_m)$.
- the initial state is $[i]$,
- the labelling is given by $\lambda(\alpha) = \lambda(e(\pi))$ for $\pi \in \alpha$.

Following ideas from [4] again, the unfolding can be seen as the glueing of all possible executions of a system, but with care needed to handle confluent homotopy. Concretely:

Proposition 5. *The unfolding of a pHDA is a tree.*

We can also define $\mathrm{unf}_X : U(X) \longrightarrow X$ as the function that maps $[\pi]$ to $e(\pi)$.

Proposition 6. *unf_X is a covering, and so, $U(X)$ is $\boldsymbol{PS_L}$-bisimilar to X.*

The Unique Path Property Characterises Trees. When X has exactly one class of paths modulo confluent homotopy from the initial state to any state, it is possible to define a function $\eta_X : X \longrightarrow U(X)$ that maps any element x of X to the unique confluent homotopy class to x. When furthermore X does not have shortcuts, then η is actually a morphism of pHDA.

Proposition 7. *When X has the unique path property modulo confluent homotopy, then η_X is the inverse of unf_X. In particular, X is a tree.*

Together with Proposition 4, this implies the following:

Theorem 2. *Trees are exactly the pHDA that have the unique path property modulo confluent homotopy.*

Another consequence is that this isomorphism η_X is actually natural (in the categorical sense) and is part of an adjunction, which implies that trees form a coreflective subcategory of pHDA:

Corollary 1. *U extends to a functor, which is the right adjoint of the embedding $\iota : \boldsymbol{Tr_L} \longrightarrow \boldsymbol{pHDA_L}$. Furthermore, this is a coreflection.*

5 Cofibrant Objects

Cofibrant objects are another type of 'simple objects', coming from homotopy theory, more particularly the language of model categories from [24]. Those cofibrant objects are those whose unique morphism from the initial object is a cofibration. Intuitively (intuition which holds at least in cofibrantly generated model structures [15]), this means that cofibrant objects are those objects constructed from 'nothing', using only very basic constructions (generators of cofibrations). In the case of the classical model structure on topological spaces (Kan-Quillen), those spaces are those constructed from the empty space by adding 'cells', which produces what is called CW-complexes. In this section, we want to mimic this idea with trees: trees are those pHDA constructed from an initial state by only extending paths. We also want to emphasize that much as CW-complexes gives a kind of homotopy type of a space, trees gives a concurrency type of a pHDA, in the sense that there is a canonical way to produce an equivalent cofibrant object out of any object, which is called the **cofibrant replacement** in homotopy theory. In concurrency theory, this is the unfolding.

5.1 Cofibrant Objects in pHDA$_L$

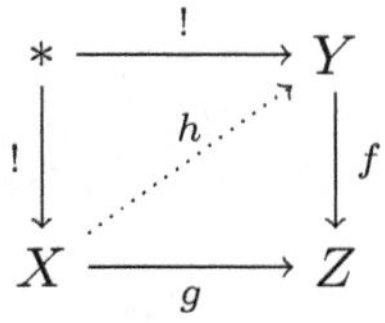

Following the language of model structures from [24], we say that a pHDA X is **cofibrant** if for every $\mathbf{PS_L}$-open morphism $f : Y \longrightarrow Z$ and every morphism $g : X \longrightarrow Z$, there is a morphism $h : X \longrightarrow Y$, such that $f \circ h = g$. That is, a partial HDA X is cofibrant if and only if every $\mathbf{PS_L}$-open morphism has the right lifting property with respect to the unique morphism from $*$ to X.

$$
\begin{array}{ccc}
* & \xrightarrow{\;!\;} & Y \\
{\scriptstyle !}\downarrow & \nearrow{\scriptstyle h} & \downarrow{\scriptstyle f} \\
X & \xrightarrow{\;g\;} & Z
\end{array}
$$

5.2 Cofibrant Objects Are Exactly Trees

In this section, we would like to prove the following:

Theorem 3. *The cofibrant objects are exactly trees.*

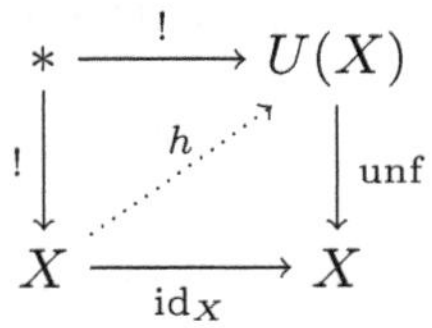

Let us start by giving the idea of the proof of the fact that cofibrant objects are trees. By Proposition 6, unf$_X$ is a covering, so is open. This means that for every cofibrant object X, there is a morphism $h : X \longrightarrow U(X)$ such that unf$_X \circ h = \mathrm{id}_X$, that is, X is a retract of its unfolding. Since

we know that the unfolding is a tree by Proposition 5, it is enough to observe the following:

Lemma 3. *A retract of a tree is a tree.*

Intuitively, a pHDA is the retract of a tree only when it is obtain by retracting branches. This can only produce a tree. For the converse:

Proposition 8. *A tree is a cofibrant object. Furthermore, if $f : Y \longrightarrow Z$ is a covering, then the lift $h : X \longrightarrow Y$ is unique.*

The lift h is constructed by induction as follows. We define X_n as the restriction of X to elements whose depth is smaller than n, and the face maps $\partial^{\alpha_1,\ldots,\alpha_m}_{j_1 < \ldots < j_m}(x)$ are defined if and only if $\partial^{\alpha_1,\ldots,\alpha_m}_{j_1 < \ldots < j_m}(x)$ is defined in X and belongs to X_n. We then construct $h_n : X_n \longrightarrow Y$ using the unique path property modulo confluent homotopy, in a natural way (in the categorical meaning), i.e., such that $h_n \circ \kappa_n = h_{n-1}$, where $\kappa_n : X_{n-1} \longrightarrow X_n$ is the inclusion. h is then the inductive limit of those h_n. This proof can be seen as a small object argument.

5.3 The Unfolding Is Universal

As an application of the previous theorem, we would like to prove that the unfolding is universal. As in the case of covering spaces in algebraic topology, a covering corresponds to a partial unrolling of a system, in the sense that we can unroll some loops or even partially unroll a loop (imagine for example executing a few steps of a while-loop). In this sense, we can describe the fact that a covering unrolls more than another one, and that, an unfolding is a complete unrolling: since the domain is a tree, it is impossible to unroll more. Actually, much as the topological and the groupoidal cases (see [18] for example), unfoldings are the only such maximal unrollings among coverings: they are initial among coverings, that is why we call them 'universal'. In a way, this says that our definition of unfolding is the only reasonable one. Concretely, we say that a $\mathbf{PS_L}$-covering is **universal** if its domain is a tree.

Corollary 2. *If* $f : Y \longrightarrow X$ *is a universal covering, then for every covering* $g : Z \longrightarrow X$ *there is a unique map* $h : Y \longrightarrow X$ *such that* $f = g \circ h$. *Furthermore,* h *is itself a covering. Consequently, the universal covering is unique up-to isomorphism, and is given by the unfolding.*

This whole story is similar to the universal covering of a topological space: just replace pHDA by spaces and trees by simply-connected spaces [2].

6 Conclusion and Future Work

In this paper, we have given a cleaner definition of partial precubical sets and partial Higher Dimensional Automata, as they really correspond to collections of cubes with missing faces. From this categorical definition, we derived that pHDA can be completed, giving rise to a geometric realisation. We also describe the first premisses of a homotopy theory of the concurrency of pHDA where the cofibrant objects are trees, and replacement is the unfolding. As a future work, we could look at wider class of paths, typically allowing shortcuts as paths, or introducing general homotopies in the path category, which is possible because we can encode those inside the category of pHDA. Another direction would be to continue the description of this homotopy theory, to see if it corresponds to some kind of Quillen's model structure, or at least to some weaker version (e.g., category of cofibrant objects).

References

1. Bednarczyk, M.A.: Categories of asynchronous systems. Ph.D. thesis, University of Sussex (1987)
2. tom Dieck, T.: Algebraic Topology. Textbooks in Mathematics. European Mathematical Society, Zürich (2008)
3. Dubut, J.: Directed homotopy and homology theories for geometric models of true concurrency. Ph.D. thesis, ENS Paris-Saclay (2017)
4. Dubut, J., Goubault, E., Goubault-Larrecq, J.: Bisimulations and unfolding in P-accessible categorical models. In: Proceedings of the 27th International Conference on Concurrency Theory (CONCUR 2016). Leibniz International Proceedings in Informatics (LIPIcs), vol. 59, pp. 1–14. Schloss Dagstuhl-Leibniz-Zentrum fuer Informatik (2016)
5. Fahrenberg, U.: A category of higher-dimensional automata. In: Sassone, V. (ed.) FoSSaCS 2005. LNCS, vol. 3441, pp. 187–201. Springer, Heidelberg (2005). https://doi.org/10.1007/978-3-540-31982-5_12
6. Fahrenberg, U., Legay, A.: History-preserving bisimilarity for higher-dimensional automata via open maps. Electron. Notes Theor. Comput. Sci. **298**, 165–178 (2013)

7. Fahrenberg, U., Legay, A.: Partial higher-dimensional automata. In: CALCO 2015, pp. 101–115 (2015)
8. Fajstrup, L.: Dipaths and dihomotopies in a cubical complex. Adv. Appl. Math. **35**(2), 188–206 (2005)
9. Fajstrup, L., Goubault, E., Haucourt, E., Mimram, S., Raussen, M.: Directed Algebraic Topology and Concurrency. Springer, Cham (2016). https://doi.org/10.1007/978-3-319-15398-8
10. Gaucher, P.: Towards a homotopy theory of higher dimensional transition systems. Theory Appl. Categ. **25**, 295–341 (2011)
11. van Glabbeek, R.J.: Bisimulations for higher dimensional automata, June 1991. http://theory.stanford.edu/~rvg/hda
12. van Glabbeek, R.J.: On the expresiveness of higher dimensional automata: (extended abstract). Electron. Notes Theor. Comput. Sci. **128**(2), 5–34 (2005)
13. Goubault, E.: Géométrie du parallélisme. Ph.D. thesis, Ecole Polytechnique (1995)
14. Grandis, M.: Directed Algebraic Topology: Models of Non-Reversible Worlds. New Mathematical Monographs, vol. 13. Cambridge University Press, Cambridge (2009)
15. Hirschhorn, P.S.: Model Categories and Their Localizations. Mathematical Surveys and Monographs, vol. 99. American Mathematical Society, Providence (2003)
16. Jacobs, B.: Introduction to Coalgebra: Towards Mathematics of States and Observation. Cambridge Tracts in Theoretical Computer Science. Cambridge University Press, New York (2016)
17. Joyal, A., Nielsen, M., Winskel, G.: Bisimulation from open maps. Inf. Comput. **127**(2), 164–185 (1996)
18. May, J.P.: A Concise Course in Algebraic Topology. Chicago Lectures in Mathematics. University of Chicago Press, Chicago (1999)
19. Milner, R. (ed.): A Calculus of Communicating Systems. LNCS, vol. 92. Springer, Heidelberg (1980). https://doi.org/10.1007/3-540-10235-3
20. Niefield, S.: Lax presheaves and exponentiability. Theory Appl. Categ. **24**(12), 288–301 (2010)
21. Nielsen, M., Plotkin, G., Winskel, G.: Petri nets, event structures and domains, part I. Theor. Comput. Sci. **13**(1), 85–108 (1981)
22. Nielsen, M., Sassone, V., Winskel, G.: Relationships between models of concurrency. In: de Bakker, J.W., de Roever, W.-P., Rozenberg, G. (eds.) REX 1993. LNCS, vol. 803, pp. 425–476. Springer, Heidelberg (1994). https://doi.org/10.1007/3-540-58043-3_25
23. Pratt, V.: Modeling concurrency with geometry. In: Proceedings of the 18th ACM SIGPLAN-SIGACT Symposium on Principles of Programming Languages (POPL), pp. 311–322, January 1991
24. Quillen, D.G.: Homotopical Algebra. LNM, vol. 43. Springer, Heidelberg (1967). https://doi.org/10.1007/BFb0097438
25. Shields, M.W.: Concurrent machines. Comput. J. **28**(5), 449–465 (1985)

7

Partial and Conditional Expectations in Markov Decision Processes with Integer Weights

Jakob Piribauer(✉) and Christel Baier

Technische Universität Dresden, Dresden, Germany
{jakob.piribauer,christel.baier}@tu-dresden.de

Abstract. The paper addresses two variants of the stochastic shortest path problem ("optimize the accumulated weight until reaching a goal state") in Markov decision processes (MDPs) with integer weights. The first variant optimizes partial expected accumulated weights, where paths not leading to a goal state are assigned weight 0, while the second variant considers conditional expected accumulated weights, where the probability mass is redistributed to paths reaching the goal. Both variants constitute useful approaches to the analysis of systems without guarantees on the occurrence of an event of interest (reaching a goal state), but have only been studied in structures with non-negative weights. Our main results are as follows. There are polynomial-time algorithms to check the finiteness of the supremum of the partial or conditional expectations in MDPs with arbitrary integer weights. If finite, then optimal weight-based deterministic schedulers exist. In contrast to the setting of non-negative weights, optimal schedulers can need infinite memory and their value can be irrational. However, the optimal value can be approximated up to an absolute error of ϵ in time exponential in the size of the MDP and polynomial in $\log(1/\epsilon)$.

1 Introduction

Stochastic shortest path (SSP) problems generalize the shortest path problem on graphs with weighted edges. The SSP problem is formalized using finite state Markov decision processes (MDPs), which are a prominent model combining probabilistic and nondeterministic choices. In each state of an MDP, one is allowed to choose nondeterministically from a set of actions, each of them is augmented with probability distributions over the successor states and a weight (cost or reward). The SSP problem asks for a policy to choose actions (here called a scheduler) maximizing or minimizing the expected accumulated weight until reaching a goal state. In the classical setting, one seeks an optimal *proper* scheduler where proper means that a goal state is reached almost surely. Polynomial-time solutions exist exploiting the fact that optimal memoryless deterministic schedulers exist (provided the optimal value is finite) and can be computed using linear programming techniques, possibly in combination with model transformations (see [1,5,10]). The restriction to proper schedulers, however, is often too restrictive. First, there are models that have no proper scheduler. Second, even if proper schedulers exist, the expectation of the accumulated weight of schedulers missing the goal with a positive probability should be taken into account as well. Important such applications include the semantics of probabilistic programs (see e.g. [4,7,12,14,16]) where no guarantee for almost sure termination can be given and the analysis of program properties at termination time gives rise to stochastic shortest (longest) path problems in which the goal (halting configuration) is not reached almost surely. Other examples are the fault-tolerance analysis (e.g., expected costs of repair mechanisms) in selected error scenarios that can appear with some positive, but small probability or the trade-off analysis with conjunctions of utility and cost constraints that are achievable with positive probability, but not almost surely (see e.g. [2]).

This motivates the switch to variants of classical SSP problems where the restriction to proper schedulers is relaxed. One option (e.g., considered in [8]) is to seek a scheduler optimizing the expectation of the random variable that assigns weight 0 to all paths not reaching the goal and the accumulated weight of the shortest prefix reaching the goal to all other paths. We refer to this expectation as *partial expectation*. Second, we consider the *conditional expectation* of the accumulated weight until reaching the goal under the condition that the goal is reached. In general, partial expectations describe situations in which some reward (positive and negative) is accumulated but only retrieved if a certain goal is met. In particular, partial expectations can be an appropriate replacement for the classical expected weight before reaching the goal if we want to include schedulers which miss the goal with some (possibly very small) probability. In contrast to conditional expectations, the resulting scheduler still has an incentive to reach the goal with a high probability, while schedulers maximizing the conditional expectation might reach the goal with a very small positive probability.

Previous work on partial or conditional expected accumulated weights was restricted to the case of non-negative weights. More precisely, partial expectations have been studied in the setting of stochastic multiplayer games with non-negative weights [8]. Conditional expectations in MDPs with non-negative weights have been addressed in [3]. In both cases, optimal values are achieved by weight-based deterministic schedulers that depend on the current state and the weight that has been accumulated so far, while memoryless schedulers are not sufficient. Both [8] and [3] prove the existence of a *saturation point* for the accumulated weight from which on optimal schedulers behave memoryless and maximize the probability to reach a goal state. This yields exponential-time algorithms for computing optimal schedulers using an iterative linear programming approach. Moreover, [3] proves that the threshold problem for conditional expectations ("does there exist a scheduler $\mathfrak{S}$ such that the conditional expectation under $\mathfrak{S}$ exceeds a given threshold?") is PSPACE-hard even for acyclic MDPs.

The purpose of the paper is to study partial and conditional expected accumulated weights for MDPs with integer weights. The switch from non-negative to integer weights indeed causes several additional difficulties. We start with the following observation. While optimal partial or conditional expectations in non-negative MDPs are rational, they can be irrational in the general setting:

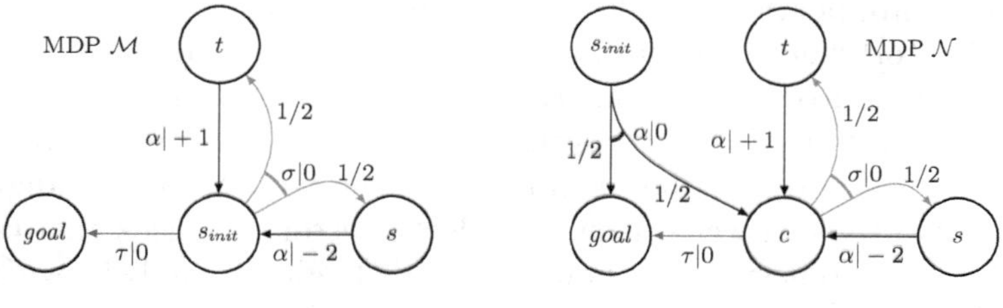

Fig. 1. Enabled actions are denoted by Greek letters and the weight associated to the action is stated after the bar. Probabilistic choices are marked by a bold arc and transition probabilities are denoted next to the arrows.

Example 1. Consider the MDP $\mathcal{M}$ depicted on the left in Fig. 1. In the initial state s_{init}, two actions are enabled. Action τ leads to *goal* with probability 1 and weight 0. Action σ leads to the states s and t with probability 1/2 from where we will return to s_{init} with weight -2 or $+1$, respectively. The scheduler choosing τ immediately leads to an expected weight of 0 and is optimal among schedulers reaching the goal almost surely. As long as we choose σ in s_{init}, the accumulated weight follows an asymmetric random walk increasing by 1 or decreasing by 2 with probability 1/2 before we return to s_{init}. It is well known that the probability to ever reach accumulated weight $+1$ in this random walk is $1/\Phi$ where $\Phi = \frac{1+\sqrt{5}}{2}$ is the golden ratio. Likewise, ever reaching accumulated weight n has probability $1/\Phi^n$ for all $n \in \mathbb{N}$. Consider the scheduler $\mathfrak{S}_k$ choosing τ as soon as the accumulated weight reaches k in s_{init}. Its partial expectation is k/Φ^k as the paths which never reach weight k are assigned weight 0. The maximum is reached at $k = 2$. In Sect. 4, we prove that there are optimal schedulers whose decisions only depend on the current state and the weight accumulated so far. With this result we can conclude that the maximal partial expectation is indeed $2/\Phi^2$, an irrational number.

The conditional expectation of $\mathfrak{S}_k$ in $\mathcal{M}$ is k as $\mathfrak{S}_k$ reaches the goal with accumulated weight k if it reaches the goal. So, the conditional expectation is not bounded. If we add a new initial state making sure that the goal is reached with positive probability as in the MDP $\mathcal{N}$, we can obtain an irrational maximal conditional expectation as well: The scheduler $\mathfrak{T}_k$ choosing τ in c as soon as the weight reaches k has conditional expectation $\frac{k/2\Phi^k}{1/2+1/2\Phi^k}$. The maximum is obtained for $k = 3$; the maximal conditional expectation is $\frac{3/\Phi^3}{1+1/\Phi^3} = \frac{3}{3+\sqrt{5}}$.

Moreover, while the proposed algorithms of [3,8] crucially rely on the monotonicity of the accumulated weights along the prefixes of paths, the accumulated weights of prefixes of path can oscillate when there are positive and negative weights. As we will see later, this implies that the existence of saturation points is no longer ensured and optimal schedulers might require infinite memory (more precisely, a counter for the accumulated weight). These observations provide evidence why linear-programming techniques as used in the case of non-negative MDPs [3,8] cannot be expected to be applicable for the general setting.

Contributions. We study the problem of maximizing the partial and conditional expected accumulated weight in MDPs with integer weights. Our first result is that the finiteness of the supremum of partial and conditional expectations in MDPs with integer weights can be checked in polynomial time (Sect. 3). For both variants we show that there are optimal weight-based deterministic schedulers if the supremum is finite (Sect. 4). Although the suprema might be irrational and optimal schedulers might need infinite memory, the suprema can be ϵ-approximated in time exponential in the size of the MDP and polynomial in $\log(1/\epsilon)$ (Sect. 5). By duality of maximal and minimal expectations, analogous results hold for the problem of minimizing the partial or conditional expected accumulated weight. (Note that we can multiply all weights by -1 and then apply the results for maximal partial resp. conditional expectations.)

Related Work. Closest to our contribution is the above mentioned work on partial expected accumulated weights in stochastic multiplayer games with non-negative weights in [8] and on computation schemes for maximal conditional expected accumulated weights in non-negative MDPs [3]. Conditional expected termination time in probabilistic push-down automata has been studied in [11], which can be seen as analogous considerations for a class of infinite-state Markov chains with non-negative weights. The recent work on notions of conditional value at risk in MDPs [15] also studies conditional expectations, but the considered random variables are limit averages and a notion of (non-accumulated) weight-bounded reachability.

2 Preliminaries

We give basic definitions and present our notation. More details can be found in textbooks, e.g. [18].

Notations for Markov Decision Processes. A *Markov decision process* (MDP) is a tuple $\mathcal{M} = (S, Act, P, s_{init}, wgt)$ where S is a finite set of states, Act a finite set of actions, $s_{init} \in S$ the initial state, $P : S \times Act \times S \to [0,1] \cap \mathbb{Q}$ is the transition probability function and $wgt : S \times Act \to \mathbb{Z}$ the weight function. We require that $\sum_{t \in S} P(s, \alpha, t) \in \{0, 1\}$ for all $(s, \alpha) \in S \times Act$. We write $Act(s)$ for the set of actions that are enabled in s, i.e., $\alpha \in Act(s)$ iff $\sum_{t \in S} P(s, \alpha, t) = 1$. We assume that $Act(s)$ is non-empty for all s and that all states are reachable from s_{init}. We call a state absorbing if the only enabled action leads to the state itself with probability 1 and weight 0. The paths of $\mathcal{M}$ are finite or infinite sequences $s_0\, \alpha_0\, s_1\, \alpha_1\, s_2\, \alpha_2 \ldots$ where states and actions alternate such that $P(s_i, \alpha_i, s_{i+1}) > 0$ for all $i \geq 0$. If $\pi = s_0\, \alpha_0\, s_1\, \alpha_1 \ldots \alpha_{k-1}\, s_k$ is finite, then

$wgt(\pi) = wgt(s_0, \alpha_0) + \ldots + wgt(s_{k-1}, \alpha_{k-1})$ denotes the accumulated weight of π, $P(\pi) = P(s_0, \alpha_0, s_1) \cdot \ldots \cdot P(s_{k-1}, \alpha_{k-1}, s_k)$ its probability, and $last(\pi) = s_k$ its last state. The *size* of $\mathcal{M}$, denoted $size(\mathcal{M})$, is the sum of the number of states plus the total sum of the logarithmic lengths of the non-zero probability values $P(s, \alpha, s')$ as fractions of co-prime integers and the weight values $wgt(s, \alpha)$.

Scheduler. A *(history-dependent, randomized) scheduler* for $\mathcal{M}$ is a function $\mathfrak{S}$ that assigns to each finite path π a probability distribution over $Act(last(\pi))$. $\mathfrak{S}$ is called memoryless if $\mathfrak{S}(\pi) = \mathfrak{S}(\pi')$ for all finite paths π, π' with $last(\pi) = last(\pi')$, in which case $\mathfrak{S}$ can be viewed as a function that assigns to each state s a distribution over $Act(s)$. $\mathfrak{S}$ is called deterministic if $\mathfrak{S}(\pi)$ is a Dirac distribution for each path π, in which case $\mathfrak{S}$ can be viewed as a function that assigns an action to each finite path π. Scheduler $\mathfrak{S}$ is said to be *weight-based* if $\mathfrak{S}(\pi) = \mathfrak{S}(\pi')$ for all finite paths π, π' with $wgt(\pi) = wgt(\pi')$ and $last(\pi) = last(\pi')$. Thus, deterministic weight-based schedulers can be viewed as functions that assign actions to state-weight-pairs. By $HR^{\mathcal{M}}$ we denote the class of all schedulers, by $WR^{\mathcal{M}}$ the class of weight-based schedulers, by $WD^{\mathcal{M}}$ the class of weight-based, deterministic schedulers, and by $MD^{\mathcal{M}}$ the class of memoryless deterministic schedulers. Given a scheduler $\mathfrak{S}$, $\varsigma = s_0\, \alpha_0\, s_1\, \alpha_1 \ldots$ is a $\mathfrak{S}$-path iff ς is a path and $\mathfrak{S}(s_0\, \alpha_0\, s_1\, \alpha_1 \ldots \alpha_{k-1}\, s_k)(\alpha_k) > 0$ for all $k \geq 0$.

Probability Measure. We write $\Pr^{\mathfrak{S}}_{\mathcal{M},s}$ or briefly $\Pr^{\mathfrak{S}}_{s}$ to denote the probability measure induced by $\mathfrak{S}$ and s. For details, see [18]. We will use LTL-like formulas to denote measurable sets of paths and also write $\lozenge(wgt \bowtie x)$ to describe the set of infinite paths having a prefix π with $wgt(\pi) \bowtie x$ for $x \in \mathbb{Z}$ and $\bowtie \in \{<, \leq, =, \geq, >\}$. Given a measurable set ψ of infinite paths, we define $\Pr^{\min}_{\mathcal{M},s}(\psi) = \inf_{\mathfrak{S}} \Pr^{\mathfrak{S}}_{\mathcal{M},s}(\psi)$ and $\Pr^{\max}_{\mathcal{M},s}(\psi) = \sup_{\mathfrak{S}} \Pr^{\mathfrak{S}}_{\mathcal{M},s}(\psi)$ where $\mathfrak{S}$ ranges over all schedulers for $\mathcal{M}$. Throughout the paper, we suppose that the given MDP has a designated state *goal*. Then, $p^{\max}_s$ and $p^{\min}_s$ denote the maximal resp. minimal probability of reaching *goal* from s. That is, $p^{\max}_s = \sup_{\mathfrak{S}} \Pr^{\mathfrak{S}}_s(\lozenge goal)$ and $p^{\min}_s = \inf_{\mathfrak{S}} \Pr^{\mathfrak{S}}_s(\lozenge goal)$. Let $Act^{\max}(s) = \{\alpha \in Act(s) | \sum_{t \in S} P(s, \alpha, t) \cdot p^{\max}_t = p^{\max}_s\}$, and $Act^{\min}(s) = \{\alpha \in Act(s) | \sum_{t \in S} P(s, \alpha, t) \cdot p^{\min}_t = p^{\min}_s\}$.

Mean Payoff. A well-known measure for the long-run behavior of a scheduler $\mathfrak{S}$ in an MDP $\mathcal{M}$ is the *mean payoff.* Intuitively, the mean payoff is the amount of weight accumulated per step on average in the long run. Formally, we define the mean payoff as the following random variable on infinite paths $\zeta = s_0\alpha_0 s_1\alpha_1 \ldots$: $MP(\zeta) := \liminf_{k \to \infty} \frac{\sum_{i=0}^{k} wgt(s_i, \alpha_i)}{k+1}$. The mean payoff of the scheduler $\mathfrak{S}$ starting in s_{init} is then defined as the expected value $\mathbb{E}^{\mathfrak{S}}_{s_{init}}(MP)$. The maximal mean payoff is the supremum over all schedulers which is equal to the maximum over all MD-schedulers: $\mathbb{E}^{\max}_{s_{init}}(MP) = \max_{\mathfrak{S} \in MD} \mathbb{E}^{\mathfrak{S}}_{s_{init}}(MP)$. In strongly connected MDPs, the maximal mean payoff does not depend on the initial state.

End Components, MEC-Quotient. An *end component* of $\mathcal{M}$ is a strongly connected sub-MDP. End components can be formalized as pairs $\mathcal{E} = (E, \mathfrak{A})$ where E is a nonempty subset of S and $\mathfrak{A}$ a function that assigns to each state $s \in E$ a nonempty subset of $Act(s)$ such that the graph induced by $\mathcal{E}$ is strongly connected. $\mathcal{E}$ is called *maximal* if there is no end component $\mathcal{E}' = (E', \mathfrak{A}')$ with $\mathcal{E} \neq \mathcal{E}'$, $E \subseteq E'$ and $\mathfrak{A}(s) \subseteq \mathfrak{A}'(s)$ for all $s \in E$. The *MEC-quotient* of an MDP $\mathcal{M}$ is the MDP $MEC(\mathcal{M})$ arising from $\mathcal{M}$ by collapsing all states that belong to the same maximal end component $\mathcal{E}$ to a state $s_{\mathcal{E}}$. All actions enabled in some state in $\mathcal{E}$ not belonging to $\mathcal{E}$ are enabled in $s_{\mathcal{E}}$. Details and the formal construction can be found in [9]. We call an end component $\mathcal{E}$ *positively weight-divergent* if there is a scheduler $\mathfrak{S}$ for $\mathcal{E}$ such that $\Pr^{\mathfrak{S}}_{\mathcal{E},s}(\Diamond(wgt \geq n)) = 1$ for all $s \in \mathcal{E}$ and $n \in \mathbb{N}$. In [1], it is shown that the existence of positively weight-divergent end components can be decided in polynomial time.

3 Partial and Conditional Expectations in MDPs

We define *partial* and *conditional expectations* in MDPs. We extend the definition of [8] by introducing partial expectations with *bias* which are closely related to conditional expectations. Afterwards, we sketch the computation of maximal partial expectations in MDPs with non-negative weights and in Markov chains.

Partial and Conditional Expectation. In the sequel, let $\mathcal{M}$ be an MDP with a designated absorbing goal state *goal*. Furthermore, we collapse all states from which *goal* is not reachable to one absorbing state *fail*. Let $b \in \mathbb{R}$. We define the random variable $\oplus^b goal$ on infinite paths ζ by

$$\oplus^b goal(\zeta) = \begin{cases} wgt(\zeta) + b & \text{if } \zeta \vDash \Diamond goal, \\ 0 & \text{if } \zeta \nvDash \Diamond goal. \end{cases}$$

We call the expectation of this random variable under a scheduler $\mathfrak{S}$ the *partial expectation with bias b* of $\mathfrak{S}$ and write $PE^{\mathfrak{S}}_{\mathcal{M},s_{init}}[b] := \mathbb{E}^{\mathfrak{S}}_{\mathcal{M},s_{init}}(\oplus^b goal)$ as well as $PE^{\sup}_{\mathcal{M},s_{init}}[b] := \sup_{\mathfrak{S}\in HR^{\mathcal{M}}} PE^{\mathfrak{S}}_{\mathcal{M},s_{init}}[b]$. If $b = 0$, we sometimes drop the argument b; if $\mathcal{M}$ is clear from the context, we drop the subscript. In order to maximize the partial expectation, intuitively one has to find the right balance between reaching *goal* with high probability and accumulating a high positive amount of weight before reaching *goal*. The bias can be used to shift this balance by additionally rewarding or penalizing a high probability to reach *goal*.

The *conditional expectation* of $\mathfrak{S}$ is defined as the expectation of $\oplus^0 goal$ under the condition that *goal* is reached. It is defined if $\Pr^{\mathfrak{S}}_{\mathcal{M},s_{init}}(\Diamond goal) > 0$. We write $CE^{\mathfrak{S}}_{\mathcal{M},s_{init}} := \mathbb{E}^{\mathfrak{S}}_{\mathcal{M},s_{init}}(\oplus^0 goal|\Diamond goal)$ and $CE^{\sup}_{\mathcal{M},s_{init}} = \sup_{\mathfrak{S}} CE^{\mathfrak{S}}_{\mathcal{M},s_{init}}$ where the supremum is taken over all schedulers $\mathfrak{S}$ with $\Pr^{\mathfrak{S}}_{\mathcal{M},s_{init}}(\Diamond goal) > 0$. We can express the conditional expectation as $CE^{\mathfrak{S}}_{\mathcal{M},s_{init}} = PE^{\mathfrak{S}}_{\mathcal{M},s_{init}}/\Pr^{\mathfrak{S}}_{\mathcal{M},s_{init}}(\Diamond goal)$. The following proposition establishes a close connection between conditional expectations and partial expectations with bias.

Proposition 2. *Let $\mathcal{M}$ be an MDP, $\mathfrak{S}$ a scheduler with $\Pr^{\mathfrak{S}}_{s_{init}}(\Diamond goal) > 0$, $\theta \in \mathbb{Q}$, and $\bowtie \in \{<, \leq, \geq, >\}$. Then we have $PE^{\mathfrak{S}}_{s_{init}}[-\theta] \bowtie 0$ iff $CE^{\mathfrak{S}}_{s_{init}} \bowtie \theta$. Further, if $\Pr^{\min}_{s_{init}}(\Diamond goal) > 0$, then $PE^{\sup}_{s_{init}}[-\theta] \bowtie 0$ iff $CE^{\sup}_{s_{init}} \bowtie \theta$.*

Proof. The first claim follows from $PE^{\mathfrak{S}}_{s_{init}}[-\theta] = PE^{\mathfrak{S}}_{s_{init}}[0] - \Pr^{\mathfrak{S}}_{s_{init}}(\Diamond goal) \cdot \theta$. The second claim follows by quantification over all schedulers. □

In [3], it is shown that deciding whether $CE^{\sup}_{s_{init}} \bowtie \theta$ for $\bowtie \in \{<, \leq, \geq, >\}$ and $\theta \in \mathbb{Q}$ is PSPACE-hard even for acyclic MDPs. We conclude:

Corollary 3. *Given an MDP $\mathcal{M}$, $\bowtie \in \{<, \leq, \geq, >\}$, and $\theta \in \mathbb{Q}$, deciding whether $PE^{\sup}_{\mathcal{M},s_{init}} \bowtie \theta$ is PSPACE-hard.*

Finiteness. We present criteria for the finiteness of $PE^{\sup}_{s_{init}}[b]$ and $CE^{\sup}_{s_{init}}$. Detailed proofs can be found in Appendix A.1 of [17]. By slightly modifying the construction from [1] which removes end components only containing 0-weight cycles, we obtain the following result.

Proposition 4. *Let $\mathcal{M}$ be an MDP which does not contain positively weight-divergent end components and let $b \in \mathbb{Q}$. Then there is a polynomial time transformation to an MDP $\mathcal{N}$ containing all states from $\mathcal{M}$ and possibly an additional absorbing state fail such that*

- *all end components of $\mathcal{N}$ have negative maximal expected mean payoff,*
- *for any scheduler $\mathfrak{S}$ for $\mathcal{M}$ there is a scheduler $\mathfrak{S}'$ for $\mathcal{N}$ with $\Pr^{\mathfrak{S}}_{\mathcal{M},s}(\Diamond goal) = \Pr^{\mathfrak{S}'}_{\mathcal{N},s}(\Diamond goal)$ and $PE^{\mathfrak{S}}_{\mathcal{M},s}[b] = PE^{\mathfrak{S}'}_{\mathcal{N},s}[b]$ for any state s in $\mathcal{M}$, and vice versa.*

Hence, we can restrict ourselves to MDPs in which all end components have negative maximal expected mean payoff if there are no positively weight divergent end components. The following result is now analogous to the result in [1] for the classical SSP problem.

Proposition 5. *Let $\mathcal{M}$ be an MDP and $b \in \mathbb{R}$ arbitrary. The optimal partial expectation $PE^{\sup}_{s_{init}}[b]$ is finite if and only if there are no positively weight-divergent end components in $\mathcal{M}$.*

To obtain an analogous result for conditional expectations, we observe that the finiteness of the maximal partial expectation is necessary for the finiteness of the maximal conditional expectation. However, this is not sufficient. In [3], a *critical scheduler* is defined as a scheduler $\mathfrak{S}$ for which there is a path containing a positive cycle and for which $\Pr^{\mathfrak{S}}_{s_{init}}(\Diamond goal) = 0$. Given a critical scheduler, it is easy to construct a sequence of schedulers with unbounded conditional expectation (see Appendix A.1 of [17] and [3]). On the other hand, if $\Pr^{\min}_{\mathcal{M},s_{init}}(\Diamond goal) > 0$, then $CE^{\sup}_{s_{init}}$ is finite if and only if $PE^{\sup}_{s_{init}}$ is finite. We will show how we can restrict ourselves to this case if there are no critical schedulers:

So, let $\mathcal{M}$ be an MDP with $\Pr^{\min}_{\mathcal{M},s_{init}}(\Diamond goal) = 0$ and suppose there are no critical schedulers for $\mathcal{M}$. Let S_0 be the set of all states reachable from s_{init} while only choosing actions in $Act^{\min}$. As there are no critical schedulers, $(S_0, Act^{\min})$ does not contain positive cycles. So, there is a finite maximal weight w_s among paths leading from s_{init} to s in S_0. Consider the following MDP $\mathcal{N}$: It contains the MDP $\mathcal{M}$ and a new initial state t_{init}. For each $s \in S_0$ and each $\alpha \in Act(s) \setminus Act^{\min}(s)$, $\mathcal{N}$ also contains a new state $t_{s,\alpha}$ which is reachable from

t_{init} via an action $\beta_{s,\alpha}$ with weight w_s and probability 1. In $t_{s,\alpha}$, only action α with the same probability distribution over successors and the same weight as in s is enabled. So in $\mathcal{N}$, one has to decide immediately in which state to leave S_0 and one accumulates the maximal weight which can be accumulated in $\mathcal{M}$ to reach this state in S_0. In this way, we ensure that $\Pr^{\min}_{\mathcal{N},t_{init}}(\Diamond goal) > 0$.

Proposition 6. *The constructed MDP $\mathcal{N}$ satisfies $CE^{\sup}_{\mathcal{N},t_{init}} = CE^{\sup}_{\mathcal{M},s_{init}}$.*

We can rely on this reduction to an MDP in which *goal* is reached with positive probability for ϵ-approximations and the exact computation of the optimal conditional expectation. In particular, the values w_s for $s \in S_0$ are easy to compute by classical shortest path algorithms on weighted graphs. Furthermore, we can now decide the finiteness of the maximal conditional expectation.

Proposition 7. *For an arbitrary MDP $\mathcal{M}$, $CE^{\sup}_{\mathcal{M},s_{init}}$ is finite if and only if there are no positively weight-divergent end components and no critical schedulers.*

Partial and Conditional Expectations in Markov Chains. Markov chains with integer weights can be seen as MDPs with only one action α enabled in every state. Consequently, there is only one scheduler for a Markov chain. Hence, we drop the superscripts in $p^{\max}$ and $PE^{\sup}$.

Proposition 8. *The partial and conditional expectation in a Markov chain $\mathcal{C}$ are computable in polynomial time.*

Proof. Let α be the only action available in $\mathcal{C}$. Assume that all states from which *goal* is not reachable have been collapsed to an absorbing state *fail*. Then $PE_{\mathcal{C},s_{init}}$ is the value of $x_{s_{init}}$ in the unique solution to the following system of linear equations with one variable x_s for each state s:

$$x_{goal} = x_{fail} = 0,$$
$$x_s = wgt(s,\alpha) \cdot p_s + \sum_t P(s,\alpha,t) \cdot x_t \text{ for } s \in S \setminus \{goal, fail\}.$$

The existence of a unique solution follows from the fact that $\{goal\}$ and $\{fail\}$ are the only end components (see [18]). It is straight-forward to check that $(PE_{\mathcal{C},s})_{s\in S}$ is this unique solution. The conditional expectation is obtained from the partial expectation by dividing by the probability $p_{s_{init}}$ to reach the goal. □

This result can be seen as a special case of the following result. Restricting ourselves to schedulers which reach the goal with maximal or minimal probability in an MDP without positively weight-divergent end components, linear programming allows us to compute the following two memoryless deterministic schedulers (see [3,8]).

Proposition 9. *Let $\mathcal{M}$ be an MDP without positively weight-divergent end components. There is a scheduler $\mathfrak{Max} \in MD^{\mathcal{M}}$ such that for each $s \in S$ we have $\Pr_s^{\mathfrak{Max}}(\lozenge goal) = p_s^{\max}$ and $PE_s^{\mathfrak{Max}} = \sup_{\mathfrak{S}} PE_s^{\mathfrak{S}}$ where the supremum is taken over all schedulers $\mathfrak{S}$ with $\Pr_s^{\mathfrak{S}}(\lozenge goal) = p_s^{\max}$. Similarly, there is a scheduler $\mathfrak{Min} \in MD^{\mathcal{M}}$ maximizing the partial expectation among all schedulers reaching the goal with minimal probability. Both these schedulers and their partial expectations are computable in polynomial time.*

These schedulers will play a crucial role for the approximation of the maximal partial expectation and the exact computation of maximal partial expectations in MDPs with non-negative weights.

Partial Expectations in MDPs with Non-negative Weights. In [8], the computation of maximal partial expectations in stochastic multiplayer games with non-negative weights is presented. We adapt this approach to MDPs with non-negative weights. A key result is the existence of a *saturation point*, a bound on the accumulated weight above which optimal schedulers do not need memory.

In the sequel, let $R \in \mathbb{Q}$ be arbitrary, let $\mathcal{M}$ be an MDP with non-negative weights, $PE_{s_{init}}^{\sup} < \infty$, and assume that end components have negative maximal mean payoff (see Proposition 4). A saturation point for bias R is a natural number $\mathfrak{p}$ such that there is a scheduler $\mathfrak{S}$ with $PE_{s_{init}}^{\mathfrak{S}}[R] = PE_{s_{init}}^{\sup}[R]$ which is memoryless and deterministic as soon as the accumulated weight reaches $\mathfrak{p}$. I.e. for any two paths π and π', with $last(\pi) = last(\pi')$ and $wgt(\pi), wgt(\pi') > \mathfrak{p}$, $\mathfrak{S}(\pi) = \mathfrak{S}(\pi')$.

Transferring the idea behind the saturation point for conditional expectations given in [3], we provide the following saturation point which can be considerably smaller than the saturation point given in [8] in stochastic multiplayer games. Detailed proofs to this section are given in Appendix A.2 of [17].

Proposition 10. *We define $p_{s,\alpha}^{\max} := \sum_{t \in S} P(s,\alpha,t) \cdot p_t^{\max}$ and $PE_{s,\alpha}^{\mathfrak{Max}} := p_{s,\alpha}^{\max} \cdot wgt(s,\alpha) + \sum_{t \in S} P(s,\alpha,t) \cdot PE_t^{\mathfrak{Max}}$. Then,*

$$\mathfrak{p}_R := \sup \left\{ \frac{PE_{s,\alpha}^{\mathfrak{Max}} - PE_s^{\mathfrak{Max}}}{p_s^{\max} - p_{s,\alpha}^{\max}} \middle| s \in S, \alpha \in Act(s) \setminus Act^{\max}(s) \right\} - R$$

is an upper saturation point for bias R in $\mathcal{M}$.

The saturation point $\mathfrak{p}_R$ is chosen such that, as soon as the accumulated weight exceeds $\mathfrak{p}_R$, the scheduler $\mathfrak{Max}$ is better than any scheduler deviating from $\mathfrak{Max}$ for only one step. So, the proposition states that $\mathfrak{Max}$ is then also better than any other scheduler.

As all values involved in the computation can be determined by linear programming, the saturation point $\mathfrak{p}_R$ is computable in polynomial time. This also means that the logarithmic length of $\mathfrak{p}_R$ is polynomial in the size of $\mathcal{M}$ and hence $\mathfrak{p}_R$ itself is at most exponential in the size of $\mathcal{M}$.

Proposition 11. *Let $R \in \mathbb{Q}$ and let B_R be the least integer greater or equal to $\mathfrak{p}_R + \max_{s \in S, \alpha \in Act(s)} wgt(s,\alpha)$ and let $S' := S \setminus \{goal, fail\}$. The values*

$(PE^{\sup}_{s_{init}}[r+R])_{s\in S',0\le r\le B_R}$ *form the unique solution to the following linear program in the variables* $(x_{s,r})_{s\in S',0\le r\le B_R}$ *(r ranges over integers):*

Minimize $\sum_{s\in S',0\le r\le B_R} x_{s,r}$ *under the following constraints:*

$$\text{For } r \ge \mathfrak{p}_R : x_{s,r} = p_s^{\max} \cdot (r+R) + E_s^{\mathfrak{Max}},$$

$$\text{for } r < \mathfrak{p}_R \text{ and } \alpha \in Act(s) :$$

$$x_{s,r} \ge P(s,\alpha,goal)\cdot(r+R+wgt(s,\alpha)) + \sum_{t\in S'} P(s,\alpha,t)\cdot x_{t,r+wgt(s,\alpha)}.$$

From a solution x to the linear program, we can easily extract an optimal weight-based deterministic scheduler. This scheduler only needs finite memory because the accumulated weight increases monotonically along paths and as soon as the saturation point is reached $\mathfrak{Max}$ provides the optimal decisions. As B_R is exponential in the size of $\mathcal{M}$, the computation of the optimal partial expectation via this linear program runs in time exponential in the size of $\mathcal{M}$.

4 Existence of Optimal Schedulers

We prove that there are optimal weight-based deterministic schedulers for partial and conditional expectations. After showing that, if finite, $PE^{\sup}_{s_{init}}$ is equal to $\sup_{\mathfrak{S}\in WD^{\mathcal{M}}} PE^{\mathfrak{S}}_{s_{init}}$, we take an analytic approach to show that there is a weight-based deterministic scheduler maximizing the partial expectation. We define a metric on $WD^{\mathcal{M}}$ turning it into a compact space. Then, we prove that the function assigning the partial expectation to schedulers is upper semi-continuous. We conclude that there is a weight-based deterministic scheduler obtaining the maximum. Proofs to this section can be found in Appendix B of [17].

Proposition 12. *Let* $\mathcal{M}$ *be an MDP with* $PE^{\sup}_{s_{init}} < \infty$. *Then we have* $PE^{\sup}_{s_{init}} = \sup_{\mathfrak{S}\in WD^{\mathcal{M}}} PE^{\mathfrak{S}}_{s_{init}}$.

Proof sketch. We can assume that all end components have negative maximal expected mean payoff (see Proposition 4). Given a scheduler $\mathfrak{S} \in HR^{\mathcal{M}}$, we take the expected number of times $\theta_{s,w}$ that s is visited with accumulated weight w under $\mathfrak{S}$ for each state-weight pair (s,w), and the expected number of times $\theta_{s,w,\alpha}$ that $\mathfrak{S}$ then chooses α. These values are finite due to the negative maximal mean payoff in end components. We define the scheduler $\mathfrak{T} \in WR^{\mathcal{M}}$ choosing α in s with probability $\theta_{s,w,\alpha}/\theta_{s,w}$ when weight w has been accumulated. Then, we show by standard arguments that we can replace all probability distributions that $\mathfrak{T}$ chooses by Dirac distributions to obtain a scheduler $\mathfrak{T}' \in WD^{\mathcal{M}}$ such that $PE^{\mathfrak{T}'}_{s_{init}} \ge PE^{\mathfrak{S}}_{s_{init}}$. □

It remains to show that the supremum is obtained by a weight-based deterministic scheduler. Given an MDP $\mathcal{M}$ with arbitrary integer weights, we define the following metric $d^{\mathcal{M}}$ on the set of weight-based deterministic schedulers, i.e. on the set of functions from $S \times \mathbb{Z} \to Act$: For two such schedulers $\mathfrak{S}$ and

$\mathfrak{T}$, we let $d^{\mathcal{M}}(\mathfrak{S},\mathfrak{T}) := 2^{-R}$ where R is the greatest natural number such that $\mathfrak{S} \upharpoonright S \times \{-(R-1),\ldots,R-1\} = \mathfrak{T} \upharpoonright S \times \{-(R-1),\ldots,R-1\}$ or ∞ if there is no greatest such natural number.

Lemma 13. *The metric space $(Act^{S\times\mathbb{Z}}, d^{\mathcal{M}})$ is compact.*

Having defined this compact space of schedulers, we can rely on the analytic notion of upper semi-continuity.

Lemma 14 (Upper Semi-Continuity of Partial Expectations). *If $PE^{\sup}_{s_{init}}$ is finite in $\mathcal{M}$, then the function $PE : (WD, d^{WD}) \to (\mathbb{R}_\infty, d^{euclid})$ assigning $PE^{\mathfrak{S}}_{s_{init}}$ to a weight-based deterministic scheduler $\mathfrak{S}$ is upper semi-continuous.*

The technical proof of this lemma can be found in Appendix B of [17]. We arrive at the main result of this section.

Theorem 15 (Existence of Optimal Schedulers for Partial Expectations). *If $PE^{\sup}_{s_{init}}$ is finite in an MDP $\mathcal{M}$, then there is a weight-based deterministic scheduler $\mathfrak{S}$ with $PE^{\sup}_{s_{init}} = PE^{\mathfrak{S}}_{s_{init}}$.*

Proof. If $PE^{\sup}_{s_{init}}$ is finite, then the map $PE : (WD, d^{WD}) \to (\mathbb{R}_\infty, d^{euclid})$ is upper semi-continuous. So, this map has a maximum because (WD, d^{WD}) is a compact metric space. □

Corollary 16 (Existence of Optimal Schedulers for Conditional Expectations). *If $CE^{\sup}_{s_{init}}$ is finite in an MDP $\mathcal{M}$, then there is a weight-based deterministic scheduler $\mathfrak{S}$ with $CE^{\sup}_{s_{init}} = CE^{\mathfrak{S}}_{s_{init}}$.*

Proof. By Proposition 6, we can assume that $\Pr^{\min}_{s_{init}}(\Diamond goal) > 0$. We know that $PE^{\sup}_{s_{init}}[-CE^{\sup}_{s_{init}}] = 0$ and that there is a weight-based deterministic scheduler $\mathfrak{S}$ with $PE^{\mathfrak{S}}_{s_{init}}[-CE^{\sup}_{s_{init}}] = 0$. By Proposition 2, $\mathfrak{S}$ maximizes the conditional expectation as it reaches *goal* with positive probability. □

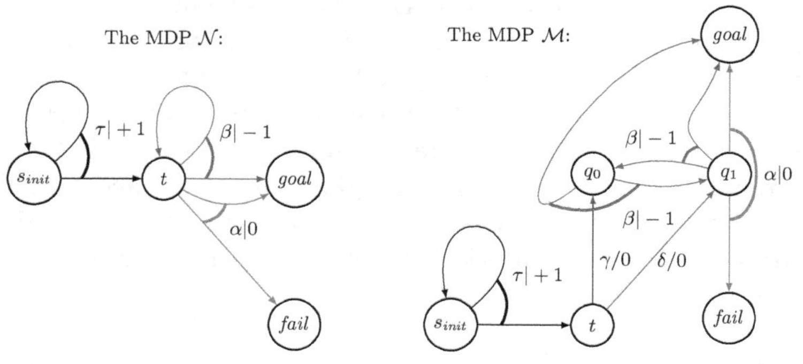

Fig. 2. All non-trivial transition probabilities are 1/2. In the MDP $\mathcal{M}$, the optimal choice to maximize the partial expectation in t depends on the parity of the accumulated weight.

In MDPs with non-negative weights, the optimal decision in a state s only depends on s as soon as the accumulated weight exceeds a saturation point. In MDPs with arbitrary integer weights, it is possible that the optimal choice of action does not become stable for increasing values of accumulated weight as we see in the following example.

Example 17. Let us first consider the MDP $\mathcal{N}$ depicted in Fig. 2. Let π be a path reaching t for the first time with accumulated weight r. Consider a scheduler which chooses β for the first k times and then α. In this situation, the partial expectation from this point on is:

$$\frac{1}{2^{k+1}}(r-k) + \sum_{i=1}^{k} \frac{1}{2^i}(r-i) = \frac{1}{2^{k+1}} + \sum_{i=1}^{k+1} \frac{1}{2^i}(r-i) = \frac{k-r+4}{2^{k+1}} + r-2.$$

For $r \geq 2$, this partial expectation has its unique maximum for the choice $k = r-2$. This already shows that an optimal scheduler needs infinite memory. No matter how much weight r has been accumulated when reaching t, the optimal scheduler has to count the $r-2$ times it chooses β.

Furthermore, we can transfer the optimal scheduler for the MDP $\mathcal{N}$ to the MDP $\mathcal{M}$. In state t, we have to make a nondeterministic choice between two action leading to the states q_0 and q_1, respectively. In both of these states, action β is enabled which behaves like the same action in the MDP $\mathcal{N}$ except that it moves between the two states if *goal* is not reached. So, the action α is only enabled every other step. As in $\mathcal{N}$, we want to choose α after choosing β $r-2$ times if we arrived in t with accumulated weight $r \geq 2$. So, the choice in t depends on the parity of r: For $r = 1$ or r even, we choose δ. For odd $r \geq 3$, we choose γ. This shows that the optimal scheduler in the MDP $\mathcal{M}$ needs specific information about the accumulated weight, in this case the parity, no matter how much weight has been accumulated.

In the example, the optimal scheduler has a periodic behavior when fixing a state and looking at optimal decisions for increasing values of accumulated weight. The question whether an optimal scheduler always has such a periodic behavior remains open.

5 Approximation

As the optimal values for partial and conditional expectation can be irrational, there is no hope to compute these values by linear programming as in the case of non-negative weights. In this section, we show how we can nevertheless approximate the values. The main result is the following.

Theorem 18. *Let $\mathcal{M}$ be an MDP with $PE^{\sup}_{\mathcal{M},s_{init}} < \infty$ and $\epsilon > 0$. The maximal partial expectation $PE^{\sup}_{\mathcal{M},s_{init}}$ can be approximated up to an absolute error of ϵ in time exponential in the size of $\mathcal{M}$ and polynomial in $\log(1/\epsilon)$. If further, $CE^{\sup}_{\mathcal{M},s_{init}} < \infty$, also $CE^{\sup}_{\mathcal{M},s_{init}}$ can be approximated up to an absolute error of ϵ in time exponential in the size of $\mathcal{M}$ and polynomial in $\log(1/\epsilon)$.*

We first prove that upper bounds for $PE^{\sup}_{\mathcal{M},s_{init}}$ and $CE^{\sup}_{\mathcal{M},s_{init}}$ can be computed in polynomial time. Then, we show that there are ϵ-optimal schedulers for the partial expectation which become memoryless as soon as the accumulated weight leaves a sufficiently large weight window around 0. We compute the optimal partial expectation of such a scheduler by linear programming. The result can then be extended to conditional expectations.

Upper Bounds. Let $\mathcal{M}$ be an MDP in which all end components have negative maximal mean payoff. Let δ be the minimal non-zero transition probability in $\mathcal{M}$ and $W := \max_{s\in S,\alpha\in Act(s)} |wgt(s,\alpha)|$. Moving through the MEC-quotient, the probability to reach an accumulated weight of $|S| \cdot W$ is bounded by $1-\delta^{|S|}$ as *goal* or *fail* is reached within S steps with probability at least $1-\delta^{|S|}$. It remains to show similar bounds inside an end component.

We will use the characterization of the maximal mean payoff in terms of super-harmonic vectors due to Hordijk and Kallenberg [13] to define a super-martingale controlling the growth of the accumulated weight in an end component under any scheduler. As the value vector for the maximal mean payoff in an end component is constant and negative in our case, the results of [13] yield:

Proposition 19 (Hordijk, Kallenberg). *Let $\mathcal{E} = (S, Act)$ be an end component with maximal mean payoff $-t$ for some $t > 0$. Then there is a vector $(u_s)_{s\in S}$ such that $-t + u_s \geq wgt(s,\alpha) + \sum_{s'\in S} P(s,\alpha,s') \cdot u_{s'}$.*

Furthermore, let v be the vector $(-t,\ldots,-t)$ in $\mathbb{R}^S$. Then, (v,u) is the solution to a linear program with $2|S|$ variables, $2|S||Act|$ inequalities, and coefficients formed from the transition probabilities and weights in $\mathcal{E}$.

We will call the vector u a *super-potential* because the expected accumulated weight after i steps is at most $u_s - \min_{t\in S} u_t - i \cdot t$ when starting in state s. Let $\mathfrak{S}$ be a scheduler for $\mathcal{E}$ starting in some state s. We define the following random variables on $\mathfrak{S}$-runs in $\mathcal{E}$: let $s(i) \in S$ be the state after i steps, let $\alpha(i)$ be the action chosen after i steps, let $w(i)$ be the accumulated weight after i steps, and let $\pi(i)$ be the history, i.e. the finite path after i steps.

Lemma 20. *The sequence $m(i) := w(i) + u_{s(i)}$ satisfies $\mathbb{E}(m(i+1)|\pi(0),\ldots,\pi(i)) \leq m(i) - t$ for all i.*[1]

Proof. By Proposition 19, $\mathbb{E}(m(i+1)|\pi(0),\ldots,\pi(i)) - m(i) = wgt(s(i),\mathfrak{S}(\pi(i))) + \sum_{s'\in S} P(s(i),\mathfrak{S}(\pi(i)),s') \cdot u_{s'} - u_{s(i)} \leq -t$. □

We are going to apply the following theorem by Blackwell [6].

Theorem 21 (Blackwell [6]). *Let $X_1, X_2, \ldots$ be random variables, and let $S_n := \sum_{k=1}^{n} X_k$. Assume that $|X_i| \leq 1$ for all i and that there is a $u > 0$ such that $\mathbb{E}(X_{n+1}|X_1,\ldots,X_n) \leq -u$. Then, $\Pr(\sup_{n\in\mathbb{N}} S_n \geq t) \leq \left(\frac{1-u}{1+u}\right)^t$.*

[1] This means that $m(i) + i \cdot t$ is a super-martingale with respect to the history $\pi(i)$.

We denote $\max_{s'\in S} u_{s'} - \min_{s'\in S} u_{s'}$ by $\|u\|$. Observe that $|m(i+1)-m(i)| \leq \|u\| + W =: c_{\mathcal{E}}$. We can rescale the sequence $m(i)$ by defining $m'(i) := (m(i) - m(0))/c_{\mathcal{E}}$. This ensures that $m'(0) = 0$, $|m'(i+1) - m'(i)| \leq 1$ and $\mathbb{E}(m'(i+1)|m'(0),\ldots,m'(i)) \leq -t/c_{\mathcal{E}}$ for all i. In this way, we arrive at the following conclusion, putting $\lambda_{\mathcal{E}} := \frac{1-t/c_{\mathcal{E}}}{1+t/c_{\mathcal{E}}}$.

Corollary 22. *For any scheduler $\mathfrak{S}$ and any starting state s in $\mathcal{E}$, we have* $\Pr_s^{\mathfrak{S}}(\Diamond wgt \geq (k+1) \cdot c_{\mathcal{E}}) \leq \lambda_{\mathcal{E}}^k$.

Proof. By Theorem 21, $\Pr_s^{\mathfrak{S}}(\Diamond wgt \geq (k+1) \cdot c_{\mathcal{E}}) \leq \Pr_s^{\mathfrak{S}}(\Diamond wgt \geq \|u\| + k \cdot c_{\mathcal{E}}) \leq \Pr_s^{\mathfrak{S}}(\exists i : m(i) - m(0) \geq k \cdot c_{\mathcal{E}}) = \Pr_s^{\mathfrak{S}}(\sup_{i\in\mathbb{N}} m'(i) \geq k) \leq \left(\frac{1-t/c_{\mathcal{E}}}{1+t/c_{\mathcal{E}}}\right)^k$. □

Let MEC be the set of maximal end components in $\mathcal{M}$. For each $\mathcal{E} \in MEC$, let $\lambda_{\mathcal{E}}$ and $c_{\mathcal{E}}$ be as in Corollary 22. Define $\lambda_{\mathcal{M}} := 1 - (\delta^{|S|} \cdot \prod_{\mathcal{E}\in MEC}(1 - \lambda_{\mathcal{E}}))$, and $c_{\mathcal{M}} := |S| \cdot W + \sum_{\mathcal{E}\in MEC} c_{\mathcal{E}}$. Then an accumulated weight of $c_{\mathcal{M}}$ cannot be reached with a probability greater than $\lambda_{\mathcal{M}}$ because reaching accumulated weight $c_{\mathcal{M}}$ would require reaching weight $c_{\mathcal{E}}$ in some end component $\mathcal{E}$ or reaching weight $|S|\cdot W$ in the MEC-quotient and $1-\lambda_{\mathcal{M}}$ is a lower bound on the probability that none of this happens (under any scheduler).

Proposition 23. *Let $\mathcal{M}$ be an MDP with $PE_{s_{init}}^{\sup} < \infty$. There is an upper bound PE^{ub} for the partial expectation in $\mathcal{M}$ computable in polynomial time.*

Proof. In any end component $\mathcal{E}$, the maximal mean payoff $-t$ and the super-potential u are computable in polynomial time. Hence, $c_{\mathcal{E}}$ and $\lambda_{\mathcal{E}}$, and in turn also $c_{\mathcal{M}}$ and $\lambda_{\mathcal{M}}$ are also computable in polynomial time. When we reach accumulated weight $c_{\mathcal{M}}$ for the first time, the actual accumulated weight is at most $c_{\mathcal{M}} + W$. So, we conclude that $\Pr_s^{\max}(\Diamond wgt \geq k \cdot (c_{\mathcal{M}} + W)) \leq \lambda_{\mathcal{M}}^k$. The partial expectation can now be bounded by $\sum_{k=0}^{\infty}(k+1) \cdot (c_{\mathcal{M}} + W) \cdot \lambda_{\mathcal{M}}^k = \frac{c_{\mathcal{M}}+W}{(1-\lambda_{\mathcal{M}})^2}$. □

Corollary 24. *Let $\mathcal{M}$ be an MDP with $CE_{\mathcal{M},s_{init}}^{\sup} < \infty$. There is an upper bound CE^{ub} for the conditional expectation in $\mathcal{M}$ computable in polynomial time.*

Proof. By Proposition 6, we can construct an MDP $\mathcal{N}$ in which *goal* is reached with probability $q > 0$ in polynomial time with $CE_{\mathcal{M},s_{init}}^{\sup} = CE_{\mathcal{N},s_{init}}^{\sup}$. Now, $CE^{ub} := PE^{ub}/q$ is an upper bound for the conditional expectation in $\mathcal{M}$. □

Approximating Optimal Partial Expectations. The idea for the approximation is to assume that the partial expectation is $PE_{s_{init}}^{\mathfrak{Max}} + w \cdot p_s^{\max}$ if a high weight w has been accumulated in state s. Similarly, for small weights w', we use the value $PE_{s_{init}}^{\mathfrak{Min}} + w \cdot p_s^{\min}$. We will first provide a lower "saturation point" making sure that only actions minimizing the probability to reach the goal are used by an optimal scheduler as soon as the accumulated weight drops below this saturation point. For the proofs to this section, see Appendix C.1 of [17].

Proposition 25. *Let $\mathcal{M}$ be an MDP with $PE^{\sup}_{s_{init}} < \infty$. Let $s \in S$ and let $\mathfrak{q}_s := \frac{PE^{ub} - PE^{\mathfrak{Min}}_s}{p^{\min}_s - \min_{\alpha \notin Act^{\min}(s)} p^{\min}_{s,\alpha}}$. Then any weight-based deterministic scheduler $\mathfrak{S}$ maximizing the partial expectation in $\mathcal{M}$ satisfies $\mathfrak{S}(s,w) \in Act^{\min}(s)$ if $w \leq \mathfrak{q}_s$.*

Let $\mathfrak{q} := \min_{s \in S} \mathfrak{q}_s$ and let $D := PE^{ub} - \min\{PE^{\mathfrak{Max}}_s, PE^{\mathfrak{Min}}_s | s \in S\}$. Given $\epsilon > 0$, we define $R^+_\epsilon := (c_{\mathcal{M}} + W) \cdot \left\lceil \frac{\log(2D) + \log(1/\epsilon)}{\log(1/\lambda_{\mathcal{M}})} \right\rceil$ and $R^-_\epsilon := \mathfrak{q} - R^+_\epsilon$.

Theorem 26. *There is a weight-based deterministic scheduler $\mathfrak{S}$ such that the scheduler $\mathfrak{T}$ defined by*

$$\mathfrak{T}(\pi) = \begin{cases} \mathfrak{S}(\pi) & \text{if any prefix } \pi' \text{ of } \pi \text{ satisfies } R^-_\epsilon \leq wgt(\pi') \leq R^+_\epsilon, \\ \mathfrak{Max}(\pi) & \text{if the shortest prefix } \pi' \text{ of } \pi \text{ with } wgt(\pi') \notin [R^-_\epsilon, R^+_\epsilon] \\ & \text{satisfies } wgt(\pi') > R^+_\epsilon, \\ \mathfrak{Min}(\pi) & \text{otherwise,} \end{cases}$$

satisfies $PE^{\mathfrak{T}}_{s_{init}} \geq PE^{\sup}_{s_{init}} - \epsilon$.

This result now allows us to compute an ϵ-approximation and an ϵ-optimal scheduler with finite memory by linear programming, similar to the case of non-negative weights, in a linear program with $R^+_\epsilon + R^-_\epsilon$ many variables and $|Act|$-times as many inequalities.

Corollary 27. *$PE^{\sup}_{s_{init}}$ can be approximated up to an absolute error of ϵ in time exponential in the size of $\mathcal{M}$ and polynomial in $\log(1/\epsilon)$.*

If the logarithmic length of $\theta \in \mathbb{Q}$ is polynomial in the size of $\mathcal{M}$, we can also approximate $PE^{\sup}_{s_{init}}[\theta]$ up to an absolute error of ϵ in time exponential in the size of $\mathcal{M}$ and polynomial in $\log(1/\epsilon)$: We can add a new initial state s with a transition to s_{init} with weight θ and approximate $PE^{\sup}_s$ in the new MDP.

Transfer to Conditional Expectations. Let $\mathcal{M}$ be an MDP with $CE^{sup}_{s_{init}} < \infty$ and $\epsilon > 0$. By Proposition 6, we can assume that $\Pr^{\min}_{\mathcal{M},s_{init}}(\Diamond goal) =: p$ is positive. Clearly, $CE^{sup}_{s_{init}} \in [CE^{\mathfrak{Max}}_{s_{init}}, CE^{ub}]$. We perform a binary search to approximate $CE^{sup}_{s_{init}}$: We put $A_0 := CE^{\mathfrak{Max}}_{s_{init}}$ and $B_0 := CE^{ub}$. Given A_i and B_i, let $\theta_i := (A_i + B_i)/2$. Then, we approximate $PE^{\sup}_{s_{init}}[-\theta_i]$ up to an absolute error of $p \cdot \epsilon$. Let E_i be the value of this approximation. If $E_i \in [-2p \cdot \epsilon, 2p \cdot \epsilon]$, terminate and return θ_i as the approximation for $CE^{\sup}_{s_{init}}$. If $E_i < -2p \cdot \epsilon$, put $A_{i+1} := A_i$ and $B_{i+1} := \theta_i$, and repeat. If $E_i > 2p \cdot \epsilon$, put $A_{i+1} := \theta_i$ and $B_{i+1} := B_i$, and repeat.

Proposition 28. *The procedure terminates after at most $\lceil \log((A_0 - B_0)/(p \cdot \epsilon)) \rceil$ iterations and returns an 3ϵ-approximation of $CE^{\sup}_{s_{init}}$ in time exponential in the size of $\mathcal{M}$ and polynomial in $\log(1/\epsilon)$.*

The proof can be found in Appendix C.2 of [17]. This finishes the proof of Theorem 18.

6 Conclusion

Compared to the setting of non-negative weights, the optimization of partial and conditional expectations faces substantial new difficulties in the setting of integer weights. The optimal values can be irrational showing that the linear programming approaches from the setting of non-negative weights cannot be applied for the computation of optimal values. We showed that this approach can nevertheless be adapted for approximation algorithms. Further, we were able to show that there are optimal weight-based deterministic schedulers. These schedulers, however, can require infinite memory and it remains open whether we can further restrict the class of schedulers necessary for the optimization. In examples, we have seen that optimal schedulers can switch periodically between actions they choose for increasing values of accumulated weight. Further insights on the behavior of optimal schedulers would be helpful to address threshold problems ("Is $PE^{\sup}_{s_{init}} \geq \theta$?").

References

1. Baier, C., Bertrand, N., Dubslaff, C., Gburek, D., Sankur, O.: Stochastic shortest paths and weight-bounded properties in Markov decision processes. In: Proceedings of the 33rd Annual ACM/IEEE Symposium on Logic in Computer Science (LICS), pp. 86–94. ACM (2018)
2. Baier, C., Dubslaff, C., Klein, J., Klüppelholz, S., Wunderlich, S.: Probabilistic model checking for energy-utility analysis. In: van Breugel, F., Kashefi, E., Palamidessi, C., Rutten, J. (eds.) Horizons of the Mind. A Tribute to Prakash Panangaden. LNCS, vol. 8464, pp. 96–123. Springer, Cham (2014). https://doi.org/10.1007/978-3-319-06880-0_5
3. Baier, C., Klein, J., Klüppelholz, S., Wunderlich, S.: Maximizing the conditional expected reward for reaching the goal. In: Legay, A., Margaria, T. (eds.) TACAS 2017. LNCS, vol. 10206, pp. 269–285. Springer, Heidelberg (2017). https://doi.org/10.1007/978-3-662-54580-5_16
4. Barthe, G., Espitau, T., Ferrer Fioriti, L.M., Hsu, J.: Synthesizing probabilistic invariants via Doob's decomposition. In: Chaudhuri, S., Farzan, A. (eds.) CAV 2016. LNCS, vol. 9779, pp. 43–61. Springer, Cham (2016). https://doi.org/10.1007/978-3-319-41528-4_3
5. Bertsekas, D.P., Tsitsiklis, J.N.: An analysis of stochastic shortest path problems. Math. Oper. Res. **16**(3), 580–595 (1991)
6. Blackwell, D.: On optimal systems. Ann. Math. Stat. **25**, 394–397 (1954)
7. Chatterjee, K., Fu, H., Goharshady, A.K.: Termination analysis of probabilistic programs through Positivstellensatz's. In: Chaudhuri, S., Farzan, A. (eds.) CAV 2016. LNCS, vol. 9779, pp. 3–22. Springer, Cham (2016). https://doi.org/10.1007/978-3-319-41528-4_1
8. Chen, T., Forejt, V., Kwiatkowska, M., Parker, D., Simaitis, A.: Automatic verification of competitive stochastic systems. Formal Methods Syst. Des. **43**(1), 61–92 (2013)
9. Ciesinski, F., Baier, C., Größer, M., Klein, J.: Reduction techniques for model checking Markov decision processes. In: Proceedings of the Fifth International Conference on Quantitative Evaluation of Systems (QEST), pp. 45–54. IEEE (2008)

10. de Alfaro, L.: Computing minimum and maximum reachability times in probabilistic systems. In: Baeten, J.C.M., Mauw, S. (eds.) CONCUR 1999. LNCS, vol. 1664, pp. 66–81. Springer, Heidelberg (1999). https://doi.org/10.1007/3-540-48320-9_7
11. Esparza, J., Kucera, A., Mayr, R.: Quantitative analysis of probabilistic pushdown automata: expectations and variances. In: Proceedings of the 20th Annual IEEE Symposium on Logic in Computer Science (LICS), pp. 117–126. IEEE (2005)
12. Gretz, F., Katoen, J.-P., McIver, A.: Operational versus weakest pre-expectation semantics for the probabilistic guarded command language. Perform. Eval. **73**, 110–132 (2014)
13. Hordijk, A., Kallenberg, L.: Linear programming and Markov decision chains. Manage. Sci. **25**(4), 352–362 (1979)
14. Katoen, J.-P., Gretz, F., Jansen, N., Kaminski, B.L., Olmedo, F.: Understanding probabilistic programs. In: Meyer, R., Platzer, A., Wehrheim, H. (eds.) Correct System Design. LNCS, vol. 9360, pp. 15–32. Springer, Cham (2015). https://doi.org/10.1007/978-3-319-23506-6_4
15. Kretínský, J., Meggendorfer, T.: Conditional value-at-risk for reachability and mean payoff in Markov decision processes. In: Proceedings of the 33rd Annual ACM/IEEE Symposium on Logic in Computer Science (LICS), pp. 609–618. ACM (2018)
16. Olmedo, F., Gretz, F., Jansen, N., Kaminski, B.L., Katoen, J.-P., Mciver, A.: Conditioning in probabilistic programming. ACM Trans. Program. Lang. Syst. (TOPLAS) **40**(1), 4:1–4:50 (2018)
17. Piribauer, J., Baier, C.: Partial and conditional expectations in Markov decision processes with integer weights (extended version). arXiv:1902.04538 (2019)
18. Puterman, M.L.: Markov Decision Processes: Discrete Stochastic Dynamic Programming. Wiley, New York (1994)

8

Resource-Tracking Concurrent Games

Aurore Alcolei(✉), Pierre Clairambault, and Olivier Laurent

Université de Lyon, ENS de Lyon, CNRS, UCB Lyon 1, LIP, Lyon, France
{Aurore.Alcolei,Pierre.Clairambault,Olivier.Laurent}@ens-lyon.fr

Abstract. We present a framework for game semantics based on concurrent games, that keeps track of *resources* as data modified throughout execution but not affecting its control flow. Our leading example is *time*, yet the construction is in fact parametrized by a *resource bimonoid* $\mathcal{R}$, an algebraic structure expressing resources and the effect of their consumption either sequentially or in parallel. Relying on our construction, we give a sound resource-sensitive denotation to $\mathcal{R}$-IPA, an affine higher-order concurrent programming language with shared state and a primitive for resource consumption in $\mathcal{R}$. Compared with general operational semantics parametrized by $\mathcal{R}$, our resource analysis turns out to be finer, leading to non-adequacy. Yet, our model is not degenerate as adequacy holds for an operational semantics specialized to time.

In regard to earlier semantic frameworks for tracking resources, the main novelty of our work is that it is based on a non-interleaving semantics, and as such accounts for *parallel* use of resources accurately.

1 Introduction

Since its inception, *denotational semantics* has grown into a very wide subject. Its developments now cover numerous programming languages or paradigms, using approaches that range from the extensionality of *domain semantics* [24] (recording the input-output behaviour) to the intensionality of *game semantics* [1,17] (recording execution traces, formalized as *plays* in a 2-players game between the program ("Player") and its execution environment ("Opponent")). Denotational semantics has had significant influence on the theory of programming languages, with contributions ranging from program logics or reasoning principles to new language constructs and verification algorithms.

Most denotational models are *qualitative* in nature, meaning that they ignore efficiency of programs in terms of time, or other resources such as power or bandwith. To our knowledge, the first denotational model to cover time was Ghica's *slot games* [13], an extension of Ghica and Murawski's fully abstract model for a higher-order language with concurrency and shared state [14]. Slot games exploit the intensionality of game semantics and represent time via special moves called *tokens* matching the *ticks* of a clock. They are fully abstract *w.r.t.* the notion of observation in Sands' operational theory of *improvement* [26].

More recently, there has been a growing interest in capturing quantitative aspects denotationally. Laird *et al.* constructed [18] an enrichment of the relational model of Linear Logic [11], using weights from a *resource semiring* given as parameter. This way, they capture in a single framework several notions of resources for extensions of PCF, ranging from time to probabilistic weights. Two type systems with similar parametrizations were introduced simultaneously by, on the one hand, Ghica and Smith [15] and, on the other hand, Brunel, Gaboardi *et al.* [4]; the latter with a quantitative realizability denotational model.

In this paper, we give a resource-sensitive denotational model for $\mathcal{R}$-*IPA*, an affine higher-order programming language with concurrency, shared state, and with a primitive for resource consumption. With respect to slot games our model differs in that our resource analysis accounts for the fact that resource consumption may combine differently in parallel and sequentially – simply put, we mean to express that $\mathbf{wait}(1) \parallel \mathbf{wait}(1)$ may terminate in 1 s, rather than 2. We also take inspiration from weighted relational models [18] in that our construction is parametrized by an algebraic structure representing resources and their usage. Our *resource bimonoids* $\langle \mathcal{R}, 0, ;, \parallel, \leq \rangle$ differ however significantly from their resource semiring $\langle \mathcal{R}, 0, 1, +, \cdot \rangle$: while ; matches $\cdot$, $\parallel$ is a new operation expressing the consumption of resources in parallel. We have no counterpart for the $+$, which agglomerates distinct non-deterministically co-existing executions leading to the same value: instead our model keeps them separate.

Capturing parallel resource usage is technically challenging, as it can only be attempted relying on a representation of execution where parallelism is explicit. Accordingly, our model belongs to the family of *concurrent* or *asynchronous* game semantics pioneered by Abramsky and Melliès [2], pushed by Melliès [20] and later with Mimram [22], and by Faggian and Piccolo [12]; actively developed in the past 10 years prompted by the introduction of a more general framework by Rideau and Winskel [7,25]. In particular, our model is a refinement of the (qualitative) truly concurrent interpretation of *affine IPA* described in [5]. Our methodology to record resource usage is inspired by game semantics for first-order logic [3,19] where moves carry first-order terms from a signature – instead here they carry explicit *functions*, *i.e.* terms up to a congruence (it is also reminiscent of Melliès' construction of the free dialogue category over a category [21]).

As in [5] we chose to interpret an affine language: this lets us focus on the key phenomena which are already at play, avoiding the technical hindrance caused by replication. As suggested by recent experience with concurrent games [6,10], we expect the developments presented here to extend transparently in the presence of *symmetry* [8,9]; this would allow us to move to the general (non-affine) setting.

Outline. We start Sect. 2 by introducing the language $\mathcal{R}$-IPA. We equip it first with an interleaving semantics and sketch its interpretation in slot games. We then present resource bimonoids, give a new parallel operational semantics, and hint at our truly concurrent games model. In Sect. 3, we construct this model and prove its soundness. Finally in Sect. 4, we show adequacy for an operational semantics specialized to time, noting first that the general parallel operational semantics is too coarse *w.r.t.* our model.

2 From $\mathcal{R}$-IPA to $\mathcal{R}$-Strategies

2.1 Affine IPA

Terms and Types. We start by introducing the basic language under study, *affine Idealized Parallel Algol* (IPA). It is an affine variant of the language studied in [14], a call-by-name concurrent higher-order language with shared state. Its **types** are given by the following grammar:

$$A, B ::= \mathbf{com} \mid \mathbf{bool} \mid \mathbf{mem}_W \mid \mathbf{mem}_R \mid A \multimap B$$

Here, $\mathbf{mem}_W$ is the type of *writeable* references and $\mathbf{mem}_R$ is the type of *readable* references; the distinction is necessary in this affine setting as it allows to share accesses to a given state over subprocesses; this should make more sense in the next paragraph with the typing rules. In the sequel, non-functional types are called **ground types** (for which we use notation $\mathbb{X}$). We define terms directly along with their typing rules in Fig. 1. **Contexts** are simply lists $x_1 : A_1, \ldots, x_n : A_n$ of variable declarations (in which each variable occurs at most once), and the exchange rule is kept implicit. Weakening is not a rule but is admissible. We comment on a few aspects of these rules.

$$\frac{}{\Gamma \vdash \mathbf{skip} : \mathbf{com}} \qquad \frac{}{\Gamma \vdash \mathbf{tt} : \mathbf{bool}} \qquad \frac{}{\Gamma \vdash \mathbf{ff} : \mathbf{bool}} \qquad \frac{}{\Gamma \vdash \bot : \mathbb{X}} \qquad \frac{(x : A) \in \Gamma}{\Gamma \vdash x : A}$$

$$\frac{\Gamma, x : A \vdash M : B}{\Gamma \vdash \lambda x.\, M : A \multimap B} \qquad \frac{\Gamma \vdash M : A \multimap B \qquad \Delta \vdash N : A}{\Gamma, \Delta \vdash M\, N : B} \qquad \frac{\Gamma \vdash M : \mathbf{mem}_R}{\Gamma \vdash !M : \mathbf{bool}}$$

$$\frac{\Gamma \vdash M : \mathbf{com} \qquad \Delta \vdash N : \mathbb{X}}{\Gamma, \Delta \vdash M;\, N : \mathbb{X}} \qquad \frac{\Gamma \vdash M : \mathbf{com} \qquad \Delta \vdash N : \mathbb{X}}{\Gamma, \Delta \vdash M \parallel N : \mathbb{X}} \qquad \frac{\Gamma \vdash M : \mathbf{mem}_W}{\Gamma \vdash M := \mathbf{tt} : \mathbf{com}}$$

$$\frac{\Gamma \vdash M : \mathbf{bool} \qquad \Delta \vdash N_1 : \mathbb{X} \qquad \Delta \vdash N_2 : \mathbb{X}}{\Gamma, \Delta \vdash \mathbf{if}\, M\, N_1\, N_2 : \mathbb{X}} \qquad \frac{\Gamma, x : \mathbf{mem}_W, y : \mathbf{mem}_R \vdash M : \mathbb{X}}{\Gamma \vdash \mathbf{new}\, x, y\, \mathbf{in}\, M : \mathbb{X}}$$

Fig. 1. Typing rules for affine IPA

Firstly, observe that the reference constructor $\mathbf{new}\, x, y\, \mathbf{in}\, M$ binds two variables x and y, one with a write permission and the other with a read permission. In this way, the permissions of a shared state can be distributed in different components of *e.g.* an application or a parallel composition, causing interferences despite the affine aspect of the language. Secondly, the assignment command, $M := \mathbf{tt}$, seems quite restrictive. Yet, the language is affine, so a variable can only be written to once, and, as we choose to initialize it to **ff**, the only useful thing to write is **tt**. Finally, many rules seem restrictive in that they apply only at ground type $\mathbb{X}$. More general rules can be defined as syntactic sugar; for instance we give (all other constructs extend similarly): $M;_{A\multimap B} N = \lambda x^A.\,(M;_B (N\,x))$.

Operational Semantics. We fix a countable set L of **memory locations**. Each location ℓ comes with two associated variable names ℓ_W and ℓ_R distinct from other variable names. Usually, stores are partial maps from L to $\{\mathbf{tt}, \mathbf{ff}\}$. Instead, we find it more convenient to introduce the notion of **state** of a memory location. A state corresponds to a history of memory actions (reads or writes) and follows the *state diagram* of Fig. 2 (ignoring for now the annotations with α, β). We write $(\mathsf{M}, \leq_{\mathsf{M}})$ for the induced set of states and accessibility relation on it. For each $m \in \mathsf{M}$, its set of **available actions** is $\mathrm{act}(m) = \{W, R\} \setminus m$ (the letters not occurring in m, annotations being ignored); and its **value** (in $\{\mathbf{tt}, \mathbf{ff}\}$) is $\mathrm{val}(m) = \mathbf{tt}$ iff W occurs in m.

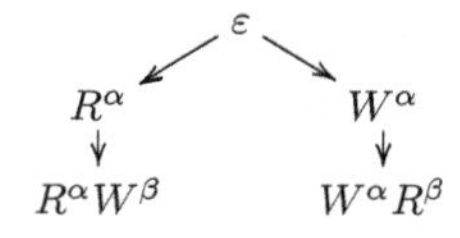

Fig. 2. State diagram

Finally, a **store** is a partial map $s : \mathsf{L} \to \mathsf{M}$ with finite domain, mapping each memory location to its current state. To each store corresponds a *typing context*

$$\Omega(s) = \{\ell_X : \mathbf{mem}_X \mid \ell \in \mathrm{dom}(s) \ \&\ X \in \mathrm{act}(s(\ell))\}.$$

The operational semantics operates on **configurations** defined as pairs $\langle M, s\rangle$ with s a store and $\Gamma \vdash M : A$ a term whose free variables are all memory locations with $\Gamma \subseteq \Omega(s)$. This property will be preserved by our rather standard small-step, call-by-name operational semantics. We refrain for now from giving the details, they will appear in Sect. 2.2 in the presence of resources.

2.2 Interleaving Cost Semantics, and $\mathcal{R}$-IPA

Ghica and Murawski [14] have constructed a *fully abstract*(for may-equivalence) model for (non-affine) IPA, relying on an extension of Hyland-Ong games [17].

Their model takes an *interleaving* view of the execution of concurrent programs: a program is represented by the set of all its possible executions, as decided non-deterministically by the scheduler. In game semantics, this is captured by lifting the standard requirement that the two players alternate. For instance, Fig. 3 shows a *play* in the interpretation of the program $x : \mathbf{com}, y : \mathbf{bool} \vdash x \parallel y : \mathbf{bool}$. The diagram is read from top to bottom, chronologically. Each line comprises one computational event ("move"), annotated with "−" if due to the execution environment ("Opponent") and with "+" if due to the program ("Player"); each move corresponds to a certain type component, under which it is placed. With the first move $\mathbf{q}^-$, the environment initiates the computation.

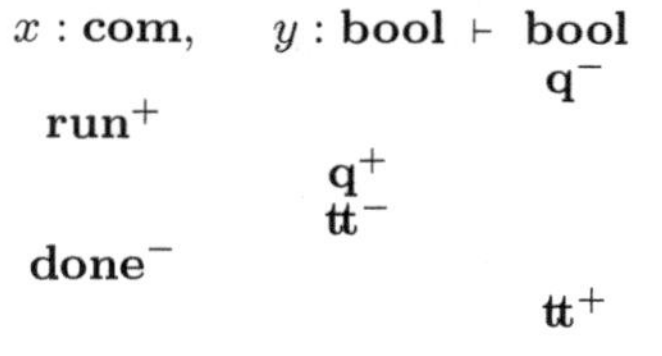

Fig. 3. A non-alternating play

Player then plays $\mathbf{run}^+$, triggering the evaluation of x. In standard game semantics, the control would then go back to the execution environment – Player would be stuck until Opponent plays. Here instead, due to parallelism Player can play a second move $\mathbf{q}^+$ immediately. At this point of execution, x and y are both running in parallel. Only when they have both returned (moves $\mathbf{done}^-$ and $\mathbf{tt}^-$) is Player able to respond $\mathbf{tt}^+$, terminating the computation. The full interpretation of $x : \mathbf{com}, y : \mathbf{bool} \vdash x \parallel y : \mathbf{bool}$, its *strategy*, comprises numerous plays like that, one for each interleaving.

As often in denotational semantics, Ghica and Murawski's model is invariant under reduction: if $\langle M, s\rangle \to \langle M', s'\rangle$, both have the same denotation. The model adequately describes the result of computation, but not its *cost* in terms, for instance, of time. Of course this cost is not yet specified: one must, for instance, define a *cost model* assigning a cost to all basic operations (*e.g.* memory operations, function calls, *etc*). In this paper we instead enrich the language with a primitive for *resource consumption* – cost models can then be captured by inserting this primitive concomitantly with the costly operations (see for example [18]).

$\mathcal{R}$-IPA. Consider a set $\mathcal{R}$ of **resources**. The language $\mathcal{R}$-IPA is obtained by adding to affine IPA a new construction, $\mathbf{consume}(\alpha)$, typed as in Fig. 4. When evaluated, $\mathbf{consume}(\alpha)$ triggers the consumption of resource $\mathcal{R}$. Time consumption will be a running example throughout the paper. In that case, we will consider the non-negative reals $\mathbb{R}_+$ as set $\mathcal{R}$, and for $t \in \mathbb{R}_+$ we will use $\mathbf{wait}(t)$ as a synonym for $\mathbf{consume}(t)$.

$$\frac{(\alpha \in \mathcal{R})}{\Gamma \vdash \mathbf{consume}(\alpha) : \mathbf{com}}$$

Fig. 4. Typing **consume**

$$\begin{array}{rlrl}
\langle \mathbf{skip};\, M, s, \alpha\rangle \to \langle M, s, \alpha\rangle & & \langle (\lambda x.\, M)\, N, s, \alpha\rangle \to \langle M[N/x], s, \alpha\rangle \\
\langle \mathbf{skip} \parallel M, s, \alpha\rangle \to \langle M, s, \alpha\rangle & & \langle !\ell_R, s, \alpha\rangle \to \langle \mathrm{val}(s(\ell)), s[\ell \mapsto s(\ell).R^\alpha], \alpha\rangle \\
\langle M \parallel \mathbf{skip}, s, \alpha\rangle \to \langle M, s, \alpha\rangle & & \langle \ell_W := \mathbf{tt}, s, \alpha\rangle \to \langle \mathbf{skip}, s[\ell \mapsto s(\ell).W^\alpha], \alpha\rangle \\
\langle \mathbf{if\,tt}\, N_1\, N_2, s, \alpha\rangle \to \langle N_1, s, \alpha\rangle & & \langle \mathbf{new}\, x, y\, \mathbf{in}\, M, s, \alpha\rangle \to \langle M[\ell_W/x, \ell_R/y], s \uplus \{\ell \mapsto \varepsilon\}, \alpha\rangle \\
\langle \mathbf{if\,ff}\, N_1\, N_2, s, \alpha\rangle \to \langle N_2, s, \alpha\rangle & & \langle \mathbf{consume}(\beta), s, \alpha\rangle \to \langle \mathbf{skip}, s, \alpha; \beta\rangle
\end{array}$$

Fig. 5. Operational semantics: basic rules

To equip $\mathcal{R}$-IPA with an operational semantics we need operations on $\mathcal{R}$, they are introduced throughout this section. First we have $0 \in \mathcal{R}$, the null resource; if $\alpha, \beta \in \mathcal{R}$, we have some $\alpha; \beta \in \mathcal{R}$, the resource taken by consuming α, then β – for $\mathcal{R} = \mathbb{R}_+$, this is simply addition. To evaluate $\mathcal{R}$-IPA, the **configurations** are now triples $\langle M, s, \alpha\rangle$ with $\alpha \in \mathcal{R}$ tracking resources already spent. With that, we give in Fig. 5 the basic operational rules. The only rule affecting current resources is that for $\mathbf{consume}(\beta)$, the others leave it unchanged. However note that we store the current state of resources when performing memory operations, explaining the annotations in Fig. 2. These annotations do not impact the operational behaviour, but will be helpful in relating with the game semantics in Sect. 3. As usual, these rules apply within call-by-name evaluation contexts – we omit the details here but they will appear for our final operational semantics.

Slot Games. In [13], Ghica extends Ghica and Murawski's model to *slot games* in order to capture resource consumption. Slot games introduce a new action called a *token*, representing an atomic resource consumption, and written $\textcircled{\$}$ – writing $\textcircled{n}$ for n successive occurrences of $\textcircled{\$}$. A model of $\mathbb{N}_+$-IPA using slot games would have for instance the play in Fig. 6 in the interpretation of

$$H = (\mathbf{wait}(1);\ x;\ \mathbf{wait}(2)) \parallel (\mathbf{wait}(2);\ y;\ \mathbf{wait}(1))$$

in context $x : \mathbf{com}, y : \mathbf{bool}$, among with many others. Note, in examples, we use a more liberal typing rule for ';' allowing $y^{\mathbf{bool}};\ z^{\mathbf{com}} : \mathbf{bool}$ to avoid clutter: it can be encoded as $\mathbf{if}\, y\, (z;\ \mathbf{tt})\, (z;\ \mathbf{ff})$. Following the methodology of game semantics, the interpretation of $(\lambda xy.\, H)\, \mathbf{skip}\, \mathbf{tt}$ would yield, by composition, the strategy with only maximal play $\mathbf{q}^-\textcircled{6}\mathbf{tt}^+$, where $\textcircled{6}$ reflects the overall 6 time units (say "seconds") that have to pass in total before we see the result (3 in each thread). This seems wasteful, but it is indeed an adequate computational analysis, because both slot games and the operational semantics given so far implicitly assume a sequential operational model, *i.e.* that both threads compete to be scheduled on a *single* processor. Let us now question that assumption.

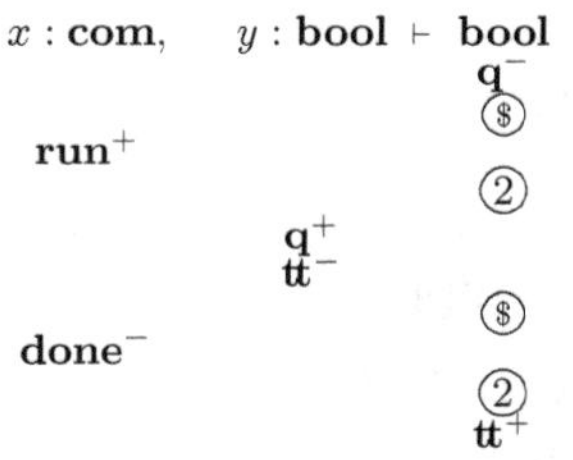

Fig. 6. A play with tokens

Parallel Resource Consumption. With a truly concurrent evaluation in mind, we should be able to prove that the program above may terminate in 3 s, rather than 6; as nothing prevents the threads from evaluating in parallel. Before we update the operational semantics to express that, we enrich our resource structure to allow it to express the effect of consuming resources in parallel.

We now introduce the full algebraic structure we require for resources.

Definition 1. *A* ***resource bimonoid*** *is* $\langle \mathcal{R}, 0, ;, \parallel, \leq \rangle$ *where* $\langle \mathcal{R}, 0, ;, \leq \rangle$ *is an ordered monoid,* $\langle \mathcal{R}, 0, \parallel, \leq \rangle$ *is an ordered commutative monoid,* 0 *is bottom for* $\leq$*, and* $\parallel$ *is* ***idempotent****,* i.e. *it satisfies* $\alpha \parallel \alpha = \alpha$.

A resource bimonoid is in particular a *concurrent monoid* in the sense of *e.g.* [16] (though we take $\leq$ in the opposite direction: we read $\alpha \leq_{\mathcal{R}} \alpha'$ as "α is *better/more efficient* than α'"). Our *Idempotence* assumption is rather strong as it entails that $\alpha \parallel \beta$ is the supremum of $\alpha, \beta \in \mathcal{R}$. This allows to recover a number of simple laws, *e.g.* $\alpha \parallel \beta \leq \alpha; \beta$, or the exchange rule $(\alpha; \beta) \parallel (\alpha'; \beta') \leq (\alpha \parallel \alpha'); (\beta \parallel \beta')$. Idempotence, which would not be needed for a purely functional language, is used crucially in our interpretation of state.

Our leading examples are $\langle \mathbb{N}_+, 0, +, \max, \leq \rangle$ and $\langle \mathbb{R}_+, 0, +, \max, \leq \rangle$ – we call the latter the *time bimonoid.* Others are the *permission bimonoid* $\langle \mathcal{P}(P), \emptyset, \cup, \cup, \subseteq \rangle$ for some set P of *permissions*: if reaching a state requires certain permissions, it does not matter whether these have been requested sequentially or in parallel;

the bimonoid of *parametrized time* $\langle \mathcal{M}, 0, ;, \|, \leq \rangle$ with $\mathcal{M}$ the monotone functions from positive reals to positive reals, 0 the constant function, $\|$ the pointwise maximum, and $(f;\, g)(x) = f(x) + g(x + f(x))$: it tracks time consumption in a context where the time taken by $\mathbf{consume}(\alpha)$ might grow over time.

Besides time-based bimonoids, it would be appealing to cover resources such as *power*, *bandwith* or *heapspace*. Those, however, clearly fail idempotence of $\|$, and are therefore not covered. It is not clear how to extend our model to those.

$$\frac{}{\langle M, s, \alpha\rangle \rightrightarrows \langle M, s, \alpha\rangle} \qquad \frac{\langle M, s, \alpha\rangle \to \langle M', s', \alpha'\rangle}{\langle M, s, \alpha\rangle \rightrightarrows \langle M', s', \alpha'\rangle} \qquad \frac{\langle M, s, \alpha\rangle \rightrightarrows \langle M', s', \alpha'\rangle}{\langle C[M], s, \alpha\rangle \rightrightarrows \langle C[M'], s', \alpha'\rangle}$$

$$\frac{\langle M, s, \alpha\rangle \rightrightarrows \langle M', s', \alpha'\rangle \qquad \langle M', s', \alpha'\rangle \rightrightarrows \langle M'', s'', \alpha''\rangle}{\langle M, s, \alpha\rangle \rightrightarrows \langle M'', s'', \alpha''\rangle} \qquad \frac{\langle M, s, \alpha\rangle \rightrightarrows \langle M', s', \alpha'\rangle \qquad \langle N, s, \alpha\rangle \rightrightarrows \langle N', s'', \alpha''\rangle}{\langle M \parallel N, s, \alpha\rangle \rightrightarrows \langle M' \parallel N', s' \uparrow s'', \alpha' \parallel \alpha''\rangle}$$

Fig. 7. Rules for parallel reduction

Parallel Operational Semantics. Let us fix a resource bimonoid $\mathcal{R}$. To express parallel resource consumption, we use the many-step *parallel reductions* defined in Fig. 7, with **call-by-name evaluation contexts** given by

$$C[] ::= [] \mid []\,N \mid [];\,N \mid \mathbf{if}\,[]\,N_1\,N_2 \mid [] := \mathbf{tt} \mid ![] \mid ([] \parallel N) \mid (M \parallel [])$$

The rule for parallel composition carries some restrictions regarding memory: M and N can only reduce concurrently if they do not access the same memory cells. This is achieved by requiring that the *partial* operation $s \uparrow s'$ – that intuitively corresponds to "merging" two memory stores s and s' whenever there are no conflicts – is defined. More formally, the partial order $\leq_{\mathsf{M}}$ on memory states induces a partial order (also written $\leq_{\mathsf{M}}$) on stores, defined by $s \leq_{\mathsf{M}} s'$ iff $\mathrm{dom}(s) \subseteq \mathrm{dom}(s')$ and for all $\ell \in \mathrm{dom}(s)$ we have $s(\ell) \leq_{\mathsf{M}} s'(\ell)$. This order is a cpo in which s' and s'' are *compatible* (*i.e.* have an upper bound) iff for all $\ell \in \mathrm{dom}(s') \cap \mathrm{dom}(s'')$, $s'(\ell) \leq_{\mathsf{M}} s''(\ell)$ or $s''(\ell) \leq_{\mathsf{M}} s'(\ell)$ – so there has been no interference going to s' and s'' from their last common ancestor. When compatible, $s' \uparrow s''$ maps s' and s'' to their lub, and is undefined otherwise.

For $\vdash M : \mathbf{com}$, we set $M \Downarrow_\alpha$ if $\langle M, \emptyset, 0\rangle \rightrightarrows \langle \mathbf{skip}, s, \alpha\rangle$. For instance, instantiating the rules with the time bimonoid, we have

$$(\mathbf{wait}(1);\, \mathbf{wait}(2)) \parallel (\mathbf{wait}(2);\, \mathbf{wait}(1)) \Downarrow_3$$

2.3 Non-interleaving Semantics

To capture this parallel resource usage semantically, we build on the games model for affine IPA presented in [5]. Rather than presenting programs as collections of *sequences* of moves expressing all observable sequences of computational actions, this model adopts a *truly concurrent* view using collections of *partially ordered* plays. For each Player move, the order specifies its *causal dependencies*, *i.e.* the Opponent moves that need to have happened before. For instance, ignoring the subscripts, Fig. 8 displays a typical partially ordered play in the strategy for the term H of Sect. 2.2. One partially ordered play does not fully specify a sequential execution: that in Fig. 8 stands for *many* sequential executions, one of which is in Fig. 3. Behaviours expressed by partially ordered plays are deterministic *up to* choices of the scheduler irrelevant for the eventual result. Because $\mathcal{R}$-IPA is non-deterministic (via concurrency and shared state), our strategies will be *sets* of such partial orders.

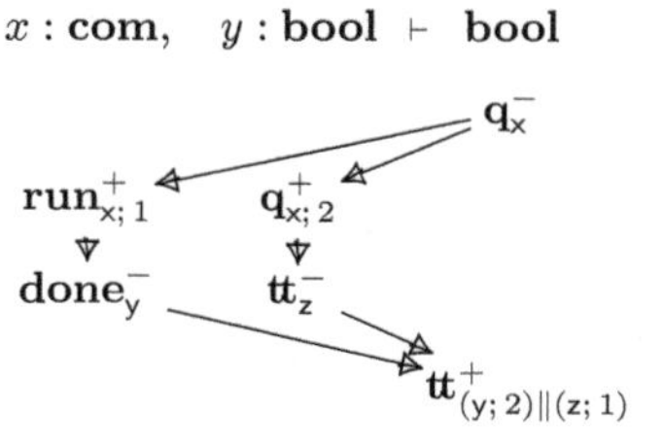

Fig. 8. A parallel $\mathcal{R}$-play

To express resources, we leverage the causal information and indicate, in each partially ordered play and for each positive move, an $\mathcal{R}$-expression representing its *additional cost* in function of the cost of its negative dependencies. Figure 8 displays such a *$\mathcal{R}$-play*: each Opponent move introduces a fresh variable, which can be used in annotations for Player moves. As we will see further on, once applied to strategies for values **skip** and **tt** (with no additional cost), this $\mathcal{R}$-play will answer to the initial Opponent move $\mathbf{q}_{\mathsf{x}}^-$ with $\mathbf{tt}^+_{\mathsf{x};\,\alpha}$ where $\alpha = (1;\, 2) \parallel (2;\, 1) =_{\mathbb{R}_+} 3$, as prescribed by the more efficient parallel operational semantics.

We now go on to define formally our semantics.

3 Concurrent Game Semantics of IPA

3.1 Arenas and $\mathcal{R}$-Strategies

Arenas. We first introduce *arenas*, the semantic representation of types in our model. As in [5], an arena will be a certain kind of *event structure* [27].

Definition 2. *An* ***event structure*** *comprises* $(E, \leq_E, \#_E)$ *where* E *is a set of* events, $\leq_E$ *is a partial order called* causal dependency, *and* $\#_E$ *is an irreflexive symmetric binary relation called* conflict, *subject to the two axioms:*

$$\forall e \in E, [e]_E = \{e' \in E \mid e' \leq_E e\} \textit{ is finite}$$
$$\forall e_1 \#_E e_2, \forall e_1 \leq_E e_1', e_1' \#_E e_2$$

We will use some vocabulary and notations from event structures. A **configuration** $x \subseteq E$ is a down-closed, consistent (*i.e.* for all $e, e' \in x$, $\neg(e \#_E e')$) finite set of events. We write $\mathscr{C}(E)$ for the set of configurations of E. We write $\rightarrowtriangle_E$ for **immediate causality**, *i.e.* $e \rightarrowtriangle_E e'$ iff $e <_E e'$ with nothing in between – this is the relation represented in diagrams such as Fig. 8. A conflict $e_1 \#_E e_2$ is **minimal** if for all $e_1' <_E e_1$, $\neg(e_1' \#_E e_2)$ and symmetrically. We write $e_1 \sim_E e_2$ to indicate that e_1 and e_2 are in minimal conflict.

With this, we now define arenas.

Definition 3. *An* ***arena*** *is* $(A, \leq_A, \#_A, \mathrm{pol}_A)$*, an event structure along with a* ***polarity function*** $\mathrm{pol}_A : A \longrightarrow \{-, +\}$ *subject to: (1)* $\leq_A$ *is forest-shaped, (2)* $\rightarrowtriangle_A$ *is alternating: if* $a_1 \rightarrowtriangle_A a_2$*, then* $\mathrm{pol}_A(a_1) \neq \mathrm{pol}_A(a_2)$*, and (3) it is race-free,* i.e. *if* $a_1 \sim_A a_2$*, then* $\mathrm{pol}_A(a_1) = \mathrm{pol}_A(a_2)$*.*

Arenas present the computational actions available on a type, following a call-by-name evaluation strategy. For instance, the observable actions of a closed term on **com** are that it can be ran, and it may terminate, leading to the arena $\mathbf{com} = \mathbf{run}^- \rightarrowtriangle \mathbf{done}^+$. Likewise, a boolean can be evaluated, and can terminate on **tt** or **ff**, yielding the arena on the right of Fig. 9 (when drawing arenas, immediate causality is written with a dotted line, from top to bottom). We present some simple arena constructions. The **empty arena**, written 1, has no events. If A is an arena, then its **dual** $A^\perp$ has the same components, but polarity reversed. The **parallel composition** of A and B, written $A \parallel B$, has as events the tagged disjoint union $\{1\} \times A \cup \{2\} \times B$, and all other components inherited. For $x_A \in \mathscr{C}(A)$ and $x_B \in \mathscr{C}(B)$, we also write $x_A \parallel x_B \in \mathscr{C}(A \parallel B)$. Figure 9 displays the arena $\mathbf{com}^\perp \parallel \mathbf{bool}^\perp \parallel \mathbf{bool}$.

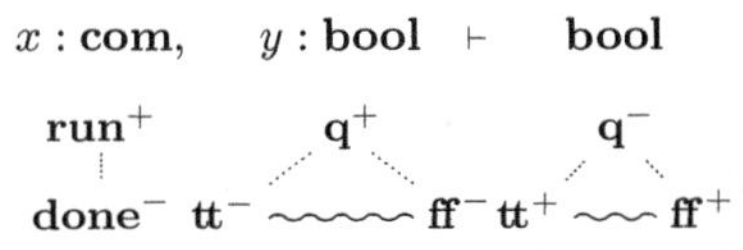

Fig. 9. An arena for a sequent

$\mathcal{R}$-Augmentations. As hinted before, $\mathcal{R}$-strategies will be collections of partially ordered plays with resource annotations in $\mathcal{R}$, called *$\mathcal{R}$-augmentations.*

Definition 4. *An* ***augmentation*** *[5] on arena A is a finite partial order* $\mathbb{q} = (|\mathbb{q}|, \leq_{\mathbb{q}})$ *such that* $\mathscr{C}(\mathbb{q}) \subseteq \mathscr{C}(A)$ *(concerning configurations, augmentations are considered as event structures with empty conflict), which is* ***courteous****, in the sense that for all* $a_1 \rightarrowtriangle_{\mathbb{q}} a_2$*, if* $\mathrm{pol}_A(a_1) = +$ *or* $\mathrm{pol}_A(a_2) = -$*, then* $a_1 \rightarrowtriangle_A a_2$*.*

A ***$\mathcal{R}$-augmentation*** *also has (with* $[a]^-_{\mathbb{q}} = \{a' \leq_{\mathbb{q}} a \mid \mathrm{pol}_A(a') = -\}$*)*

$$\lambda_{\mathbb{q}} : (a \in |\mathbb{q}|) \quad \longrightarrow \quad \left(\mathcal{R}^{[a]^-_{\mathbb{q}}} \to \mathcal{R}\right)$$

such that if $\mathrm{pol}_A(a) = -$*, then* $\lambda_{\mathbb{q}}(a)(\rho) = \rho_a$*, the projection on a of* $\rho \in \mathcal{R}^{[a]^-_{\mathbb{q}}}$*, and for all* $a \in |\mathbb{q}|$*,* $\lambda_{\mathbb{q}}(a)$ *is monotone* w.r.t. *all of its variables.*

We write $\mathcal{R}$-Aug(A) *for the set of* $\mathcal{R}$*-augmentations on A.*

If $\mathbb{q}, \mathbb{q}' \in \mathcal{R}$-Aug$(A)$, $\mathbb{q}$ is **rigidly embedded** in $\mathbb{q}'$, or a **prefix** of $\mathbb{q}'$, written $\mathbb{q} \hookrightarrow \mathbb{q}'$, if $|\mathbb{q}| \in \mathscr{C}(\mathbb{q}')$, for all $a, a' \in |\mathbb{q}|$, $a \leq_{\mathbb{q}} a'$ iff $a \leq_{\mathbb{q}'} a'$, and for all $a \in |\mathbb{q}|$, $\lambda_{\mathbb{q}}(a) = \lambda_{\mathbb{q}'}(a)$. The *$\mathcal{R}$-plays* of Sect. 2.3 are formalized as $\mathcal{R}$-augmentations: Fig. 8 presents an $\mathcal{R}$-augmentation on the arena of Fig. 9. The functional dependency in the annotation of positive events is represented by using the free variables introduced alongside negative events, however this is only a symbolic representation: the formal annotation is a function for each positive event. In the model of $\mathcal{R}$-IPA, we will only use the particular case where the annotations of positive events only depend on the annotations of their immediate predecessors.

$\mathcal{R}$-Strategies. We start by defining $\mathcal{R}$-strategies on arenas.

Definition 5. *A **$\mathcal{R}$-strategy** on A is a non-empty prefix-closed set of $\mathcal{R}$-augmentations $\sigma \subseteq \mathcal{R}\text{-Aug}(A)$ which is **receptive** [5]: for $\mathbb{q} \in \sigma$ such that $|\mathbb{q}|$ extends with $a^- \in A$ (*i.e. $\mathrm{pol}(a) = -$*, $a \notin |\mathbb{q}|$, and $|\mathbb{q}| \cup \{a\} \in \mathscr{C}(A)$), there is $\mathbb{q} \hookrightarrow \mathbb{q}' \in \sigma$ such that $|\mathbb{q}'| = |\mathbb{q}| \cup \{a\}$.*

If σ is a $\mathcal{R}$-strategy on arena A, we write $\sigma : A$.

Observe that $\mathcal{R}$-strategies are fully described by their *maximal* augmentations, *i.e.* augmentations that are the prefix of no other augmentations in the strategy. Our interpretation of new will use the $\mathcal{R}$-strategy cell : $[\![\mathbf{mem}_W]\!] \parallel [\![\mathbf{mem}_R]\!]$ (with arenas presented in Fig. 10), comprising all the $\mathcal{R}$-augmentations rigidly included in either of the two from Fig. 11. These two match the race when reading and writing simultaneously: if both $\mathbf{wtt}^-$ and $\mathbf{r}^-$ are played the read may return $\mathbf{tt}^+$ or $\mathbf{ff}^+$, but it can only return $\mathbf{tt}^+$ in the presence of $\mathbf{wtt}^-$.

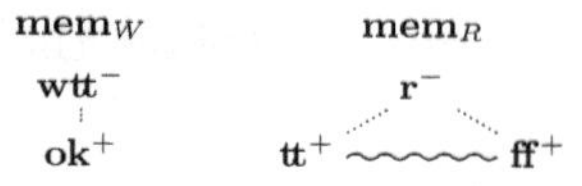

Fig. 10. $[\![\mathbf{mem}_W]\!]$ and $[\![\mathbf{mem}_R]\!]$

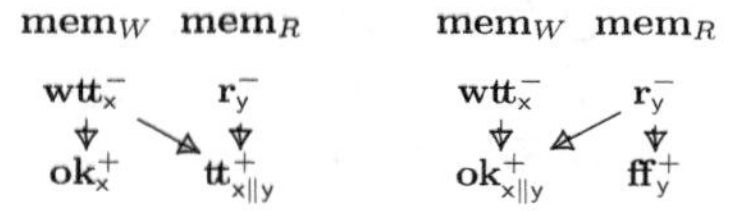

Fig. 11. Maximal $\mathcal{R}$-augmentations of cell

3.2 Interpretation of $\mathcal{R}$-IPA

Categorical Structure. In order to define the interpretation of terms of $\mathcal{R}$-IPA as $\mathcal{R}$-strategies, a key step is to show how to form a *category* of $\mathcal{R}$-strategies. To do that we follow the standard idea of considering **$\mathcal{R}$-strategies from A to B** to be simply $\mathcal{R}$-strategies on the compound arena $A^\perp \parallel B$. As usual, our first example of a $\mathcal{R}$-strategy between arenas is the *copycat $\mathcal{R}$-strategy.*

Definition 6. *Let A be an arena. We define a partial order $\leq_{\mathbb{C}_A}$ on $A^\perp \parallel A$:*

$$\leq_{\mathbb{C}_A} = (\{((1,a),(1,a')) \mid a \leq_A a'\} \cup \{((2,a),(2,a')) \mid a \leq_A a'\} \cup \\ \{((1,a),(2,a)) \mid \mathrm{pol}_A(a) = +\} \cup \{((2,a),(1,a)) \mid \mathrm{pol}_A(a) = -\})^+$$

where $(-)^+$ denotes the transitive closure of a relation. Note that if $a \in A^\perp \parallel A$ is positive, it has a unique immediate predecessor $\mathrm{pred}(a) \in A^\perp \parallel A$ *for $\leq_{\mathbb{C}_A}$.*

If $x \parallel y \in \mathscr{C}(A^\perp \parallel A)$ is down-closed for $\leq_{\mathbb{C}_A}$ (write $\leq_{x,y}$ for the restriction of $\leq_{\mathbb{C}_A}$ to $x \parallel y$), we define an $\mathcal{R}$-augmentation $\mathbb{q}_{x,y} = (x \parallel y, \leq_{x,y}, \lambda_{x,y})$ where

$$\lambda_{x,y} : (a \in x \parallel y) \quad \longrightarrow \quad \left(\mathcal{R}^{[a]^-_{x\parallel y}} \to \mathcal{R}\right)$$

with $\lambda_{x,y}(a^-)(\rho) = \rho_a$, and $\lambda_{x,y}(a^+)(\rho) = \rho_{\mathrm{pred}(a)}$. Then, $\mathbb{C}_A$ is the $\mathcal{R}$-strategy comprising all $\mathbb{q}_{x,y}$ for $x \parallel y \in \mathscr{C}(A^\perp \parallel A)$ down-closed in A.

We first define *interactions* of $\mathcal{R}$-augmentations, extending [5].

Definition 7. *We say that $\mathbb{q} \in \mathcal{R}\text{-Aug}(A^\perp \parallel B)$, and $\mathbb{p} \in \mathcal{R}\text{-Aug}(B^\perp \parallel C)$ are* ***causally compatible*** *if $|\mathbb{q}| = x_A \parallel x_B$, $|\mathbb{p}| = x_B \parallel x_C$, and the preorder $\leq_{\mathbb{p}\circledast\mathbb{q}}$ on $x_A \parallel x_B \parallel x_C$ defined as $(\leq_\mathbb{q} \cup \leq_\mathbb{p})^+$ is a partial order.*

Say $e \in x_A \parallel x_B \parallel x_C$ is negative *if it is negative in $A^\perp \parallel C$. We define*

$$\lambda_{\mathbb{p}\circledast\mathbb{q}} : (e \in x_A \parallel x_B \parallel x_C) \quad \longrightarrow \quad \left(\mathcal{R}^{[e]^-_{\mathbb{p}\circledast\mathbb{q}}} \to \mathcal{R}\right)$$

as follows, by well-founded induction on $<_{\mathbb{p}\circledast\mathbb{q}}$, for $\rho \in \mathcal{R}^{[e]^-_{\mathbb{p}\circledast\mathbb{q}}}$:

$$\lambda_{\mathbb{p}\circledast\mathbb{q}}(e)(\rho) = \begin{cases} \lambda_\mathbb{p}(e)\left(\langle \lambda_{\mathbb{p}\circledast\mathbb{q}}(e')(\rho) \mid e' \in [e]^-_\mathbb{p}\rangle\right) & \text{if } \mathrm{pol}_{B^\perp\parallel C}(e) = +, \\ \lambda_\mathbb{q}(e)\left(\langle \lambda_{\mathbb{p}\circledast\mathbb{q}}(e')(\rho) \mid e' \in [e]^-_\mathbb{q}\rangle\right) & \text{if } \mathrm{pol}_{A^\perp\parallel B}(e) = +, \\ \rho_e & \text{otherwise, i.e. } e \text{ negative} \end{cases}$$

The ***interaction*** *$\mathbb{p} \circledast \mathbb{q}$ of compatible $\mathbb{q}, \mathbb{p}$ is $(x_A \parallel x_B \parallel x_C, \leq_{\mathbb{p}\circledast\mathbb{q}}, \lambda_{\mathbb{p}\circledast\mathbb{q}})$.*

If $\sigma : A^\perp \parallel B$ and $\tau : B^\perp \parallel C$, we write $\tau \circledast \sigma$ for the set comprising all $\mathbb{p} \circledast \mathbb{q}$ such that $\mathbb{p} \in \tau$ and $\mathbb{q} \in \sigma$ are causally compatible. For $\mathbb{q} \in \sigma$ and $\mathbb{p} \in \tau$ causally compatible with $|\mathbb{p} \circledast \mathbb{q}| = x_A \parallel x_B \parallel x_C$, their **composition** is $\mathbb{p} \odot \mathbb{q} = (x_A \parallel x_C, \leq_{\mathbb{p}\odot\mathbb{q}}, \lambda_{\mathbb{p}\odot\mathbb{q}})$ where $\leq_{\mathbb{p}\odot\mathbb{q}}$ and $\lambda_{\mathbb{p}\odot\mathbb{q}}$ are the restrictions of $\leq_{\mathbb{p}\circledast\mathbb{q}}$ and $\lambda_{\mathbb{p}\circledast\mathbb{q}}$. Finally, the **composition** of $\sigma : A^\perp \parallel B$ and $\tau : B^\perp \parallel C$ is the set comprising all $\mathbb{p} \odot \mathbb{q}$ for $\mathbb{q} \in \sigma$ and $\mathbb{p} \in \tau$ causally compatible.

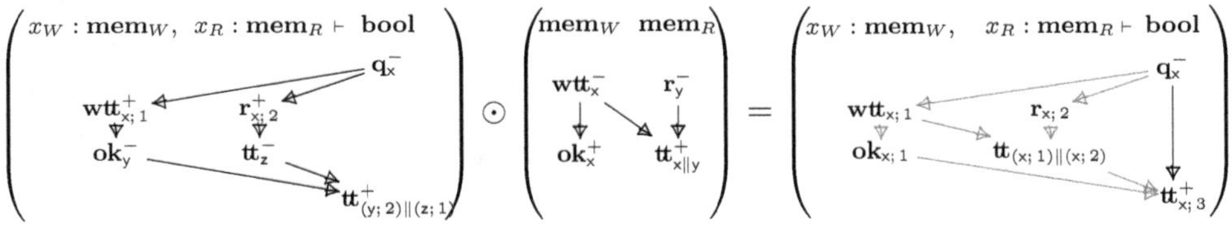

Fig. 12. Example of interaction and composition between $\mathbb{R}_+$-augmentations

In Fig. 12, we display an example composition between $\mathbb{R}_+$-augmentations – with also in gray the underlying interaction. The reader may check that the variant of the left $\mathbb{R}_+$-augmentation with **tt** replaced with **ff** is causally compatible with the other augmentation in Fig. 11, with composition $\mathbf{q}_x^- \rightarrow \mathbf{ff}^+_{x;4}$.

We also have a tensor operation: on arenas, $A \otimes B$ is simply a synonym for $A \parallel B$. If $\mathbb{q}_1 \in \mathcal{R}\text{-Aug}(A_1^\perp \parallel B_1)$ and $\mathbb{q}_2 \in \mathcal{R}\text{-Aug}(A_2^\perp \parallel B_2)$, their **tensor product** $\mathbb{q}_1 \otimes \mathbb{q}_2 \in \mathcal{R}\text{-Aug}((A_1 \otimes A_2)^\perp \parallel (B_1 \otimes B_2))$ is defined in the obvious way. This is lifted to $\mathcal{R}$-strategies element-wise. As is common when constructing basic categories of games and strategies, we have:

Proposition 1. *There is a compact closed category* $\mathcal{R}$-Strat *having arenas as objects, and as morphisms,* $\mathcal{R}$*-strategies between them.*

Negative Arenas and $\mathcal{R}$*-Strategies.* As a compact closed category, $\mathcal{R}$-Strat is a model of the linear λ-calculus. However, we will (as usual for call-by-name) instead interpret $\mathcal{R}$-IPA in a sub-category of *negative* arenas and strategies, in which the empty arena 1 is terminal, providing the interpretation of weakening. We will stay very brief here, as this proceeds exactly as in [5].

A partial order with polarities is **negative** if all its minimal events are. This applies in particular to arenas, and $\mathcal{R}$-augmentations. A $\mathcal{R}$-strategy is **negative** if all its $\mathcal{R}$-augmentations are. A negative $\mathcal{R}$-augmentation $\mathbb{q} \in \mathcal{R}\text{-Aug}(A)$ is **well-threaded** if for all $a \in |\mathbb{q}|$, $[a]_{\mathbb{q}}$ has exactly one minimal event; a $\mathcal{R}$-strategy is **well-threaded** iff all its $\mathcal{R}$-augmentations are. We have:

Proposition 2. Negative arenas *and* negative well-threaded $\mathcal{R}$*-strategies form a cartesian symmetric monoidal closed category* $\mathcal{R}$-Strat_-*, with* 1 *terminal.*

We also write $\sigma : A \twoheadrightarrow B$ *for morphisms in* $\mathcal{R}$-Strat_-.

The closure of $\mathcal{R}$-Strat does not transport to $\mathcal{R}$-Strat_- as $A^\perp \parallel B$ is never negative if A is non-empty, thus we replace it with a negative version. Here we describe only a restricted case of the general construction in [5], which is however sufficient for the types of $\mathcal{R}$-IPA. If A, B are negative arenas and B is **well-opened**, *i.e.* it has exactly one minimal event b, we form $A \multimap B$ as having all components as in $A^\perp \parallel B$, with additional dependencies $\{((2,b),(1,a)) \mid a \in A\}$.

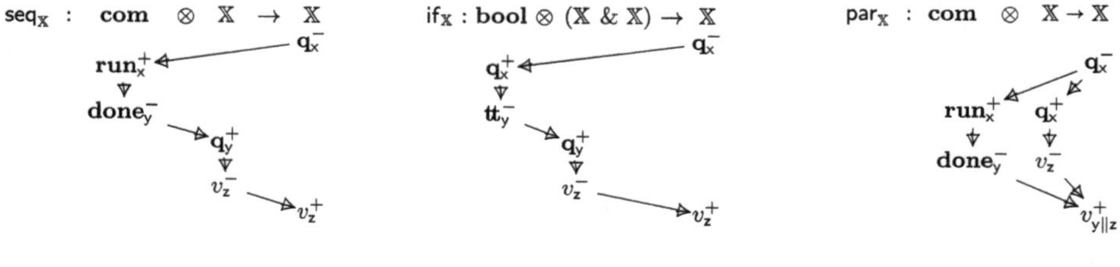

Fig. 13. Maximal $\mathcal{R}$-augmentations of $\mathcal{R}$-strategies used in the interpretation

Using the compact closed structure of $\mathcal{R}$-Strat it is easy to build a copycat $\mathcal{R}$-strategy $\mathsf{ev}_{A,B} : (A \multimap B) \otimes A \twoheadrightarrow B$, and to associate to any $\sigma : C \otimes A \twoheadrightarrow B$ some $\Lambda(\sigma) : C \twoheadrightarrow A \multimap B$ providing the monoidal closure. The cartesian product of A and B is $A \& B$ with components the same as $A \parallel B$, except for $(1,a) \# (2,b)$ for all $a \in A, b \in B$. We write $\pi_i : A_1 \& A_2 \twoheadrightarrow A_i$ for the projections, and $\langle \sigma, \tau \rangle : A \twoheadrightarrow B \& C$ for the pairing of $\sigma : A \twoheadrightarrow B$, and $\tau : A \twoheadrightarrow C$.

Interpretation of $\mathcal{R}$-IPA. We set $[\![\mathbf{com}]\!] = \mathbf{run}^- \rightarrow \mathbf{done}^+$, $[\![\mathbf{bool}]\!]$ as in the right-hand side of Fig. 9, $[\![\mathbf{mem}_W]\!]$ and $[\![\mathbf{mem}_R]\!]$ as in Fig. 10, and $[\![A \multimap B]\!] = [\![A]\!] \multimap [\![B]\!]$ as expected. Contexts $\Gamma = x_1 : A_1, \ldots, x_n : A_n$ are interpreted as $[\![\Gamma]\!] = \otimes_{1 \leq i \leq n} [\![A_i]\!]$. Terms $\Gamma \vdash M : A$ are interpreted as $[\![t]\!] : [\![\Gamma]\!] \nrightarrow [\![A]\!]$ as follows: $[\![\bot]\!]$ is the diverging $\mathcal{R}$-strategy (no player move), $[\![\mathbf{consume}(\alpha)]\!]$ has only maximal $\mathcal{R}$-augmentation $\mathbf{run}_{\mathsf{x}}^- \rightarrow \mathbf{done}_{\mathsf{x};\alpha}^+$, $[\![\mathbf{skip}]\!]$ is $[\![\mathbf{consume}(0)]\!]$, and $\mathbf{tt}$ and $\mathbf{ff}$ are interpreted similarly with the adequate constant $\mathcal{R}$-strategies. The rest of the interpretation is given on the left, using the two obvious isos $\mathsf{deref} : [\![\mathbf{mem}_R]\!] \nrightarrow [\![\mathbf{bool}]\!]$ and $\mathsf{assign} : [\![\mathbf{mem}_W]\!] \nrightarrow [\![\mathbf{com}]\!]$; the $\mathcal{R}$-strategy cell introduced in Fig. 11; and additional $\mathcal{R}$-strategies with typical $\mathcal{R}$-augmentations in Fig. 13. We omit the (standard) clauses for the λ-calculus.

$$[\![M; N : \mathbb{X}]\!] = \mathsf{seq}_{\mathbb{X}} \odot ([\![M]\!] \otimes [\![N]\!])$$

$$[\![M \parallel N : \mathbb{X}]\!] = \mathsf{par}_{\mathbb{X}} \odot ([\![M]\!] \otimes [\![N]\!])$$

$$[\![\mathbf{if}\, M\, N_1\, N_2 : \mathbb{X}]\!] = \mathsf{if}_{\mathbb{X}} \odot ([\![M]\!] \otimes \langle [\![N_1]\!], [\![N_2]\!] \rangle)$$

$$[\![!M : \mathbf{bool}]\!] = \mathsf{deref} \odot [\![M]\!]$$

$$[\![M := \mathbf{tt} : \mathbf{com}]\!] = \mathsf{assign} \odot [\![M]\!]$$

$$[\![\mathbf{new}\, x, y\, \mathbf{in}\, M : \mathbb{X}]\!] = [\![M]\!] \odot ([\![\Gamma]\!] \otimes \mathsf{cell})$$

3.3 Soundness

Now that we have defined the game semantics of $\mathcal{R}$-IPA, we set to prove that it is sound with respect to the operational semantics given in Sect. 2.2.

We first introduce a useful notation. For any type A, $[\![A]\!]$ has a unique minimal event; write $(\!|A|\!)$ for the arena without this minimal event. Likewise, if $\Gamma \vdash M : A$, then by construction, $[\![M]\!] : [\![\Gamma]\!]^\perp \parallel [\![A]\!]$ is a negative $\mathcal{R}$-strategy whose augmentations all share the same minimal event $\mathbf{q}_{\mathsf{x}}^-$ where $\mathbf{q}^-$ is minimal in A. For $\alpha \in \mathcal{R}$, write $(\!|M|\!)_\alpha$ for $[\![M]\!]$ without $\mathbf{q}_{\mathsf{x}}^-$, with x replaced by α. Then we have $(\!|M|\!)_\alpha : [\![\Gamma]\!]^\perp \parallel (\!|A|\!)$ – one may think of $(\!|M|\!)_\alpha$ as "M started with consumed resource α".

Naively, one may expect soundness to state that for all $\vdash M : \mathbf{com}$, if $M \Downarrow_\alpha$, then $(\!|M|\!)_0 = \mathbf{done}_\alpha^+$. However, whereas the resource annotations in the semantics are always as good as permitted by the causal constraints, derivations in the operational semantics may be sub-optimal. For instance, we may derive $M \Downarrow_\alpha$ not using the parallel rule at all. So our statement is:

Theorem 1. *If* $\vdash M : \mathbf{com}$ *with* $M \Downarrow_\alpha$, *there is* $\beta \leq_{\mathcal{R}} \alpha$ s.t. $(\!|M|\!)_0 = \mathbf{done}_\beta^+$.

Our proof methodology is standard: we replay operational derivations as augmentations in the denotational semantics. Stating the invariant successfully proved by induction on operational derivations requires some technology.

If s is a store, then write $\mathsf{cell}_s : [\![\Omega(s)]\!]$ for the memory strategy for store s. It is defined as $\otimes_{\ell \in \mathrm{dom}(s)} \mathsf{cell}_{s(\ell)}$ where $\mathsf{cell}_\varepsilon = \mathsf{cell}$, cell_{R^α} is the $\mathcal{R}$-strategy with only maximal $\mathcal{R}$-augmentation $\mathbf{wtt}_{\mathsf{x}}^- \rightarrow \mathbf{ok}_{\mathsf{x}\parallel\alpha}^+$, cell_{W^α} has maximal $\mathcal{R}$-augmentation $\mathbf{r}_{\mathsf{y}}^- \rightarrow \mathbf{tt}_{\alpha\parallel\mathsf{y}}^+$, and the empty $\mathcal{R}$-strategy for the other cases. If $s \leq_{\mathsf{M}} s'$, then

s' can be obtained from s using memory operations and there is a matching $\mathcal{R}$-augmentation $\mathbb{q}_{s \triangleright s'} \in \mathsf{cell}_s$ defined location-wise in the obvious way.

Now, if $\sigma : [\![\Omega(s)]\!]^\perp \parallel (\!|A|\!)$ is a $\mathcal{R}$-strategy and $\mathbb{q} \in \sigma$ with moves only in $[\![\Omega(s)]\!]^\perp$ is causally compatible with $\mathbb{q}_{s \triangleright s'}$, we define the **residual** of σ after $\mathbb{q}$:

$$\sigma/(\mathbb{q} \circledast \mathbb{q}_{s \triangleright s'}) : [\![\Omega(s')]\!]^\perp \parallel (\!|A|\!)$$

If $\mathbb{p} \in \sigma$ with $\mathbb{q} \hookrightarrow \mathbb{p}$, we write first $\mathbb{p}' = \mathbb{p}/(\mathbb{q} \circledast \mathbb{q}_{s \triangleright s'})$ the $\mathcal{R}$-augmentation with $|\mathbb{p}'| = |\mathbb{p}| \setminus |\mathbb{q}|$, and with causal order the restriction of that of $\mathbb{p}$. For $e \in |\mathbb{p}'|$, we set $\lambda_{\mathbb{p}'}(e)$ to be $\lambda_{\mathbb{p}}(e)$ whose arguments corresponding to negative events e' in $\mathbb{q}$ are instantiated with $\lambda_{\mathbb{q} \circledast \mathbb{q}_{s \triangleright s'}}(e') \in \mathcal{R}$. With that, we set $\sigma/(\mathbb{q} \circledast \mathbb{q}_{s \triangleright s'})$ as comprising all $\mathbb{p}/(\mathbb{q} \circledast \mathbb{q}_{s \triangleright s'})$ for $\mathbb{p} \in \sigma$ with $\mathbb{q} \hookrightarrow \mathbb{p}$.

Informally, this means that, considering some $\mathbb{q}$ which represents a scheduling of the memory operations turning s into s', we extract from σ its behavior after the execution of these memory operations. Finally, we generalize $\leq_{\mathcal{R}}$ to $\mathcal{R}$-augmentations by setting $\mathbb{q} \leq_{\mathcal{R}} \mathbb{q}'$ iff they have the same underlying partial order and for all $e \in |\mathbb{q}|$, $\lambda_{\mathbb{q}}(e) \leq_{\mathcal{R}} \lambda_{\mathbb{q}'}(e)$. With that, we can finally state:

Lemma 1. *Let* $\Omega(s) \vdash M : A$, $\langle M, s_1, \alpha\rangle \rightrightarrows \langle M', s_1' \uplus s_2', \alpha'\rangle$ *with* $\mathrm{dom}(s_1) = \mathrm{dom}(s_1')$, *and all resource annotations in* s_1 *lower than* α. *Then, there is* $\mathbb{q} \in (\!|M|\!)_\alpha$ *with events in* $[\![\Omega(s)]\!]$, *causally compatible with* $\mathbb{q}_{s_1 \triangleright s_1'}$, *and a function*

$$\varphi : (\!|M'|\!)_{\alpha'} \circledast \mathsf{cell}_{s_2'} \quad \longrightarrow \quad (\!|M|\!)_\alpha/(\mathbb{q} \circledast \mathbb{q}_{s_1 \triangleright s_1'})$$

preserving $\hookrightarrow$ *and* s.t. *for all* $\mathbb{p} \circledast \mathbb{q}_{s_2'} \in (\!|M'|\!)_{\alpha'} \circledast \mathsf{cell}_{s_2'}$, $\varphi(\mathbb{p} \circledast \mathbb{q}_{s_2'}) \leq_{\mathcal{R}} \mathbb{p} \odot \mathbb{q}_{s_2'}$.

This is proved by induction on the operational semantics – the critical cases are: assignment and dereferenciation exploiting that if $\alpha \leq_{\mathcal{R}} \beta$, then $\alpha \parallel \beta = \beta$ (which boils down to idempotence); and parallel composition where compatibility of s' and s'' entails that the corresponding augmentations of cell_s are compatible.

Lemma 1, instantiated with $\langle M, \emptyset, 0\rangle \rightrightarrows \langle \mathbf{skip}, s, \alpha\rangle$, yields soundness.

Non-adequacy. Our model is not adequate. To see why, consider:

$$\vdash \mathbf{new}\, x_W, x_R\, \mathbf{in} \left(\begin{array}{r} \mathbf{wait}(1); \\ x_W := \mathtt{tt}; \\ \mathbf{wait}(2) \end{array} \middle\| \begin{array}{l} \mathbf{wait}(2); \\ !x_R; \\ \mathbf{wait}(1) \end{array} \right) : \mathbf{bool}$$

Our model predicts that this may evaluate to $\mathtt{tt}$ in 3 s (see Fig. 12) and to $\mathtt{ff}$ in 4 s. However, the operational semantics can only evaluate it (both to $\mathtt{tt}$ and $\mathtt{ff}$) in 4 s. Intuitively, the reason is that the causal shapes implicit in the reduction $\rightrightarrows$ are all series-parallel (generated with sequential and parallel composition), whereas the interaction in Fig. 12 is not.

Our causal semantic approach yields a finer resource analysis than achieved by the parallel operational semantics. The operational semantics, rather than our model, is to blame for non-adequacy: indeed, we now show that for $\mathcal{R} = \mathbb{R}_+$ our model is adequate *w.r.t.* an operational semantics specialized for time.

4 Adequacy for Time

For time, we may refine the operational semantics by adding the following rule

$$\langle \mathbf{wait}(t_1 + t_2), s, t_0 \rangle \to \langle \mathbf{wait}(t_2), s, t_0 + t_1 \rangle$$

using which the program above evaluates to $\mathbf{tt}$ in 3 s. It is clear that the soundness theorem of the previous section is retained.

We first focus on adequacy for first-order programs without abstraction or application, written $\Omega(s) \vdash_1 M : \mathbf{com}$. For any $t_0 \in \mathbb{R}_+$ there is $\langle M, s, t_0 \rangle \rightrightarrows \langle M', s \uplus s', t_0 \rangle$ where $(\!|M|\!)_{t_0} = (\!|M'|\!)_{t_0} \odot \mathsf{cell}_{s'}$ and M' is in **canonical form**: it cannot be decomposed as $C[\mathbf{skip}; N]$, $C[\mathbf{skip} \parallel N]$, $C[N \parallel \mathbf{skip}]$, $C[\mathbf{if}\,\mathbf{tt}\, N_1\, N_2]$, $C[\mathbf{if}\,\mathbf{ff}\, N_1\, N_2]$, $C[\mathbf{wait}(0)]$ and $C[\mathbf{new}\, x, y\, \mathbf{in}\, N]$ for $C[]$ an evaluation context.

Consider $\Omega(s) \vdash_1 M : \mathbf{com}$, and $\mathfrak{q} \in (\!|M|\!)_{t_0} \circledast \mathsf{cell}_s$ with a top element $\mathbf{done}^+_{t_\mathsf{f}}$ in $(\!|\mathbf{com}|\!)$, the **result** – *i.e.* $\mathfrak{q}$ describes an interaction between $(\!|M|\!)_{t_0}$ and the memory leading to a successful evaluation to **done** at time t_f. To prove adequacy, we must extract from it a derivation from $\langle M, s, t_0 \rangle$, at time t_f.

Apart from the top $\mathbf{done}^+_{t_\mathsf{f}}$, $\mathfrak{q}$ only records memory operations, which we must replicate operationally in the adequate order. A **minimal operation with timing** t is either the top $\mathbf{done}^+_t$ if it is the only event in $\mathfrak{q}$, or a prefix $(m_t \twoheadrightarrow n_t) \hookrightarrow \mathfrak{q}$ corresponding to a memory operation (for instance, in augmentations of Fig. 14, the only minimal operation has timing 2). If $t = t_0$, this operation should be performed immediately. If $t > t_0$ we need to spend time to trigger it – it is then critical to spend time on *all available* **wait***s in parallel*:

Lemma 2. *For* $\Omega(s) \vdash_1 M : \mathbf{com}$ *in canonical form,* $t_0 \in \mathbb{R}_+$, $\mathfrak{q} \in (\!|M|\!)_{t_0} \circledast \mathsf{cell}_s$ *with result* $\mathbf{done}^+_{t_\mathsf{f}}$, *if all minimal operations have timing strictly greater than* t_0,

$$\langle M, s, t_0 \rangle \rightrightarrows \langle M', s, t_0 + t \rangle$$

for some $t > 0$ *and* M' *only differing from* M *by having smaller annotations in* **wait** *commands and at least one* **wait** *changed to* **skip**.

Furthermore, there is $\mathfrak{q} \leq_{\mathcal{R}} \mathfrak{q}'$ *with* $\mathfrak{q}' \in (\!|M'|\!)_{t_0+t} \circledast \mathsf{cell}_s$ *with result* $\mathbf{done}^+_{t_\mathsf{f}}$.

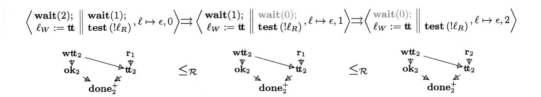

$$\left\langle \begin{array}{l}\mathbf{wait}(2);\\ \ell_W := \mathbf{tt}\end{array} \middle\| \begin{array}{l}\mathbf{wait}(1);\\ \mathbf{test}\,(!\ell_R)\end{array}, \ell \mapsto \epsilon, 0 \right\rangle \rightrightarrows \left\langle \begin{array}{l}\mathbf{wait}(1);\\ \ell_W := \mathbf{tt}\end{array} \middle\| \begin{array}{l}\mathbf{wait}(0);\\ \mathbf{test}\,(!\ell_R)\end{array}, \ell \mapsto \epsilon, 1 \right\rangle \rightrightarrows \left\langle \begin{array}{l}\mathbf{wait}(0);\\ \ell_W := \mathbf{tt}\end{array} \middle\| \mathbf{test}\,(!\ell_R), \ell \mapsto \epsilon, 2 \right\rangle$$

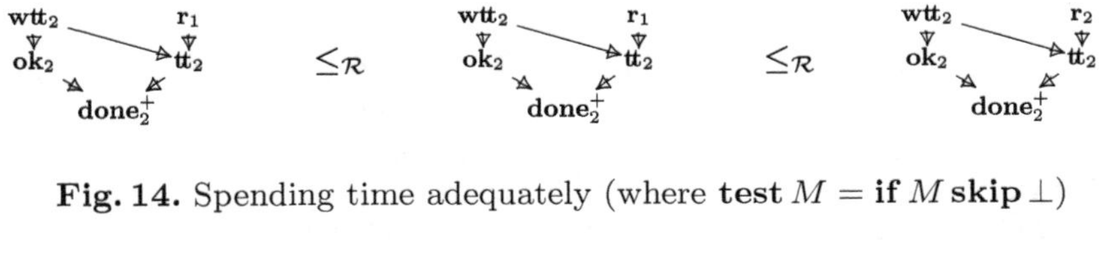

Fig. 14. Spending time adequately (where $\mathbf{test}\, M = \mathbf{if}\, M\, \mathbf{skip}\, \bot$)

Proof. As M is in canonical form, all delays in minimal operations are impacted by $\mathbf{wait}(t)$ commands in head position (*i.e.* such that $M = C[\mathbf{wait}(t)]$). Let $t_{\min}$ be the minimal time appearing in those $\mathbf{wait}(-)$ commands in head position. Using our new rule and parallel composition, we remove $t_{\min}$ to all such instances of $\mathbf{wait}(-)$; then transform the resulting occurrences of $\mathbf{wait}(0)$ to $\mathbf{skip}$.

A representative example is displayed in Fig. 14. In the second step, though $!\ell_R$ is available immediately, we must wait to get the right result.

With that we can prove the key lemma towards adequacy.

Lemma 3. *Let* $\Omega(s) \vdash_1 M : \mathbf{com}$, $t_0 \in \mathbb{R}_+$, *and* $\mathbb{q} \in (\!|M|\!)_{t_0} \circledast \mathsf{cell}_s$ *with result* $\mathbf{done}^+_{t_f}$ *in* $(\!|\mathbf{com}|\!)$. *Then, there is* $\langle M, s, t_0\rangle \rightrightarrows \langle \mathbf{skip}, -, t_f\rangle$.

Proof. By induction on the size of M. First, we convert M to canonical form. If all minimal operations in $\mathbb{q} \in (\!|M|\!)_{t_0}$ have timing strictly greater than t_0, we apply Lemma 2 and conclude by induction hypothesis.

Otherwise, at least one minimal operation has timing t_0. If it is the result $\mathbf{done}^+_{t_0}$ in $(\!|\mathbb{X}|\!)$, then M is the constant $\mathbf{skip}$. Otherwise, it is a memory operation, say $\mathbb{p} \hookrightarrow \mathbb{q}$ with $\mathbb{p} = (\mathbf{r}_{t_0} \twoheadrightarrow b_{t_0})$ and write also $s' = s[\ell \mapsto s(\ell).R^{t_0}]$. It follows then by an induction on M that $M = C[!\ell_R]$ for some $C[]$, with

$$\mathbb{q}/(\mathbb{p} \circledast \mathbb{q}_{s \rhd s'}) \in (\!|C[b]|\!)_{t_0} \circledast \mathsf{cell}_s$$

so $\langle M, s, t_0\rangle \rightrightarrows \langle C[b], s', t_0\rangle \rightrightarrows \langle \mathbf{skip}, -, t_f\rangle$ by induction hypothesis.

Adequacy follows for higher-order programs: in general, any $\vdash M : \mathbf{com}$ can be β-reduced to first-order M', leaving the interpretation unchanged. By Church-Rosser, M' behaves like M operationally, up to weak bisimulation. Hence:

Theorem 2. *Let* $\vdash M : \mathbf{com}$. *For any* $t \in \mathbb{R}_+$, *if* $\mathbf{done}^+_t \in (\!|M|\!)_0$ *then* $M \Downarrow_t$.

5 Conclusion

It would be interesting to compare our model with structures used in timing analysis, for instance [23] relies on a concurrent generalization of control flow graphs that is reminiscent of event structures. In future work we also plan to investigate whether our annotated model construction could be used for other purposes, such as symbolic execution or abstract interpretation.

References

1. Abramsky, S., Jagadeesan, R., Malacaria, P.: Full abstraction for PCF. Inf. Comput. **163**(2), 409–470 (2000). https://doi.org/10.1006/inco.2000.2930
2. Abramsky, S., Melliès, P.: Concurrent games and full completeness. In: 14th Annual IEEE Symposium on Logic in Computer Science, Trento, Italy, 2–5 July 1999, pp. 431–442 (1999). https://doi.org/10.1109/LICS.1999.782638

3. Alcolei, A., Clairambault, P., Hyland, M., Winskel, G.: The true concurrency of Herbrand's theorem. In: 27th EACSL Annual Conference on Computer Science Logic, CSL 2018, Birmingham, UK, 4–7 September 2018, pp. 5:1–5:22 (2018). https://doi.org/10.4230/LIPIcs.CSL.2018.5
4. Brunel, A., Gaboardi, M., Mazza, D., Zdancewic, S.: A core quantitative coeffect calculus. In: Shao, Z. (ed.) ESOP 2014. LNCS, vol. 8410, pp. 351–370. Springer, Heidelberg (2014). https://doi.org/10.1007/978-3-642-54833-8_19
5. Castellan, S., Clairambault, P.: Causality vs. interleavings in concurrent game semantics. In: Desharnais, J., Jagadeesan, R. (eds.) 27th International Conference on Concurrency Theory, CONCUR 2016, Québec City, Canada, 23–26 August 2016. LIPIcs, vol. 59, pp. 32:1–32:14. Schloss Dagstuhl - Leibniz-Zentrum fuer Informatik (2016). https://doi.org/10.4230/LIPIcs.CONCUR.2016.32
6. Castellan, S., Clairambault, P., Paquet, H., Winskel, G.: The concurrent game semantics of probabilistic PCF. In: Proceedings of the 33rd Annual ACM/IEEE Symposium on Logic in Computer Science, LICS 2018, Oxford, UK, 09–12 July 2018, pp. 215–224 (2018). https://doi.org/10.1145/3209108.3209187
7. Castellan, S., Clairambault, P., Rideau, S., Winskel, G.: Games and strategies as event structures. Logical Methods Comput. Sci. **13**(3) (2017). https://doi.org/10.23638/LMCS-13(3:35)2017
8. Castellan, S., Clairambault, P., Winskel, G.: The parallel intensionally fully abstract games model of PCF. In: 30th Annual ACM/IEEE Symposium on Logic in Computer Science, LICS 2015, Kyoto, Japan, 6–10 July 2015, pp. 232–243 (2015). https://doi.org/10.1109/LICS.2015.31
9. Castellan, S., Clairambault, P., Winskel, G.: Thin games with symmetry and concurrent hyland-ong games. Logical Methods Comput. Sci. (to appear, 2019)
10. Clairambault, P., de Visme, M., Winskel, G.: Game semantics for quantum programming. PACMPL **3**(POPL), 32:1–32:29 (2019). https://doi.org/10.1145/3290345
11. Ehrhard, T.: The Scott model of linear logic is the extensional collapse of its relational model. Theor. Comput. Sci. **424**, 20–45 (2012). https://doi.org/10.1016/j.tcs.2011.11.027
12. Faggian, C., Piccolo, M.: Partial orders, event structures and linear strategies. In: Curien, P.-L. (ed.) TLCA 2009. LNCS, vol. 5608, pp. 95–111. Springer, Heidelberg (2009). https://doi.org/10.1007/978-3-642-02273-9_9
13. Ghica, D.R.: Slot games: a quantitative model of computation. In: Proceedings of the 32nd ACM SIGPLAN-SIGACT Symposium on Principles of Programming Languages, POPL 2005, Long Beach, California, USA, 12–14 January 2005, pp. 85–97 (2005). https://doi.org/10.1145/1040305.1040313
14. Ghica, D.R., Murawski, A.S.: Angelic semantics of fine-grained concurrency. Ann. Pure Appl. Logic **151**(2–3), 89–114 (2008). https://doi.org/10.1016/j.apal.2007.10.005
15. Ghica, D.R., Smith, A.I.: Bounded linear types in a resource semiring. In: Shao, Z. (ed.) ESOP 2014. LNCS, vol. 8410, pp. 331–350. Springer, Heidelberg (2014). https://doi.org/10.1007/978-3-642-54833-8_18
16. Hoare, T., Möller, B., Struth, G., Wehrman, I.: Concurrent Kleene algebra and its foundations. J. Log. Algebr. Program. **80**(6), 266–296 (2011). https://doi.org/10.1016/j.jlap.2011.04.005
17. Hyland, J.M.E., Ong, C.L.: On full abstraction for PCF: I, II, and III. Inf. Comput. **163**(2), 285–408 (2000). https://doi.org/10.1006/inco.2000.2917

18. Laird, J., Manzonetto, G., McCusker, G., Pagani, M.: Weighted relational models of typed lambda-calculi. In: 28th Annual ACM/IEEE Symposium on Logic in Computer Science (LICS), New Orleans, USA, Proceedings, pp. 301–310 (2013)
19. Laurent, O.: Game semantics for first-order logic. Logical Methods Comput. Sci. **6**(4) (2010). https://doi.org/10.2168/LMCS-6(4:3)2010
20. Melliès, P.: Asynchronous games 4: a fully complete model of propositional linear logic. In: 20th IEEE Symposium on Logic in Computer Science (LICS 2005), Chicago, IL, USA, 26–29 June 2005, Proceedings, pp. 386–395 (2005). https://doi.org/10.1109/LICS.2005.6
21. Melliès, P.: Game semantics in string diagrams. In: Proceedings of the 27th Annual IEEE Symposium on Logic in Computer Science, LICS 2012, Dubrovnik, Croatia, 25–28 June 2012, pp. 481–490 (2012). https://doi.org/10.1109/LICS.2012.58
22. Melliès, P.-A., Mimram, S.: Asynchronous games: innocence without alternation. In: Caires, L., Vasconcelos, V.T. (eds.) CONCUR 2007. LNCS, vol. 4703, pp. 395–411. Springer, Heidelberg (2007). https://doi.org/10.1007/978-3-540-74407-8_27
23. Mittermayr, R., Blieberger, J.: Timing analysis of concurrent programs. In: Vardanega, T. (ed.) 12th International Workshop on Worst-Case Execution Time Analysis, WCET 2012, Pisa, Italy, 10 July 2012. OASICS, vol. 23, pp. 59–68. Schloss Dagstuhl - Leibniz-Zentrum fuer Informatik (2012). https://doi.org/10.4230/OASIcs.WCET.2012.59
24. Plotkin, G.D.: Post-graduate lecture notes in advanced domain theory (incorporating the "Pisa notes"). Department of Computer Science, University of Edinburgh (1981)
25. Rideau, S., Winskel, G.: Concurrent strategies. In: Proceedings of the 26th Annual IEEE Symposium on Logic in Computer Science, LICS 2011, Toronto, Ontario, Canada, 21–24 June 2011, pp. 409–418 (2011). https://doi.org/10.1109/LICS.2011.13
26. Sands, D.: Operational theories of improvement in functional languages (extended abstract). In: Heldal, R., Holst, C.K., Wadler, P. (eds.) Functional Programming, Glasgow 1991, pp. 298–311. Springer, London (1991). https://doi.org/10.1007/978-1-4471-3196-0_24
27. Winskel, G.: Event structures. In: Brauer, W., Reisig, W., Rozenberg, G. (eds.) ACPN 1986. LNCS, vol. 255, pp. 325–392. Springer, Heidelberg (1987). https://doi.org/10.1007/3-540-17906-2_31

9

Languages Ordered by the Subword Order

Dietrich Kuske[1(✉)] and Georg Zetzsche[2]

[1] Technische Universität Ilmenau, Ilmenau, Germany
dietrich.kuske@tu-ilmenau.de
[2] Max Planck Institute for Software Systems (MPI-SWS), Kaiserslautern, Germany
georg@mpi-sws.org

Abstract. We consider a language together with the subword relation, the cover relation, and regular predicates. For such structures, we consider the extension of first-order logic by threshold- and modulo-counting quantifiers. Depending on the language, the used predicates, and the fragment of the logic, we determine four new combinations that yield decidable theories. These results extend earlier ones where only the language of all words without the cover relation and fragments of first-order logic were considered.

Keywords: Subword order · First-order logic · Counting quantifiers · Decidable theories

1 Introduction

The subword relation (sometimes called scattered subword relation) is a simple example of a well-quasi ordering [7]. This property allows its prominent use in the verification of infinite-state systems [4]. The subword relation can be understood as embeddability of one word into another. This embeddability relation has been considered for other classes of structures like trees, posets, semilattices, lattices, graphs etc. [8–11,14–16,22,23].

We are interested in logics over the subword order. Prior work on this has concentrated on first-order logic where the universe consists of all words over some alphabet. In this setting, we already have a rather precise picture about the border between decidability and undecidability: For the subword order alone, the $\exists^*$-theory is decidable [17] and the $\exists^*\forall^*$-theory is undecidable [6,12]. If we add constants to the signature, already the $\exists^*$-theory becomes undecidable [6]. With regular predicates, the two-variable theory is decidable, but the three-variable theory is undecidable [12].

Thus, the decidable theories identified so far leave little room to express natural properties. First, the universe is confined to the set of all words and

Part of the results were obtained when the second author was affiliated with the Laboratoire Spécification et Vérification (ENS Paris-Saclay) and supported by a fellowship within the Postdoc-Program of the German Academic Exchange Service (DAAD) and by Labex DigiCosme, Université Paris-Saclay, project VERICONISS.

predicates for subsets quickly incur undecidability. Moreover, neither in the $\exists^*$-, nor in the two-variable fragment of first-order logic, one can express the cover relation $\sqsubset\!\!\cdot$ (i.e., "u is a proper subword of v and there is no word properly between these two"). As another example, one cannot express threshold properties like "there are at most k subwords with a given property" in any of these two logics.

In this paper, we aim to identify decidable logics that are more expressive. To that end, we consider four additions to the expressivity of the logic:

- Instead of all words over some alphabet, the universe is a language L.
- We add regular predicates or constants to the structure.
- Besides the subword order, we also consider the cover relation $\sqsubset\!\!\cdot$.
- We add threshold and modulo counting quantifiers to the logic.

Formally, this means we consider structures of the form

$$(L, \sqsubseteq, \sqsubset\!\!\cdot, (K \cap L)_{K \text{ regular}}, (w)_{w \in L}),$$

where the universe is a language $L \subseteq \Sigma^*$, $\sqsubseteq$ is the subword ordering, $\sqsubset\!\!\cdot$ is the cover relation, there is a predicate $K \cap L$ for each regular $K \subseteq \Sigma^*$, and a constant symbol for each $w \in L$. Moreover, we consider fragments of the logic C+MOD, which extends first-order logic by threshold- and modulo-counting quantifiers.

The key idea of this paper is to find decidable theories by varying the universe L and thereby either (i) simplify the structure $(L, \sqsubseteq)$ enough to obtain decidability even with the extensions above or (ii) generalize existing results that currently only apply to $L = \Sigma^*$. This leads to the following results.

1. First, we require L to be bounded. This means, we have $L \subseteq w_1^* \cdots w_m^*$ for some words $w_1, \ldots, w_m \in \Sigma^*$. Then, as soon as L is context-free, the C+MOD-theory of the whole structure is decidable (Theorem 3.4).
2. To lift the boundedness restriction, we show that if L is regular, we still obtain decidability for the whole structure if we stay within the two-variable fragment C+MOD^2 (Corollary 4.8). This generalizes the decidability of the FO^2-theory without the cover relation as shown in [12, Theorem 5.5].
3. Moreover, we consider a regular universe, but lift the two-variable requirement. To get decidability, we restrict quantifiers and available predicates: We show that for regular L, the Σ_1-theory of the structure $(L, \sqsubseteq)$ is decidable (Theorem 5.1). In the case $L = \Sigma^*$, this had been shown in [17, Prop. 2.2].
4. Finally, we place a further restriction on L, but in return obtain decidability with constants. We show that if L is regular and every letter is "frequent" in L (see Sect. 6), then the Σ_1-theory of the structure $(L, \sqsubseteq, (w)_{w \in L})$ is decidable (Theorem 6.2). Note that, by [6, Theorem 3.3], this theory is undecidable if $L = \Sigma^*$.

Our first result is shown by a first-order interpretation of the structure in $(\mathbb{N}, +)$. Since $L \subseteq w_1^* \cdots w_n^*$, instead of words, one can argue about vectors $(x_1, \ldots, x_n) \in \mathbb{N}^n$ for which $w_1^{x_1} \cdots w_n^{x_n} \in L$. For the interpretation, we use the fact that semilinearity of context-free languages yields a Presburger formula expressing $w_1^{x_1} \cdots w_n^{x_n} \in L$ for $(x_1, \ldots, x_n) \in \mathbb{N}^n$. Moreover, Presburger definability of $w_1^{x_1} \cdots w_n^{x_n} \sqsubseteq w_1^{y_1} \cdots w_n^{y_n}$ for $(x_1, \ldots, x_n) \in \mathbb{N}^n$ and $(y_1, \ldots, y_n) \in \mathbb{N}^n$ is a simple consequence of the subword relation being rational, which was observed in [12]. The first-order interpretation of our structure in $(\mathbb{N}, +)$ then enables us to employ decidability of the C+MOD-theory of the latter structure [1,5,21]. (Note that this decidability does not follow directly from Presburger's result since in first-order logic, one cannot make statements like "the number of witnesses $x \in \mathbb{N}$ satisfying ... is even"). A similar interpretation in $(\mathbb{N}, +)$ was used in [6] for various algorithms concerning $(\Sigma^*, \sqsubseteq, (w)_{w \in \Sigma^*})$ for fragments of FO related to bounded languages.

Our second result extends an approach from [12] for decidability of the FO^2-theory of the structure $(\Sigma^*, \sqsubseteq, (L)_{L \text{ regular}})$. The authors of [12] provide a quantifier elimination procedure showing that every unary relation FO^2-definable in this structure is regular. Our extended quantifier-elimination procedure uses the same invariant, now relying on the following two properties:

- The class of regular languages is closed under *counting* images under *unambiguous* rational relations.
  This can be shown either directly or (as we do here) using weighted automata [20].
- The proper subword, the cover, and the incomparability relation are *unambiguous* rational.

Our third result extends the decidability of the Σ_1-theory of $(\Sigma^*, \sqsubseteq)$ from [17]. In [17], decidability is a consequence of the fact that every finite partial order can be embedded into $(\Sigma^*, \sqsubseteq)$ if $|\Sigma| \geq 2$. This certainly fails for general regular languages: $(a^*, \sqsubseteq)$ can only accomodate linear orders. However, we can distinguish two cases: If L is a bounded language, then decidability of the Σ_1-theory of $(L, \sqsubseteq)$ follows from our first result. If L is not bounded, then we show that again every finite partial order embeds into $(L, \sqsubseteq)$. To this end, we first extend a well-known property of unbounded regular languages, namely that there are $x, u, v, y \in \Sigma^*$ with $x\{u, v\}^*y \subseteq L$ such that $|u| = |v|$ and $u \neq v$. We show that here, u, v can be chosen so that uv is a primitive word. We then observe that for large enough n, any embedding of the word $(uv)^{n-1}$ into $(uv)^n$ must hit either the left-most position or the right-most position in $(uv)^n$. This enables us to argue that for large enough n, sending a tuple $(t_1, \ldots, t_m) \in \{0,1\}^m$ to $xv^{t_1}(uv)^n \cdots v^{t_m}(uv)^n y$ is in fact an embedding of $(\{0,1\}^m, \leq)$ into $(L, \sqsubseteq)$, where $\leq$ denotes coordinate-wise comparison. Since any partial order with $\leq m$ elements embeds into $(\{0,1\}^m, \leq)$, this completes the proof.

Regarding our fourth result, we know from [6] that decidability of the Σ_1-theory of $(L, \sqsubseteq, (w)_{w \in L})$ does not hold for every regular L: Undecidability holds already for $L = \{a, b\}^*$. Therefore, we require that every letter is frequent in L, meaning that in some automaton for L, every letter occurs in every cycle. In case L is bounded, we can again invoke our first result. If L is not bounded, we deduce from the frequency condition that for every $w \in \Sigma^*$, there are only finitely many words in L that do not have w as a subword. Removing those finitely many words preserves unboundedness, so that every finite partial order embeds in L above w. We then proceed to show that for such languages, any Σ_1-sentence is effectively equivalent to a sentence where constants are only used to express that all variables take values above a certain word w. Since every finite partial order embeds above w, this implies decidability.

The full version of this work is available as [18].

2 Preliminaries

Throughout this paper, let Σ be some finite alphabet. A word $u = a_1a_2 \dots a_m$ with $a_1, a_2, \dots, a_m \in \Sigma$ is a *subword* of a word $v \in \Sigma^*$ if there are words $v_0, v_1, \dots, v_m \in \Sigma^*$ with $v = v_0a_1v_1a_2v_2 \cdots a_mv_m$. In that case, we write $u \sqsubseteq v$; if, in addition, $u \neq v$, then we write $u \sqsubset v$ and call u a *proper* subword of v. If $u, w \in \Sigma^*$ such that $u \sqsubset w$ and there is no word v with $u \sqsubset v \sqsubset w$, then we say that w is a *cover* of u and write $u \mathrel{\sqsubset\!\!\cdot}\, w$. This is equivalent to saying $u \sqsubseteq w$ and $|u| + 1 = |w|$ where $|u|$ is the length of the word u. If neither u is a subword of v nor *vice versa*, then the words u and v are *incomparable* and we write $u \parallel v$. For instance, $aa \sqsubset babbba$, $aa \mathrel{\sqsubset\!\!\cdot}\, aba$, and $aba \parallel aabb$.

Let $\mathcal{S} = (L, (R_i)_{i\in I}, (w_j)_{j\in J})$ be a *structure*, i.e., L is a set, $R_i \subseteq L^{n_i}$ is a relation of arity n_i (for all $i \in I$), and $w_j \in L$ for all $j \in J$. Then, formulas φ of the logic C+MOD are defined by the following grammar:

$$\varphi ::= (s = t) \mid R_i(s_1, \dots, s_{n_i}) \mid \neg\varphi \mid \varphi \vee \varphi \mid \exists x\, \varphi \mid \exists^{\geq k} x\, \varphi \mid \exists^{p \bmod q} x\, \varphi$$

where $s, t, s_1, \dots, s_{n_i}$ are variables or constants w_j with $j \in J$, $i \in I$, $k \in \mathbb{N}$, and $p, q \in \mathbb{N}$ with $p < q$. We call $\exists^{\geq k}$ a *threshold counting quantifier* and $\exists^{p \bmod q}$ a *modulo counting quantifier*. The semantics of these quantifiers is defined as follows:

- $\mathcal{S} \models \exists^{\geq k} x\, \alpha$ iff $|\{w \in L \mid \mathcal{S} \models \alpha(w)\}| \geq k$
- $\mathcal{S} \models \exists^{p \bmod q} x\, \alpha$ iff $|\{w \in L \mid \mathcal{S} \models \alpha(w)\}| \in p + q\mathbb{N}$

For instance, $\exists^{0 \bmod 2} x\, \alpha$ expresses that the number of elements of the structure satisfying α is even. Then $(\exists^{0 \bmod 2} x\, \alpha) \vee (\exists^{1 \bmod 2} x\, \alpha)$ holds iff only finitely many elements of the structure satisfy α. The fragment FO+MOD of C+MOD comprises all formulas not containing any threshold counting quantifier. First-order logic FO is the set of formulas from C+MOD not mentioning any counting quantifier. Let Σ_1 denote the set of first-order formulas of the form $\exists x_1\, \exists x_2 \dots \exists x_n \colon \psi$ where ψ is quantifier-free; these formulas are also called *existential*.

The threshold quantifier $\exists^{\geq k}$ can be expressed using the existential quantifier, only. Consequently, the logics FO+MOD and C+MOD are equally expressive. The situation changes when we restrict the number of variables that can be used in a formula: Let FO+MOD^2 and C+MOD^2 denote the set of formulas from FO+MOD and C+MOD, respectively, that use the variables x and y, only. Then, the existence of $\geq$3 elements in the structure is expressible in C+MOD^2, but not in FO+MOD^2.

In this paper, we will consider the following structures:

- The largest one is $(L, \sqsubseteq, \sqsubset, (K \cap L)_{K \text{ regular}}, (w)_{w \in L})$ for some $L \subseteq \Sigma^*$. The universe of this structure is the language L, we have two binary predicates ($\sqsubseteq$ and $\sqsubset$), a unary predicate $K \cap L$ for every regular language K, and we can use every word from L as a constant.
- The other extreme is the structure $(L, \sqsubseteq)$ for some $L \subseteq \Sigma^*$ where we consider only the binary predicate $\sqsubseteq$.
- Finally, we will also prove results on the intermediate structure $(L, \sqsubseteq, (w)_{w \in L})$ that has a binary relation and any word from the language as a constant.

For any structure $\mathcal{S}$ and any of the logics $\mathcal{L}$, the *$\mathcal{L}$-theory* of $\mathcal{S}$ is the set of sentences from $\mathcal{L}$ that hold in $\mathcal{S}$.

A non-deterministic finite automaton is called *non-degenerate* if every state lies on a path from an initial to a final state. A language $L \subseteq \Sigma^*$ is *bounded* if there are a number $n \in \mathbb{N}$ and words $w_1, w_2, \ldots, w_n \in \Sigma^*$ such that $L \subseteq w_1^* w_2^* \cdots w_n^*$. Otherwise, it is *unbounded.*

For a monoid M, a subset $S \subseteq M$ is called *rational* if it is a homomorphic image of a regular language. In other words, there exists an alphabet Δ, a regular $R \subseteq \Delta^*$, and a homomorphism $h\colon \Delta^* \to M$ with $S = h(R)$. In particular, if Σ_1, Σ_2 are alphabets and $M = \Sigma_1^* \times \Sigma_2^*$, then a subset $S \subseteq \Sigma_1^* \times \Sigma_2^*$ is rational iff there is an alphabet Δ, a regular $R \subseteq \Delta^*$, and homomorphisms $h_i\colon \Delta^* \to \Sigma_i^*$ with $S = \{(h_1(w), h_2(w)) \mid w \in R\}$. This fact is known as *Nivat's theorem* [2].

For an alphabet Γ, a word $w \in \Gamma^*$, and a letter $a \in \Gamma$, let $|w|_a$ denote the number of occurrences of the letter a in the word w. The *Parikh vector* of w is the tuple $\Psi_\Gamma(w) = (|w|_a)_{a \in \Gamma} \in \mathbb{N}^\Gamma$. Note that Ψ_Γ is a homomorphism from the free monoid Γ^* onto the additive monoid $(\mathbb{N}^\Gamma, +)$.

3 The FO+MOD-Theory with Regular Predicates

The aim of this section is to prove that the full FO+MOD-theory of the structure

$$(L, \sqsubseteq, \sqsubset, (K \cap L)_{K \text{ regular}}, (w)_{w \in L})$$

is decidable for L bounded and context-free. This is achieved by interpreting this structure in $(\mathbb{N}, +)$, i.e., in Presburger arithmetic whose FO+MOD-theory is known to be decidable [1,5,21]. We start with three preparatory lemmas.

Lemma 3.1. *Let $K \subseteq \Sigma^*$ be context-free, $w_1, \ldots, w_n \in \Sigma^*$, and $g\colon \mathbb{N}^n \to \Sigma^*$ be defined by $g(\overline{m}) = w_1^{m_1} w_2^{m_2} \cdots w_n^{m_n}$ for all $\overline{m} = (m_1, m_2, \ldots, m_n) \in \mathbb{N}^n$. The set $g^{-1}(K) = \{\overline{m} \in \mathbb{N}^n \mid g(\overline{m}) \in K\}$ is effectively semilinear.*

Proof. Let $\Gamma = \{a_1, a_2, \ldots, a_n\}$ be an alphabet and define the monoid homomorphism $f\colon \Gamma^* \to \Sigma^*$ by $f(a_i) = w_i$ for all $i \in [1, n]$.

Since the class of context-free languages is effectively closed under inverse homomorphisms and under intersections with regular languages, the language

$$L = f^{-1}(K) \cap a_1^* a_2^* \cdots a_n^* = \{u \in a_1^* a_2^* \cdots a_n^* \mid f(u) \in K\}$$

is effectively context-free. Its Parikh image $\Psi_\Gamma(L) \subseteq \mathbb{N}^n$ is effectively semilinear [19]. Moreover, $\Psi_\Gamma(L)$ equals the set $g^{-1}(K)$ from the lemma. $\square$

Lemma 3.2. *Let $w_1, \dots, w_n \in \Sigma^*$ and $g\colon \mathbb{N}^n \to \Sigma^*$ be defined by $g(\overline{m}) = w_1^{m_1} w_2^{m_2} \cdots w_n^{m_n}$ for all $\overline{m} = (m_1, m_2, \dots, m_n) \in \mathbb{N}^n$. The set $\{(\overline{m}, \overline{n}) \in \mathbb{N}^n \times \mathbb{N}^n \mid g(\overline{m}) \sqsubseteq g(\overline{n})\}$ is semilinear.*

Proof. Let $\Gamma = \{a_1, a_2, \dots, a_n\}$ be an alphabet and define the monoid homomorphism $f\colon \Gamma^* \to \Sigma^*$ by $f(a_i) = w_i$ for all $i \in [1, n]$. One first shows that

$$S_2 = \{(u, v) \mid u, v \in a_1^* a_2^* \dots a_n^*,\ f(v) \sqsubseteq f(v)\}$$

is rational. We now employ Nivat's theorem. It tells us that there are a regular language R over some alphabet Δ and two homomorphisms $h_1, h_2\colon \Delta^* \to \Gamma^*$ so that we can write $S_2 = \{(h_1(w), h_2(w)) \mid w \in R\}$. Since R is regular, its Parikh-image $\Psi_\Delta(R) = \{\Psi_\Delta(w) \mid w \in R\}$ is semilinear [19]. There are monoid homomorphisms $p_1, p_2\colon \mathbb{N}^\Delta \to \mathbb{N}^n$ with $\Psi_\Gamma(h_i(w)) = p_i(\Psi_\Delta(w))$ for all $i \in \{1, 2\}$ and $w \in \Delta^*$. With these, the image $H = \{(p_1(\Psi_\Delta(w)), p_2(\Psi_\Delta(w))) \mid w \in R\}$ of the set $\Psi_\Delta(R)$ under the monoid homomorphism $(p_1, p_2)\colon \mathbb{N}^\Delta \to \mathbb{N}^n \times \mathbb{N}^n$ is semilinear. It turns out that this set equals the set from the lemma. $\square$

Lemma 3.3. *Let $w_1, w_2, \dots, w_n \in \Sigma^*$, $L \subseteq w_1^* w_2^* \cdots w_n^*$ be context-free, and $g\colon \mathbb{N}^n \to \Sigma^*$ be defined by $g(\overline{m}) = w_1^{m_1} w_2^{m_2} \cdots w_n^{m_n}$ for every tuple $\overline{m} = (m_1, m_2, \dots, m_n) \in \mathbb{N}^n$. Then there exists a semilinear set $U \subseteq \mathbb{N}^n$ such that g maps U bijectively onto L.*

Proof. The set U contains, for each $u \in L$, the lexicographically minimal tuple $\overline{m} \in \mathbb{N}^n$ with $g(\overline{m}) = u$. Then, Lemmas 3.1 and 3.2 and the closure of the class of semilinear sets under first-order definitions imply the required properties. $\square$

Now we can prove the main result of this section.

Theorem 3.4. *Let $L \subseteq \Sigma^*$ be context-free and bounded. Then the* FO+MOD*-theory of $(L, \sqsubseteq, \sqsubset\!\!\cdot, (K \cap L)_{K \text{ regular}}, (w)_{w \in L})$ is decidable.*

Proof. It suffices to prove the decidability for the structure $\mathcal{S} = (L, \sqsubseteq, (K \cap L)_{K \text{ regular}})$ since the theory of the structure from the theorem can be reduced to that of $\mathcal{S}$ ($x \sqsubset\!\!\cdot\, y$ gets replaced by its definition and $x\theta w$ by $\exists y\colon y \in \{w\} \wedge x\theta y$ where θ is any binary relation symbol).

Since L is bounded, there are words $w_1, w_2, \dots, w_n \in \Sigma^*$ such that L is included in $w_1^* w_2^* \cdots w_n^*$. For an n-tuple $\overline{m} = (m_1, m_2, \dots, m_n) \in \mathbb{N}^n$ we define $g(\overline{m}) = w_1^{m_1} w_2^{m_2} \cdots w_n^{m_n} \in \Sigma^*$.

1. By Lemma 3.3, there is a semilinear set $U \subseteq \mathbb{N}^n$ that is mapped by g bijectively onto L.
2. The set $\{(\overline{m}, \overline{n}) \mid g(\overline{m}) \sqsubseteq g(\overline{n})\}$ is semilinear by Lemma 3.2.
3. For any regular language $K \subseteq \Sigma^*$ the set $\{\overline{m} \in \mathbb{N}^n \mid g(\overline{m}) \in K\} \subseteq \mathbb{N}^n$ is effectively semilinear by Lemma 3.1.

From these semilinear sets, we obtain first-order formulas $\lambda(\overline{x})$, $\sigma(\overline{x},\overline{y})$, and $\kappa_K(\overline{x})$ in the language of $(\mathbb{N},+)$ such that, for any $\overline{m},\overline{n} \in \mathbb{N}^n$, we have

1. $(\mathbb{N},+) \models \lambda(\overline{m}) \iff \overline{m} \in U$,
2. $(\mathbb{N},+) \models \sigma(\overline{m},\overline{n}) \iff g(\overline{m}) \sqsubseteq g(\overline{n})$, and
3. $(\mathbb{N},+) \models \kappa_K(\overline{m}) \iff g(\overline{m}) \in K$.

One then defines, from an FO+MOD-formula $\varphi(x_1,\dots,x_k)$ in the language of $\mathcal{S}$, an FO+MOD-formula $\varphi'(\overline{x_1},\dots,\overline{x_k})$ in the language of $(\mathbb{N},+)$ such that

$$(\mathbb{N},+) \models \varphi'(\overline{m_1},\dots,\overline{m_k}) \iff \mathcal{S} \models \varphi(g(\overline{m_1}),\dots,g(\overline{m_k})).$$

(This construction can be found in the full version [18] and increases the formula size at least exponentially.)

Consequently, any sentence φ from FO+MOD in the language of $\mathcal{S}$ is translated into an equivalent sentence φ' in the language of $(\mathbb{N},+)$. By [1,5,21], validity of the sentence φ' in $(\mathbb{N},+)$ is decidable. □

4 The C+MOD^2-Theory with Regular Predicates

It is the aim of this section to show that the C+MOD^2-theory of the structure $(L,\sqsubseteq,\sqsubset\!\!\cdot,(K\cap L)_{K \text{ regular}},(w)_{w\in L})$ is decidable for any regular language L. To this aim, we first show that the C+MOD^2-theory of

$$\mathcal{S} = (\Sigma^*,\sqsubseteq,\sqsubset\!\!\cdot,(L)_{L \text{ regular}})$$

is decidable. This decidability proof extends the proof from [12] for the decidability of the FO^2-theory of $(\Sigma^*,\sqsubseteq,(L)_{L \text{ regular}})$. It provides a quantifier-elimination procedure (see Sect. 4.3) that relies on the following two properties:

1. The class of regular languages is closed under *counting* images under *unambiguous* rational relations (Sect. 4.2) and
2. the proper subword, the cover, and the incomparability relation are *unambiguous* rational (Sect. 4.1).

4.1 Unambiguous Rational Relations

Recall that, by Nivat's theorem, a relation $R \subseteq \Sigma^* \times \Sigma^*$ is rational if there exist an alphabet Γ, a homomorphism $h\colon \Gamma^* \to \Sigma^* \times \Sigma^*$, and a regular language $S \subseteq \Gamma^*$ such that h maps S surjectively onto R. We call R an *unambiguous rational relation* if, in addition, h maps S *injectively* (and therefore bijectively) onto R. Note that these are precisely the relations accepted by unambiguous 2-tape-automata.

While the class of rational relations is closed under unions, this is not the case for unambiguous rational relations (e.g., $R = \{(a^m ba^n, a^m) \mid m,n \in \mathbb{N}\} \cup \{(a^m ba^n, a^n) \mid m,n \in \mathbb{N}\}$ is the union of unambiguous rational relations but not unambiguous). But it is closed under *disjoint* unions.

Lemma 4.1. *For any alphabet Σ, the cover relation $\sqsubset\!\!\cdot$ and the relation $\sqsubset \setminus \sqsubset\!\!\cdot$ are unambiguous rational.*

Proof. For $i \in \{1,2\}$, let $\Sigma_i = \Sigma \times \{i\}$ and $\Gamma = \Sigma_1 \cup \Sigma_2$. Furthermore, let the homomorphism $\mathrm{proj}_i : \Gamma^* \to \Sigma^*$ be defined by $\mathrm{proj}_i(a,i) = a$ and $\mathrm{proj}_i(a, 3-i) = \varepsilon$ for all $a \in \Sigma$. Finally, let the homomorphism $\mathrm{proj} : \Gamma^* \to \Sigma^* \times \Sigma^*$ be defined by $\mathrm{proj}(w) = (\mathrm{proj}_1(w), \mathrm{proj}_2(w))$.

- The regular language

$$\mathrm{Sub} = \left(\bigcup_{a \in \Sigma} \left((\Sigma_2 \setminus \{(a,2)\})^* \, (a,2)\, (a,1) \right) \right)^* {\Sigma_2}^*.$$

  is mapped bijectively onto the subword relation.
- Let S be the regular language of words from Sub with precisely one more occurrence of letters from Σ_2 than from Σ_1. Then S is mapped bijectively onto the relation $\sqsubset\!\!\cdot$, hence this relation is unambiguous rational.
- Similarly, let S' denote the regular language of all words from Sub with at least two more occurrences of letters from Σ_2 than from Σ_1. It is mapped bijectively onto the relation $\sqsubset \setminus \sqsubset\!\!\cdot$, i.e., $\sqsubset \setminus \sqsubset\!\!\cdot$ is unambiguous rational. □

Lemma 4.2. *For any alphabet Σ, the incomparability relation*

$$\| = \{(u,v) \in \Sigma^* \times \Sigma^* \mid \textit{neither } u \sqsubseteq v \textit{ nor } v \sqsubseteq u\}$$

is unambiguous rational.

Proof. We will show that the following three relations are unambiguous rational:

1. $R_1 = \{(u,v) \mid |u| < |v| \text{ and not } u \sqsubseteq v\}$,
2. $R_2 = \{(u,v) \mid |u| = |v| \text{ and } u \neq v\}$, and
3. $R_3 = \{(u,v) \mid |u| > |v| \text{ and not } v \sqsubseteq u\}$.

The result follows since $\|$ is the disjoint union of these relations. Let Σ_i, Γ, proj_i, and proj be defined as in the previous proof. First, the regular language

$$\mathrm{Inc}_2 = (\Sigma_2\Sigma_1)^* \cdot \{(a,2)(b,1) \mid a,b \in \Sigma, a \neq b\} \cdot (\Sigma_2\Sigma_1)^*.$$

is mapped by proj bijectively onto R_2.

From [12, Lemma 5.2], we learn that $(u,v) \in R_1 \cup R_2$ if, and only if,

- $u = a_1 a_2 \ldots a_\ell u'$ for some $\ell \geq 1$, $a_1, \ldots, a_\ell \in \Sigma$, $u' \in \Sigma^*$, and
- $v \in (\Sigma \setminus \{a_1\})^* a_1 \, (\Sigma \setminus \{a_2\})^* a_2 \cdots (\Sigma \setminus \{a_{\ell-1}\})^* a_{\ell-1} \, (\Sigma \setminus \{a_\ell\})^+ v'$ for some word $v' \in \Sigma^*$ with $|u'| = |v'|$.

Consequently, proj maps the following language bijectively onto $R_1 \cup R_2$:

$$\mathrm{Inc}_{1,2} = \left(\bigcup_{a \in \Sigma} \left((\Sigma_2 \setminus \{(a,2)\})^* (a,2)(a,1) \right) \right)^* \cdot \bigcup_{a \in \Sigma} \left((\Sigma_2 \setminus \{(a,2)\})^+ (a,1) \right) \cdot (\Sigma_2\Sigma_1)^*$$

and since $\mathrm{Inc}_2 \subseteq \mathrm{Inc}_{1,2}$, proj maps $\mathrm{Inc}_1 = \mathrm{Inc}_{1,2} \setminus \mathrm{Inc}_2$ bijectively onto R_1. The claim regarding R_3 follows analogously. □

4.2 Closure Properties of the Class of Regular Languages

Let $R \subseteq \Sigma^* \times \Sigma^*$ be an unambiguous rational relation and $L \subseteq \Sigma^*$ a regular language. We want to show that the languages of all words $u \in \Sigma^*$

$$\text{with } |\{v \in L \mid (u,v) \in R\}| \geq k \tag{1}$$
$$(\text{with } |\{v \in L \mid (u,v) \in R\}| \in p + q\mathbb{N}, \text{ respectively}) \tag{2}$$

are effectively regular for all $k \in \mathbb{N}$ and all $0 \leq p < q$, respectively (this does not hold for arbitrary rational relations). It is straightforward to work out direct automata constructions for this. However, the full details of this are somewhat cumbersome. Instead, we provide a proof via weighted automata, which enables us to split the two constructions into several simple steps.

Let S be a semiring. A function $r \colon \Sigma^* \to S$ is *realizable over* S if there are $n \in \mathbb{N}$, $\lambda \in S^{1\times n}$, a homomorphism $\mu \colon \Sigma^* \to S^{n\times n}$, and $\nu \in S^{n\times 1}$ with $r(w) = \lambda \cdot \mu(w) \cdot \nu$ for all $w \in \Sigma^*$. The triple (λ, μ, ν) is a *presentation of dimension* n or a *weighted automaton for* r.

In the following, we consider the semiring $\mathbb{N}^\infty$, i.e., the set $\mathbb{N} \cup \{\infty\}$ together with the commutative operations $+$ and $\cdot$ (with $x + \infty = \infty$ for all $x \in \mathbb{N} \cup \{\infty\}$, $x \cdot \infty = \infty$ for all $x \in (\mathbb{N} \cup \{\infty\}) \setminus \{0\}$, and $0 \cdot \infty = 0$). Sometimes, we will argue about sums of infinitely many elements from $\mathbb{N}^\infty$, which are defined as expected.

Proposition 4.3. *Let Γ and Σ be alphabets, $f \colon \Gamma^* \to \Sigma^*$ a homomorphism, and $\chi \colon \Gamma^* \to \mathbb{N}^\infty$ a realizable function over $\mathbb{N}^\infty$. Then the following function r is effectively realizable over $\mathbb{N}^\infty$:*

$$r = \chi \circ f^{-1} \colon \Sigma^* \to \mathbb{N}^\infty \colon u \mapsto \sum_{\substack{w \in \Gamma^* \\ f(w) = u}} \chi(w)$$

Proof. The homomorphism f can be written as $f = f_2 \circ f_1$ where $f_1 \colon \Gamma^* \to \Gamma^*$ is non-expanding (i.e., $f_1(a) \in \Gamma \cup \{\varepsilon\}$ for all $a \in \Gamma$) and $f_2 \colon \Gamma^* \to \Sigma^*$ is non-erasing (i.e., $f_2(a) \in \Sigma^+$ for all $a \in \Gamma$). Then $r = (\chi \circ f_1^{-1}) \circ f_2^{-1}$. Then $\chi' = \chi \circ f_1^{-1}$ is effectively realizable by [3, Lemma 2.2(b)].

Let (λ, μ, ν) be a presentation of dimension n for χ'. For $\sigma \in \Sigma \cup \{\varepsilon\}$, set $\Gamma_\sigma = \{b \in \Gamma \mid f_2(b) = \sigma\}$. Furthermore, define the matrix $M \in (\mathbb{N}^\infty)^{n\times n}$ by

$$M_{ij} = \begin{cases} \infty & \text{if there is } w \in \Gamma_\varepsilon^* \text{ with } n < |w| \leq 2n \text{ and } \mu(w)_{ij} > 0 \\ \sum_{w \in \Gamma_\varepsilon^{\leq n}} \mu(w)_{ij} & \text{otherwise.} \end{cases}$$

Then $M_{ij} = \sum_{w \in \Gamma_\varepsilon^*} \mu(w)_{ij}$ for all $i, j \in [1, n]$. Setting $\lambda' = \lambda \cdot M$ and

$$\mu'(a) = \sum_{b \in \Gamma_a} \big(\mu(b) \cdot M\big) \text{ for all } a \in \Sigma$$

defines the presentation (λ', μ', ν) for the function $r = \chi' \circ f_2^{-1}$. □

Lemma 4.4. *Let $R \subseteq \Sigma^* \times \Sigma^*$ be an unambiguous rational relation and $L \subseteq \Sigma^*$ be regular. Then the following function r is effectively realizable over $\mathbb{N}^\infty$:*

$$r \colon \Sigma^* \to \mathbb{N}^\infty \colon u \mapsto |\{v \in L \mid (u,v) \in R\}|$$

Proof. Since R is unambiguous rational, so is $R \cap (\Sigma^* \times L)$, i.e., there are an alphabet Γ, homomorphisms $f, g \colon \Gamma^* \to \Sigma^*$, and a regular language $S_L \subseteq \Gamma^*$ such that

$$(f,g) \colon \Gamma^* \to \Sigma^* \times \Sigma^* \colon w \mapsto \big(f(w), g(w)\big)$$

maps S_L bijectively onto $R \cap (\Sigma^* \times L)$. Since S_L is regular, its characteristic function χ is effectively realizable by [20, Prop. 3.12]. One then shows that r is the function $\chi \circ f^{-1}$ as in Proposition 4.3. □

We now come to the main result of this section.

Proposition 4.5. *Let $R \subseteq \Sigma^* \times \Sigma^*$ be an unambiguous rational relation and $L \subseteq \Sigma^*$ be regular. Then, for $k \in \mathbb{N}$ and for $p, q \in \mathbb{N}$ with $p < q$, the set H of words w satisfying* (1) *and* (2)*, respectively, is effectively regular.*

Let R denote the rational relation mentioned before Lemma 4.1. Then a word $a^m b a^n$ has ≥ 2 "R-partners" iff it has an even number of "R-partners" iff $m \neq n$. Hence, the above proposition does not hold for arbitrary rational relations.

Proof. Let r be the function from Lemma 4.4. Setting $x \equiv y$ iff $x = y$ or $k \leq x, y < \infty$ defines a congruence $\equiv$ on $\mathbb{N}^\infty$. Then $S_k^\infty = \mathbb{N}^\infty/{\equiv}$ is a finite semiring and the function $s \colon \Sigma^* \to S_k^\infty \colon u \mapsto [r(u)]$ is effectively realizable. Since the semiring S_k^∞ is finite, the "level sets" $s^{-1}([i]) = \{u \in \Sigma^* \mid s(u) \equiv i\}$ are effectively regular by [20, Prop. 4.5]. Since $s^{-1}([k]) \cup s^{-1}([\infty])$ is the language of words u satisfying (1), the first result follows.

For the second language, we consider the congruence $\equiv \subseteq \mathbb{N}^\infty \times \mathbb{N}^\infty$ with $x \equiv y$ iff $x = y$ or $q \leq x, y < \infty$ and $x - y \in q\mathbb{N}$. □

4.3 Quantifier Elimination for C+MOD²

Our decision algorithm employs a quantifier alternation procedure, i.e., we will transform an arbitrary formula into an equivalent one that is quantifier-free. As usual, the heart of this procedure handles formulas $\psi = \mathrm{Q}y\,\varphi$ where Q is a quantifier and φ is quantifier-free. Since the logic C+MOD² has only two variables, any such formula ψ has at most one free variable. In other words, it defines a language K. The following lemma shows that this language is effectively regular, such that ψ is equivalent to the quantifier-free formula $x \in K$.

Lemma 4.6. *Let $\varphi(x,y)$ be a quantifier-free formula from* C+MOD² *in the language of the structure $\mathcal{S} = (\Sigma^*, \sqsubseteq, \sqsubset, (L)_{L \text{ regular}})$. Then the sets*

$$\{x \in \Sigma^* \mid \mathcal{S} \models \exists^{\geq k} y\, \varphi\} \text{ and } \{x \in \Sigma^* \mid \mathcal{S} \models \exists^{p \bmod q} y\, \varphi\}$$

are effectively regular for all $k \in \mathbb{N}$ and all $p, q \in \mathbb{N}$ with $p < q$.

Proof. Since φ is quantifier-free, we can rewrite it into a Boolean combination of formulas of the form $x \in K$ and $y \in L$ for some regular languages K and L, $x \sqsubseteq y$ and $y \sqsubseteq x$, and $x \sqsubset\!\!\cdot\, y$ and $y \sqsubset\!\!\cdot\, x$.

There are six possible relations between the two variables x and y in the partial order: we can have $x = y$, $x \sqsubset\!\!\cdot\, y$ or *vice versa*, $x \sqsubset y \wedge \neg x \sqsubset\!\!\cdot\, y$ or *vice versa*, or $x \parallel y$. Let $\theta_i(x, y)$ for $1 \leq i \leq 6$ be formulas describing these relations.

Hence φ is equivalent to $\bigvee_{1 \leq i \leq 6}(\theta_i \wedge \varphi)$. In this formula, any occurrence of φ appears in conjunction with precisely one of the formulas θ_i. Depending on this formula θ_i (i.e., the relation between x and y), we can simplify φ to φ_i by replacing the atomic subformulas that compare x and y by true or false. As a result, the formula φ is equivalent to $\bigvee_{1 \leq i \leq 6}(\theta_i \wedge \varphi_i)$ where the formulas φ_i are Boolean combinations of formulas of the form $x \in K$ and $y \in L$ for some regular languages K and L.

Now let $k \in \mathbb{N}$. Since the formulas θ_i are mutually exclusive, we get

$$\exists^{\geq k} y\, \varphi \equiv \exists^{\geq k} y \bigvee_{1 \leq i \leq 6} (\theta_i \wedge \varphi_i) \equiv \bigvee_{(*)} \bigwedge_{1 \leq i \leq 6} \exists^{\geq k_i} y\, (\theta_i \wedge \varphi_i)$$

where the disjunction $(*)$ extends over all $(k_1, \ldots, k_6) \in \mathbb{N}^6$ with $\sum_{1 \leq i \leq 6} k_i = k$.

Hence it suffices to show that

$$\{x \in \Sigma^* \mid \exists^{\geq k} y\, (\theta_i \wedge \varphi)\} \tag{3}$$

is effectively regular for all $1 \leq i \leq 6$, all $k \in \mathbb{N}$, and all Boolean combinations φ of formulas of the form $x \in K$ and $y \in L$ where K and L are regular languages. We can find regular languages K_M and L_M and a finite set I such that φ is equivalent to $\bigvee_{M \in I} (x \in K_M \wedge y \in L_M)$ and such that this disjunction is exclusive. Hence the set from (3) equals the union of the sets

$$\{x \in \Sigma^* \mid \exists^{\geq k} y\, (\theta_i \wedge x \in K_M \wedge y \in L_M)\} = K_M \cap \underbrace{\{x \in \Sigma^* \mid \exists^{\geq k} y \in L_M \colon \theta_i\}}_{H_M}$$

for $M \in I$. The set H_M is effectively regular by Proposition 4.5 and Lemmas 4.1 and 4.2. Since the language in the claim of the lemma is a Boolean combination of such sets, the first claim is demonstrated; the second follows similarly. □

The only atomic formulas with a single variable x are $x \in L$ with L regular, $x = x$, $x \sqsubseteq x$ (which are equivalent to $x \in \Sigma^*$), and $x \sqsubset\!\!\cdot\, x$ (which is equivalent to $x \in \emptyset$). Hence, any quantifier-free formula with a single free variable x is a Boolean combination of statements of the form $x \in L$. Lemma 4.6 thus implies:

Theorem 4.7. *Let* $\mathcal{S} = (\Sigma^*, \sqsubseteq, \sqsubset\!\!\cdot, (L)_{L \text{ regular}})$. *Let* $\varphi(x)$ *be a formula from* C+MOD^2. *Then the set* $\{x \in \Sigma^* \mid \mathcal{S} \models \varphi\}$ *is effectively regular.*

Corollary 4.8. *Let* $L \subseteq \Sigma^*$ *be a regular language. Then the* C+MOD^2*-theory of the structure* $\mathcal{S}_L = (L, \sqsubseteq, \sqsubset\!\!\cdot, (K \cap L)_{K \text{ regular}}, (w)_{w \in L})$ *is decidable.*

Proof. Let $\varphi \in$ C+MOD^2 be a sentence. We build φ_L by (1) restricting all quantifications to L, (2) replace $x\theta w$ by $\exists y\colon y \in \{w\} \wedge x\theta y$, and dually for $y\theta w$ for all $w \in L$ and all binary relations θ.

With $\mathcal{S}$ the structure from Theorem 4.7, we obtain $\mathcal{S} \models \varphi_L \iff \mathcal{S}_L \models \varphi$. By Theorem 4.7, the language $\{x \mid \mathcal{S} \models \varphi_L\}$ is regular (since φ_L is a sentence, it is $\emptyset$ or Σ^*). Hence φ_L holds iff this set is nonempty, which is decidable. □

5 The Σ_1-Theory

In this section, we study for which regular languages L the Σ_1-theory of the structure $(L, \sqsubseteq)$ is decidable. If L is bounded, then decidability follows from Theorem 3.4. In the case of $(\Sigma^*, \sqsubseteq)$, decidability is known as well [17]. Here, we prove decidability for every regular language L. Note that in terms of quantifier block alternation, this is optimal: The Σ_2-theory is undecidable already in the simple case of $(\{a, b\}^*, \sqsubseteq)$ [6].

Theorem 5.1. *For every regular $L \subseteq \Sigma^*$, the Σ_1-theory of $(L, \sqsubseteq)$ is decidable.*

Observe that very generally, the Σ_1-theory of a partially ordered set $(P, \leq)$ is decidable if every finite partial order embeds into $(P, \leq)$: In that case, a formula with n variables is satisfied in $(P, \leq)$ if and only if it is satisfied for some finite partial order with at most n elements. This is used to obtain decidability for the case $L = \Sigma^*$ with $|\Sigma| \geq 2$ in [17].

As mentioned above, if L is bounded, decidability follows from Theorem 3.4. If L is unbounded, it is well-known that there is a subset $x\{p, q\}^*y \subseteq L$ such that $|p| = |q|$ and $p \neq q$ (see Lemma 5.2). Since in that case, the monoids $(\{a, b\}^*, \cdot)$ and $(\{p, q\}^*, \cdot)$ are isomorphic, it is tempting to assume that $(\{a, b\}^*, \sqsubseteq)$ embeds into $(\{p, q\}^*, \sqsubseteq)$ and thus into $(x\{p, q\}^*y, \sqsubseteq)$. However, that is not the case. If $L = \{ab, ba\}^*$, then the downward closure of any infinite subset of L includes all of L. Since, on the other hand, $(\{a, b\}^*, \sqsubseteq)$ has infinite downward closed strict subsets such as a^*, it cannot embed into $(L, \sqsubseteq)$. Nevertheless, the rest of this section demonstrates that every finite partial order embeds into $(L, \sqsubseteq)$ whenever L is an unbounded regular language. By the previous paragraph, this implies Theorem 5.1.

We recall a well-known property of unbounded regular languages.

Lemma 5.2. *If $L \subseteq \Sigma^*$ is not bounded, then there are $x, y, p, q \in \Sigma^*$ such that $|p| = |q|$, $p \neq q$, and $x\{p, q\}^*y \subseteq L$.*

Proof. Let A be any non-degenerate deterministic finite automaton accepting L. Then at least one strongly connected component of A is not a cycle since otherwise, L would be bounded. Hence, there is a state s and prefix-incomparable words u, v, each of which is read on a cycle starting in s. Since u and v are prefix-incomparable, the words $p = uv$ and $q = vu$ are distinct, but equally long. Since A is non-degenerate, there are words $x, y \in \Sigma^*$ with $x\{p, q\}^*y \subseteq L$. □

To have some control over how words can embed, we prove a stronger version of Lemma 5.2. Two words $p, q \in \Sigma^*$ are *conjugate* if there are $x, y \in \Sigma^*$ with $p = xy$ and $q = yx$. A word $p \in \Sigma^*$ is *primitive* if there is no $q \in \Sigma^*$ with $p \in qq^+$.

Proposition 5.3. *For every unbounded regular language $L \subseteq \Sigma^*$, there are $x, u, v, y \in \Sigma^*$ such that $|u| = |v|$, the word uv is primitive, and $x\{u, v\}^*y \subseteq L$.*

Proof. Since L is unbounded and regular, Lemma 5.2 yields words $x, y, p, q \in \Sigma^*$ with $|p| = |q|$, $p \neq q$, and $x\{p, q\}^*y \subseteq L$. Then the words $r = pq$ and $s = pp$ are not conjugate, because every conjugate of a square is a square. Moreover, $|r| = |s|$, and $x\{r, s\}^*y \subseteq x\{p, q\}^*y \subseteq L$. Let $n = |r|$, $u = rs^{n-1}$, and $v = s^n$. Towards a contradiction, suppose $uv = rs^{2n-1}$ is not primitive. Then there is a word $w \in \Sigma^*$ with $rs^{2n-1} \in ww^+$. Depending on whether $|w| \geq n$ or $|w| < n$, we have $n \leq |w^t| \leq n^2$ either for $t = 1$ or for $t = n$. It follows that r is a prefix of w^t and that w^t is a suffix of s^n, implying that r is a factor of s^n. Since r and s are not conjugate, this is impossible. □

We are now ready to describe how to embed a finite partial order into $(L, \sqsubseteq)$. Observe that every finite partial order with m elements embeds into $(\{0, 1\}^m, \leq)$ where $\leq$ is the componentwise order. Hence, it suffices to embed this partial order into $(\{u, v\}^*, \sqsubseteq)$. We do this as follows. Let $n = |uv| + m + 3$ and define, for a tuple $t = (t_1, \ldots, t_m) \in \{0, 1\}^m$,

$$\varphi_m(t_1, \ldots, t_m) = v^{t_1}(uv)^n \cdots v^{t_m}(uv)^n.$$

Then, clearly, $s \leq t$ implies $\varphi_m(s) \sqsubseteq \varphi_m(t)$. The converse requires a careful analysis of how prefixes of $\varphi_m(s)$ can embed into prefixes of $\varphi_m(t)$. For $x, y \in \Sigma^*$, we write $x \hookrightarrow y$ if x, but no word xa with $a \in \Sigma$ is a subword of y. In other words, $x \hookrightarrow y$ if x is a *prefix-maximal subword of* y. This gives us a criterion for non-embeddability: If x has a strict prefix x_0 with $x_0 \hookrightarrow y$, then certainly $x \not\sqsubseteq y$. In this case, the word x_1 with $x = x_0x_1$ is called *residue*. We show the following:

Lemma 5.4. *Let $u, v \in \Sigma^*$ be words such that $|u| = |v|$ and uv is primitive. Then, for all $\ell, n \in \mathbb{N}$ with $n > |uv| + \ell + 2$, we have*

(i) $(uv)^n \hookrightarrow v(uv)^n$,
(ii) $(uv)^\ell v(uv)^{n-\ell-1} \hookrightarrow (uv)^n$, *and*
(iii) $(uv)^{1+\ell}v(uv)^{n-\ell-2} \hookrightarrow v(uv)^n$.

For this lemma, it is crucial to observe that for a primitive word w and $n > |w|+1$, any embedding of w^{n-1} into w^n must either hit the left-most or the right-most position in w^n. To conclude that $s \not\leq t$ implies $\varphi_m(s) \not\sqsubseteq \varphi_m(t)$, we argue about prefixes of the form $p_i = v^{s_1}(uv)^n \cdots v^{s_i}(uv)^n$ and $q_i = v^{t_1}(uv)^n \cdots v^{t_i}(uv)^n$ for $i \in [1, m]$. If $s \not\leq t$, let $i \in [1, m]$ be the index with $s_i = 1$, $t_i = 0$ and $s_j \leq t_j$ for all $j \in [1, i-1]$. Then clearly $p_{i-1} \sqsubseteq q_{i-1}$. In fact, Lemma 5.4 (i) implies that even $p_{i-1} \hookrightarrow q_{i-1}$, since $x \hookrightarrow y$ and $x' \hookrightarrow y'$ imply $xy \hookrightarrow x'y'$. Then, by

Lemma 5.4 (ii), $p_i = p_{i-1}v(uv)^{n-1}(uv)$ has a residue of uv in $q_i = q_{i-1}(uv)^n$. To conclude $\varphi_m(s) \not\sqsubseteq \varphi_m(t)$, it remains to be shown that this can never be rectified when considering prefixes p_j and q_j for $j = i+1, \ldots, m$. To this end, Lemma 5.4 (ii) and (iii) tell us that if p_j has a residue of $(uv)^\ell$ in q_j, then the word p_{j+1} has a residue of $(uv)^\ell$ or even $(uv)^{\ell+1}$ in q_{j+1}.

6 The Σ_1-Theory with Constants

In this section, we study for which languages L the structure $(L, \sqsubseteq, (w)_{w \in L})$ has a decidable Σ_1-theory. From Theorem 3.4, we know that this is the case whenever L is bounded. However, there are very simple languages for which decidability is lost: If $|\Sigma| \geq 2$, then the Σ_1-theory of $(\Sigma^*, \sqsubseteq, (w)_{w \in \Sigma^*})$ is undecidable [6]. Here, we present a sufficient condition for the Σ_1-theory of $(L, \sqsubseteq, (w)_{w \in \Sigma^*})$ to be decidable.

Let $L \subseteq \Sigma^*$. We say that a letter $a \in \Sigma$ is *frequent* in L if there is a real constant $\delta > 0$ so that $|w|_a \geq \delta \cdot |w|$ for all but finitely many $w \in L$. Our sufficient condition requires that all letters be frequent in L. If L is regular, this is equivalent to saying that in every non-degenerate automaton for L, every cycle contains every letter. An example of such a language is $\{ab, ba\}^*$.

We shall prove that this condition implies decidability of the Σ_1-theory of $(L, \sqsubseteq, (w)_{w \in \Sigma^*})$. If L is bounded, decidability already follows from Theorem 3.4. In case L is unbounded, we employ our results from Sect. 5 to show another embeddability result. For $w \in \Sigma^*$, let $w\!\uparrow = \{u \in \Sigma^* \mid w \sqsubseteq u\}$ denote the upward closure of $\{w\}$ in $(\Sigma^*, \sqsubseteq)$. We will show that if L is unbounded, then for each $w \in \Sigma^*$, the decomposition of $L = (L \setminus w\!\uparrow) \cup (L \cap w\!\uparrow)$ yields two simple parts: The set $L \setminus w\!\uparrow$ is finite and the set $L \cap w\!\uparrow$ embeds every finite partial order. This simplifies the conditions under which a Σ_1-sentence is satisfied.

Lemma 6.1. *Let $L \subseteq \Sigma^*$ be an unbounded regular language where every letter is frequent. For every $w \in \Sigma^*$, the set $L \setminus w\!\uparrow$ is finite and $L \cap w\!\uparrow$ is unbounded.*

Proof. In a non-degenerate automaton A for L, every cycle must contain every letter. Therefore, if A has n states and $v \in L$ has $|v| > n \cdot |w|$, then a computation for v must contain some state more than $|w|$ times, which implies $w \sqsubseteq v$ and hence $v \notin L \setminus w\!\uparrow$. Therefore, $L \setminus w\!\uparrow$ is finite. This implies that $L \cap w\!\uparrow$ is unbounded: Otherwise $L = (L \cap w\!\uparrow) \cup (L \setminus w\!\uparrow)$ would be bounded as well. □

Theorem 6.2. *Let $L \subseteq \Sigma^*$ be an unbounded regular language where every letter is frequent. Then the Σ_1-theory of $(L, \sqsubseteq, (w)_{w \in L})$ is decidable.*

Proof. For decidability, we may assume that we are given a formula φ that is a disjunction of conjunctions of literals of the following forms (where x and y are arbitrary variables and w an arbitrary word from L):

(i) $x \sqsubseteq w$	(iii) $w \sqsubseteq x$	(v) $x \sqsubseteq y$
(ii) $x \not\sqsubseteq w$	(iv) $w \not\sqsubseteq x$	(vi) $x \not\sqsubseteq y$

Step 1. We first show that literals of types (i) and (iv) can be eliminated. To this end, we observe that for each $w \in L$, both of the sets $\{u \in L \mid u \sqsubseteq w\}$, and $\{u \in L \mid w \not\sqsubseteq u\}$ are finite (in the latter case, this follows from Lemma 6.1). Thus, every conjunction that contains a literal $x \sqsubseteq w$ or $w \not\sqsubseteq x$, constrains x to finitely many values. Therefore, we can replace this conjunction with a disjunction of conjunctions that result from replacing x by one of these values. (Here, we might obtain literals $u \sqsubseteq v$ or $u \not\sqsubseteq v$, but those can be replaced by other equivalent formulas). We repeat this until there are no more literals of the form (i) and (iv). *Step 2.* We now eliminate literals of the form (ii). Note that the language $\{u \in L \mid u \not\sqsubseteq w\}$ is upward closed in $(L, \sqsubseteq)$. Since L is regular, we can compute the finite set of minimal elements of this set. Thus, $x \not\sqsubseteq w$ is equivalent to a finite disjunction of literals of the form $w' \sqsubseteq x$. The resulting formula ψ is a disjunction of conjunction of literals of the form (iii), (v), (vi).

Step 3. To check satisfiability, we may assume that ψ is a conjunction of literals of the form (iii), (v), (vi). We can write ψ as $\gamma_1 \wedge \gamma_2$, where γ_1 is a conjunction of literals of the form (iii) and γ_2 is a conjunction of literals of the form (v) and (vi). We claim that ψ is satisfiable if and only if γ_2 is satisfiable in some partial order. The "only if" direction is trivial, so suppose γ_2 is satisfied by some finite partial order $(P, \leq)$ and let $w \in \Sigma^*$ be a concatenation of all words occurring in γ_1. By Lemma 6.1, $L \cap w\!\uparrow$ is unbounded, which implies that $(P, \leq)$ can be embedded into $(L \cap w\!\uparrow, \sqsubseteq)$ (see Sect. 5). This means, there exists a satisfying assignment where even $w \sqsubseteq x$ for every variable x. In particular, it satisfies $\psi = \gamma_1 \wedge \gamma_2$. □

Open Questions

We did not consider complexity issues. In particular, from [13], we know that the FO^2-theory of the structure $(\Sigma^*, \sqsubseteq, (w)_{w \in \Sigma^*})$ can be decided in elementary time. We are currently working out the details for the extension of this result to the $\mathrm{C{+}MOD}^2$-theory of the structure $(L, \sqsubseteq, (w)_{w \in L})$ for regular languages L. We reduced the FO+MOD-theory of the full structure (for L context-free and bounded) to the FO+MOD-theory of $(\mathbb{N}, +)$, which is known to be decidable in elementary time [5]. Our reduction increases the formula exponentially due to the need of handling statements of the form "there is an even number of pairs $(x, y) \in \mathbb{N}^2$ such that ..." It should be checked whether the proof from [5] can be extended to handle such statements in FO+MOD for $(\mathbb{N}, +)$ directly.

Finally, our results raise an interesting question: For which regular languages L does the structure $(L, \sqsubseteq, (w)_{w \in L})$ have a decidable Σ_1-theory? If every letter is frequent in L, we have decidability. For example, this applies to $L = \{ab, ba\}^*$ or $L = \{ab, baa\}^* \cup bb\{abb\}^*$. If $L = \Sigma^*$ for $|\Sigma| \geq 2$, we have undecidability [6].

References

1. Apelt, H.: Axiomatische Untersuchungen über einige mit der Presburgerschen Arithmetik verwandten Systeme. Z. Math. Logik Grundlagen Math. **12**, 131–168 (1966)
2. Berstel, J.: Transductions and Context-Free Languages. Teubner Studienbücher, Stuttgart (1979)
3. Droste, M., Gastin, P.: Weighted automata and weighted logics. In: Droste, M., Kuich, W., Vogler, H. (eds.) Handbook of Weighted Automata, pp. 176–211. Springer, Heidelberg (2009). https://doi.org/10.1007/978-3-642-01492-5_5
4. Finkel, A., Schnoebelen, Ph.: Well-structured transition systems everywhere! Theor. Comput. Sci. **256**, 63–92 (2001)
5. Habermehl, P., Kuske, D.: On Presburger arithmetic extended with modulo counting quantifiers. In: Pitts, A. (ed.) FoSSaCS 2015. LNCS, vol. 9034, pp. 375–389. Springer, Heidelberg (2015). https://doi.org/10.1007/978-3-662-46678-0_24
6. Halfon, S., Schnoebelen, Ph., Zetzsche, G.: Decidability, complexity, and expressiveness of first-order logic over the subword ordering. In: Proceedings of the Thirty-Second Annual ACM/IEEE Symposium on Logic in Computer Science (LICS 2017), pp. 1–12. IEEE Computer Society (2017)
7. Higman, G.: Ordering by divisibility in abstract algebras. Proc. London Math. Soc. **2**, 326–336 (1952)
8. Ježek, J., McKenzie, R.: Definability in substructure orderings. I: finite semilattices. Algebra Univers. **61**(1), 59–75 (2009)
9. Ježek, J., McKenzie, R.: Definability in substructure orderings. III: finite distributive lattices. Algebra Univers. **61**(3–4), 283–300 (2009)
10. Ježek, J., McKenzie, R.: Definability in substructure orderings. IV: finite lattices. Algebra Univers. **61**(3–4), 301–312 (2009)
11. Ježek, J., McKenzie, R.: Definability in substructure orderings. II: finite ordered sets. Order **27**(2), 115–145 (2010)
12. Karandikar, P., Schnoebelen, Ph.: Decidability in the logic of subsequences and supersequences. In: Harsha, P., Ramalingam, G. (eds.) Proceedings of the 35th Conference on Foundations of Software Technology and Theoretical Computer Science (FSTTCS 2015). Leibniz International Proceedings in Informatics, vol. 45, pp. 84–97. Leibniz-Zentrum für Informatik (2015)
13. Karandikar, P., Schnoebelen, Ph.: The height of piecewise-testable languages with applications in logical complexity. In: Talbot, J.-M., Regnier, L. (eds.) Proceedings of the 25th EACSL Annual Conference on Computer Science Logic (CSL 2016). Leibniz International Proceedings in Informatics, vol. 62, pp. 37:1–37:22 (2016)
14. Kudinov, O.V., Selivanov, V.L.: Undecidability in the homomorphic quasiorder of finite labelled forests. J. Log. Comput. **17**(6), 1135–1151 (2007)
15. Kudinov, O.V., Selivanov, V.L., Yartseva, L.V.: Definability in the subword order. In: Ferreira, F., Löwe, B., Mayordomo, E., Mendes Gomes, L. (eds.) CiE 2010. LNCS, vol. 6158, pp. 246–255. Springer, Heidelberg (2010). https://doi.org/10.1007/978-3-642-13962-8_28
16. Kudinov, O.V., Selivanov, V.L., Zhukov, A.V.: Definability in the h-quasiorder of labeled forests. Ann. Pure Appl. Logic **159**(3), 318–332 (2009)
17. Kuske, D.: Theories of orders on the set of words. Theor. Inf. Appl. **40**, 53–74 (2006)
18. Kuske, D., Zetzsche, G.: Languages ordered by the subword order. CoRR, abs/1901.02194 (2019)

19. Parikh, R.: On context-free languages. J. ACM **13**(4), 570–581 (1966)
20. Sakarovitch, J.: Rational and recognisable power series. In: Droste, M., Kuich, W., Vogler, H. (eds.) Handbook of Weighted Automata, pp. 105–174. Springer, Heidelberg (2009). https://doi.org/10.1007/978-3-642-01492-5_4
21. Schweikardt, N.: Arithmetic, first-order logic, and counting quantifiers. ACM Trans. Comput. Log. **6**(3), 634–671 (2005)
22. Thinniyam, R.S.: Definability of recursive predicates in the induced subgraph order. In: Ghosh, S., Prasad, S. (eds.) ICLA 2017. LNCS, vol. 10119, pp. 211–223. Springer, Heidelberg (2017). https://doi.org/10.1007/978-3-662-54069-5_16
23. Thinniyam, R.S.: Defining recursive predicates in graph orders. Logical Methods Comput. Sci. **14**(3:21), 1–38 (2018)

10

Causality in Linear Logic Full Completeness and Injectivity (Unit-Free Multiplicative-Additive Fragment)

Simon Castellan(✉) and Nobuko Yoshida

Imperial College London, London, UK
simon@phis.me

Abstract. Commuting conversions of Linear Logic induce a notion of dependency between rules inside a proof derivation: a rule depends on a previous rule when they cannot be permuted using the conversions. We propose a new interpretation of proofs of Linear Logic as *causal invariants* which captures *exactly* this dependency. We represent causal invariants using game semantics based on general event structures, carving out, inside the model of [6], a submodel of causal invariants. This submodel supports an interpretation of unit-free Multiplicative Additive Linear Logic with MIX ($MALL^-$) which is (1) *fully complete*: every element of the model is the denotation of a proof and (2) *injective*: equality in the model characterises exactly commuting conversions of $MALL^-$. This improves over the standard fully complete game semantics model of $MALL^-$.

Keywords: Event structures · Linear Logic · Proof nets · Game semantics

1 Introduction

Proofs up to commuting conversions. In the sequent calculus of Linear Logic, the order between rules need not always matter: allowed reorderings are expressed by *commuting conversions*. These conversions are necessary for confluence of cut-elimination by mitigating the sequentiality of the sequent calculus. The real proof object is often seen as an equivalence class of proofs modulo commuting conversions. The problem of providing a canonical representation of proofs up to those commuting conversions is as old as Linear Logic itself, and proves to be a challenging problem. The traditional solution interprets a proof by a graphical representation called *proof net* and dates back to Girard [17]. Girard's solution is only satisfactory in the multiplicative-exponential fragment of Linear Logic. For additives, a well-known solution is due to Hughes and van Glabbeck [22], where proofs are reduced to their set of axiom linkings. However, the correctness criterion relies on the difficult *toggling* condition.

Proof nets tend to be based on specific representations such as graphs or sets of linkings. Denotational semantics has not managed to provide a semantic counterpart to proof nets, which would be a model where every element is

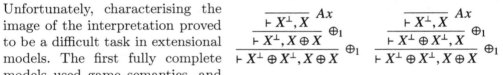

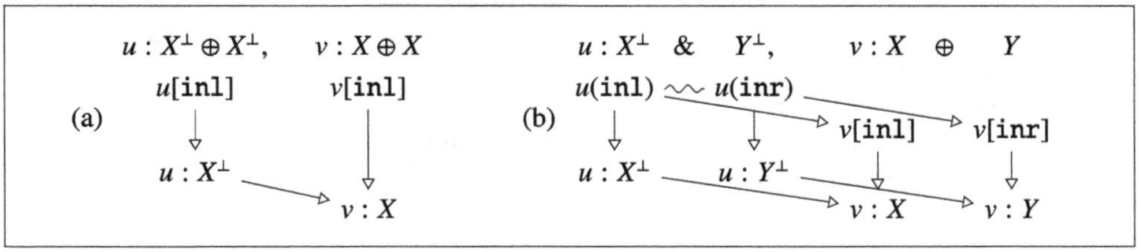

Fig. 1. Examples of causal invariants

the interpretation of a proof (*full completeness*) and whose equational theory coincides with commuting conversions (*injectivity*). We believe this is because denotational semantics views conversions as extensional principles, hence models proofs with extensional objects (relations, functions) too far from the syntax.

Conversions essentially state that the order between rules applied to different premises does not matter, as evidenced in the two equivalent proofs of the sequent $\vdash X^\perp \oplus X^\perp, X \oplus X$ depicted on the right. These two proofs are equal in extensional models of Linear Logic because *they have the same extensional behaviour.* Unfortunately, characterising the image of the interpretation proved to be a difficult task in extensional models. The first fully complete models used game semantics, and are due to Abramsky and Melliès (MALL) [1] and Melliès (Full LL) [24]. However, their models use an *extensional* quotient on strategies to satisfy the conversions, blurring the concrete nature of strategies.

$$\dfrac{\dfrac{\overline{\vdash X^\perp, X}\ Ax}{\vdash X^\perp, X \oplus X}\ \oplus_1}{\vdash X^\perp \oplus X^\perp, X \oplus X}\ \oplus_1 \qquad \dfrac{\dfrac{\overline{\vdash X^\perp, X}\ Ax}{\vdash X^\perp \oplus X^\perp, X}\ \oplus_1}{\vdash X^\perp \oplus X^\perp, X \oplus X}\ \oplus_1$$

The true concurrency of conversions. Recent work [5] highlights an interpretation of Linear Logic as communicating processes. Rules become actions whose polarity (input or output) is tied to the polarity of the connective (negative or positive), and cut-elimination becomes communication. In this interpretation, each assumption in the context is assigned a channel on which the proof communicates. Interestingly, commuting conversions can be read as asynchronous permutations. For instance, the conversion mentioned above becomes the equation in the syntax of Wadler [27]:

$$(1)\quad u[\mathtt{inl}].\, v[\mathtt{inl}].\, [u \leftrightarrow v] \equiv v[\mathtt{inl}].\, u[\mathtt{inl}].\, [u \leftrightarrow v] \ \triangleright\ u : X^\perp \oplus X^\perp, v : X \oplus X,$$

where $u[\mathtt{inl}]$ corresponds to a $\oplus_1$-introduction rule on (the assumption corresponding to) u, and $[u \leftrightarrow v]$ is the counterpart to an axiom between the hypothesis corresponding to u and v. It becomes then natural to consider that the canonical object representing these two proofs should be a concurrent process issuing the two outputs in parallel. A notion of causality emerges from this interpretation, where a rule *depends on* a previous rule below in the tree when these two rules cannot be permuted using the commuting conversions. This leads us to causal models to make this dependency explicit. For instance, the two processes in (1) can be represented as the partial order depicted in Fig. 1a, where dependency between rules is marked with $\twoheadrightarrow$.

In presence of &, a derivation stands for several execution (slices), given by different premises of a &-rule (whose process equivalent is $u.\mathtt{case}\,(P, Q)$ and represents pattern matching on an incoming message). The identity on $X \oplus Y$, corresponding to the proof

$$u.\mathtt{case}\,(v[\mathtt{inl}].\,[u \leftrightarrow v],\quad v[\mathtt{inr}].\,[u \leftrightarrow v]) \;\triangleright\; u : X^{\perp} \,\&\, Y^{\perp}, v : X \oplus Y,$$

is interpreted by the *event structure* depicted in Fig. 1b. Event structures [28] combine a partial order, representing causality, with a conflict relation representing when two events cannot belong to the same execution (here, same slice). Conflict here is indicating with $\sim\!\sim$ and separates the slices. The &-introduction becomes two conflicting events.

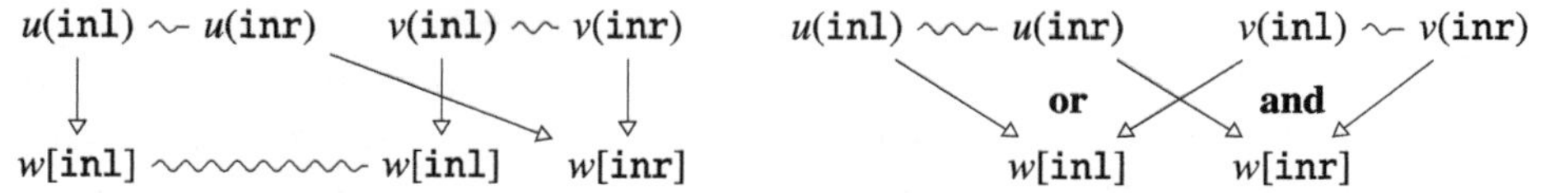

(a) as prime event structures (b) as general event structures

Fig. 2. Representations of or

Conjunctive and disjunctive causalities. Consider the process on the context $u : (X \oplus X)^{\perp}, v : (Y \oplus Y)^{\perp}, w : (X \otimes Y) \oplus (X \otimes Y)$ implementing disjunction:

$$\mathtt{or} = u.\mathtt{case}\begin{pmatrix} v.\mathtt{case}\,(w[\mathtt{inl}].\,P, w[\mathtt{inl}].\,P), \\ v.\mathtt{case}\,(w[\mathtt{inl}].\,P, w[\mathtt{inr}].\,P) \end{pmatrix} \text{ where } P = w[x].\,([u \leftrightarrow w] \mid [v \leftrightarrow x]).$$

Cuts of or against a proof starting with $u[\mathtt{inl}]$ or $v[\mathtt{inl}]$ answer on w after reduction:

$$(\nu u)(\mathtt{or} \mid u[\mathtt{inl}]) \to^{*} w[\mathtt{inl}].v.\mathtt{case}\,(P, P) \quad (\nu v)(\mathtt{or} \mid v[\mathtt{inl}]) \to^{*} w[\mathtt{inl}].u.\mathtt{case}\,(P, P)$$

where $(\nu u)(P \mid Q)$ is the process counterpart to logical cuts. This operational behaviour is related to *parallel or*, evaluating its arguments in parallel and returning true as soon as one returns true. Due to this intentional behaviour, the interpretation of or in prime event structures is nondeterministic (Fig. 2a), as causality in event structures is *conjunctive* (an event may only occur after all its predecessors have occurred). By moving to *general* event structures, however, we can make the disjunctive causality explicit and recover determinism (Fig. 2b).

Contributions and outline. Drawing inspiration from the interpretation of proofs in terms of processes, we build a fully complete and injective model of unit-free Multiplicative Additive Linear Logic with MIX (MALL^{-}), interpreting proofs as general event structures living in a submodel of the model introduced by [6]. Moreover, our model captures the dependency between rules, which makes sequentialisation a local operation, unlike in proof nets, and has a more uniform acyclicity condition than [22].

We first recall the syntax of MALL$^-$ and its reading in terms of processes in Sect. 2. Then, in Sect. 3, we present a slight variation on the model of [6], where we call the (pre)strategies *causal structures*, by analogy with proof structures. Each proof tree can be seen as a (sequential) causal structure. However, the space of causal structures is too broad and there are many causal structures which do not correspond to any proofs. A major obstacle to sequentialisation is the presence of *deadlocks*. In Sect. 4, we introduce a condition on causal structures, ensuring deadlock-free composition, inspired by the interaction between $⅋$ and $\otimes$ in Linear Logic. Acyclic causal structures are still allowed to only explore partially the game, contrary to proofs which must explore it exhaustively, hence in Sect. 5, we introduce further conditions on causal structures, ensuring a *strong* sequentialisation theorem (Theorem 2): we call them *causal nets*. In Sect. 6, we define causal invariants as maximal causal nets. Every causal net embeds in a *unique* causal invariant; and a particular proof P embeds inside a unique causal invariant which forms its denotation $[\![P]\!]$. Moreover, two proofs embed in the same causal invariant if and only if they are convertible (Theorem 4). Finally, we show how to equip causal invariants with the structure of $*$-autonomous category with products and deduce that they form a fully complete model of MALL$^-$ (Theorem 6) for which the interpretation is injective.

The proofs are available in the technical report [7].

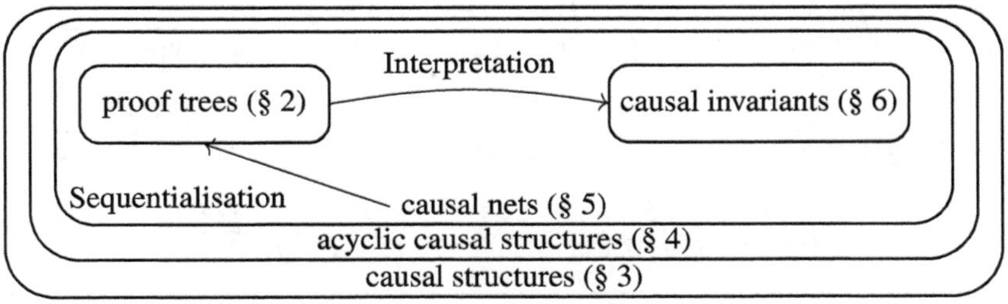

2 MALL$^-$ and Its Commuting Conversions

In this section, we introduce MALL$^-$ formulas and proofs as well as the standard commuting conversions and cut elimination for this logic. As mentioned in the introduction, we use a process-like presentation of proofs following [27]. This highlights the communicating aspect of proofs which is an essential intuition for the model; and it offers a concise visualisation of proofs and conversions.

Formulas. We define the formulas of MALL$^-$: $T, S ::= X \mid X^\perp \mid T \otimes S \mid T ⅋ S \mid T \oplus S \mid T \,\&\, S$, where X and $X^\perp$ are *atomic formulas* (or *ltterals*) belonging to a set $\mathbb{A}$. Formulas come with the standard notion of duality $(\cdot)^\perp$ given by the De Morgan rules: $\otimes$ is dual to $⅋$, and $\oplus$ to $\&$. An *environment* is a partial mapping of *names* to formulas, instead of a multiset of formulas – names disambiguate which assumption a rule acts on.

Proofs as processes. We see proofs of MALL^- (with MIX) as typing derivations for a variant of the π-calculus [27]. The (untyped) syntax for the processes is as follows:

$$
\begin{array}{rll}
P, Q ::= & u(v).\, P \mid u[v].\, (P \mid Q) & \text{(multiplicatives)} \\
\mid & u.\mathtt{case}\,(P, Q) \mid u[\mathtt{inl}].\, P \mid u[\mathtt{inr}].\, P & \text{(additives)} \\
\mid & [u \leftrightarrow v] \mid (\nu u)(P \mid Q) \mid \ (P \mid Q) & \text{(logical and mix)}
\end{array}
$$

$u(v).P$ denotes an input of v on channel u (used in $⅋$-introduction) while $u[v].(P \mid Q)$ denotes output of a fresh channel v along channel u (used in $\otimes$-introduction); The term $[u \leftrightarrow v]$ is a *link*, forwarding messages received on u to v, corresponds to axioms, and conversely; and $(\nu u)(P \mid Q)$ represents a restriction of u in P and Q and corresponds to cuts; $u.\mathtt{case}\,(P, Q)$ is an input branching representing &-introductions, which interacts with selection, either $u[\mathtt{inl}].\, R$ or $u[\mathtt{inr}].\, R$; in $(\nu u)(P \mid Q)$, u is bound in both P and Q, in $u(v).\, P$, v is bound in P, and in $u[v].\, (P \mid Q)$, v is only bound in Q.

We now define MALL^- proofs as typing derivations for processes. The inference rules, recalled in Fig. 3, are from [27]. The links (axioms) are restricted to literals – for composite types, one can use the usual η-expansion laws. There is a straightforward bijection between standard (η-expanded) proofs of MALL^- and typing derivations.

$$
\frac{P \triangleright u : T, v : S, \Gamma}{u(v).\, P \triangleright u : T ⅋ S, \Gamma}
\qquad
\frac{P \triangleright u : T, \Gamma \quad Q \triangleright v : S, \Delta}{u[v].\, (P|Q) \triangleright u : T \otimes S, \Gamma, \Delta}
\qquad
\frac{}{[u \leftrightarrow v] \triangleright u : X^\perp, v : X}
$$

$$
\frac{P \triangleright \Gamma, u : T \quad Q \triangleright \Delta, u : T^\perp}{(\nu u)(P \mid Q) \triangleright \Gamma, \Delta}
\qquad
\frac{P \triangleright \Gamma, u : T \qquad Q \triangleright \Gamma, u : S}{u.\mathtt{case}\,(P, Q) \triangleright \Gamma, u : T \& S}
\qquad
\frac{P \triangleright \Gamma, u : T}{u[\mathtt{inl}].\, P \triangleright \Gamma, u : T \oplus S}
$$

$$
\frac{P \triangleright \Gamma, u : S}{u[\mathtt{inr}].\, P \triangleright \Gamma, u : T \oplus S}
\qquad
\frac{P \triangleright \Gamma \qquad Q \triangleright \Delta}{P \mid Q \triangleright \Gamma, \Delta}
$$

$$
\frac{}{\vdash u[\mathtt{inl}].\, [] : \Gamma, u : T \Rightarrow \Gamma, u : T \oplus S}
\qquad
\frac{Q \triangleright \Delta, v : S}{\vdash u[v].\, ([] \mid Q) : \Gamma, u : T \Rightarrow u : T \otimes S, \Gamma, \Delta}
$$

$$
\frac{}{\vdash u[\mathtt{inr}].\, [] : \Gamma, u : S \Rightarrow \Gamma, u : T \oplus S}
\qquad
\frac{P \triangleright \Gamma, u : T}{\vdash u[v].\, (P \mid []) : \Delta, v : S \Rightarrow u : T \otimes S, \Gamma, \Delta}
$$

$$
\frac{}{\vdash u.\mathtt{case}\,([]_1, []_2) : (\Gamma, u : T) \times (\Gamma, u : S) \Rightarrow \Gamma, u : T \,\&\, S}
$$

$$
\frac{}{\vdash u(v).\, [] : \Gamma, u : T, v : S \Rightarrow \Gamma, u : T ⅋ S}
\qquad
\frac{P \triangleright \Delta}{\vdash ([] \mid P) : \Gamma \Rightarrow \Gamma, \Delta}
\qquad
\frac{P \triangleright \Gamma}{\vdash (P \mid []) : \Delta \Rightarrow \Gamma, \Delta}
$$

Fig. 3. Typing rules for MALL^- (above) and contexts (below)

Commutation rules and cut elimination. We now explain the valid commutations rules in our calculus. We consider contexts $C\,[[]_1, \ldots, []_n]$ with several holes to accomodate & which has two branches. Contexts are defined in Fig. 3, and are assigned a type $\Gamma_1 \times \ldots \times \Gamma_n \Rightarrow \Delta$. It intuitively means that if we plug proofs of Γ_i in the holes, we get back a proof of Δ. We use the notation $C[P_i]_i$ for $C[P_1, \ldots, P_n]$ when (P_i) is a family of processes. Commuting conversion is the smallest congruence $\equiv$ satisfying all well-typed instances of the rule $C[D[P_{i,j}]_j]_i \equiv D[C[P_{i,j}]_i]_j$ for C and D two contexts. For instance $a[\mathtt{inl}]. b.\mathtt{case}\,(P, Q) \equiv b.\mathtt{case}\,(a[\mathtt{inl}]. P, a[\mathtt{inl}]. Q)$. Figure 4 gives reduction rules $P \to Q$. The first four rules are the *principal* cut rules and describe the interaction of two dual terms, while the last one allows cuts to move inside contexts.

3 Concurrent Games Based on General Event Structures

This section introduces a slight variation on the model of [6]. In Sect. 3.1, we define *games* as prime event structures with polarities, which are used to interpret formulas. We then introduce general event structures in Sect. 3.2, which are used to define causal structures.

$$(\nu u)([u \leftrightarrow v] \mid P) \to P[v/u] \qquad (\nu u)(u[x].(P \mid Q) \mid u(x).R) \to (\nu u)(P \mid (\nu x)(Q \mid R))$$

$$(\nu u)(u[\mathtt{inl}].R \mid u.\mathtt{case}\,(P, Q)) \to (\nu u)(R \mid P) \qquad (\nu u)(u[\mathtt{inr}].R \mid u.\mathtt{case}\,(P, Q)) \to (\nu u)(R \mid Q)$$

$$(\nu u)(C[P_i]_i \mid Q) \to C[(\nu u)(P_i \mid Q)]_i \quad (u \notin C)$$

Fig. 4. Cut elimination in MALL$^-$

3.1 Games as Prime Event Structures with Polarities

Definition of games. Prime event structures [28] (simply event structures in the rest of the paper) are a causal model of nondeterministic and concurrent computation. We use here prime event structures *with binary conflict.* An **event structure** is a triple $(E, \leq_E, \#_E)$ where $(E, \leq_E)$ is a partial order and $\#_E$ is an irreflexive symmetric relation (representing **conflict**) satisfying: (1) if $e \in E$, then $[e] := \{e' \in E \mid e' \leq_E e\}$ is finite; and (2) if $e \#_E e'$ and $e \leq_E e''$ then $e'' \#_E e'$. We often omit the E subscripts when clear from the context.

A **configuration** of E is a downclosed subset of E which does not contain two conflicting events. We write $\mathscr{C}(E)$ for the set of *finite* configurations of E. For any $e \in E$, $[e]$ is a configuration, and so is $[e) := [e] \setminus \{e\}$. We write $e \rightarrowtriangle e'$ for the immediate causal relation of E defined as $e < e'$ with no event between. Similarly, a conflict $e \# e'$ is **minimal**, denoted $e \sim e'$, when the $[e] \cup [e')$ and $[e) \cup [e']$ are configurations. When drawing event structures, only $\rightarrowtriangle$ and $\sim$ are represented. We write $\max(E)$ for the set of maximal events of E for $\leq_E$. An event e is maximal in x when it has no successor for $\leq_E$ in x. We write $\max_E x$ for the maximal events of a configuration $x \in \mathscr{C}(E)$.

An event structure E is **confusion-free** when (1) for all $e \sim_E e'$ then $[e) = [e')$ and (2) if $e \sim_E e'$ and $e' \sim_E e''$ then $e = e''$ or $e \sim_E e''$. As a result, the relation "$e \sim e'$ or $e = e'$" is an equivalence relation whose equivalent classes $\mathfrak{a}$ are called **cells**.

Definition 1. *A* ***game*** *is a confusion-free event structure A along with an assignment $pol : A \to \{-, +\}$ such that cells contain events of the same polarity, and a function atom*: $\max(A) \to \mathbb{A}$ *mapping every maximal event of A to an atom. Events with polarity $-$ (resp. $+$) are* ***negative*** *(resp.* ***positive****).*

Events of a game are usually called *moves*. The restriction imposes branching to be polarised (*i.e.* belonging to a player). A game is **rooted** when two minimal events are in conflict. Single types are interpreted by rooted games, while contexts are interpreted by arbitrary games. When introducing moves of a game, we will indicate their polarity in exponent, *e.g.* "let $a^+ \in A$" stands for assuming a positive move of A.

Interpretation of formulas. To interpret formulas, we make use of standard constructions on prime event structures. The event structure $a \cdot E$ is E prefixed with a, *i.e.* $E \cup \{a\}$ where *all* events of E depends on a. The parallel composition of E and E' represents parallel executions of E and E' without interference:

Definition 2. *The parallel composition of event structures A_0 and A_1 is the event structure $A_0 \parallel A_1 = (\{0\} \times A_0 \cup \{1\} \times A_1, \leq_{A_0\parallel A_1}, \#_{A_0\parallel A_1})$ with $(i, a) \leq_{A_0\parallel A_1} (j, a')$ iff $i = j$ and $a \leq_{A_i} a'$; and $(i, a) \#_{A_0\parallel A_1} (j, a')$ when $i = j$ and $a \#_{A_j} a'$.*

The sum of event structure $E + F$ is the nondeterministic analogue of parallel composition.

Definition 3. *The sum $A_0 + A_1$ of the two event structures A_0 and A_1 has the same partial order as $A_0 \parallel A_1$, and conflict relation $(i, a) \#_{A_0+A_1} (j, a')$ iff $i \neq j$ or $i = j$ and $a \#_{A_j} a'$.*

Prefixing, parallel composition and sum of event structures extend to games. The dual of a game A, obtained by reversing the polarity labelling, is written $A^\perp$. Given $x \in \mathscr{C}(A)$, we define A/x ("A after x") as the subgame of A comprising the events $a \in A \setminus x$ not in conflict with events in x.

Interpretation of formulas. The interpretation of the atom X is the game with a single positive event simply written X with $atom(X) = X$, and the interpretation of $X^\perp$ is $[\![X]\!]^\perp$, written simply $X^\perp$ in diagrams. For composite formulas, we let (where `send`, `inl` and `inr` are simply labels):

$$[\![S \otimes T]\!] = \mathtt{send}^+ \cdot ([\![S]\!] \parallel [\![T]\!]) \qquad [\![S \parr T]\!] = \mathtt{send}^- \cdot ([\![S]\!] \parallel [\![T]\!])$$
$$[\![S \oplus T]\!] = (\mathtt{inl}^+ \cdot [\![S]\!]) + (\mathtt{inr}^+ \cdot [\![T]\!]) \qquad [\![S \,\&\, T]\!] = (\mathtt{inl}^- \cdot [\![S]\!]) + (\mathtt{inr}^- \cdot [\![T]\!])$$

Parallel composition is used to interpret contexts: $[\![u_1 : T_1, \ldots, u_n : T_n]\!] = [\![T_1]\!] \parallel \ldots \parallel [\![T_n]\!]$. The interpretation commutes with duality: $[\![T]\!]^\perp = [\![T^\perp]\!]$.

In diagrams, we write moves of a context following the syntactic convention: for instance $u[\mathtt{inl}]$ denotes the minimal `inl` move of the u component. For tensors and pars, we use the notation $u[v]$ and $u(v)$ to make explicit the variables we use in the rest of the diagram, instead of $\mathtt{send}^+$ and $\mathtt{send}^-$ respectively. For atoms, we use $u : X$ and $u : X^\perp$.

3.2 Causal Structures as Deterministic General Event Structures

As we discussed in Sect. 1, prime event structures cannot express disjunctive causalities deterministically, hence fail to account for the determinism of LL. Our notion of causal structure is based on *general event structures*, which allow more complex causal patterns. We use a slight variation on the definition of deterministic general event structures given by [6], to ensure that composition is well-defined without further assumptions.

Instead of using the more concrete representation of general event structures in terms of a set of events and an enabling relation, we use the following formulation in terms of set of configurations, more adequate for mathematical reasoning. Being only sets of configurations, they can be reasoned on with very simple set-theoretic arguments.

Definition 4. *A* ***causal structure*** *(abbreviated as causal struct) on a game A is a subset $\sigma \subseteq \mathscr{C}(A)$ containing $\emptyset$ and satisfying the following conditions:*

Coincidence-freeness *If $e, e' \in x \in \sigma$ then there exists $y \in \sigma$ with $y \subseteq x$ and $y \cap \{e, e'\}$ is a singleton.*

Determinism *for $x, y \in \sigma$ such that $x \cup y$ does not contain any minimal negative conflict, then $x \cup y \in \sigma$.*

Configurations of prime event structures satisfy a further axiom, *stability*, which ensures the absence of disjunctive causalities. When σ is a causal struct on A, we write $\sigma : A$. We draw as regular event structures, using $\rightarrowtriangle$ and $\sim$. To indicate disjunctive causalities, we annotate joins with **or**. This convention is not powerful enough to draw *all* causal structs, but enough for the examples in this paper. As an example, on $A = a \parallel b \parallel c$ the diagram on the right denotes the following causal struct $\sigma = \{x \in \mathscr{C}(A) \mid c \in x \Rightarrow x \cap \{a, b\} \neq \emptyset\}$.

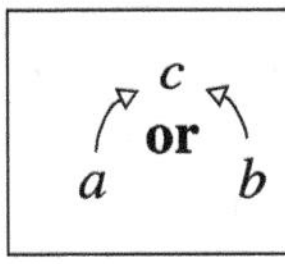

A **minimal event** of $\sigma : A$ is an event $a \in A$ with $\{a\} \in \sigma$. An event $a \in x \in \sigma$ is **maximal** in x when $x \setminus \{a\} \in \sigma$. A **prime configuration** of $a \in A$ is a configuration $x \in \sigma$ such that a is its unique maximal event. Because of disjunctive causalities, an event $a \in A$ can have several distinct prime configurations in σ (unlike in event structures). In the previous example, since c can be caused by either a or b, it has two prime configurations: $\{a, c\}$ and $\{b, c\}$. We write $\max \sigma$ for the set of **maximal configurations** of σ, ie. those configurations that cannot be further extended.

Even though causality is less clear in general event structures than in prime event structures, we give here a notion of immediate causal dependence that will be central to define acyclic causal structs. Given a causal struct $\sigma : A$ and $x \in \sigma$, we define a relation $\rightarrowtriangle_{x,\sigma}$ on x as follows: $a \rightarrowtriangle_{x,\sigma} a'$ when there exists a prime configuration y of a' such that $x \cup y \in \sigma$, and that a is maximal in $y \setminus \{a'\}$. This notion is compatible with the drawing above: we have $a \rightarrowtriangle_{\emptyset} c$ and $b \rightarrowtriangle_{\emptyset} c$ as c has two prime configurations: $\{a, c\}$ and $\{b, c\}$. Causality needs to be contextual, since different slices can implement different causal patterns. Parallel composition and prefixing structures extend to causal structs:

$$\sigma \parallel \tau = \{x \parallel y \in \mathscr{C}(A \parallel B) \mid (x, y) \in \sigma \times \tau\} \qquad a \cdot \sigma = \{x \in \mathscr{C}(a \cdot A) \mid x \cap A \in \sigma\}.$$

Categorical setting. Causal structs can be composed using the definitions of [6]. Consider $\sigma : A^\perp \parallel B$ and $\tau : B^\perp \parallel C$. A **synchronised configuration** is a configuration $x \in \mathscr{C}(A \parallel B \parallel C)$ such that $x \cap (A \parallel B) \in \sigma$ and $x \cap (B \parallel C) \in \tau$. A synchronised configuration x is **reachable** when there exists a sequence (**covering chain**) of synchronised configurations $x_0 = \emptyset \subseteq x_1 \subseteq \ldots \subseteq x_n = x$ such that $x_{i+1} \setminus x_i$ is a singleton. The reachable configurations are used to define the interaction $\tau \circledast \sigma$, and then after hiding, the composition $\tau \odot \sigma$:

$$\tau \circledast \sigma = \{x \text{ is a reachable synchronised configuration}\} \quad \tau \odot \sigma = \{x \cap (A \parallel C) \mid x \in \tau \circledast \sigma\}.$$

Unlike in [6], our determinism is strong enough for $\tau \odot \sigma$ to be a causal struct.

Lemma 1. *If $\sigma : A^\perp \parallel B$ and $\tau : B^\perp \parallel C$ are causal structs then $\tau \odot \sigma$ is a causal struct.*

Composition of causal structs will be used to interpret cuts between proofs of Linear Logic. In concurrent game semantics, composition has a natural identity, asynchronous copycat [25], playing on the game $A^\perp \parallel A$, forwarding negative moves on one side to the positive occurrence on the other side. Following [6], we define $\text{\ae}_A = \{x \parallel y \in \mathscr{C}(A^\perp \parallel A) \mid y \supseteq_A^- x \cap y \subseteq_A^+ x\}$ where $x \subseteq^p y$ means $x \subseteq y$ and $pol(y \setminus x) \subseteq \{p\}$.

However, in general copycat is not an identity on all causal structs, only $\sigma \subseteq \text{\ae}_A \odot \sigma$ holds. Indeed, copycat represents an asynchronous buffer, and causal structs which expects messages to be transmitted synchronously may be affected by composition with copycat. We call causal structs that satisfy the equality **asynchronous**. From [6], we know that asynchronous causal structs form a compact-closed category.

The syntactic tree. The syntactic tree of a derivation $P \triangleright \Delta$ can be read as a causal struct $Tr(P)$ on $[\![\Delta]\!]$, which will be the basis for our interpretation. It is defined by induction:

$$Tr(u(v).\,P) = u(v) \cdot Tr(P) \qquad Tr(u[v].\,(P \mid Q)) = u[v] \cdot (Tr(P) \parallel Tr(Q))$$

$$Tr(a.\mathtt{case}\,(P, Q)) = (a(\mathtt{inl}) \cdot Tr(P)) \cup (a(\mathtt{inr}) \cdot Tr(Q))$$

$$Tr(a[\mathtt{inl}].\,P) = a[\mathtt{inl}] \cdot Tr(P) \qquad Tr(a[\mathtt{inr}].\,P) = a[\mathtt{inr}] \cdot Tr(P)$$

$$Tr([a \leftrightarrow b]) = \text{\ae}_{[\![X]\!]} \text{ where } \Delta = a : X^\perp, b : X \qquad Tr(P \mid Q) = Tr(P) \parallel Tr(Q)$$

$$Tr((\nu a)(P \mid Q)) = Tr(P) \odot Tr(Q)$$

We use the convention in the diagram, for instance $u[v]$ means the initial **send** move of the u component. An example of this construction is given in Fig. 5a. Note that it is not asynchronous.

4 Acyclicity of Causal Structures

The space of causal structs is unfortunately too broad to provide a notion of causal nets, due in particular to the presence of deadlocks during composition.

As a first step towards defining causal nets, we introduce in this section a condition on causal structs inspired by the tensor rule in Linear Logic. In Sect. 4.1, we propose a notion of communication between actions, based on causality. In Sect. 4.2, we introduce a notion of acyclicity which is shown to be stable under composition and ensure deadlock-free composition.

4.1 Communication in Causal Structures

The tensor rule of Linear Logic says that after a tensor $u[v]$, the proof splits into two independent subproofs, one handling u and the other v. This syntactic condition is there to ensure that there are no communications between u and v. More precisely, we want to prevent any dependence between subsequent actions on u and an action v. Indeed such a causal dependence could create a deadlock when facing a par rule $u(v)$, which is allowed to put arbitrary dependence between such subsequent actions.

Communication in MLL. Let us start by the case of MLL, which corresponds to the case where games do not have conflicts. Consider the following three causal structs:

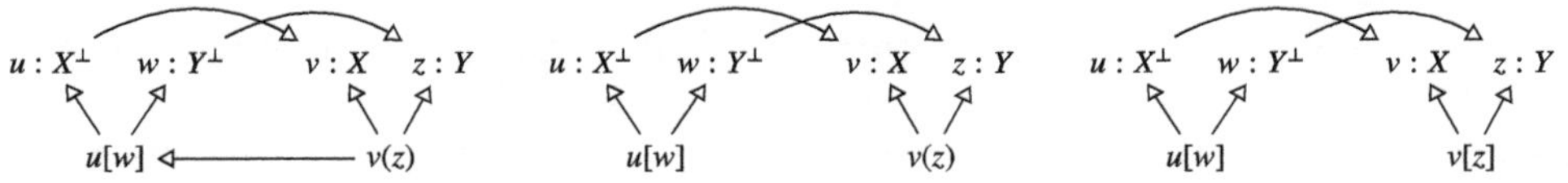

σ_1 σ_2 σ_3

The causal structs σ_1 and σ_2 play on the game $[\![u : X^\perp \otimes Y^\perp, v : X \parr Y]\!]$, while σ_3 plays on the game $[\![u : X^\perp \otimes Y^\perp, v : X \otimes Y]\!]$. The causal structs σ_2 and σ_3 are very close to proof nets, and it is easy to see that σ_2 represents a correct proof net while σ_3 does not. In particular, there exists a proof P such that $Tr(P) \subseteq \sigma_2$ but there are no such proof Q for σ_3. Clearly, σ_3 should not be acyclic. But should σ_2? After all it is sequentialisable. But, in all sequentialisations of σ_2, the par rule $v(z)$ is applied *before* the tensor $u[w]$, and this dependency is not reflected by σ_2. Since our goal is exactly to compute these implicit dependencies, we will only consider σ_1 to be acyclic, by using a stronger sequentialisation criterion:

Definition 5. *A causal struct $\sigma : [\![\Gamma]\!]$ is* ***strongly sequentialisable*** *when for all $x \in \sigma$, there exists $P \triangleright \Gamma$ with $x \in Tr(P)$ and $Tr(P) \subseteq \sigma$.*

To understand the difference between σ_1 and σ_2, we need to look at causal chains. In both σ_1 and σ_2, we can go from $u : X^\perp$ to $w : Y^\perp$ by following immediate causal links $\rightarrowtriangle$ in any direction, but observe that in σ_1 they must all cross an event below $u[w]$ (namely $v(z)$ or $u[w]$). This prompts us to define a notion of communication *outside a configuration* x:

Definition 6. *Given $\sigma : A$ and $x \in \sigma$ we say that $a, a' \in A \setminus x$ communicate* outside x *(written $a \leftrightsquigarrow_{x,\sigma} a'$) when there exists a chain $a \leftrightarrowtriangle_{x,\sigma} a_0 \leftrightarrowtriangle_\sigma \cdots \leftrightarrowtriangle_{x,\sigma} a_n \leftrightarrowtriangle_\sigma a'$ where all the $a_i \in A \setminus x$, and $\leftrightarrowtriangle_{x,\sigma}$ denotes the symmetric closure of $\rightarrowtriangle_{x,\sigma}$.*

Communication in MALL. In presence of additives, immediate causality is not the only vector of communication. Consider the following causal struct σ_4, playing on the context $u : (A \,\&\, A) \otimes (A \,\&\, A), v : (A \oplus A) \,\&\, (A \oplus A)$ where A is irrelevant:

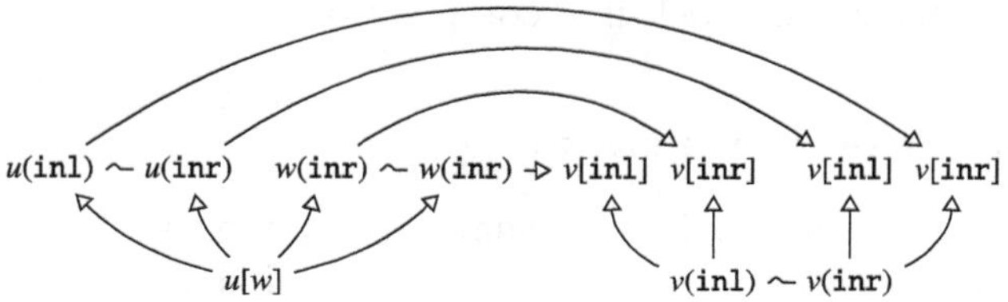

This pattern is not strongly sequentialisable: the tensor $u[w]$ must always go after the &-introduction on v, since we need this information to know how whether v should go with u or w when splitting the context. Yet, it is not possible to find a communication path from one side to the other by following purely causal links without crossing $u[w]$. There is however a path that uses both immediate causality and *minimal conflict.* This means that we should identify events in minimal conflict, since they represent the same (&-introduction rule). Concretely, this means lifting the previous definition at the level of cells. Given an causal struct $\sigma : A$ and $x \in \sigma$, along with two cells $\mathfrak{a}, \mathfrak{a}'$ of A/x, we define the relation $\mathfrak{a} \leftrightarrow_{x,\sigma} \mathfrak{a}'$ when there exists $a \in \mathfrak{a}$ and $a' \in \mathfrak{a}'$ such that $a \leftrightarrow_{x,\sigma} a'$; and $\mathfrak{a} \leftrightsquigarrow_{x,\sigma} \mathfrak{a}'$ when there exists $\mathfrak{a} \leftrightarrow_{x,\sigma} \mathfrak{a}_0 \leftrightarrow_{x,\sigma} \cdots \leftrightarrow_{\sigma} \mathfrak{a}_n \leftrightarrow_{\sigma} \mathfrak{a}'$ where all the $\mathfrak{a}_i$ do not intersect x. For instance, the two cells which are successors of the tensor $u[w]$ in σ_4 communicate outside the configuration $\{u[w]\}$ by going through the cell $\{v(\mathtt{inl}), v(\mathtt{inr})\}$.

4.2 Definition of Acyclicity on Casual Structures

Since games are trees, two events a, a' are either incomparable or have a meet $a \wedge a'$. If $a \wedge a'$ is defined and positive, we say that a and a' **have positive meet**, and means that they are on two distinct branches of a tensor. If $a \wedge a'$ is undefined, or defined and negative, we say that $a \wedge a'$ has a **negative meet**. When the meet is undefined, it means that a and a' are events of different components of the context. We consider the meet to be negative in this case, since components of a context are related by an implicit par.

These definitions are easily extended to cells. The meet $\mathfrak{a} \wedge \mathfrak{a}'$ of two cells $\mathfrak{a}$ and $\mathfrak{a}'$ of A is the meet $a \wedge a'$ for $a \in \mathfrak{a}$ and $a' \in \mathfrak{a}'$: by confusion-freeness, it does not matter which ones are chosen. Similarly, we say that $\mathfrak{a}$ and $\mathfrak{a}'$ have positive meet if $\mathfrak{a} \wedge \mathfrak{a}'$ is defined and positive; and have negative meet otherwise. These definitions formalise the idea of "the two sides of a tensor", and allow us to define acyclicity.

Definition 7. *A causal struct $\sigma : A$ is* **acyclic** *when for all $x \in \sigma$, for any cells $\mathfrak{a}, \mathfrak{a}'$ not intersecting x and with positive meet, if $\mathfrak{a} \leftrightsquigarrow_{x,\sigma} \mathfrak{a}'$ then $\mathfrak{a} \wedge \mathfrak{a}' \notin x$.*

This captures the desired intuition: if $\mathfrak{a}$ and $\mathfrak{a}'$ are on two sides of a tensor a (ie. have positive meet), and there is a communication path outside x relating them, then a must also be outside x (and implicitly, the communication path must be going through a).

Reasoning on the interaction of acyclic strategies proved to be challenging. We prove that acyclic strategies compose, and their interaction are deadlock-free, when composition is on a rooted game B. This crucial assumption arises from the fact that in linear logic, cuts are on *formulas*. It entails that for any $b, b' \in B$, $b \wedge b'$ is defined, hence must be positive either from the point of view of σ or of τ.

Theorem 1. *For acyclic causal structs $\sigma : A^{\perp} \parallel B$ and $\tau : B^{\perp} \parallel C$, (1) their interaction is* deadlock-free*: $\tau \circledast \sigma = (\sigma \parallel C) \cap (A \parallel \tau)$; and (2) the causal struct $\tau \odot \sigma$ is acyclic.*

As a result, acyclic and asynchronous causal structs form a category. We believe this intermediate category is interesting in its own right since it generalises the deadlock-freeness argument of Linear Logic without having to assume other constraints coming from Linear Logic, such as linearity. In the next section, we study further restriction on acyclic causal structs which guarantee strong sequentialisability.

5 Causal Nets and Sequentialisation

We now ready to introduce causal nets. In Sect. 5.1, we give their definition by restricting acyclic causal structs and in Sect. 5.2 we prove that causal nets are strongly sequentialisable.

5.1 Causal Nets: Totality and Well-Linking Casual Structs

To ensure that our causal structs are strongly sequentialisable, acyclicity is not enough. First, we need to require causal structs to respect the linearity discipline of Linear Logic:

Definition 8. *A causal struct $\sigma : A$ is* ***total*** *when* (1) *for $x \in \sigma$, if x is maximal in σ, then it is maximal in $\mathscr{C}(A)$; and* (2) *for $x \in \sigma$ and $a^- \in A \setminus x$ such that $x \cup \{a\} \in \sigma$, then whenever $\boldsymbol{a} \sim_A \boldsymbol{a'}$, we also have $x \cup \{a'\} \in \sigma$ as well.*

The first condition forces a causal struct to play until there are no moves to play, and the second forces an causal struct to be receptive to all Opponent choices, not a subset.

Our last condition constrains axiom links. A **linking** of a game A is a pair (x, ℓ) of a $x \in \max \mathscr{C}(A)$, and a bijection $\ell : (\max_A x)^- \simeq (\max_A x)^+$ preserving the *atom* labelling.

Definition 9. *A total causal struct $\sigma : A$ is* ***well-linking*** *when for each $x \in \max(\sigma)$, there exists a linking ℓ_x of x, such that if y is a prime configuration of $\ell_x(e)$ in x, then $\max(y \setminus \{\ell_x(e)\}) = \{e\}$.*

This ensures that every positive atom has a unique predecessor which is a negative atom.

Definition 10. *A* ***causal net*** *is an acyclic, total and well-linking causal struct.*

A causal net $\sigma : A$ induces a set of linkings A, $\mathsf{link}(\sigma) := \{\ell_x \mid x \in \max \sigma\}$. The mapping $\mathsf{link}(\cdot)$ maps causal nets to the proof nets of [22].

5.2 Strong Sequentialisation of Causal Nets

Our proof of sequentialisation relies on an induction on causal nets. To this end, we provide an inductive deconstruction of parallel proofs. Consider $\sigma : A$ a causal net and a minimal event $a \in \sigma$ not an atom. We write A/a for $A/\{a\}$. Observe that if $A = [\![\Delta]\!]$, it is easy to see that there exists a context Δ/a such that $[\![\Delta/a]\!] \cong A/a$. Given a causal struct $\sigma : A$, we define the causal struct $\sigma/a = \{x \in \mathscr{C}(A/a) \mid x \cup \{a\} \in \sigma\} : A/a$.

Lemma 2. *σ/a is a causal net on A/a.*

When a is positive, we can further decompose σ/a in disjoint parts thanks to acyclicity. Write $\mathfrak{a}_1, \ldots, \mathfrak{a}_n$ for the minimal cells of A/a and consider for $n \geq k > 0$, $A_k = \{a' \in A/a \mid \mathrm{cell}(a') \leftrightsquigarrow_{\{a\},\sigma} \mathfrak{a}_k\}$. A_k contains the events of A/a which σ connects to the k-th successor of a. We also define the set $A_0 = A/a \setminus \bigcup_{1 \leq k \leq n} A_k$, of events not connected to any successor of a (this can happen with MIX). It inherits a game structure from A.

Each subset inherits a game structure from A/a. By acyclicity of σ, the A_k are pairwise disjoint, so $A/a \cong A_0 \parallel \ldots \parallel A_n$. For $0 \leq k \leq n$, define $\sigma_k = \mathscr{C}(A_k) \cap \sigma/a$.

Lemma 3. *σ_k is a causal net on A_k and we have $\sigma/a = \sigma_0 \parallel \ldots \parallel \sigma_n$.*

This formalises the intuition that after a tensor, an acyclic causal net must be a parallel composition of proofs (following the syntactic shape of the tensor rule of Linear Logic). From this result, we show by induction that any causal net is strongly sequentialisable.

Theorem 2. *If $\sigma : A$ is a causal net, then σ is strongly sequentialisable.*

We believe sequentialisation without MIX requires causal nets to be *connected*: two cells with negative meets always communicate outside any configuration they are absent from. We leave this lead for future work.

6 Causal Invariants and Completeness

Causal nets are naturally ordered by inclusion. When $\sigma \subseteq \tau$, we can regard τ as a less sequential implementation of σ. Two causal nets which are upper bounded by a causal net should represent the same proof, but with varying degrees of sequentiality. Causal nets which are maximal for inclusion (among causal nets) are hence most parallel implementations of a certain behaviour and capture our intuition of causal invariants.

Definition 11. *A* ***causal invariant*** *is a causal net $\sigma : A$ maximal for inclusion.*

6.1 Causal Invariants as Maximal Causal Nets

We start by characterising when two causal nets are upper-bounded for inclusion:

Proposition 1. *Given two causal nets $\sigma, \tau : A$, the following are equivalent:*

1. *there exists a causal net $\upsilon : A$ such that $\sigma \subseteq \upsilon$ and $\tau \subseteq \upsilon$,*
2. *the set $\sigma \vee \tau = \{x \cup y \mid x \in \sigma, y \in \tau, x \cup y \in \mathscr{C}(A)\}$ is a causal net on A,*
3. *$\mathsf{link}(\sigma) = \mathsf{link}(\tau)$.*

In this case we write $\sigma \uparrow \tau$ and $\sigma \vee \tau$ is the least upper bound of σ and τ for $\subseteq$.

It is a direct consequence of Proposition 1 that any causal net σ is included in a unique causal invariant $\sigma^{\uparrow} : A$, defined as: $\sigma^{\uparrow} = \bigvee_{\sigma \subseteq \tau} \tau$, where τ ranges over causal nets.

Lemma 4. *For $\sigma, \tau : A$ causal nets, $\sigma \uparrow \tau$ iff $\sigma^{\uparrow} = \tau^{\uparrow}$. Moreover, if σ and τ are causal invariants, $\sigma \uparrow \tau$ if and only if $\sigma = \tau$.*

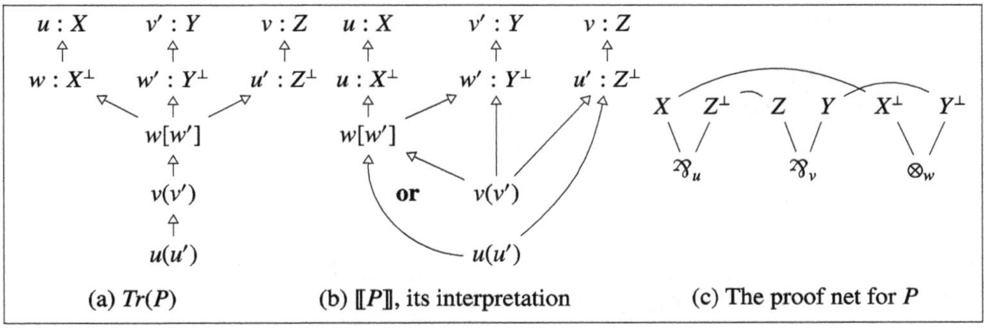
u : X
v′ : Y
v : Z
w : X⊥
w′ : Y⊥
u′ : Z⊥
w[w′]
v(v′)
u(u′)
u : X
v′ : Y
v : Z
u : X⊥
w′ : Y⊥
u′ : Z⊥
w[w′]
or
v(v′)
u(u′)
X
Z⊥
Z
Y
X⊥
Y⊥
⅋u
⅋v
⊗w
(a) Tr(P)
(b) [[P]], its interpretation
(c) The proof net for P

Fig. 5. Interpreting $P = u(u').\,v(v').\,w[w'].\,([u \leftrightarrow w] \mid ([w' \leftrightarrow v'] \mid [u' \leftrightarrow v]))$ in the context $u : X \parr Z^{\perp}, v : Z \parr Y, w : X^{\perp} \otimes Y^{\perp}$

The interpretation of a proof $P \triangleright \Delta$ is simply defined as $[\![P]\!] = \mathit{Tr}(P)^{\uparrow}$. Figure 5c illustrates the construction on a proof of MLL+mix. The interpretation features a disjunctive causality, as the tensor can be introduced as soon as *one* of the two pars has been.

Defining $\mathsf{link}(P) = \mathsf{link}(\mathit{Tr}(P))$, we have from Lemma 4: $\mathsf{link}(P) = \mathsf{link}(Q)$ if and only if $[\![P]\!] = [\![Q]\!]$. This implies that our model has the same equational theory than the proof nets of [22]. Such proof nets are already complete:

Theorem 3 ([22]). *For P, Q two proofs of Γ, we have $P \equiv Q$ iff $\mathsf{link}(P) = \mathsf{link}(Q)$.*

As a corollary, we get:

Theorem 4. *For cut-free proofs P, Q we have $P \equiv Q$ iff $[\![P]\!] = [\![Q]\!]$.*

The technical report [7] also provides an inductive proof not using the result of [22]. A consequence of this result, along with *strong* sequentialisation is: $[\![P]\!] = \bigcup_{Q \equiv P} Tr(Q)$. This equality justifies our terminology of "causal completeness", as for instance it implies that the minimal events of $[\![P]\!]$ correspond exactly the possible rules in P that can be pushed to the front using the commuting conversions.

6.2 The Category of Causal Invariants

So far we have focused on the static. Can we integrate the dynamic aspect of proofs as well? In this section, we show that causal invariants organise themselves in a category. First, we show that causal nets are stable under composition:

Lemma 5. *If $\sigma : A^\perp \parallel B$ and $\tau : B^\perp \parallel C$ are causal nets, then so is $\tau \odot \sigma$.*

Note that totality requires acyclicity (and deadlock-freedom) to be stable under composition. However, causal invariants are not stable under composition: $\tau \odot \sigma$ might not be maximal, even if τ and σ are. Indeed, during the interaction, some branches of τ will not be explored by σ and vice-versa which can lead to new allowed reorderings. However, we can always embed $\tau \odot \sigma$ into $(\tau \odot \sigma)^\uparrow$:

Lemma 6. *Rooted games and causal invariants form a category **CInv**, where the composition of $\sigma : A^\perp \parallel B$ and $\tau : B^\perp \parallel C$ is $(\tau \odot \sigma)^\uparrow$ and the identity on A is $\text{\ae}_A^\uparrow$.*

Note that the empty game is an object of **CInv**, as we need a monoidal unit.

Monoidal-closed structure. Given two games A and B we define $A \otimes B$ as $\texttt{send}^+ \cdot (A \parallel B)$, and 1 as the empty game. There is an obvious isomorphism $A \otimes 1 \cong A$ and $A \otimes (B \otimes C) \cong (A \otimes B) \otimes C$ in **CInv**. We now show how to compute directly the functorial action of $\otimes$, without resorting to $^\uparrow$. Consider $\sigma \in \mathbf{CInv}(A, B)$ and $\tau \in \mathbf{CInv}(C, D)$. Given $x \in \mathscr{C}((A \otimes C)^\perp \parallel (B \otimes D))$, we define $x\langle\sigma\rangle = x \cap (A^\perp \parallel B)$ and $x\langle\tau\rangle = x \cap (C^\perp \parallel D)$. If $x\langle\sigma\rangle \in \sigma$ and $x\langle\tau\rangle \in \tau$, we say that x is connected when there exists cells $\mathfrak{a}, \mathfrak{b}, \mathfrak{c}$ and $\mathfrak{d}$ of A, B, C and D respectively such that $\mathfrak{a} \leftrightsquigarrow_{x\langle\sigma\rangle,\sigma} \mathfrak{c}$ and $\mathfrak{b} \leftrightsquigarrow_{x\langle\tau\rangle,\tau} \mathfrak{d}$. We define:

$$\sigma \otimes \tau = \left\{ \begin{array}{l} x \in \mathscr{C}((A \otimes C)^\perp \parallel (B \otimes D)) \text{ such that :} \\ \quad (1)\ x\langle\sigma\rangle \in \sigma \text{ and } x\langle\tau\rangle \in \tau \\ \quad (2) \text{ if } x \text{ is connected and contains } \texttt{send}^+, \text{ then } \texttt{send}^- \in x \end{array} \right\}$$

In (2), $\texttt{send}^-$ refers to the minimal move of $(A \otimes C)^\perp$ and $\texttt{send}^+$ to the one of $B \otimes D$. (2) ensures that $\sigma \otimes \tau$ is acyclic.

Lemma 7. *The tensor product defines a symmetric monoidal structure on **CInv**.*

Define $A \parr B = (A^\perp \otimes B^\perp)^\perp$, $\perp = 1 = \emptyset$ and $A \multimap B = A^\perp \parr B$.

Lemma 8. *We have a bijection* $⅋_{B,C}$ *between causal invariants on* $A \parallel B \parallel C$ *and on* $A \parallel (B ⅋ C)$. *As a result, there is an adjunction* $A \otimes \_ \dashv A \multimap \_$.

Lemma 8 implies that $\mathbf{CInv}((A \multimap \bot) \multimap \bot) \simeq \mathbf{CInv}(A)$, and **CInv** is $*$-autonomous.

Cartesian products. Given two games A, B in **CInv**, we define their product $A \,\&\, B = \mathtt{inl}^- \cdot A + \mathtt{inr}^- \cdot B$. We show how to construct the pairing of two causal invariants concretely. Given $\sigma \in \mathbf{CInv}(A, B)$ and $\tau \in \mathbf{CInv}(A, C)$, we define the common behaviour of σ and τ on A to be those $x \in \mathscr{C}(A^\perp) \cap \sigma \cap \tau$ such that for all $\mathfrak{a}, \mathfrak{a}'$ outside of x with positive meet, $\mathfrak{a} \leftsquigarrow\!\!\rightsquigarrow_{x,\sigma} \mathfrak{a}'$ iff $\mathfrak{a} \leftsquigarrow\!\!\rightsquigarrow_{x,\tau} \mathfrak{a}'$. We write $\sigma \cap_A \tau$ for the set of common behaviours of σ and τ and define: $\langle \sigma, \tau \rangle = (L^- \cdot \sigma) \cup (R^- \cdot \tau) \cup \sigma \cap_A \tau$. The projections are defined using copycat: $\pi_1 = \{x \in \mathscr{C}((A \,\&\, B)^\perp \parallel A) \mid x \cap (A^\perp \parallel A) \in \mathbb{c}_A^\uparrow\}$ (and similarly for π_2).

Theorem 5. ***CInv*** *has products. As it is also* $*$*-autonomous, it is a model of MALL.*

It is easy to see that the interpretation of MALL$^-$ in **CInv** following the structure is the same as $[\![\cdot]\!]$, however it is computed compositionally without resorting to the $^\uparrow$ operator. We deduce that our interpretation is invariant by cut-elimination: if $P \to Q$, then $[\![P]\!] = [\![Q]\!]$. Putting the pieces together, we get the final result.

Theorem 6. ***CInv*** *is an injective and fully complete model of MALL*$^-$.

7 Extensions and Related Work

The model provides a representation of proofs which retains only the necessary sequentiality. We study the phenomenon in Linear Logic, but commuting conversions of additives arise in other languages, eg. in functional languages with sums and products, where proof nets do not necessarily exist. Having an abstract representation of which reorderings are allowed could prove useful (reasoning on the possible commuting conversions in a language with sum types is notoriously difficult).

Extensions. Exponentials are difficult to add, as their conversions are not as canonical as those of MALL. Cyclic proofs [2] could be accomodated via recursive event structures.

Adding multiplicative units while keep determinism is difficult, as their commuting conversion is subtle (*e.g.* conversion for MLL is PSPACE-complete [18]), and exhibit apparent nondeterminism. For instance the following proofs are convertible in MLL:

$$a().\, b[] \mid c[] \equiv a().\, (b[] \mid c[]) \equiv b[] \mid a().\, c[] \rhd a : \bot, b : 1, c : 1$$

where $a().\, P$ is the process counterpart to introduction of $\bot$ and $a[]$ of 1. Intuitively, $b[]$ and $c[]$ can be performed at the start, but as soon as one is performed, the other has to wait for the input on a. This cannot be modelled inside deterministic general event structures, as it is only deterministic against an environment that will emit on b. In contrast, proofs of MALL$^-$ remain deterministic even if their environment is not total.

We would also be interested in recast multifocusing [9] in our setting by defining a class of focussed causal nets, where there are no concurrency between positive and negative events, and show that sequentialisation always give a focused proof.

Related work. The first fully complete model of MALL$^-$ is based on closure operators [1], later extended to full Linear Logic [24]. True concurrency is used to define innocence, on which the full completeness result rests. However their model does not take advantage of concurrency to account for permutations, as strategies are sequential. This investigation has been extended to concurrent strategies by Mimram and Melliès [25, 26]. De Carvalho showed that the relational model is injective for MELL [11]. In another direction, [4] provides a fully complete model for MALL without game semantics, by using a glueing construction on the model of hypercoherences. [21] explores proof nets a weaker theory of commuting conversions for MALL.

The idea of having intermediate representations between proof nets and proofs has been studied by Faggian and coauthors using l-nets [10, 13–16], leading to a similar analysis to ours: they define a space of causal nets as partial orders and compare different versions of proofs with varying degree of parallelism. Our work recasts this idea using event structures and adds the notion of causal completeness: keeping jumps that cannot be undone by a permutation, which leads naturally to step outside partial orders, as well as full completeness: which causal nets can be strongly sequentialised?

The notion of dependency between logical rules has also been studied in [3] in the case of MLL. From a proof net R, they build a partial order $D_{⅋,\otimes}(R)$ which we believe is very related to $[\![P]\!]$ where P is a sequentialisation of R. Indeed, in the case of MLL *without MIX* a partial order is enough to capture the dependency between rules. The work [12] shows that permutation rules of Linear Logic, understood as asynchronous optimisations on processes, are included in the observational equivalence. [19] studies mutual embedding between polarised proof nets [23] and the control π-calculus [20]. In another direction, we have recently built a fully-abstract, concurrent game semantics model of the synchronous session π-calculus [8]. The difficulty there was to understand name passing and the synchrony of the π-calculus, which is the dual of our objective here: trying to understand the asynchrony behind the conversions of MALL$^-$.

Acknowledgements. We would like to thank Willem Heijltjes, Domenico Ruoppolo, and Olivier Laurent for helpful discussions, and the anonymous referees for their insightful comments. This work has been partially sponsored by: EPSRC EP/K034413/1, EP/K011715/1, EP/L00058X/1, EP/N027833/1, and EP/N028201/1.

References

1. Abramsky, S., Melliès, P.-A.: Concurrent games and full completeness. In: 14th Annual IEEE Symposium on Logic in Computer Science, Trento, Italy, 2–5 July 1999, pp. 431–442 (1999). http://dx.doi.org/10.1109/LICS.1999.782638
2. Baelde, D., Doumane, A., Saurin, A.: Infinitary proof theory: the multiplicative additive case. In: CSL. Leibniz International Proceedings in Informatics (LIPIcs), vol. 62, pp. 42:1–42:17. Schloss Dagstuhl-Leibniz-Zentrum fuer Informatik (2016)
3. Bagnol, M., Doumane, A., Saurin, A.: On the dependencies of logical rules. In: Pitts, A. (ed.) FoSSaCS 2015. LNCS, vol. 9034, pp. 436–450. Springer, Heidelberg (2015). https://doi.org/10.1007/978-3-662-46678-0_28
4. Blute, R., Hamano, M., Scott, P.J.: Softness of hypercoherences and MALL full completeness. Ann. Pure Appl. Logic **131**(1–3), 1–63 (2005). https://doi.org/10.1016/j.apal.2004.05.002
5. Caires, L., Pfenning, F.: Session types as intuitionistic linear propositions. In: Gastin, P., Laroussinie, F. (eds.) CONCUR 2010. LNCS, vol. 6269, pp. 222–236. Springer, Heidelberg (2010). https://doi.org/10.1007/978-3-642-15375-4_16
6. Castellan, S., Clairambault, P., Winskel, G.: Observably deterministic concurrent strategies and intensional full abstraction for parallel-or. In: 2nd International Conference on Formal Structures for Computation and Deduction, FSCD 2017, Oxford, UK, 3–9 September 2017, pp. 12:1–12:16 (2017). https://doi.org/10.4230/LIPIcs.FSCD.2017.12
7. Castellan, S., Yoshida, N.: Causality in linear logic: full completeness and injectivity (unit-free multiplicative-additive fragment). Technical report (2019). http://iso.mor.phis.me/publis/Causality_in_Linear_Logic_FOSSACS19.pdf
8. Castellan, S., Yoshida, N.: Two sides of the same coin: session types and game semantics. Accepted for publication at POPL 2019 (2019)
9. Chaudhuri, K., Miller, D., Saurin, A.: Canonical sequent proofs via multi-focusing. In: Ausiello, G., Karhumäki, J., Mauri, G., Ong, L. (eds.) TCS 2008. IIFIP, vol. 273, pp. 383–396. Springer, Boston, MA (2008). https://doi.org/10.1007/978-0-387-09680-3_26
10. Curien, P.-L., Faggian, C.: L-nets, strategies and proof-nets. In: Ong, L. (ed.) CSL 2005. LNCS, vol. 3634, pp. 167–183. Springer, Heidelberg (2005). https://doi.org/10.1007/11538363_13
11. de Carvalho, D.: The relational model is injective for multiplicative exponential linear logic. In: 25th EACSL Annual Conference on Computer Science Logic, CSL 2016, Marseille, France, 29 August–1 September 2016, pp. 41:1–41:19 (2016). https://doi.org/10.4230/LIPIcs.CSL.2016.41
12. DeYoung, H., Caires, L., Pfenning, F., Toninho, B.: Cut reduction in linear logic as asynchronous session-typed communication. In: CSL, pp. 228–242 (2012)
13. Giamberardino, P.D.: Jump from parallel to sequential proofs: additives. Technical report (2011). https://hal.archives-ouvertes.fr/hal-00616386
14. Faggian, C., Maurel, F.: Ludics nets, a game model of concurrent interaction. In: 20th IEEE Symposium on Logic in Computer Science (LICS 2005), Chicago, IL, USA, 26–29 June 2005, Proceedings, pp. 376–385. IEEE Computer Society (2005). http://dx.doi.org/10.1109/LICS.2005.25
15. Faggian, C., Piccolo, M.: A graph abstract machine describing event structure composition. Electr. Notes Theor. Comput. Sci. **175**(4), 21–36 (2007). https://doi.org/10.1016/j.entcs.2007.04.014

16. Di Giamberardino, P., Faggian, C.: Jump from parallel to sequential proofs: multiplicatives. In: Ésik, Z. (ed.) CSL 2006. LNCS, vol. 4207, pp. 319–333. Springer, Heidelberg (2006). https://doi.org/10.1007/11874683_21
17. Girard, J.Y.: Linear logic. Theor. Comput. Sci. **50**(1), 1–101 (1987)
18. Heijltjes, W., Houston, R.: No proof nets for MLL with units: proof equivalence in MLL is PSPACE-complete. In: CSL-LICS 2014, pp. 50:1–50:10. ACM (2014)
19. Honda, K., Laurent, O.: An exact correspondence between a typed pi-calculus and polarised proof-nets. Theor. Comput. Sci. **411**(22–24), 2223–2238 (2010). https://doi.org/10.1016/j.tcs.2010.01.028
20. Honda, K., Yoshida, N., Berger, M.: Process types as a descriptive tool for interaction. In: Dowek, G. (ed.) RTA 2014. LNCS, vol. 8560, pp. 1–20. Springer, Cham (2014). https://doi.org/10.1007/978-3-319-08918-8_1
21. Hughes, D.J.D., Heijltjes, W.: Conflict nets: efficient locally canonical MALL proof nets. In: Proceedings of the 31st Annual ACM/IEEE Symposium on Logic in Computer Science, LICS 2016, New York, NY, USA, 5–8 July 2016, pp. 437–446 (2016). http://doi.acm.org/10.1145/2933575.2934559
22. Hughes, D.J.D., van Glabbeek, R.J.: Proof nets for unit-free multiplicative-additive linear logic. ACM Trans. Comput. Logic **6**(4), 784–842 (2005)
23. Laurent, O.: Polarized proof-nets and $\lambda\mu$-calculus. Theor. Comput. Sci. **290**(1), 161–188 (2003). https://doi.org/10.1016/S0304-3975(01)00297-3
24. Melliès, P.-A.: Asynchronous games 4: a fully complete model of propositional linear logic. In: 20th IEEE Symposium on Logic in Computer Science (LICS 2005), Chicago, IL, USA, 26–29 June 2005, Proceedings, pp. 386–395 (2005). http://dx.doi.org/10.1109/LICS.2005.6
25. Melliès, P.-A., Mimram, S.: Asynchronous games: innocence without alternation. In: Caires, L., Vasconcelos, V.T. (eds.) CONCUR 2007. LNCS, vol. 4703, pp. 395–411. Springer, Heidelberg (2007). https://doi.org/10.1007/978-3-540-74407-8_27
26. Mimram, S.: Sémantique des jeux asynchrones et réécriture 2-dimensionnelle (asynchronous game semantics and 2-dimensional rewriting systems). Ph.D. thesis, Paris Diderot University, France (2008). https://tel.archives-ouvertes.fr/tel-00338643
27. Wadler, P.: Propositions as sessions. J. Funct. Program. **24**(2–3), 384–418 (2014)
28. Winskel, G.: Event structures. In: Brauer, W., Reisig, W., Rozenberg, G. (eds.) ACPN 1986. LNCS, vol. 255, pp. 325–392. Springer, Heidelberg (1987). https://doi.org/10.1007/3-540-17906-2_31

11

Continuous Reachability for Unordered Data Petri Nets is in PTime

Utkarsh Gupta[1], Preey Shah[1], S. Akshay[1(✉)], and Piotr Hofman[2]

[1] Department of CSE, IIT Bombay, Mumbai, India
akshayss@cse.iitb.ac.in
[2] University of Warsaw, Warsaw, Poland

Abstract. Unordered data Petri nets (UDPN) are an extension of classical Petri nets with tokens that carry data from an infinite domain and where transitions may check equality and disequality of tokens. UDPN are well-structured, so the coverability and termination problems are decidable, but with higher complexity than for Petri nets. On the other hand, the problem of reachability for UDPN is surprisingly complex, and its decidability status remains open. In this paper, we consider the continuous reachability problem for UDPN, which can be seen as an over-approximation of the reachability problem. Our main result is a characterization of continuous reachability for UDPN and polynomial time algorithm for solving it. This is a consequence of a combinatorial argument, which shows that if continuous reachability holds then there exists a run using only polynomially many data values.

Keywords: Petri nets · Continuous reachability · Unordered data · Polynomial time

1 Introduction

The theory of Petri nets has been developing since more than 50 years. On one hand, from a theory perspective, Petri nets are interesting due to their deep mathematical structure and despite exhibiting nice properties, like being a well structured transition system [1], we still don't understand them well. On the other hand, Petri nets are a useful pictorial formalism for modeling and thus found their way to the industry. To connect this theory and practice, it would be desirable to use the developed theory of Petri nets [2–4] for the symbolic analysis and verification of Petri nets models. However, we already know that this is difficult in its full generality. It suffices to recall two results that were proved more than 30 years apart. An old but classical result by Lipton [5] shows that even coverability is ExpSpace-hard, while the non-elementary hardness of the reachability relation has just been established this year [6]. Moreover, when we look at Petri nets based formalisms that are needed to model various aspects of industrial systems, we see that they go beyond the expressivity of Petri nets. For instance, colored Petri nets, which are used in modeling workflows [7], allow the tokens to be colored with an infinite set of colors, and introduce a complex formalism to describe dependencies between colors. This makes all verification problems undecidable for this generic model. Given the basic nature and importance of the reachability problem in Petri nets (and its extensions), there have been several efforts to sidestep the complexity-theoretic hardness results. One common approach is to look for easy subclasses (such as bounded nets [8], free-choice nets [9] etc.). The other approach, which we adopt in this work, is to compute over-approximations of the reachability relation.

Continuous Reachability. A natural question regarding the dynamics of a Petri net is to ask what would happen if tokens instead of behaving like discrete units start to behave like a continuous fluid? This simple question led to an elegant theory of so-called continuous Petri nets [10–12]. Petri nets with continuous semantics allow markings to be functions from places to *nonnegative rational numbers* (i.e., in $\mathbb{Q}^+$) instead of natural numbers. Moreover, whenever a transition is fired a positive rational coefficient is chosen and both the number of consumed and produced tokens are multiplied with the coefficient. This allows to split tokens into arbitrarily small parts and process them independently. This may occur, e.g., in applications related to hybrid systems where the discrete part is used to control the continuous system [13,14]. Interestingly, this makes things simpler to analyze. For example reachability under the continuous semantics for Petri nets is *PTime*-complete [11]. However, when one wants to analyze extensions of Petri nets, e.g., reset Petri nets with continuous semantics, it turns out that reachability is as hard as reachability in reset Petri nets under the usual semantics i.e. it is undecidable[1]. In this paper we identify an extension of Petri nets with unordered data, for which this is not the case and continuous semantics leads to a substantial reduction in the complexity of the reachability problem.

Unordered Data Petri Nets. The possibility of equipping tokens with some additional information is one of the main lines of research regarding extensions of Petri nets, the best known being Colored Petri nets [15] and various types of timed Petri nets [16,17]. In [18] authors equipped tokens with data and restricted interactions between data in a way that allow to transfer techniques for well structured transition systems. They identified various classes of nets exhibiting interesting combinatorial properties which led to a number of results [19–23]. Unordered Data Petri Nets (UDPN), are simplest among them: every token carries a single datum like a barcode and transitions may check equality or disequality of data in consumed and produced tokens. UDPN are the only class identified in [18] for which the reachability is still unsolved, although in [20] authors show that the problem is at least Ackermannian-hard (for all other data extensions, reachability is undecidable). A recent attempt to over-approximate the reachability relation for UDPN in [22]

[1] This can be seen on the same lines as the proof of undecidability of continuous reachability for Petri nets with zero tests [12].

considers integer reachability i.e. number of tokens may get negative during the run (also called solution of the state equation). From the above perspective, this paper is an extension of the mentioned line of research.

Our Contribution. Our main contribution is a characterization of continuous reachability in UDPN and a polynomial time algorithm for solving it. Observe that if we find an upper bound on the minimal number of data required by a run between two configurations (if any run exists), then we can reduce continuous reachability in UDPN to continuous reachability in vanilla Petri nets with an exponential blowup and use the already developed characterization from [11]. In Sect. 5 we prove such a bound on the minimal number of required data. The bound is novel and exploits techniques that did not appear previously in the context of data nets. Further, the obtained bounds are lower than bounds on the number of data values required to solve the state equation [22], which is surprising considering that existence of a continuous run requires a solution of a sort of state equation. Precisely, the difference is that we are looking for solutions of the state equation over $\mathbb{Q}^+$ instead of $\mathbb{N}$ and in this case we prove better bounds for the number of data required. This also gives us an easy polytime algorithm for finding $\mathbb{Q}^+$-solutions of state equations of UDPN (we remark that for Petri nets without data, this appears among standard algebraic techniques [24]).

Finally, with the above bound, we solve continuous reachability in UDPN by adapting the techniques from the non-data setting of [12,25]. We adapt the characterization of continuous reachability to the data setting and next encode it as system of linear equations with implications. In doing so, however, we face the problem that a naive encoding (representing data explicitly) gives a system of equations of exponential size, giving only an ExpTime-algorithm. To improve the complexity, we use histograms, a combinatorial tool developed in [22], to compress the description of solutions of state equations in UDPNs. However, this may lead to spurious solutions for continuous reachability. To eliminate them, we show that it suffices to first transform the net and then apply the idea of histograms to characterize continuous runs in the modified net. The whole procedure is described in Sect. 7.3 and leads us to our *PTime* algorithm for continuous reachability in UDPN. Note that since we easily have *PTime* hardness for the problem (even without data), we obtain that the problem of continuous reachability in UDPN is *PTime*-complete.

Towards Verification. Over-approximations are useful in verification of Petri nets and their extensions: as explained in [24], for many practical problems, over-approximate solutions are already correct. Further, we can use them as a sub-routine to improve the practical performance of verification algorithms. A remarkable example is the recent work in [25], where the *PTime* continuous reachability algorithm for Petri nets from [11] is used as a subroutine to solve the *ExpSpace* hard coverability problem in Petri nets, outperforming the best known tools for this problem, such as Petrinizer [26]. Our results can be seen as a first step in the same spirit towards handling practical instances of coverability, but for the extended model of UDPN, where the coverability problem for UDPN is known to be Ackermannian-hard [20].

Omitted proofs and details can be found in the extended version at [27].

2 Preliminaries

We denote integers, non-negative integers, rationals, and reals as $\mathbb{Z}, \mathbb{N}, \mathbb{Q}$, and $\mathbb{R}$, respectively. For a set $\mathbb{X} \subseteq \mathbb{R}$ denote by $\mathbb{X}^+$, the set of all non-negative elements of $\mathbb{X}$. We denote by $\mathbf{0}$, a vector whose entries are all zero. We define in a standard point-wise way operations on vectors i.e. *scalar multiplication* $\cdot$, *addition* $+$, *subtraction* $-$, *and vector comparison* $\leq$. In this paper, we use functions of the type $X \to (Y \to Z)$, and instead of $(f(x))(y)$, we write $f(y, x)$. For functions f, g where the range of g is a subset of the domain of f, we denote their composition by $f \circ g$. If π is an injection then by π^{-1} we mean a partial function such that $\pi^{-1} \circ \pi$ is the identity function. Let $f : X_1 \to Y$, $g : X_2 \to Y$ be two functions with addition and scalar multiplication operations defined on Y. A *scalar multiplication* of a function is defined as follows $(a \cdot f)(x) = a \cdot f(x)$ for all $x \in X_1$. We lift *addition* operation to functions pointwise, i.e. $f+g : X_1 \cup X_2 \to Y$ such that

$$(f+g)(x) = \begin{cases} f(x) & \text{if } x \in X_1 \setminus X_2 \\ g(x) & \text{if } x \in X_2 \setminus X_1 \\ f(x) + g(x) & \text{if } x \in X_1 \cap X_2. \end{cases}$$

Similarly for *subtraction* $(f - g)(x) = f(x) + -1 \cdot g(x)$, and $f \leq g$ if for all $x \in X_1 \cup X_2, (g - f)(x) \leq 0$.

We use *matrices* with *rows and columns* indexed by sets $\mathbb{S}_1, \mathbb{S}_2$, possibly infinite. For a matrix M, let $M(r, c)$ denote the entry at column c and row r, and $M(r, \bullet)$, $M(\bullet, c)$ denote the row vector indexed by r and column vector indexed by c, respectively. Denote by $col(M)$, $row(M)$ the set of indices of nonzero columns and nonzero rows of the matrix M, respectively. Even if we have infinitely many rows or columns, our matrices will have only finitely many *nonzero* rows and columns, and only this nonzero part will be represented. Following our nonstandard matrix definition we precisely define operations on them, although they are natural. First, a *multiplication by a constant number* produces a new matrix with row and columns labelled with the same sets $\mathbb{S}_1, \mathbb{S}_2$ and defined as follows $(a \cdot M)(r, c) = a \cdot (M(r, c))$ for all $(r, c) \in \mathbb{S}_1 \times \mathbb{S}_2$. *Addition* of two matrices is only defined if the sets indexing rows $\mathbb{S}_1$ and columns $\mathbb{S}_2$ are the same for both summands M_1 and M_2, $\forall(r, c) \in \mathbb{S}_1 \times \mathbb{S}_2$ the sum $(M_1 + M_2)(r, c) = M_1(r, c) + M_2(r, c)$, the *subtraction* $M_1 - M_2$ is a shorthand for $M_1 + (-1) \cdot M_2$. Observe that all but finitely many entries in matrices are 0, and therefore when we do computation on matrices we can restrict to rows $row(M_1) \cup row(M_2)$ and columns $col(M_1) \cup col(M_2)$. Similarly the *comparison* for two matrices M_1, M_2 is defined as follows $M_1 \leq M_2$ if $\forall(r, c) \in (row(M_1) \cup row(M_2)) \times (col(M_1) \cup col(M_2))$ $M_1(r, c) \leq M_2(r, c)$; relations $>, \geq, \leq$ are defined analogically. The last operation which we need is matrix multiplication $M_1 \cdot M_2 = M_3$, it is only allowed if the set of columns of the first matrix M_1 is the same as the set of rows of the second matrix M_2, the sets of rows and columns of the resulting matrix M_3 are rows of the matrix M_1 and columns of M_2, respectively. $M_3(r, c) = \sum_k M_1(r, k) M_2(k, c)$

where k runs through columns of M_1. Again, observe that if the row or a column is equal to 0 for all entries then the effect of multiplication is 0, thus we may restrict to $row(M_1)$ and $col(M_2)$. Moreover in the sum it suffices to write $\sum_{k \in col(M_1)} M_1(r,k)M_2(k,c)$.

3 UDPN, Reachability and Its Variants: Our Main Results

Unordered data Petri nets extend the classical model of Petri nets by allowing each token to hold a data value from a countably-infinite domain $\mathbb{D}$. Our definition is closest to the definition of ν-Petri nets from [28]. For simplicity we choose this one instead of using the equivalent but complex one from [18].

Definition 1. *Let $\mathbb{D}$ be a countably infinite set. An unordered data Petri net (UDPN) over domain $\mathbb{D}$ is a tuple (P, T, F, Var) where P is a finite set of places, T is a finite set of transitions, Var is a finite set of variables, and $F : (P \times T) \cup (T \times P) \to (Var \to \mathbb{N})$ is a flow function that assigns each place $p \in P$ and transition $t \in T$ a function over variables in Var.*

For each transition $t \in T$ we define functions $F(\bullet, t)$ and $F(t, \bullet)$, $Var \to (P \to \mathbb{N})$ as $F(\bullet, t)(p, x) = F(p, t)(x)$ and analogously $F(t, \bullet)(p, x) = F(t, p)(x)$. *Displacement* of the transition t is a function $\Delta(t) : Var \to (P \to \mathbb{Z})$ defined as $\Delta(t) \stackrel{\text{def}}{=} F(t, \bullet) - F(\bullet, t)$.

For $\mathbb{X} \in \{\mathbb{N}, \mathbb{Z}, \mathbb{Q}, \mathbb{Q}^+\}$, we define an $\mathbb{X}$-*marking* as a function $M : \mathbb{D} \to (P \to \mathbb{X})$ that is constant 0 on all except finitely many values of $\mathbb{D}$. Intuitively, $M(p, \alpha)$ denotes the number of *tokens* with the data value α at place p. The fact that it is 0 at all but finitely many data means that the number of tokens in any $\mathbb{X}$-marking is finite. We denote the infinite set of all $\mathbb{X}$-markings by $\mathcal{M}_{\mathbb{X}}$.

We define an $\mathbb{X}$-*step* as a triple (c, t, π) for a transition $t \in T$, *mode* π being an injective map $\pi : Var \to \mathbb{D}$, and a scalar constant $c \in \mathbb{X}^+$. An $\mathbb{X}$-step (c, t, π) is *fireable* at a $\mathbb{X}$-marking $\boldsymbol{i}$ if $\boldsymbol{i} - c \cdot F(\bullet, t) \circ \pi^{-1} \in \mathcal{M}_{\mathbb{X}}$.

The $\mathbb{X}$-marking $\boldsymbol{f}$ reached after *firing* an $\mathbb{X}$-step (c, t, π) at $\boldsymbol{i}$ is given as $\boldsymbol{f} = \boldsymbol{i} + c \cdot \Delta(t) \circ \pi^{-1}$. We also say that an $\mathbb{X}$-step (c, t, π) when fired *consumes* tokens $c \cdot F(\bullet, t) \circ \pi^{-1}$ and *produces* tokens $c \cdot F(t, \bullet) \circ \pi^{-1}$. We define an $\mathbb{X}$-run as a sequence of $\mathbb{X}$-steps and we can represent it as $\{(c_i, t_i, \pi_i)\}_{|\rho|}$ where (c_i, t_i, π_i) is the ith $\mathbb{X}$-step and $|\rho|$ is the number of $\mathbb{X}$-steps. A run $\rho = \{(c_i, t_i, \pi_i)\}_{|\rho|}$ is fireable at a $\mathbb{X}$-marking $\boldsymbol{i}$ if, $\forall 1 \le i \le |\rho|$, the step (c_i, t_i, π_i) is fireable at $\boldsymbol{i} + \sum_{j=1}^{i-1} c_i \Delta(t_j) \circ \pi_j^{-1}$. By $\boldsymbol{i} \xrightarrow{\rho}_{\mathbb{X}} \boldsymbol{f}$ we denote that ρ is fireable at $\boldsymbol{i}$ and after firing ρ at $\boldsymbol{i}$ we reach $\mathbb{X}$-marking $\boldsymbol{f} = \boldsymbol{i} + \sum_{i=1}^{|\rho|} c_i \cdot \Delta(t_i) \circ \pi_i^{-1}$. We call (the function computed by) the mentioned sum $\sum_{i=1}^{|\rho|} c_i \Delta(t_i) \circ \pi_i^{-1}$ as the *effect* of the run and denote it by $\Delta(\rho)$.

We fix some notations for the rest of the paper. We use Greek letters α, β, γ to denote data values from data domain $\mathbb{D}$, ρ, σ to denote a run, π to denote a mode and x, y, z to denote the variables. When clear from the context, we may omit $\mathbb{X}$ from $\mathbb{X}$-marking, $\mathbb{X}$-run and just write marking, run, etc. Further, we will use letters in bold, e.g., $\boldsymbol{m}$ to denote markings, where $\boldsymbol{i}, \boldsymbol{f}$ will be used for initial and final markings respectively. Further, throughout the paper, unless stated explicitly otherwise, we will refer to a UDPN $\mathcal{N} = (P, T, F, Var)$, therefore P, T, F, Var will denote the places, transitions, flow, and variables of this UDPN.

Example 1. An example of a simple UDPN $\mathcal{N}_1$ is given in Fig. 1. For this example, we have $P = \{p_1, p_2, p_3, p_4\}$, $T = \{t\}$, $Var = \{x, y, z\}$, and the flow relation is given by $F(p_1, t) = \{y \mapsto 1\}$, $F(p_2, t) = \{x \mapsto 1\}$, $F(t, p_3) = \{y \mapsto 2\}$, $F(t, p_4) = \{x \mapsto 1, z \mapsto 1\}$, and an assignment of 0 to every variable for the remaining of the pairs. Thus, for enabling transition p_1 and p_2 must have one token each with a different data value (since $x \neq y$) and after firing two tokens are produced in p_3 with same data value as was consumed from p_1 and two tokens are produced in p_4, one of whom has same data as consumed from p_2.

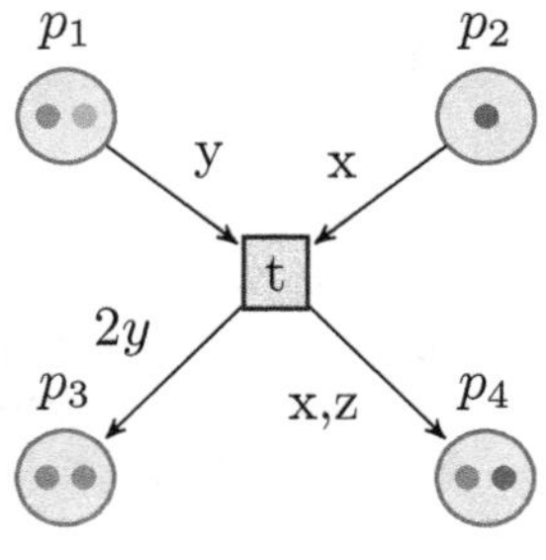

Fig. 1. A simple UDPN $\mathcal{N}_1$

Definition 2. *Given $\mathbb{X}$-markings $\boldsymbol{i}, \boldsymbol{f}$, we say $\boldsymbol{f}$ is $\mathbb{X}$-reachable from $\boldsymbol{i}$ if there exists an $\mathbb{X}$-run ρ s.t., $\boldsymbol{i} \xrightarrow{\rho}_{\mathbb{X}} \boldsymbol{f}$.*

When $\mathbb{X} = \mathbb{N}$, $\mathbb{X}$-reachability is the classical reachability problem, whose decidability is still unknown, while $\mathbb{Z}$-reachability for UDPN is in NP [22].

In this paper we tackle $\mathbb{Q}$ and $\mathbb{Q}^+$-reachability, also called *continuous* reachability in UDPN.

The first step towards the solution is showing that if a $\mathbb{Q}^+$-marking $\boldsymbol{f}$ is $\mathbb{Q}^+$-reachable from a $\mathbb{Q}^+$-marking $\boldsymbol{i}$, then there exists a $\mathbb{Q}^+$-run ρ which uses polynomially many data values and $\boldsymbol{i} \xrightarrow{\rho}_{\mathbb{Q}^+} \boldsymbol{f}$. We first formalize the set of distinct data values associated with $\mathbb{X}$-markings, data values *used* in $\mathbb{X}$-runs and variables associated with a transition.

Definition 3. *For $\mathcal{N} = (P, T, F, Var)$ a UDPN, $\mathbb{X}$-marking $\boldsymbol{m}$, $t \in T$, and $\mathbb{X}$-run $\rho = \{(c_i, t_i, \pi_i)\}_{|\rho|}$, we define*

1. $vars(t) = \{x \in Var \mid \exists p \in P : F(p, t)(x) \neq 0 \vee F(t, p)(x) \neq 0\}$.
2. $dval(\boldsymbol{m}) = \{\alpha \in \mathbb{D} \mid \exists p \in P : \boldsymbol{m}(p, \alpha) \neq 0\}$.
3. $dval(\rho) = \{\alpha \in \mathbb{D} \mid \exists i \leq |\rho| \; \exists x \in vars(t_i) : (\pi_i(x) = \alpha)\}$.

With this we state the first main result of this paper, which provides a bound on witnesses of $\mathbb{Q}, \mathbb{Q}^+$-reachability, and is proved in Sect. 5.

Theorem 1. *For $\mathbb{X} \in \{\mathbb{Q}, \mathbb{Q}^+\}$, if an $\mathbb{X}$-marking $\boldsymbol{f}$ is $\mathbb{X}$-reachable from an initial $\mathbb{X}$-marking $\boldsymbol{i}$, then there is an $\mathbb{X}$-run ρ such that $\boldsymbol{i} \xrightarrow{\rho}_{\mathbb{X}} \boldsymbol{f}$ and $|dval(\rho)| \leq |dval(\boldsymbol{i}) \cup dval(\boldsymbol{f})| + 1 + \max_{t \in T}(|vars(t)|)$.*

Using the above bound, we obtain a polynomial time algorithm for $\mathbb{Q}$-reachability, as detailed in Sect. 6.

Theorem 2. *Given $\mathcal{N} = (P, T, F, Var)$ a UDPN and two $\mathbb{Q}$-markings $\boldsymbol{i}$, $\boldsymbol{f}$, deciding if $\boldsymbol{f}$ is $\mathbb{Q}$-reachable from $\boldsymbol{i}$ in $\mathcal{N}$ is in polynomial time.*

Finally, we consider continuous, i.e., $\mathbb{Q}^+$-reachability for UDPN. We adapt the techniques used for $\mathbb{Q}^+$-reachability of Petri nets without data from [11,12] to the setting with data, and obtain a characterization of $\mathbb{Q}^+$-reachability for UDPN in Sect. 7.1. Finally, in Sect. 7.3, we show how the characterization can be combined with the above bound and compression techniques from [22] to obtain a polynomial sized system of linear equations with implications over $\mathbb{Q}^+$. To do so, we require a slight transformation of the net which is described in Sect. 7.2. This leads to our headline result, stated below.

Theorem 3 (Continuous reachability for UDPN). *Given a UDPN $\mathcal{N} = (P, T, F, Var)$ and two $\mathbb{Q}^+$-markings $\boldsymbol{i}$, $\boldsymbol{f}$, deciding if $\boldsymbol{f}$ is $\mathbb{Q}^+$-reachable from $\boldsymbol{i}$ in $\mathcal{N}$ is in polynomial time.*

The rest of this paper is dedicated to proving these theorems. First, we present an equivalent formulation via matrices, which simplifies the technical arguments.

4 Equivalent Formulation via Matrices

From now on, we restrict $\mathbb{X}$ to a symbol denoting $\mathbb{Q}$ or $\mathbb{Q}^+$. We formulate the definitions presented earlier in terms of matrices, since defining object such as $\mathbb{X}$-marking as functions is intuitive to define but difficult to operate upon.

In the following, we abuse the notation and use the same names for objects as well as matrices representing them. We remark that this is safe as all arithmetic operations on objects correspond to matching operations on matrices.

An $\mathbb{X}$-marking $\boldsymbol{m}$ is a $P \times \mathbb{D}$ matrix M, where $\forall p \in P, \forall \alpha \in \mathbb{D}, M(p, \alpha) = \boldsymbol{m}(p, \alpha)$. As a *finite representation*, we keep only a $P \times dval(\boldsymbol{m})$ matrix of non-zero columns. For a transition $t \in T$, we represent $F(t, \bullet), F(\bullet, t)$ as $P \times Var$ matrices. Note that $(t, \bullet)$ is not the position in the matrix, but is part of the name of the matrix; its entry at $(i, j) \in P \times Var$ is given by $F(t, \bullet)(i, j)$. For a place $p \in row(F(t, \bullet))$, the row $F(t, \bullet)(p, \bullet)$ is a vector in $\mathbb{N}^{Var}$, given by an equation $F(\bullet, t)(p, \bullet)(x) = F(p, t)(x)$ for $p \in P, t \in T, x \in Var$. Similarly, $\Delta(t)$ is a $P \times Var$ matrix with $\Delta(t)(p, x) = F(t, \bullet)(p, x) - F(\bullet, t)(p, x)$ for $t \in T, p \in P$, and $x \in Var$. Although, both $\Delta(t)$ and $F(\bullet, t)$ are defined as $P \times Var$ matrices, only the columns for variables in $vars(t)$ may be non-zero, so often we will iterate only over $vars(t)$ instead of Var.

Finally, we capture a mode $\pi : Var \to \mathbb{D}$ as a $Var \times \mathbb{D}$ permutation matrix $\mathcal{P}$. Although $\mathcal{P}$ may not be a square matrix, we abuse notation and call them permutation matrices. $\mathcal{P}$ basically represents assignment of variables in Var to data values just like π does. An entry of 1 represents that the corresponding variable is assigned corresponding data value in mode π. Thus, for each mode $\pi : Var \to \mathbb{D}$ there is a permutation matrix $\mathcal{P}_\pi$, such that for all $x \in Var$, $\alpha \in \mathbb{D}$, $\mathcal{P}_\pi(x, \alpha) = 1$ if $\pi(x) = \alpha$, and $\mathcal{P}_\pi(x, \alpha) = 0$ otherwise. Formulating a mode as a permutation matrix has the advantage that $\Delta(t) \circ \pi^{-1}$ is captured by $\Delta(t) \cdot \mathcal{P}_\pi$.

Example 2. In the UDPN $\mathcal{N}_1$ from Example 1, if $\mathbb{D} = \{red, blue, green, black\}$ then the initial marking $\boldsymbol{i}$ can be represented by the matrix $\boldsymbol{i}$ below and the function $\Delta(t)$ by the matrix $\Delta(t)$

$$\boldsymbol{i} = \begin{array}{c} \begin{matrix} red & blue & green & black \end{matrix} \\ \begin{pmatrix} 1 & 0 & 1 & 0 \\ 0 & 1 & 0 & 0 \\ 2 & 0 & 0 & 0 \\ 1 & 1 & 0 & 0 \end{pmatrix} \end{array} \begin{matrix} p_1 \\ p_2 \\ p_3 \\ p_4 \end{matrix} \qquad \Delta(t) = \begin{array}{c} \begin{matrix} x & y & z \end{matrix} \\ \begin{pmatrix} 0 & -1 & 0 \\ -1 & 0 & 0 \\ 0 & 2 & 0 \\ 1 & 0 & 1 \end{pmatrix} \end{array} \begin{matrix} p_1 \\ p_2 \\ p_3 \\ p_4 \end{matrix}$$

If we fire transition t with the assignment $x = blue, y = green, z = black$, we get the following net depicted below (left), with marking $\boldsymbol{f}$ (below center). The permutation matrix corresponding to the mode of fired transition is given by $\mathcal{P}$ matrix on the right. Note that the matrix $\boldsymbol{f} - \boldsymbol{i}$ is indeed the matrix $\Delta(t) \cdot \mathcal{P}$.

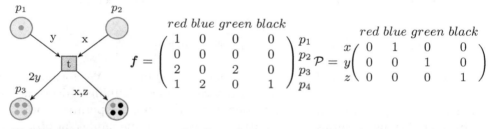

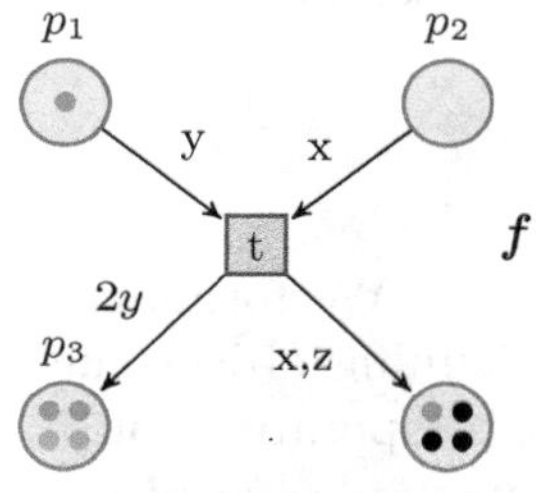

$$\boldsymbol{f} = \begin{array}{c} \begin{matrix} red & blue & green & black \end{matrix} \\ \begin{pmatrix} 1 & 0 & 0 & 0 \\ 0 & 0 & 0 & 0 \\ 2 & 0 & 2 & 0 \\ 1 & 2 & 0 & 1 \end{pmatrix} \end{array} \begin{matrix} p_1 \\ p_2 \\ p_3 \\ p_4 \end{matrix} \quad \mathcal{P} = \begin{matrix} \\ x \\ y \\ z \end{matrix} \begin{array}{c} \begin{matrix} red & blue & green & black \end{matrix} \\ \begin{pmatrix} 0 & 1 & 0 & 0 \\ 0 & 0 & 1 & 0 \\ 0 & 0 & 0 & 1 \end{pmatrix} \end{array}$$

Using the representations developed so far we can represent an $\mathbb{X}$-run ρ as $\{(c_i, t_i, \mathcal{P}_i)\}_{|\rho|}$ where $(c_i, t_i, \mathcal{P}_i)$ denotes the ith $\mathbb{X}$-step fired with coefficient c_i using transition t_i with a mode corresponding to permutation matrix $\mathcal{P}_i$. The sum of the matrices $(\sum_{i=1}^{|\rho|} c_i \Delta(t_i) \cdot \mathcal{P}_i)$ gives us the effect of the run i.e. $\Delta(\rho) = \boldsymbol{f} - \boldsymbol{i}$ where $\boldsymbol{i} \xrightarrow{\rho}_{\mathbb{X}} \boldsymbol{f}$. Effect of an $\mathbb{X}$-run ρ on a data value α is $\Delta(\rho)(\bullet, \alpha)$. Also, for an $\mathbb{X}$-run $\rho = \{(c_i, t_i, \mathcal{P}_i)\}_{|\rho|}$, define $k\rho = \{(kc_i, t_i, \mathcal{P}_i)\}_{|\rho|}$ where $k \in \mathbb{X}^+$.

5 Bounding Number of Data Values Used in $\mathbb{Q}, \mathbb{Q}^+$-run

We now prove the first main result of the paper, namely, Theorem 1, which shows a linear upper bound on the number of data values required in a $\mathbb{Q}^+$-run and a $\mathbb{Q}$-run. Theorem 1 is an immediate consequence of the following lemma, which states that if more than a linearly bounded number of data values are used in a $\mathbb{Q}$ or $\mathbb{Q}^+$ run, then there is another such run in which we use at least one less data value.

Lemma 1. *Let $\mathbb{X} \in \{\mathbb{Q}, \mathbb{Q}^+\}$. If there exists an $\mathbb{X}$-run σ such that $\boldsymbol{i} \xrightarrow{\sigma}_{\mathbb{X}} \boldsymbol{f}$ and $|dval(\sigma)| > |dval(\boldsymbol{i}) \cup dval(\boldsymbol{f})| + 1 + \max_{t \in T}(|vars(t)|)$, then there exists an $\mathbb{X}$-run ρ such that $\boldsymbol{i} \xrightarrow{\rho}_{\mathbb{X}} \boldsymbol{f}$ and $|dval(\rho)| \leq |dval(\sigma)| - 1$.*

By repeatedly applying this lemma, Theorem 1 follows immediately. The rest of this section is devoted to proving this lemma. The central idea is to take any $\mathbb{Q}$ or $\mathbb{Q}^+$-run between $\boldsymbol{i}$, $\boldsymbol{f}$ and transform it to use at least one less data value.

5.1 Transformation of an $\mathbb{X}$-run

The transformation which we call *decrease* is defined as a combination of two separate operations on an $\mathbb{X}$-run; we name them *uniformize* and *replace* and denote them by $\mathcal{U}$ and $\mathcal{R}$ respectively.

- *uniformize* takes an $\mathbb{X}$-step and a non-empty set of data values $\mathbb{E}$ as input and produces an $\mathbb{X}$-run, such that in the resultant run, the effect of the run for each data value in $\mathbb{E}$ is equal.
- *replace* takes an $\mathbb{X}$-step, a single data value α, and a non-empty set of data values $\mathbb{E}$ as input and outputs an $\mathbb{X}$-step which doesn't use data value α.

The intuition behind the decrease operation is that we would like to take two data values α and β used in the run such that effect on both of them is $\mathbf{0}$ (they exists as the effect on every data value not present in the initial of final configuration is $\mathbf{0}$) and replace usage of α by β. However, such a replacement can only be done if both data are not used together in a single step (indeed, a mode π cannot assign the same data values to two variables). Unfortunately we cannot guarantee the existence of such a β that may replace α globally. We circumvent this by applying the *replace* operation separately for every step, replacing α with different data values in different steps.

But such a transformation would not preserve the effect of the run. To repair this aspect we uniformize i.e. guarantee that the final effect after replacing α by other data values is equal for every datum that is used to replace α. As the effect on α was $\mathbf{0}$ then if we split it uniformly it adds $\mathbf{0}$ to effects of data replacing α, which is exactly what we want. We now formalize this intuition below.

The Uniformize Operator. By © we denote an operator of concatenation of two sequences. Although the data set $\mathbb{D}$ is unordered, the following definitions require access to an arbitrary but fixed linear order on its elements. The definition of the *uniformize* operator needs another operator to act on an $\mathbb{X}$-step, which we call *rotate* and denote by *rot*.

Definition 4. *For a non-empty finite set of data values $\mathbb{E} \subset \mathbb{D}$ and an $\mathbb{X}$-step, $\omega = (c, t, \mathcal{P})$, define $rot(\mathbb{E}, \omega) = (c, t, \mathcal{P}')$ where $\mathcal{P}'$ is obtained from $\mathcal{P}$ as follows.*

- $\forall \alpha \in col(\mathcal{P}) \setminus \mathbb{E}$, $\mathcal{P}'(\bullet, \alpha) = \mathcal{P}(\bullet, \alpha)$.
- $\forall \alpha \in \mathbb{E}$, $\mathcal{P}'(\bullet, \alpha) = \mathcal{P}(\bullet, next_{\mathbb{E}}(\alpha))$, *where* $next_{\mathbb{E}}(\alpha) = \min(\{\beta \in \mathbb{E} \mid \beta > \alpha\})$ *if* $|\{\beta \in \mathbb{E} \mid \beta > \alpha\}| > 0$ *and* $\min(\mathbb{E})$ *otherwise.*

For a fixed set $\mathbb{E}$, we can repeatedly apply $rot(\mathbb{E}, \bullet)$ operation on an $\mathbb{X}$-step, which we denote by $rot^k(\mathbb{E}, \omega)$, where k is the number of times we applied the operation (for example: $rot^2(\mathbb{E}, \omega) = rot(\mathbb{E}, (rot(\mathbb{E}, \omega)))$.

Definition 5. *For a finite and non-empty set of data values* $\mathbb{E} \subset \mathbb{D}$ *and an* $\mathbb{X}$*-step* $\omega = (c, t, \mathcal{P})$*, we define uniformize as follows*

$$\mathcal{U}(\mathbb{E}, \omega) = rot^0(\mathbb{E}, \tfrac{\omega}{|\mathbb{E}|}) \copyright\ rot^1(\mathbb{E}, \tfrac{\omega}{|\mathbb{E}|}) \copyright\ rot^2(\mathbb{E}, \tfrac{\omega}{|\mathbb{E}|}) \copyright \dots \copyright\ rot^{|\mathbb{E}|-1}(\mathbb{E}, \tfrac{\omega}{|\mathbb{E}|}).$$

An important property of uniformize is its effect on data values.

Lemma 2. *For a finite and non-empty set of data values* $\mathbb{E} \subset \mathbb{D}$ *and an* $\mathbb{X}$*-step* $\omega = (c, t, \mathcal{P})$, $\boldsymbol{i} \xrightarrow{\omega}_{\mathbb{Q}^+} \boldsymbol{f}$*, if* $\boldsymbol{i}' \xrightarrow{\mathcal{U}(\mathbb{E},\omega)} \boldsymbol{f}'$*, then*

1. $\forall \alpha \in dval(\omega) \backslash \mathbb{E}$, $\boldsymbol{f}'(\bullet, \alpha) - \boldsymbol{i}'(\bullet, \alpha) = \boldsymbol{f}(\bullet, \alpha) - \boldsymbol{i}(\bullet, \alpha)$
2. $\forall \alpha \in \mathbb{E}$, $, \boldsymbol{f}'(\bullet, \alpha) - \boldsymbol{i}'(\bullet, \alpha) = \frac{\sum_{\beta \in \mathbb{E}} (\boldsymbol{f}(\bullet, \beta) - \boldsymbol{i}(\bullet, \beta))}{|\mathbb{E}|}$.

This lemma tells us the effect of the run on the initial marking is equalized for data values in $\mathbb{E}$ by the $\mathcal{U}$ operation, and is unchanged for the other data values.

The Replace Operator. To define the *replace* operator it is useful to introduce $swap_{\alpha,\beta}(\mathcal{P})$ which exchanges columns α and β in the matrix $\mathcal{P}$.

Definition 6. *For a finite set of data values* $\mathbb{E}$*, an* $\mathbb{X}$*-step* $\omega = (c, t, \mathcal{P})$*, and* $\alpha \notin \mathbb{E}$ *we define replace as follows*

$$\mathcal{R}(\alpha, \mathbb{E}, \omega) = \begin{cases} (c, t, \mathcal{P}) & \textit{if } (F(t, \bullet) \cdot \mathcal{P})(\bullet, \alpha) = (F(\bullet, t) \cdot \mathcal{P})(\bullet, \alpha) = \boldsymbol{0} \\ (c, t, swap_{\alpha,\beta}(\mathcal{P})) & \textit{else, if } \beta \textit{ is the smallest datum in } \mathbb{E} \textit{ s.t.,} \\ & (F(t, \bullet) \cdot \mathcal{P})(\bullet, \beta) = (F(\bullet, t) \cdot \mathcal{P})(\bullet, \beta) = \boldsymbol{0} \\ undefined & \textit{otherwise.} \end{cases}$$

After applying the *replace* operation α is no longer used in the run, which reduces the number of data values used in the run. Observe that *replace* can not be always applied to an $\mathbb{X}$-step. It requires a zero column labelled with an element from $\mathbb{E}$ in the permutation matrix corresponding to the $\mathbb{X}$-step.

The Decrease Transformation. Finally, we define the transformation on an $\mathbb{X}$-run between two markings which we call *decrease* and denote by *dec*.

Definition 7. *For two* $\mathbb{X}$*-markings* $\boldsymbol{i}$, $\boldsymbol{f}$*, and an* $\mathbb{X}$*-run* σ *such that* $\boldsymbol{i} \xrightarrow{\sigma}_{\mathbb{X}} \boldsymbol{f}$ *and* $|dval(\sigma)| > |dval(\boldsymbol{i}) \cup dval(\boldsymbol{f})| + 1 + \max_{t \in T}(|vars(t)|)$*, let* $\{\alpha\} \cup \mathbb{E} = dval(\sigma) \setminus (dval(\boldsymbol{i}) \cup dval(\boldsymbol{f}))$ *and* $\alpha \notin \mathbb{E}$*. We define decrease by,* $dec(\mathbb{E}, \alpha, \sigma) =$

$$\mathcal{U}(\mathbb{E}, \mathcal{R}(\alpha, \mathbb{E}, \sigma(1))) \copyright\ \mathcal{U}(\mathbb{E}, \mathcal{R}(\alpha, \mathbb{E}, \sigma(2))) \copyright \dots \copyright\ \mathcal{U}(\mathbb{E}, \mathcal{R}(\alpha, \mathbb{E}, \sigma(|\sigma|))).$$

where $\sigma(j)$ *denotes the* j^{th} $\mathbb{X}$*-step of* σ.

Observe that the required size of $dval(\sigma)$ guarantees existence of a $\beta \in \mathbb{E}$ which can be replaced with α, for every application of the $\mathcal{R}$ operation. Note that the exchanged data value β could be different for each step. Finally, we can analyze the *decrease* transformation and show that if the original run allows for the *decrease* transformation (as given in the above definition), then after the application of it, the resulting sequence of transitions is a valid run of the system.

Lemma 3. *Let σ be an $\mathbb{X}$-run such that $\boldsymbol{i} \xrightarrow{\sigma}_{\mathbb{X}} \boldsymbol{f}$ and $|dval(\sigma)| > |dval(\boldsymbol{i}) \cup dval(\boldsymbol{f})| + 1 + \max_{t\in T}(|dval(t)|)$. Let $\alpha \in dval(\sigma) \setminus (dval(\boldsymbol{i}) \cup dval(\boldsymbol{f}))$ and $\mathbb{E} = dval(\sigma) \setminus (dval(\boldsymbol{i}) \cup dval(\boldsymbol{f}) \cup \{\alpha\})$. Then for $\rho = dec(\mathbb{E}, \alpha, \sigma)$, we obtain $\boldsymbol{i} \xrightarrow{\rho}_{\mathbb{X}} \boldsymbol{f}$.*

Proof. Suppose $\sigma = \sigma_1\sigma_2\ldots\sigma_l$ where each $\sigma_j = (c_j, t_j, \mathcal{P}_j)$, for $1 \le j \le l$ is an $\mathbb{X}$-step. Then $\rho = \rho_1 \copyright \ldots \copyright \rho_l$, where each ρ_j is an $\mathbb{X}$-run defined by $\rho_j = \mathcal{U}(\mathbb{E}, \mathcal{R}(\alpha, \mathbb{E}, \sigma_j))$. It will be useful to identify intermediate $\mathbb{X}$-markings

$$\boldsymbol{i} = \boldsymbol{m}_0 \xrightarrow{\sigma_1}_{\mathbb{X}} \boldsymbol{m}_1 \xrightarrow{\sigma_2}_{\mathbb{X}} \boldsymbol{m}_2 \xrightarrow{\sigma_3}_{\mathbb{X}} \ldots \xrightarrow{\sigma_l}_{\mathbb{X}} \boldsymbol{m}_l = \boldsymbol{f} \tag{1}$$

$$\boldsymbol{i} = \boldsymbol{m}'_o \xrightarrow{\mathcal{U}(\mathbb{E},\mathcal{R}(\alpha,\mathbb{E},\sigma_1))}_{\mathbb{Q}} \boldsymbol{m}'_1 \xrightarrow{\mathcal{U}(\mathbb{E},\mathcal{R}(\alpha,\mathbb{E},\sigma_2))}_{\mathbb{Q}} \boldsymbol{m}'_2 \ldots \xrightarrow{\mathcal{U}(\mathbb{E},\mathcal{R}(\alpha,\mathbb{E},\sigma_l))}_{\mathbb{Q}} \boldsymbol{m}'_l = \boldsymbol{f}' \tag{2}$$

We split the proof: first we show that $\boldsymbol{f} = \boldsymbol{f}'$ and then ρ is $\mathbb{X}$-fireable from $\boldsymbol{i}$.

Step 1: Showing that the final markings reached are the same. We prove a stronger statement which implies that $\boldsymbol{f} = \boldsymbol{f}'$, namely:

Claim 1. *For all $0 \le j \le l$,*

1. $\boldsymbol{m}'_j(\bullet, \alpha) = \boldsymbol{0}$
2. $\forall \gamma \in dval(\boldsymbol{i}) \cup dval(\boldsymbol{f})$, $\boldsymbol{m}'_j(\bullet, \gamma) = \boldsymbol{m}_j(\bullet, \gamma)$
3. $\forall \gamma \in \mathbb{E}\ \boldsymbol{m}'_j(\bullet, \gamma) = \frac{1}{|\mathbb{E}|}\left(\sum_{\delta\in\mathbb{E}\cup\{\alpha\}} \boldsymbol{m}_j(\bullet, \delta)\right)$.

The proof is obtained by induction on j. Intuitively, point 1 holds as we shift effects on α to β, point 2 holds as the transformation does not touch $\gamma \in dval(\boldsymbol{i}) \cup dval(\boldsymbol{f})$. The last and most complicated point follows from the fact that the number of tokens consumed and produced along each segment $\xrightarrow{\mathcal{U}(\mathbb{E},\mathcal{R}(\alpha,\mathbb{E},\sigma_j))}$ is the same as for σ_j, but uniformized over $\mathbb{E}$.

Step 2: Showing that ρ is an $\mathbb{X}$-run. If $\mathbb{X} = \mathbb{Q}$ then the run ρ is fireable, as any $\mathbb{Q}$-run is fireable, so in this case this step is trivial. The case when $\mathbb{X} = \mathbb{Q}^+$ is more involved. As we know from Claim 1, each m'_j is a $\mathbb{Q}^+$-marking, so it suffices to prove that for every j, $\boldsymbol{m}'_j \xrightarrow{\mathcal{U}(\mathbb{E},\mathcal{R}(\alpha,\mathbb{E},\sigma_j))}_{\mathbb{Q}^+} \boldsymbol{m}'_{j+1}$. Consider a data vector of tokens consumed along the $\mathbb{Q}^+$-run $\mathcal{U}(\mathbb{E}, \mathcal{R}(\alpha, \mathbb{E}, \sigma_j))$. If we show that it is smaller than or equal to $\boldsymbol{m}'_j$ (component-wise), then we can conclude that $\mathcal{U}(\mathbb{E}, \mathcal{R}(\alpha, \mathbb{E}, \sigma_j))$ is indeed $\mathbb{Q}^+$-fireable from $\boldsymbol{m}'_j$. To show this, we examine the consumed tokens for each datum γ separately. There are three cases:

(i) $\gamma = \alpha$. For this case, every step in $\mathcal{U}(\mathbb{E}, \mathcal{R}(\alpha, \mathbb{E}, \sigma_j))$ does not make any change on α so tokens with data value α are not consumed along the $\mathbb{Q}^+$-run $\mathcal{U}(\mathbb{E}, \mathcal{R}(\alpha, \mathbb{E}, \sigma_j))$.

(ii) $\gamma \in dval(\boldsymbol{i}) \cup dval(\boldsymbol{f})$. This is similar to the above case. Consider any data value $\gamma \in (dval(\sigma)\backslash\mathbb{E}) \setminus \{\alpha\}$. Since γ does not change on *rotate* operation, the $\mathcal{U}$ operation causes each $\mathbb{Q}$-step in $\mathcal{U}(\mathbb{E}, \mathcal{R}(\alpha, \mathbb{E}, \sigma_j))$ to consume $\frac{1}{|\mathbb{E}|}$ of the tokens with data value γ consumed when σ_j is fired. This is repeated $|\mathbb{E}|$ times and hence the vector of tokens with data value γ consumed along $\mathcal{U}(\mathbb{E}, \mathcal{R}(\alpha, \mathbb{E}, \sigma_j))$ is equal to the vector of tokens with value γ consumed by step σ_j. But we know that, it is smaller than $\boldsymbol{m}_j(\bullet, \gamma)$ and concluding smaller than $\boldsymbol{m}'_j(\bullet, \gamma)$. The last inequality is true as $\boldsymbol{m}_j(\bullet, \gamma) = \boldsymbol{m}'_j(\bullet, \gamma)$ according to Claim 1.

(iii) $\gamma \in \mathbb{E}$. Let ω be a triple $(c_j, F(\bullet, t_j), \mathcal{P}_j)$ where $(c_j, t_j, \mathcal{P}_j) = \sigma_j$. ω simply describes tokens consumed by σ_j. We slightly overload the notation and treat a triple ω like a step, where $F(\bullet, t_j)$ represents a transition "_" for which $F(\bullet, \_) = F(\bullet, t_j)$ and $F(\_, \bullet)$ is a zero matrix. We calculate the vector of consumed tokens with data value γ as follows: $\mathit{consumed}(\bullet, \gamma) =$

$$\frac{1}{|\mathbb{E}|}\sum_{k=0}^{|\mathbb{E}|-1} \Delta(\mathit{rot}^k(\mathbb{E}, \mathcal{R}(\alpha, \mathbb{E}, \omega)))(\bullet, \gamma) = \frac{1}{|\mathbb{E}|}\sum_{k=0}^{|\mathbb{E}|} \Delta(\mathit{rot}^k(\mathbb{E} \cup \{\alpha\}, \omega))(\bullet, \gamma)$$

the first equality is from definition and the second by the *replace* operation,

$$= \frac{c_j}{|\mathbb{E}|}\sum_{k=0}^{|\mathbb{E}|}(\mathit{rot}^k(\mathbb{E}\cup\{\alpha\}, (1, F(\bullet, t_j), \mathcal{P}_j)))(\bullet, \gamma) = \frac{c_j}{|\mathbb{E}|}\sum_{\delta \in \mathbb{E}\cup\{\alpha\}} (F(\bullet, t_j)\cdot\mathcal{P}_j)(\bullet, \delta)$$

Further, observe that as σ_j can fired in $\boldsymbol{m}_j$

$$c_j(F(\bullet, t_j) \cdot \mathcal{P}_j)(\bullet, \delta) \leq \boldsymbol{m}_j(\bullet, \delta) \text{ for all } \delta \in \mathbb{D},$$

summing up over $\delta \in \mathbb{E} \cup \{\alpha\}$ and multiplying with $\frac{1}{|\mathbb{E}|}$ we get

$$\frac{1}{|\mathbb{E}|}c_j \sum_{\delta \in \mathbb{E}\cup\{\alpha\}} (F(\bullet, t_j) \cdot \mathcal{P}_j)(\bullet, \delta) \leq \frac{1}{|\mathbb{E}|} \sum_{\delta \in \mathbb{E}\cup\{\alpha\}} \boldsymbol{m}_j(\bullet, \delta) = \boldsymbol{m}'_j(\delta, \gamma),$$

where the last equality comes from Claim 1 point 3. Combining inequalities we get $\mathit{consumed}(\bullet, \gamma) \leq \boldsymbol{m}'_i(\bullet, \gamma)$.

Proof (of Lemma 1). Now the proof of Lemma 1 (and hence Theorem 1) follow immediately, since we can use the *decrease* transformation, to decrease the number of data values required in an $\mathbb{X}$-run. We simply take $\alpha \in \mathit{dval}(\sigma) \setminus (\mathit{dval}(\boldsymbol{i}) \cup \mathit{dval}(\boldsymbol{f}))$ and $\mathbb{E} = \mathit{dval}(\sigma) \setminus (\mathit{dval}(\boldsymbol{i}) \cup \mathit{dval}(\boldsymbol{f})) \setminus \{\alpha\}$. Next, let $\rho = \mathit{dec}(\mathbb{E}, \alpha, \sigma)$. Due to Lemma 3 we know that $\boldsymbol{i} \xrightarrow{\rho}_{\mathbb{X}} \boldsymbol{f}$. Moreover, observe that $\mathit{dval}(\rho) \subseteq \mathit{dval}(\sigma)$. But in addition, $\alpha \notin \mathit{dval}(\rho)$ as due to the one of properties of the *decrease* operation α does not participate in the run ρ. So $\mathit{dval}(\rho) \subset \mathit{dval}(\sigma)$. Therefore $|\mathit{dval}(\rho)| \leq |\mathit{dval}(\sigma)| - 1$.

6 $\mathbb{Q}$-reachability is in PTime

We recall the definition of histograms from [22].

Definition 8. *A histogram M of order $q \in \mathbb{Q}$ is a $\mathit{Var} \times \mathbb{D}$ matrix having non-negative rational entries such that,*

1. $\sum_{\alpha \in col(M)} M(x, \alpha) = q$ *for all* $x \in row(M)$.
2. $\sum_{x \in row(M)} M(x, \alpha) \leq q$ *for all* $\alpha \in col(M)$.

A permutation matrix is a histogram of order 1.

In the following lemma, we state two properties of histograms. We say that a histogram of order a is an *[a]-histogram* if the histogram has only $\{0, a\}$ entries.

Lemma 4. *Let* $H, H_1, H_2, .., H_n$ *be histograms of order* $q, q_1, q_2, ..., q_n$ *respectively and of same row dimensions then (i)* $\sum_{i=1}^{n} H_i$ *is a histogram of order* $\sum_i^n q_i$*, (ii)* H *can be decomposed as a sum of* $[a_i]$*-histograms such that* $\sum_i a_i = q$.

Using histograms we define a representation $Hist(\rho)$ for an $\mathbb{X}$-run ρ, which captures $\Delta(\rho)$. From an $\mathbb{X}$-run $\rho = \{(c_j, t_j, \mathcal{P}_j)\}_{|\rho|}$ we obtain $Hist(\rho)$ as follows. For all transitions $t \in T$, define the set $I_t = \{j \in [1..|\rho|] |\ t_j = t\}$. Then calculate the matrix $H_t = \sum_{i \in I_t} c_i \mathcal{P}_i$. Observe that since permutation matrices are histograms and histograms are closed under scalar multiplication and addition, H_t is a histogram. If I_t is empty, then H_t is simply the null matrix. We define $Hist(\rho)$ as a mapping from T to histograms such that t is mapped to H_t.

Analogous to an $\mathbb{X}$-run we can represent $Hist(\rho)$ simply as $\{(t_j, H_{t_j})\}$, unlike an $\mathbb{X}$-run we don't indicate the length of the sequence since it is dependent on the net and not the individual run itself.

Proposition 1. *Let* $\mathcal{N} = (P, T, F, Var)$ *be a UDPN,* $\boldsymbol{i}, \boldsymbol{f}$ $\mathbb{X}$*-markings, and* σ *an* $\mathbb{X}$*-run such that* $\boldsymbol{i} \xrightarrow{\sigma}_{\mathbb{X}} \boldsymbol{f}$. *Then for each* $t \in T$ *there exists* H_t *such that:*

1. $\boldsymbol{f} - \boldsymbol{i} = \sum_{t \in T} \Delta(t) \cdot H_t$,
2. $col(H_t) \subseteq dval(\sigma)$ *for every* $t \in T$.

A PTime Procedure. We start by observing that from any $\mathbb{Q}$-marking $\boldsymbol{i}$, every $\mathbb{Q}$-step $(c, t, \mathcal{P})$ is fireable and every $\mathbb{Q}$ run is fireable. This follows from the fact that rationals are closed under addition, thus $\boldsymbol{i} + c \cdot F(\bullet, t) \cdot \mathcal{P}$ is a marking in $\mathcal{M}_{\mathbb{Q}}$. Thus if we have to find a $\mathbb{Q}$-run $\rho = \{(c_j, t_j, \mathcal{P}_j)\}_{|\rho|}$ between two $\mathbb{Q}$-markings, $\boldsymbol{i}, \boldsymbol{f}$ it is sufficient to ensure that $\boldsymbol{f} - \boldsymbol{i} = \sum_{j=1}^{|\rho|} c_j \Delta(t_j) \cdot \mathcal{P}_j$. Thus for a $\mathbb{Q}$-run all that matters is the difference in markings caused by the $\mathbb{Q}$-run which is captured succinctly by $Hist(\rho) = \{t_j, H_{t_j}\}$. This brings us to our characterization of $\mathbb{Q}$-run.

Lemma 5. *Let* $\mathcal{N} = (P, T, F, Var)$ *be a UDPN, a marking* $\boldsymbol{f}$ *is* $\mathbb{Q}$*-reachable from* $\boldsymbol{i}$ *iff there exists set* $\mathbb{E}$ *of size bounded by* $|\mathbb{E}| \leq |dval(\boldsymbol{i}) \cup dval(\boldsymbol{f})| + 1 + \max_{t \in T}(|vars(t)|)$ *and a histogram* H_t *for each* $t \in T$ *such that* $\boldsymbol{f} - \boldsymbol{i} = \sum_{t \in T} \Delta(t) \cdot H_t$ *and* $\forall t \in T$ $col(H_t) \subseteq \mathbb{E}$.

Using this characterization we can write a system of linear inequalities to encode the condition of Lemma 5. Thus, we obtain our second main result, namely, Theorem 2, with detailed proofs in [27].

7 $\mathbb{Q}^+$-reachability is in PTime

Finally, we turn to $\mathbb{Q}^+$-reachability for UDPNs and to the proof of Theorem 3. At a high level, the proof is in three steps. We start with a characterization of $\mathbb{Q}^+$-reachability in UDPNs. Then we present a polytime reduction of the continuous reachability problem to the same problem but for a special subclass of UDPN, called loop-less nets. Finally, we present how to encode the characterization for loop-less nets into a system of *linear equations with implications* to obtain a polytime algorithm for continuous reachability in UDPNs.

7.1 Characterizing $\mathbb{Q}^+$-reachability

We begin with a definition. For an $\mathbb{X}$-run we introduce the notion of the pre and post sets of $\mathbb{X}-$run. For an $\mathbb{X}$-run, $\rho = \{(c_i, t_i, \mathcal{P}_i)\}_{|\rho|}$ we define $Pre(\rho) = \{(p, \alpha) | \ \exists\ t_i, \exists\ x : F(p, t_i)(x) < 0 \wedge \mathcal{P}_i(x, \alpha) = 1\}$. We also define $Post(\rho) = \{(p, \alpha) | \ \exists\ t_i, \exists\ x : F(t_i, p)(x) > 0 \wedge \mathcal{P}_i(x, \alpha) = 1\}$. Intuitively, $Pre(\rho), Post(\rho)$ denote the set of (p, α) (place, data value) pairs describing tokens that are consumed, produced respectively by the run ρ.

Throughout this section, by a marking we denote a $\mathbb{Q}^+$-marking.

Lemma 6. *Let $\mathcal{N} = (P, T, F, Var)$ be an UDPN and $\boldsymbol{i}, \boldsymbol{f}$ are markings. For any $\mathbb{Q}^+$-run σ such that $\boldsymbol{i} \xrightarrow{\sigma}_{\mathbb{Q}^+} \boldsymbol{f}$ there exist markings $\boldsymbol{i}'$ and $\boldsymbol{f}'$ (possibly on a different run) such that*

1. *$\boldsymbol{i}'$ is $\mathbb{Q}^+$-reachable from $\boldsymbol{i}$ in at most $|P| \cdot |dval(\sigma)|$ $\mathbb{Q}^+$-steps*
2. *There is a run σ' such that $dval(\sigma') \subseteq dval(\sigma)$ and $\boldsymbol{i}' \xrightarrow{\sigma'}_{\mathbb{Q}} \boldsymbol{f}'$*
3. *$\boldsymbol{f}$ is $\mathbb{Q}^+$-reachable from $\boldsymbol{f}'$ in at most $|P| \cdot |dval(\sigma)|$ $\mathbb{Q}^+$-steps*
4. *$\forall (p, \alpha) \in Pre(\sigma'), \boldsymbol{i}'(p, \alpha) > 0$*
5. *$\forall (p, \alpha) \in Post(\sigma'), \boldsymbol{f}'(p, \alpha) > 0$*

Remark 1. If in conditions 1 and 3 we drop the requirement on the number of steps then the five conditions still imply continuous reachability.

Note that if there exist markings $\boldsymbol{i}'$ and $\boldsymbol{f}'$ and $\mathbb{Q}^+$ -runs ρ, ρ', ρ'' such that $\boldsymbol{i} \xrightarrow{\rho}_{\mathbb{Q}^+} \boldsymbol{i}', \boldsymbol{i}' \xrightarrow{\rho'}_{\mathbb{Q}^+} \boldsymbol{f}', \boldsymbol{f}' \xrightarrow{\rho''}_{\mathbb{Q}^+} \boldsymbol{f}$ then there is a $\mathbb{Q}^+$-run σ such that $\boldsymbol{i} \xrightarrow{\sigma}_{\mathbb{Q}^+} \boldsymbol{f}$. The above characterization and its proof are obtained by adapting to the data setting, the techniques developed for continuous reachability in Petri nets (without data) in [11] and [12].

7.2 Transforming UDPN to Loop-less UDPN

For a UDPN $\mathcal{N} = (P, T, F, Var)$, we construct a UDPN $\mathcal{N}'$ which is polynomial in the size of $\mathcal{N}$ and the $\mathbb{Q}^+$-reachability problem is equivalent. We define $PrePlace(t) = \{p \in P | \exists v \in Var \ s.t. \ F(p, t)(v) > 0\}$ and $PostPlace(t) = \{p \in P | \exists v \in Var \ s.t. \ F(t, p)(v) > 0\}$, where $t \in T$. The essential property of the transformed UDPN is that for every transition the sets of PrePlace and

PostPlace do not intersect. A UDPN $\mathcal{N} = (P, T, F, Var)$ is said to be *loop-less* if for all $t \in T$, $PrePlace(t) \cap PostPlace(t) = \emptyset$.

Any UDPN can easily be transformed in polynomial time into a loop-less UDPN such that $\mathbb{Q}^+$-reachability is preserved, by doubling the number of places and adding intermediate transitions. Formally, For every net $\mathcal{N}$ and two markings $\boldsymbol{i}, \boldsymbol{f}$ in polynomial time one can construct a loop-less net $\mathcal{N}'$ and two markings $\boldsymbol{i}'$, $\boldsymbol{f}'$ such that $\boldsymbol{i} \rightarrow_{\mathbb{Q}^+} \boldsymbol{f}$ in the net $\mathcal{N}$ iff $\boldsymbol{i}' \rightarrow_{\mathbb{Q}^+} \boldsymbol{f}'$ in $\mathcal{N}'$. Now, the following lemma which describes a property of loop-less nets will be crucial for our reachability algorithm:

Lemma 7. *In a loop-less net, for markings $\boldsymbol{i}$, $\boldsymbol{f}$, if there exist a histogram H, and a transition $t \in T$ such that $\boldsymbol{i} + \Delta(t) \cdot H = \boldsymbol{f}$, then there exist a $\mathbb{Q}^+$-run ρ such that $\boldsymbol{i} \xrightarrow{\rho}_{\mathbb{Q}^+} \boldsymbol{f}$.*

7.3 Encoding $\mathbb{Q}^+$-reachability as Linear Equations with Implications

Linear equations with implications, as we use them, are defined in [23], but were introduced in [12]. A system of linear equations with implications, also denoted a $\Longrightarrow$ system, is a finite set of linear inequalities over the same variables, plus a finite set of implications of the form $x > 0 \implies y > 0$, where x, y are variables appearing in the linear inequalities.

Lemma 8 *[12]. The $\mathbb{Q}^+$ solvability problem for a $\Longrightarrow$ system is in PTime.*

We then reduce the $\mathbb{Q}^+$-reachability problem to checking the solvability of a system of linear equations with implications, using the characterization established in Lemma 6 in the following lemma.

Lemma 9. *$\mathbb{Q}^+$-reachability in a UDPN $\mathcal{N} = (P, T, F, Var)$ between markings $\boldsymbol{i}, \boldsymbol{f}$ can be encoded as a set of linear equations with implications in P-time.*

Finally, we obtain Theorem 3 as a consequence of Lemmas 8 and 9.

8 Conclusion

In this paper, we provided a polynomial time algorithm for continuous reachability in UDPN, matching the complexity for Petri nets without data. This is in contrast to problems such as discrete coverability, termination, where Petri nets with and without data differ enormously in complexity, and to (discrete) reachability, where decidability is still open. As future work, we aim to implement the continuous reachability algorithm developed here, to build the first tool for discrete coverability in UDPN on the lines of what has been done for Petri nets without data. The main obstacle will be performance evaluation due to lack of benchmarks for UDPNs. Another interesting avenue for future work would be to tackle continuous reachability for Petri nets with ordered data, which would allow us to analyze continuous variants of Timed Petri nets.

Acknowledgments. We thank the anonymous reviewers for their careful reading and their helpful and insightful comments.

References

1. Finkel, A., Schnoebelen, P.: Well-structured transition systems everywhere! Theor. Comput. Sci. **256**(1–2), 63–92 (2001)
2. Rackoff, C.: The covering and boundedness problems for vector addition systems. Theor. Comput. Sci. **6**, 223–231 (1978)
3. Rao Kosaraju, S.: Decidability of reachability in vector addition systems (preliminary version). In: Proceedings of the 14th Annual ACM Symposium on Theory of Computing, San Francisco, California, USA, 5–7 May 1982, pp. 267–281 (1982)
4. Leroux, J., Schmitz, S.: Demystifying reachability in vector addition systems. In: 30th Annual ACM/IEEE Symposium on Logic in Computer Science, LICS 2015, Kyoto, Japan, 6–10 July 2015, pp. 56–67 (2015)
5. Cardoza, E., Lipton, R.J., Meyer, A.R.: Exponential space complete problems for Petri nets and commutative semigroups: preliminary report. In: Proceedings of the 8th Annual ACM Symposium on Theory of Computing, Hershey, Pennsylvania, USA, 3–5 May 1976, pp. 50–54 (1976)
6. Czerwinski, W., Lasota, S., Lazic, R., Leroux, J., Mazowiecki, F.: The reachability problem for Petri nets is not elementary (extended abstract). CoRR, abs/1809.07115 (2018)
7. van der Aalst, W.M.P.: The application of Petri nets to workflow management. J. Circ. Syst. Comput. **8**(1), 21–66 (1998)
8. Esparza, J.: Decidability and complexity of Petri net problems — an introduction. In: Reisig, W., Rozenberg, G. (eds.) ACPN 1996. LNCS, vol. 1491, pp. 374–428. Springer, Heidelberg (1998). https://doi.org/10.1007/3-540-65306-6_20
9. Desel, J., Esparza, J.: Free Choice Petri Nets. Cambridge University Press, New York (1995)
10. David, R., Alla, H.: Continuous Petri nets. In: Proceedings of the 8th European Workshop on Application and Theory of Petri Nets, Zaragoza, Spain, pp. 275–294 (1987)
11. Fraca, E., Haddad, S.: Complexity analysis of continuous Petri nets. Fundam. Inform. **137**(1), 1–28 (2015)
12. Blondin, M., Haase, C.: Logics for continuous reachability in Petri nets and vector addition systems with states. In: 32nd Annual ACM/IEEE Symposium on Logic in Computer Science, LICS 2017, Reykjavik, Iceland, 20–23 June 2017, pp. 1–12 (2017)
13. David, R., Alla, H.: Petri nets for modeling of dynamic systems: a survey. Automatica **30**(2), 175–202 (1994)
14. Alla, H., David, R.: Continuous and hybrid Petri nets. J. Circ. Syst. Comput. **8**, 159–188 (1998)
15. Jensen, K.: Coloured Petri nets - preface by the section editor. STTT **2**(2), 95–97 (1998)
16. Wang, J.: Timed Petri nets. Timed Petri Nets: Theory and Application. The Kluwer International Series on Discrete Event Dynamic Systems, vol. 9, pp. 63–123. Springer, Boston (1998). https://doi.org/10.1007/978-1-4615-5537-7_4
17. Abdulla, P.A., Nylén, A.: Timed Petri nets and BQOs. In: Colom, J.-M., Koutny, M. (eds.) ICATPN 2001. LNCS, vol. 2075, pp. 53–70. Springer, Heidelberg (2001). https://doi.org/10.1007/3-540-45740-2_5
18. Lazic, R., Newcomb, T.C., Ouaknine, J., Roscoe, A.W., Worrell, J.: Nets with tokens which carry data. Fundam. Inform. **88**(3), 251–274 (2008)

19. Rosa-Velardo, F., de Frutos-Escrig, D.: Forward analysis for Petri nets with name creation. In: Lilius, J., Penczek, W. (eds.) PETRI NETS 2010. LNCS, vol. 6128, pp. 185–205. Springer, Heidelberg (2010). https://doi.org/10.1007/978-3-642-13675-7_12
20. Lazić, R., Totzke, P.: What makes Petri nets harder to verify: stack or data? In: Gibson-Robinson, T., Hopcroft, P., Lazić, R. (eds.) Concurrency, Security, and Puzzles. LNCS, vol. 10160, pp. 144–161. Springer, Cham (2017). https://doi.org/10.1007/978-3-319-51046-0_8
21. Hofman, P., Lasota, S., Lazić, R., Leroux, J., Schmitz, S., Totzke, P.: Coverability trees for Petri nets with unordered data. In: Jacobs, B., Löding, C. (eds.) FOSSACS 2016. LNCS, vol. 9634, pp. 445–461. Springer, Heidelberg (2016). https://doi.org/10.1007/978-3-662-49630-5_26
22. Hofman, P., Leroux, J., Totzke, P.: Linear combinations of unordered data vectors. In: 32nd Annual ACM/IEEE Symposium on Logic in Computer Science, LICS 2017, Reykjavik, Iceland, 20–23 June 2017, pp. 1–11 (2017)
23. Hofman, P., Lasota, S.: Linear equations with ordered data. In: 29th International Conference on Concurrency Theory, CONCUR 2018, Beijing, China, 4–7 September 2018, pp. 24:1–24:17 (2018)
24. Silva, M., Terue, E., Colom, J.M.: Linear algebraic and linear programming techniques for the analysis of place/transition net systems. In: Reisig, W., Rozenberg, G. (eds.) ACPN 1996. LNCS, vol. 1491, pp. 309–373. Springer, Heidelberg (1998). https://doi.org/10.1007/3-540-65306-6_19
25. Blondin, M., Finkel, A., Haase, C., Haddad, S.: Approaching the coverability problem continuously. In: Chechik, M., Raskin, J.-F. (eds.) TACAS 2016. LNCS, vol. 9636, pp. 480–496. Springer, Heidelberg (2016). https://doi.org/10.1007/978-3-662-49674-9_28
26. Esparza, J., Ledesma-Garza, R., Majumdar, R., Meyer, P., Niksic, F.: An SMT-based approach to coverability analysis. In: Biere, A., Bloem, R. (eds.) CAV 2014. LNCS, vol. 8559, pp. 603–619. Springer, Cham (2014). https://doi.org/10.1007/978-3-319-08867-9_40
27. Gupta, U., Shah, P., Akshay, S., Hofman, P.: Continuous reachability for unordered data Petri nets is in PTime. CoRR abs/1902.05604 (2019). arxiv.org/abs/1902.05604
28. Rosa-Velardo, F., de Frutos-Escrig, D.: Decidability and complexity of Petri nets with unordered data. Theor. Comput. Sci. **412**(34), 4439–4451 (2011)

12

Tight Worst-Case Bounds for Polynomial Loop Programs

Amir M. Ben-Amram[1] and Geoff W. Hamilton[2(✉)]

[1] School of Computer Science, Tel-Aviv Academic College, Tel Aviv, Israel
amirben@mta.ac.il
[2] School of Computing, Dublin City University, Dublin 9, Ireland
hamilton@computing.dcu.ie

Abstract. In 2008, Ben-Amram, Jones and Kristiansen showed that for a simple programming language—representing non-deterministic imperative programs with bounded loops, and arithmetics limited to addition and multiplication—it is possible to decide precisely whether a program has certain growth-rate properties, in particular whether a computed value, or the program's running time, has a polynomial growth rate.

A natural and intriguing problem was to improve the precision of the information obtained. This paper shows how to obtain asymptotically-tight *multivariate* polynomial bounds for this class of programs. This is a complete solution: whenever a polynomial bound exists it will be found.

1 Introduction

One of the most important properties we would like to know about programs is their *resource usage*, i.e., the amount of resources (such as time, memory and energy) required for their execution. This information is useful during development, when performance bugs and security vulnerabilities exploiting performance issues can be avoided. It is also particularly relevant for mobile applications, where resources are limited, and for cloud services, where resource usage is a major cost factor.

In the literature, a lot of different "cost analysis" problems (also called "resource bound analysis," etc.) have been studied (e.g. [1,11,13,18,19,24,26,27]); several of them may be grouped under the following general definition. The *countable resource problem* asks about the maximum usage of a "resource" that accumulates during execution, and which one can explicitly count, by instrumenting the program with an accumulator variable and instructions to increment it where necessary. For example, we can estimate the *execution time* of a program by counting certain "basic steps". Another example is counting the number of visits to designated program locations. Realistic problems of this type include bounding the number of calls to specific functions, perhaps to system services; the number of I/O operations; number of accesses to memory, etc. The consumption of resources such as *energy* suits our problem formulation as long as such explicit bookkeeping is possible (we have to assume that the increments, if not constant, are given by a monotone polynomial expression).

In this paper we solve the *bound analysis problem* for a particular class of programs, defined in [7]. The bound analysis problem is to find symbolic bounds on the maximal possible value of an integer variable at the end of the program, in terms of some integer-valued variables that appear in the initial state of a computation. Thus, a solution to this problem might be used for any of the resource-bound analyses above. In this work we focus on values that grow polynomially (in the sense of being bounded by a polynomial), and our goal is to find polynomial bounds that are tight, in the sense of being precise up to a constant factor.

The programs we study are expressed by the so-called *core language*. It is imperative, including bounded loops, non-deterministic branches and restricted arithmetic expressions; the syntax is shown in Fig. 1. Semantics is explained and motivated below, but is largely intuitive; see also the illustrative example in Fig. 2. In 2008, it was proved [7] that for this language it is decidable whether a computed result is polynomially bounded or not. This makes the language an attractive target for work on the problem of computing tight bounds. However, for the past ten years there has been no improvement on [7]. We now present an algorithm to compute, for every program in the language, and every variable in the program which has a polynomial upper bound (in terms of input values), a tight polynomial bound on its largest attainable value (informally, "the worst-case value") as a function of the input values. The bound is guaranteed to be tight up to a multiplicative constant factor but constants are left implicit (for example a bound quadratic in n will always be represented as n^2). The algorithm could be extended to compute upper and lower bounds with explicit constant factors, but choosing to ignore coefficients simplifies the algorithm considerably. In fact, we have striven for a simple, comprehensible algorithm, and we believe that the algorithm we present is sufficiently simple that, beyond being comprehensible, offers insight into the structure of computations in this model.

1.1 The Core Language

Data. It is convenient to assume (without loss of generality) that the only type of data is non-negative integers. Note that a realistic (not "core") program may include many statements that manipulate non-integer data that are not relevant to loop control—so in a complexity analysis, we may be able to abstract these parts away and still analyze the variables of interest. In other cases, it is

$$
\begin{array}{rcl}
\texttt{X} \in \text{Variable} & ::= & \texttt{X}_1 \mid \texttt{X}_2 \mid \texttt{X}_3 \mid \ldots \mid \texttt{X}_n \\
\texttt{E} \in \text{Expression} & ::= & \texttt{X} \mid \texttt{E + E} \mid \texttt{E * E} \\
\texttt{C} \in \text{Command} & ::= & \texttt{skip} \mid \texttt{X:=E} \mid \texttt{C}_1\texttt{;C}_2 \mid \texttt{loop E \{C\}} \\
 & \mid & \texttt{choose C}_1\texttt{ or C}_2
\end{array}
$$

Fig. 1. Syntax of the core language.

possible to preprocess a program to replace complex data values with their size (or "norm"), which is the quantity of importance for loop control. Methods for this process have been widely studied in conjunction with termination and cost analysis.

Command Semantics. The core language is inherently non-deterministic. The `choose` command represents a non-deterministic choice, and can be used to abstract any concrete conditional command by simply ignoring the condition; this is necessary to ensure that our analysis problem is decidable. Note that what we ignore is branches within a loop body and not branches that implement the loop control, which we represent by a dedicated loop command. The command `loop E {C}` repeats `C` a (non-deterministic) number of times bounded by the value of `E`, which is evaluated just before the loop is entered. Thus, as a conservative abstraction, it may be used to model different forms of loops (for-loops, while-loops) as long as a bound on the number of iterations, as a function of the program state on loop initiation, can be determined and expressed in the language. There is an ample body of research on analysing programs to find such bounds where they are not explicitly given by the programmer; in particular, bounds can be obtained from a *ranking function* for the loop [2,3,5,6,23]. Note that the arithmetic in our language is too restricted to allow for the maintenance of counters and the creation of *while* loops, as there is no subtraction, no explicit constants and no tests. Thus, for realistic "concrete" programs which use such devices, loop-bound analysis is supposed to be performed *on the concrete program* as part of the process of abstracting it to the core language. This process is illustrated in [9, Sect. 2].

From a computability viewpoint, the use of bounded loops restricts the programs that can be represented to such that compute primitive recursive functions; this is a rich enough class to cover a lot of useful algorithms and make the analysis problem challenging. In fact, our language resembles a weakened version of Meyer and Ritchie's LOOP language [20], which computes all the primitive recursive functions, and where behavioral questions like "is the result linearly bounded" are undecidable.

```
loop X1 {
   loop X2 + X3 { choose { X3:= X1; X2:= X4 } or { X3:= X4; X2:= X1 } };
   X4:= X2 + X3
};
loop X4 { choose  { X3:= X1 + X2 + X3 } or { X3:= X2;  X2:= X1 } }
```

Fig. 2. A core-language program. `loop` n `C` means "do `C` at most n times."

1.2 The Algorithm

Consider the program in Fig. 2. Suppose that it is started with the values of the variables $\mathtt{X}_1, \mathtt{X}_2, \ldots$ being $x_1, x_2, \ldots$. Our purpose is to bound the values of all variables at the conclusion of the program in terms of those initial values. Indeed, they are all polynomially bounded, and our algorithm provides tight bounds. For instance, it establishes that the final value of $\mathtt{X}_3$ is tightly bounded (up to a constant factor) by $\max(x_4(x_4 + x_1^2), x_4(x_2 + x_3 + x_1^2))$.

In fact, it produces information in a more precise form, as *a disjunction of simultaneous bounds*. This means that it generates vectors, called *multi-polynomials*, that give simultaneous bounds on all variables; for example, with the program in Fig. 2, one such multi-polynomial is $\langle x_1, x_2, x_3, x_4 \rangle$ (this is the result of all loops taking a very early exit). This form is important in the context of a compositional analysis. To see why, suppose that we provide, for a command with variables $\mathtt{X}, \mathtt{Y}$, the bounds $\langle x, y \rangle$ and $\langle y, x \rangle$. Then we know that the *sum* of their values is always bounded by $x + y$, a result that would have not been deduced had we given the bound $\max(x, y)$ on each of the variables. The difference may be critical for the success of analyzing an enclosing or subsequent command.

Multivariate bounds are often of interest, and perhaps require no justification, but let us point out that multivariate polynomials are necessary even if we're ultimately interested in a univariate bound, in terms of some single initial value, say n. This is, again, due to the analysis being compositional. When we analyze an internal command that uses variables $\mathtt{X}, \mathtt{Y}, \ldots$ we do not know in what possible contexts the command will be executed and how the values of these variables will be related to n.

Some highlights of our solution are as follows.

- We reduce the problem of analyzing any core-language program to the problem of analyzing a single loop, whose body is already processed, and therefore presented as a collection of multi-polynomials. This is typical of algorithms that analyze a structured imperative language and do so compositionally.
- Since we are computing bounds only up to a constant factor, we work with *abstract* polynomials, that have no numeric coefficients.
- We further introduce *τ-polynomials*, to describe the evolution of values in a loop. These have an additional parameter τ (for "time"; more precisely, number of iterations). Introducing τ-polynomials was a key step in the solution.
- The analysis of a loop is simply a closure computation under two operations: ordinary composition, and *generalization* which is the operation that predicts the evolution of values by judiciously adding τ's to *idempotent* abstract multi-polynomials.

The remainder of this paper is structured as follows. In Sect. 2 we give some definitions and state our main result. In Sects. 3, 4 and 5 we present our algorithm. In Sect. 6, we outline the correctness proofs. Section 7 considers related work, and Sect. 8 concludes and discusses ideas for further work.

2 Preliminaries

In this section, we give some basic definitions, complete the presentation of our programming language and precisely state the main result.

2.1 Some Notation and Terminology

The Language. We remark that in our language syntax there is no special form for a "program unit"; in the text we sometimes use "program" for the subject of our analysis, yet syntactically it's just a command.

Polynomials and Multi-polynomials. We work throughout this article with multivariate polynomials in $x_1, \ldots, x_n$ that have non-negative integer coefficients and no variables other than $x_1, \ldots, x_n$; when we speak of a polynomial we always mean one of this kind. Note that over the non-negative integers, such polynomials are monotonically (weakly) increasing in all variables.

The post-fix substitution operator $[a/b]$ may be applied to any sort of expression containing a variable b, to substitute a instead; e.g., $(x^2 + yx + y)[2z/y] = x^2 + 2zx + 2z$.

When discussing a command, state-transition, or program trace, with a variable $\mathtt{X}_i$, x_i will denote, as a rule, the initial value of this variable, and x'_i its final value. Thus we distinguish the syntactic entity by the typewriter font. We write the polynomials manipulated by our algorithms using the variable names x_i. We presume that an implementation of the algorithm represents polynomials concretely so that ordinary operations such as composition can be applied, but otherwise we do not concern ourselves much with representation.

The parameter n always refers to the number of variables in the subject program. The set $[n]$ is $\{1, \ldots, n\}$. For a set S an n-tuple over S is a mapping from $[n]$ to S. The set of these tuples is denoted by S^n. Throughout the paper, various natural liftings of operators to collections of objects is tacitly assumed, e.g., if S is a set of integers then $S + 1$ is the set $\{s + 1 \mid s \in S\}$ and $S + S$ is $\{s + t \mid s, t \in S\}$. We use such lifting with sets as well as with tuples. If S is ordered, we extend the ordering to S^n by comparing tuples element-wise (this leads to a partial order, in general, e.g., with natural numbers, $\langle 1, 3\rangle$ and $\langle 2, 2\rangle$ are incomparable).

Definition 1. *A* polynomial transition (PT) *represents a mapping of an "input" state* $\mathbf{x} = \langle x_1, \ldots, x_n\rangle$ *to a "result" state* $\mathbf{x}' = \langle x'_1, \ldots, x'_n\rangle = \mathbf{p}(\boldsymbol{x})$ *where* $\mathbf{p} = \langle \mathbf{p}[1], \ldots, \mathbf{p}[n]\rangle$ *is an n-tuple of polynomials. Such a* $\mathbf{p}$ *is called* a a multi-polynomial (MP)*; we denote by* `MPol` *the set of multi-polynomials, where the number of variables n is fixed by context.*

Multi-polynomials are used in this work to represent the effect of a command. Various operations will be applied to MPs, mostly obvious—in particular, composition (which corresponds to sequential application of the transitions). Note that composition of multi-polynomials, $\mathbf{q} \circ \mathbf{p}$, is naturally defined since $\mathbf{p}$ supplies n values for the n variables of $\mathbf{q}$ (in other words, they are composed as functions in $\mathbb{N}^n \to \mathbb{N}^n$). We define *Id* to be the identity transformation, $\mathbf{x}' = \mathbf{x}$ (in MP notation: $\mathbf{p}[i] = x_i$ for $i = 1, \ldots, n$).

2.2 Formal Semantics of the Core Language

The semantics associates with every command C over variables $X_1, \ldots, X_n$ a relation $[\![C]\!] \subseteq \mathbb{N}^n \times \mathbb{N}^n$. In the expression $\boldsymbol{x}[\![C]\!]\boldsymbol{y}$, vector $\boldsymbol{x}$ (respectively $\boldsymbol{y}$) is the store before (after) the execution of C.

The semantics of `skip` is the identity. The semantics of an assignment X_i:=E associates to each store $\boldsymbol{x}$ a new store $\boldsymbol{y}$ obtained by replacing the component x_i by the value of the expression E when evaluated over store $\boldsymbol{x}$. This is defined in the natural way (details omitted), and is denoted by $[\![E]\!]\boldsymbol{x}$. Composite commands are described by the straight-forward equations:

$$[\![C_1; C_2]\!] = [\![C_2]\!] \circ [\![C_1]\!]$$
$$[\![\texttt{choose } C_1 \texttt{ or } C_2]\!] = [\![C_1]\!] \cup [\![C_2]\!]$$
$$[\![\texttt{loop E \{C\}}]\!] = \{(\boldsymbol{x}, \boldsymbol{y}) \mid \exists i \leq [\![E]\!]\boldsymbol{x} : \boldsymbol{x}[\![C]\!]^i \boldsymbol{y}\}$$

where $[\![C]\!]^i$ represents $[\![C]\!] \circ \cdots \circ [\![C]\!]$ (i occurrences of $[\![C]\!]$); and $[\![C]\!]^0 = Id$.

Remarks. The following two changes may enhance the applicability of the core language for simulating certain concrete programs; we include them as "options" because they do not affect the validity of our proofs.

1. The semantics of an assignment operation may be non-deterministic: X:=E assigns to X some non-negative value *bounded* by E. This is useful to abstract expressions which are not in the core language, and also to use the results of size analysis of subprograms. Such an analysis may determine invariants such as "the value of f(X,Y) is at most the sum of X and Y."
2. The domain of the integer variables may be extended to $\mathbb{Z}$. In this case the bounds that we seek are on the absolute value of the output in terms of absolute values of the inputs. This change does not affect our conclusions because of the facts $|xy| = |x| \cdot |y|$ and $|x + y| \leq |x| + |y|$. The semantics of the loop command may be defined either as doing nothing if the loop bound is not positive, or using the absolute value as a bound.

2.3 Detailed Statement of the Main Result

The *polynomial-bound analysis problem* is to find, for any given command, which output variables are bounded by a polynomial in the input values (which are simply the values of all variables upon commencement of the program), and to bound these output values tightly (up to constant factors). The problem of *identifying* the polynomially-bounded variables is completely solved by [7]. We rely on that algorithm, which is polynomial-time, to do this for us (as further explained below).

Our main result is thus stated as follows.

Theorem 1. *There is an algorithm which, for a command* C*, over variables X_1 through X_n, outputs a set $\mathcal{B}$ of multi-polynomials, such that the following hold, where PB is the set of indices i of variables X_i which are polynomially bounded under $[\![C]\!]$.*

1. *(Bounding) There is a constant* $c_{\mathbf{p}}$ *associated with each* $\mathbf{p} \in \mathcal{B}$*, such that*

$$\forall \boldsymbol{x}, \boldsymbol{y} \ . \ \boldsymbol{x}[\![\mathtt{C}]\!]\boldsymbol{y} \Longrightarrow \exists \mathbf{p} \in \mathcal{B} . \forall i \in PB . \, y_i \leq c_{\mathbf{p}}\mathbf{p}[i](\boldsymbol{x})$$

2. *(Tightness) For every* $\mathbf{p} \in \mathcal{B}$ *there are constants* $d_{\mathbf{p}} > 0$*,* $\boldsymbol{x}_0$ *such that for all* $\boldsymbol{x} \geq \boldsymbol{x}_0$ *there is a* $\boldsymbol{y}$ *such that*

$$\boldsymbol{x}[\![\mathtt{C}]\!]\boldsymbol{y} \text{ and } \forall i \in PB . \, y_i \geq d_{\mathbf{p}}\mathbf{p}[i](\boldsymbol{x}).$$

3 Analysis Algorithm: First Concepts

The following sections describe our analysis algorithm. Naturally, the most intricate part of the analysis concerns loops. In fact we break the description into stages: first we reduce the problem of analyzing any program to that of analyzing *simple disjunctive loops*, defined next. Then, we approach the analysis of such loops, which is the main effort in this work.

Definition 2. *A* simple disjunctive loop (SDL) *is a finite set of PTs.*

The loop is "disjunctive" because its meaning is that in every iteration, any of the given transitions may be applied. The semantics is formalized by *traces* (Definition 4). A SDL does not specify the number of iterations; our analysis generates polynomials which depend on the number of iterations as well as the initial state. For this purpose, we now introduce τ-polynomials where τ represents the number of iterations.

Definition 3. τ*-polynomials are polynomials in* $x_1, \ldots, x_n$ *and* τ*.*

τ has a special status and does not have a separate component in the polynomial giving its value. If p is a τ-polynomial, then $p(v_1, \ldots, v_n)$ is the result of substituting each v_i for the respective x_i; and we also write $p(v_1, \ldots, v_n, t)$ for the result of substituting t for τ as well. The set of τ-polynomials in n variables (n known from context) is denoted $\tau\mathtt{Pol}$.

Multi-polynomials and polynomial transitions are formed from τ-polynomials just as previously defined and are used to represent the effect of a variable number of iterations. For example, the τ-polynomial transition $\langle x_1', x_2' \rangle = \langle x_1, \ x_2 + \tau x_1 \rangle$ represents the effect of repeating (τ times) the assignment $\mathtt{X}_2$:= $\mathtt{X}_2 + \mathtt{X}_1$. The effect of iterating the composite command: $\mathtt{X}_2$:= $\mathtt{X}_2 + \mathtt{X}_1$; $\mathtt{X}_3$:= $\mathtt{X}_3 + \mathtt{X}_2$ has an effect described by $\mathbf{x}' = \langle x_1, \ x_2 + \tau x_1, \ x_3 + \tau x_2 + \tau^2 x_1 \rangle$ (here we already have an upper bound which is not reached precisely, but is correct up to a constant factor). We denote the set of τ-polynomial transitions by τ**MPol**. We should note that composition $\mathbf{q} \circ \mathbf{p}$ over τ**MPol** is performed by substituting $\mathbf{p}[i]$ for each occurrence of x_i in $\mathbf{q}$. Occurrences of τ are unaffected (since τ is not part of the state). We make a couple of preliminary definitions before reaching our goal which is the definition of the *simple disjunctive loop problem* (Definition 6).

Definition 4. *Let* $\mathcal{S}$ *be a set of polynomial transitions. An* (abstract) trace *over* $\mathcal{S}$ *is a finite sequence* $\mathbf{p}_1; \ldots; \mathbf{p}_{|\sigma|}$ *of elements of* $\mathcal{S}$*. Thus* $|\sigma|$ *denotes the* length *of the trace. The set of all traces is denoted* $\mathcal{S}^*$*. We write* $[\![\sigma]\!]$ *for the composed relation* $\mathbf{p}_{|\sigma|} \circ \cdots \circ \mathbf{p}_1$ *(for the empty trace,* ε*, we have* $[\![\varepsilon]\!] = Id$*).*

Definition 5. *Let $p(\mathbf{x})$ be a (concrete or abstract) τ-polynomial. We write $\dot{p}$ for the sum of* linear monomials *of p, namely any one of the form ax_i with constant coefficient a. We write $\ddot{p}$ for the rest. Thus $p = \dot{p} + \ddot{p}$.*

Definition 6 (Simple disjunctive loop problem). *The* simple disjunctive loop problem *is: given the set $\mathcal{S}$, find (if possible) a finite set $\mathcal{B}$ of τ-polynomial transitions which* tightly bound *all traces over $\mathcal{S}$. More precisely, we require:*

1. *(Bounding) There is a constant $c_{\mathbf{p}} > 0$ associated with each $\mathbf{p} \in \mathcal{B}$, such that*

$$\forall \boldsymbol{x}, \boldsymbol{y}, \sigma \;.\; \boldsymbol{x}[\![\sigma]\!]\boldsymbol{y} \Longrightarrow \exists \mathbf{p} \in \mathcal{B} \,.\, \boldsymbol{y} \leq c_{\mathbf{p}}\mathbf{p}(\boldsymbol{x}, |\sigma|)$$

2. *(Tightness) For every $\mathbf{p} \in \mathcal{B}$ there are constants $d_{\mathbf{p}} > 0$, $\boldsymbol{x}_0$ such that for all $\boldsymbol{x} \geq \boldsymbol{x}_0$ there are a trace σ and a state vector $\boldsymbol{y}$ such that*

$$\boldsymbol{x}[\![\sigma]\!]\boldsymbol{y} \wedge \boldsymbol{y} \geq \dot{\mathbf{p}}(\boldsymbol{x}, |\sigma|) + d_{\mathbf{p}}\ddot{\mathbf{p}}(\boldsymbol{x}, |\sigma|)\,.$$

Note that in the lower-bound clause (2), the linear monomials of p are not multiplied, in the left-hand side, by the coefficient $d_{\mathbf{p}}$; this sets, in a sense, a stricter requirement for them: if the trace maps x to x^2 then the bound $2x^2$ is acceptable, but if it maps x to x, the bound $2x$ is not accepted. The reader may understand this technicality by considering the effect of iteration: it is important to distinguish the transition $x_1' = x_1$, which can be iterated ad libitum, from the transition $x_1' = 2x_1$, which produces exponential growth on iteration. Distinguishing $x_1' = x_1^2$ from $x_1' = 2x_1^2$ is not as important. The result set $\mathcal{B}$ above is sometimes called a *loop summary.* We remark that Definition 6 implies that the **max** of all these polynomials provides a "big Theta" bound for the worst-case (namely biggest) results of the loop's computation. We prefer, however, to work with sets of polynomials. Another technical remark is that $c_{\mathbf{p}}, d_{\mathbf{p}}$ range over real numbers. However, our data and the coefficients of polynomials remain integers, it is only such comparisons that are performed with real numbers (specifically, to allow $c_{\mathbf{p}}$ to be smaller than one).

4 Reduction to Simple Disjunctive Loops

We show how to reduce the problem of analysing core-language programs to the analysis of polynomially-bounded simple disjunctive loops.

4.1 Symbolic Evaluation of Straight-Line Code

Straight-line code consists of atomic commands—namely assignments (or `skip`, equivalent to `X`$_1$`:=X`$_1$), composed sequentially. It is obvious that symbolic evaluation of such code leads to polynomial transitions.

Example 1. `X`$_2$`:= X`$_1$`; X`$_4$`:= X`$_2$` + X`$_3$`; X`$_1$`:= X`$_2$` * X`$_3$ is precisely represented by the transition $\langle x_1, x_2, x_3 \rangle' = \langle x_1x_3,\ x_1,\ x_3,\ x_1 + x_3 \rangle$.

4.2 Evaluation of Non-deterministic Choice

Evaluation of the command `choose` $\mathtt{C}_1$ `or` $\mathtt{C}_2$ yields a set of possible outcomes. Hence, the result of analyzing a command will be a *set* of multi-polynomial transitions. We express this in the common notation of abstract semantics:

$$[\![\mathtt{C}]\!]^S \in \wp(\mathtt{MPol}).$$

For uniformity, we consider $[\![\mathtt{C}]\!]^S$ for an atomic command to be a singleton in $\wp(\mathtt{MPol})$ (this means that we represent a transition $\boldsymbol{x}' = \mathbf{p}(\boldsymbol{x})$ by $\{\mathbf{p}\}$). Composition is naturally extended to sets, and the semantics of a choice command is now simply set union, so we have:

$$[\![\mathtt{C}_1;\mathtt{C}_2]\!]^S = [\![\mathtt{C}_2]\!]^S \circ [\![\mathtt{C}_1]\!]^S$$
$$[\![\mathtt{choose}\ \mathtt{C}_1\ \mathtt{or}\ \mathtt{C}_2]\!]^S = [\![\mathtt{C}_1]\!]^S \cup [\![\mathtt{C}_2]\!]^S$$

Example 2. $\mathtt{X}_2$`:=` $\mathtt{X}_1$`; choose {` $\mathtt{X}_4$`:=` $\mathtt{X}_2$ `+` $\mathtt{X}_3$ `} or {` $\mathtt{X}_1$`:=` $\mathtt{X}_2$ `*` $\mathtt{X}_3$ `}` is represented by the set $\{\langle x_1, x_1, x_3, x_1 + x_3\rangle,\ \langle x_1x_3, x_1, x_3, x_4\rangle\}$.

4.3 Handling Loops

The above shows that any loop-free command in our language can be precisely represented by a finite set of PTs. Consequently, the problem of analyzing *any* command is reduced to the analysis of simple disjunctive loops.

Suppose that we have an algorithm SOLVE that takes a simple disjunctive loop and computes tight bounds for it (see Definition 6). We use it to complete the analysis of any program by the following definition:

$$[\![\mathtt{loop\ E\ \{C\}}]\!]^S = (\textsc{Solve}([\![\mathtt{C}]\!]^S)[E/\tau]\ .$$

Thus, the whole solution is constructed as an ordinary abstract interpretation, following the semantics of the language, except for procedure SOLVE, described below.

Example 3. $\mathtt{X}_4$`:=` $\mathtt{X}_1$`; loop` $\mathtt{X}_4$ `{` $\mathtt{X}_2$`:=` $\mathtt{X}_1$ `+` $\mathtt{X}_2$`;` $\mathtt{X}_3$`:=` $\mathtt{X}_2$ `}`.
The loop includes just one PT. Solving the loop yields a set $\mathcal{L} = \{\langle x_1, x_2, x_3, x_4\rangle, \langle x_1, x_2 + \tau x_1, x_2 + \tau x_1, x_4\rangle\}$ (the first MP accounts for zero iterations, the second covers any positive number of iterations). We can now compute the effect of the given command as

$$\begin{aligned}\mathcal{L}[x_4/\tau] \circ [\![\mathtt{X}_4\ \mathtt{:=}\ \mathtt{X}_1]\!]^S &= \mathcal{L}[x_4/\tau] \circ \{\langle x_1, x_2, x_3, x_1\rangle\} \\ &= \{\langle x_1, x_2, x_3, x_1\rangle, \langle x_1, x_2 + x_1^2, x_2 + x_1^2, x_1\rangle\}.\end{aligned}$$

The next section describes procedure SOLVE, and operates under the assumption that all variables are polynomially bounded in the loop. However, a loop can generate exponential growth. To cover this eventuality, we first apply the algorithm of [7] which identifies which variables are polynomially bounded. If some $\mathtt{X}_i$ is *not* polynomially bounded we replace the ith component of all the loop transitions with x_n (where we assume x_n to be a dedicated, unmodified variable). Clearly, after this change, all variables are polynomially bounded; moreover, variables which are genuinely polynomial are unaffected, because they cannot depend on a super-exponential quantity (given the restricted arithmetics in our language). In reporting the results of the algorithm, we should display "`super-polynomial`" instead of all bounds that depend on x_n.

5 Simple Disjunctive Loop Analysis Algorithm

Intuitively, evaluating `loop E {C}` abstractly consists of simulating any finite number of iterations, i.e., computing

$$Q_i = \{Id\} \cup P \cup (P \circ P) \cup \cdots \cup P^{(i)} \tag{1}$$

where $P = [\![\mathtt{C}]\!]^S \in \wp(\mathtt{MPol})$. The question now is whether the sequence (1) reaches a fixed point. In fact, it often doesn't. However, it is quite easy to see that in the *multiplicative fragment* of the language, that is, where the addition operator is not used, such non-convergence is associated with exponential growth. Indeed, since there is no addition, all our polynomials are monomials with a leading coefficient of 1 (*monic monomials*)—this is easy to verify. It follows that if the sequence (1) does not converge, higher and higher exponents must appear, which indicates that some variable cannot be bounded polynomially. Taking the contrapositive, we conclude that if all variables are known to be polynomially bounded the sequence will converge. Thus we have the following easy (and not so satisfying) result:

Observation 2. *For a SDL that does not use addition, the sequence Q_i as in (1) reaches a fixed point, and the fixed point provides tight bounds for all the polynomially-bounded variables.*

When we have addition, we find that knowing that all variables are polynomially bounded does not imply convergence of the sequence (1). An example is: `loop` $\mathtt{X}_3$ `{` $\mathtt{X}_1$`:=` $\mathtt{X}_1$ `+` $\mathtt{X}_2$ `}` yielding the infinite sequence of MPs $\langle x_1, x_2, x_3\rangle$, $\langle x_1 + x_2, x_2, x_3\rangle$, $\langle x_1 + 2x_2, x_2, x_3\rangle$, ... Our solution employs two means. One is the introduction of τ-polynomials, already presented. The other is a kind of *abstraction*—intuitively, ignoring the concrete values of (non-zero) coefficients. Let us first define this abstraction:

Definition 7. `APol`*, the set of abstract polynomials, consists of formal sums of distinct monomials over $x_1, \ldots, x_n$, where the coefficient of every monomial included is* 1*. We extend the definition to an abstraction of τ-polynomials, denoted τ*`APol`.

The meaning of abstract polynomials is given by the following rules:

1. The abstraction of a polynomial p, $\alpha(p)$, is obtained by modifying all (non-zero) coefficients to 1.
2. Addition and multiplication in τ`APol` is defined in a natural way so that $\alpha(p)+\alpha(q) = \alpha(p+q)$ and $\alpha(p)\cdot\alpha(q) = \alpha(p\cdot q)$ (to carry these operations out, you just go through the motions of adding or multiplying ordinary polynomials, ignoring the coefficient values).
3. The *canonical concretization* of an abstract polynomial, $\gamma(\mathbf{p})$ is obtained by simply regarding it as an ordinary polynomial.
4. These definitions extend naturally to tuples of (abstract) polynomials.
5. The set of abstract multi-polynomials `AMPol` and their extension with τ (τ`AMPol`) are defined as n-tuples over `APol` (respectively, τ`APol`). We use AMP as an abbreviation for abstract multi-polynomial.
6. Composition $\mathbf{p} \bullet \mathbf{q}$, for $\mathbf{p}, \mathbf{q} \in$ `AMPol` (or τ`AMPol`) is defined as $\alpha(\gamma(\mathbf{p}) \circ \gamma(\mathbf{q}))$; it is easy to see that one can perform the calculation without the detour through polynomials with coefficients. The different operator symbol ("$\bullet$" versus "$\circ$") helps in disambiguating expressions.

Analysing a SDL. To analyse a SDL specified by a set of MPs $\mathcal{S}$, we start by computing $\alpha(\mathcal{S})$. The rest of the algorithm computes within τ`AMPol`. We define two operations that are combined in the analysis of loops. The first, which we call *closure*, is simply the fixed point of accumulated iterations as in the multiplicative case. It is introduced by the following two definitions.

Definition 8 (iterated composition). *Let* $\mathbf{t}$ *be any abstract* τ*-MP. We define* $\mathbf{t}^{\bullet(n)}$*, for* $n \geq 0$*, by:*

$$\mathbf{t}^{\bullet(0)} = Id$$
$$\mathbf{t}^{\bullet(n+1)} = \mathbf{t} \bullet \mathbf{t}^{\bullet(n)}.$$

For a set $\mathcal{T}$ *of abstract* τ*-MPs, we define, for* $n \geq 0$*:*

$$\mathcal{T}^{\bullet(0)} = \{Id\}$$
$$\mathcal{T}^{\bullet(n+1)} = \mathcal{T}^{\bullet(n)} \cup \bigcup_{\mathbf{q}\in\mathcal{T},\ \mathbf{p}\in\mathcal{T}^{\bullet(n)}} \mathbf{q} \bullet \mathbf{p}\,.$$

Note that $\mathbf{t}^{\bullet(n)} = \alpha(\gamma(\mathbf{t})^{(n)})$, where $\mathbf{p}^{(n)}$ is defined using ordinary composition.

Definition 9 (abstract closure). *For finite* $P \subset \tau$`AMPol`*, we define:*

$$Cl(P) = \bigcup_{i=0}^{\infty} P^{\bullet(i)}\,.$$

In the correctness proof, we argue that when all variables are polynomially bounded in a loop $\mathcal{S}$, the closure of $\alpha(\mathcal{S})$ can be computed in finite time; equivalently, it equals $\bigcup_{i=0}^{k}(\alpha(\mathcal{S}))^{\bullet(i)}$ for some k. The argument is essentially the same as in the multiplicative case.

The second operation is called *generalization* and its role is to capture the behaviour of accumulator variables, meaning variables that grow by accumulating increments in the loop, and make explicit the dependence on the number of iterations. The identification of which additive terms in a MP should be considered as increments that accumulate is at the heart of our problem, and is greatly simplified by concentrating on idempotent AMPs.

Definition 10. $\mathbf{p} \in \tau\mathtt{AMPol}$ *is called* idempotent *if* $\mathbf{p} \bullet \mathbf{p} = \mathbf{p}$.

Note that this is composition in the abstract domain. So, for instance, $\langle x_1, x_2\rangle$ is idempotent, and so is $\langle x_1 + x_2, x_2\rangle$, while $\langle x_1 x_2, x_2\rangle$ and $\langle x_1 + x_2, x_1\rangle$ are not.

Definition 11. *For* $\mathbf{p}$ *an (abstract) multi-polynomial, we say that* x_i *is* self-dependent *in* $\mathbf{p}$ *if* $\mathbf{p}[i]$ *depends on* x_i*. We call a monomial self-dependent if all the variables appearing in it are.*

Definition 12. *We define a notational convention for* τ*-MPs. Assuming that* $\mathbf{p}[i]$ *depends on* x_i*, we write*

$$\mathbf{p}[i] = x_i + \tau\mathbf{p}[i]' + \mathbf{p}[i]'' + \mathbf{p}[i]''' ,$$

where $\mathbf{p}[i]'''$ *includes all the non-self-dependent monomials of* $\mathbf{p}[i]$*, while the self-dependent monomials (other than* x_i*) are grouped into two sums:* $\tau\mathbf{p}[i]'$*, including all monomials with a positive degree of* τ*, and* $\mathbf{p}[i]''$ *which includes all the* τ*-free monomials.*

Example 4. Let $\mathbf{p} = \langle x_1 + \tau x_2 + \tau x_3 + x_3 x_4,\ x_3,\ x_3,\ x_4\rangle$. The self-dependent variables are all but x_2. Since x_1 is self-dependent, we will apply the above definition to $\mathbf{p}[1]$, so that $\mathbf{p}[1]' = x_3$, $\mathbf{p}[1]'' = x_3 x_4$ and $\mathbf{p}[1]''' = \tau x_2$. Note that a factor of τ is stripped in $\mathbf{p}[1]'$. Had the monomial been $\tau^2 x_3$, we would have $\mathbf{p}[1]' = \tau x_3$.

Definition 13 (generalization). *Let* $\mathbf{p}$ *be idempotent in* $\tau\mathtt{AMPol}$*; define* $\mathbf{p}^\tau$ *by*

$$\mathbf{p}^\tau[i] = \begin{cases} x_i + \tau\mathbf{p}[i]' + \tau\mathbf{p}[i]'' + \mathbf{p}[i]''' & \text{if } \mathbf{p}[i] \text{ depends on } x_i \\ \mathbf{p}[i] & \text{otherwise.} \end{cases}$$

Note that the arithmetic here is abstract (see examples below). Note also that in the term $\tau\mathbf{p}[i]'$ the τ is already present in $\mathbf{p}$, while in $\tau\mathbf{p}[i]''$ it is added to existing monomials. In this definition, the monomials of $\mathbf{p}[i]'''$ are treated like those of $\tau\mathbf{p}[i]'$; however, in certain steps of the proofs we treat them differently, which is why the notation separates them.

Example 5. Let $\mathbf{p} = \langle x_1 + x_3,\ x_2 + x_3 + x_4,\ x_3,\ x_3\rangle$.

Note that $\mathbf{p} \bullet \mathbf{p} = \mathbf{p}$. We have $\mathbf{p}^\tau = \langle x_1 + \tau x_3,\ x_2 + \tau x_3 + x_4,\ x_3,\ x_3\rangle$.

Example 6. Let $\mathbf{p} = \langle x_1 + \tau x_2 + \tau x_3 + \tau x_3 x_4,\ x_3,\ x_3,\ x_4 \rangle$.

Note that $\mathbf{p} \bullet \mathbf{p} = \mathbf{p}$. The self-dependent variables are all but x_2.

We have $\mathbf{p}^\tau = \langle x_1 + \tau x_2 + \tau x_3 + \tau x_3 x_4,\ x_3,\ x_3,\ x_4 \rangle = \mathbf{p}$.

Finally we can present the analysis of the loop command.

Algorithm SOLVE($\mathcal{S}$)
Input: $\mathcal{S}$, a polynomially-bounded disjunctive simple loop
Output: a set of τ-MPs which tightly approximates the effect of all $\mathcal{S}$-traces.

1. Set $T = \alpha(\mathcal{S})$.
2. Repeat the following steps until T remains fixed:
   (a) Closure: Set T to $Cl(T)$.
   (b) Generalization: For all $\mathbf{p} \in T$ such that $\mathbf{p} \bullet \mathbf{p} = \mathbf{p}$, add $\mathbf{p}^\tau$ to T.

Example 7. `loop X`$_3$` { X`$_1$`:= X`$_1$` + X`$_2$`; X`$_2$`:= X`$_2$` + X`$_3$`; X`$_4$`:= X`$_3$` }`
The body of the loop is evaluated symbolically and yields the multi-polynomial:

$$\mathbf{p} = \langle x_1 + x_2,\ x_2 + x_3,\ x_3,\ x_3 \rangle$$

Now, computing within `AMPol`,

$$\begin{aligned} \alpha(\mathbf{p})^{\bullet(2)} &= \alpha(\mathbf{p}) \bullet \alpha(\mathbf{p}) = \langle x_1 + x_2 + x_3,\ x_2 + x_3,\ x_3,\ x_3 \rangle; \\ \alpha(\mathbf{p})^{\bullet(3)} &= \alpha(\mathbf{p})^{\bullet(2)}. \end{aligned}$$

Here the closure computation stops. Since $\alpha(\mathbf{p}^{\bullet(2)})$ is idempotent, we compute

$$\mathbf{q} = (\alpha(\mathbf{p})^{\bullet(2)})^\tau = \langle x_1 + \tau x_2 + \tau x_3,\ x_2 + \tau x_3,\ x_3,\ x_3 \rangle$$

and applying closure again, we obtain some additional results:

$$\begin{aligned} \mathbf{q} \bullet \alpha(\mathbf{p}) &= \langle x_1 + x_2 + x_3 + \tau x_2 + \tau x_3,\ x_2 + x_3 + \tau x_3,\ x_3,\ x_3 \rangle \\ (\mathbf{q})^{\bullet(2)} &= \langle x_1 + \tau x_2 + \tau x_3 + \tau^2 x_3,\ x_2 + \tau x_3,\ x_3,\ x_3 \rangle \\ (\mathbf{q})^{\bullet(2)} \bullet \alpha(\mathbf{p}) &= \langle x_1 + x_2 + x_3 + \tau x_2 + \tau x_3 + \tau^2 x_3,\ x_2 + x_3 + \tau x_3,\ x_3,\ x_3 \rangle \end{aligned}$$

The last element is idempotent but applying generalization does not generate anything new. Thus the algorithm ends. The reader may reconsider the source code to verify that we have indeed obtained tight bounds for the loop.

6 Correctness

We claim that our algorithm obtains a description of the worst-case results of the program that is precise up to constant factors. That is, we claim that the set of MPs returned provides an upper bound (on all executions) which is also tight; tightness means that every MP returned is also a lower bound (up to a constant factor) on an infinite sequence of possible executions. Unfortunately, due to space constraints, we are not able to give full details of the proofs here; however, we give the main highlights. Intuitively, what we want to prove is that the multi-polynomials we compute cover all "behaviors" of the loop. More precisely, in the upper-bound part of the proof we want to cover all behaviors: upper-bounding is a universal statement. To prove that bounds are tight, we show that each such bound constitutes a *lower bound* on a certain "worst-case behavior": tightness is an existential statement. The main aspects of these proofs are as follows:

- A key notion in our proofs is that of *realizability*. Intuitively, when we come up with a bound, we want to show that there are traces that achieve (realize) this bound for arbitrarily large input values.
- In the lower-bound proof, we describe a "behavior" by a *pattern*. A pattern is constructed like a regular expression with concatenation and Kleene-star. However, they allow no nested iteration constructs, and the starred sub-expressions have to be repeated the same number of times; for example, the pattern $\mathbf{p}^*\mathbf{q}^*$ generates the traces $\{\mathbf{p}^t\mathbf{q}^t,\ t \geq 0\}$. The proof constructs a pattern for every multi-polynomial computed, showing it is realizable. It is interesting that such simple patterns suffice to establish tight lower bounds for all our programs.
- In the upper-bound proof, we describe all "behaviors" by a finite set of *well-typed regular expressions* [10]. This elegant tool channels the power of the Factorization Forest Theorem [25]; this brings out the role of idempotent elements, which is key in our algorithm.
- Interestingly, the lower-bound proof not only justifies the tightness of our upper bounds, it also justifies the termination of the algorithm and the application of the Factorization Forest Theorem in the upper-bound proof, because it shows that our abstract multi-polynomials generate a finite monoid.

7 Related Work

Bound analysis, in the sense of finding symbolic bounds for data values, iteration bounds and related quantities, is a classic field of program analysis [18,24,27]. It is also an area of active research, with tools being currently (or recently) developed including COSTA [1], AProVE [13], CiaoPP [19], C^4B [11], Loopus [26]—all for imperative programs. There is also work on functional and logic programs, term rewriting systems, recurrence relations, etc. which we cannot attempt to survey here. In the rest of this section we survey work which is more directly related to ours, and has even inspired it.

The LOOP language is due to Meyer and Ritchie [20], who note that it computes only primitive recursive functions, but complexity can rise very fast, even for programs with nesting-depth 2. Subsequent work [15–17,22] concerning similar languages attempted to analyze such programs more precisely; most of them proposed syntactic criteria, or analysis algorithms, that are sufficient for ensuring that the program lies in a desired class (often, polynomial-time programs), but are not both necessary and sufficient: thus, they do not prove decidability (the exception is [17] which has a decidability result for a weak "core" language). The core language we use in this paper is from Ben-Amram et al. [7], who observed that by introducing weak bounded loops instead of concrete loop commands and non-deterministic branching instead of "`if`", we have weakened the semantics just enough to obtain decidability of polynomial growth-rate. Justifying the necessity of these relaxations, [8] showed undecidability for a language that can only do addition and definite loops (that cannot exit early).

In the vast literature on bound analysis in various forms, there are a few other works that give a complete solution for a weak language. *Size-change programs* are considered by [12,28]. Size-change programs abstract away nearly everything in the program, leaving a control-flow graph annotated with assertions about variables which decrease (or do not increase) in a transition. Thus, it does not assume structured and explicit loops, and it cannot express information about values which increase. Both works yield tight bounds on the number of transitions until termination.

Dealing with a somewhat different problem, [14,21] both check, or find, *invariants* in the form of polynomial equations. We find it remarkable that they give complete solutions for weak languages, where the weakness lies in the non-deterministic control-flow, as in our language. If one could give a complete solution for polynomial *inequalities*, this would have implied a solution to our problem as well.

8 Conclusion and Further Work

We have solved an open problem in the area of analyzing programs in a simple language with bounded loops. For our language, it has been previously shown that it is possible to decide whether a variable's value, number of steps in the program, etc. are polynomially bounded or not. Now, we have an algorithm that computes tight polynomial bounds on the final values of variables in terms of initial values. The bounds are tight up to constant factors (suitable constants are also computable). This result improves our understanding of what is computable by, and about, programs of this form. An interesting corollary of our algorithm is that as long as variables are *polynomially bounded*, their worst-case bounds are described tightly by (multivariate) *polynomials*. This is, of course, not true for common Turing-complete languages. Another interesting corollary of the *proofs* is the definition of a simple class of patterns that suffice to realize the worst-case behaviors. This will appear in a planned extended version of this paper.

There are a number of possible directions for further work. We would like to look for decidability results for richer (yet, obviously, sub-recursive) languages. Some possible language extensions include deterministic loops, variable resets (cf. [4]), explicit constants, and procedures. The inclusion of explicit constants is a particularly challenging open problem.

Rather than extending the language, we could extend the range of bounds that we can compute. In light of the results in [17], it seems plausible that the approach can be extended to classify the Grzegorczyk-degree of the growth rate of variables when they are super-polynomial. There may also be room for progress regarding precise bounds of the form 2^{poly}.

In terms of time complexity, our algorithm is polynomial in the size of the program times n^{nd}, where d is the highest degree of any MP computed. Such exponential behavior is to be expected, since a program can be easily written to compute a multivariate polynomial that is exponentially long to write. But there is still room for finer investigation of this issue.

References

1. Albert, E., Arenas, P., Genaim, S., Puebla, G., Zanardini, D.: Cost analysis of object-oriented bytecode programs. Theor. Comput. Sci. **413**(1), 142–159 (2012). https://doi.org/10.1016/j.tcs.2011.07.009
2. Alias, C., Darte, A., Feautrier, P., Gonnord, L.: Multi-dimensional rankings, program termination, and complexity bounds of flowchart programs. In: Cousot, R., Martel, M. (eds.) SAS 2010. LNCS, vol. 6337, pp. 117–133. Springer, Heidelberg (2010). https://doi.org/10.1007/978-3-642-15769-1_8
3. Bagnara, R., Hill, P.M., Zaffanella, E.: The parma polyhedra library: toward a complete set of numerical abstractions for the analysis and verification of hardware and software systems. Sci. Comput. Program. **72**(1–2), 3–21 (2008)
4. Ben-Amram, A.M.: On decidable growth-rate properties of imperative programs. In: Baillot, P. (ed.) International Workshop on Developments in Implicit Computational complExity (DICE 2010). EPTCS, vol. 23, pp. 1–14 (2010). https://doi.org/10.4204/EPTCS.23.1
5. Ben-Amram, A.M., Genaim, S.: Ranking functions for linear-constraint loops. J. ACM **61**(4), 26:1–26:55 (2014). https://doi.org/10.1145/2629488
6. Ben-Amram, A.M., Genaim, S.: On multiphase-linear ranking functions. In: Majumdar, R., Kunčak, V. (eds.) CAV 2017. LNCS, vol. 10427, pp. 601–620. Springer, Cham (2017). https://doi.org/10.1007/978-3-319-63390-9_32
7. Ben-Amram, A.M., Jones, N.D., Kristiansen, L.: Linear, polynomial or exponential? Complexity inference in polynomial time. In: Beckmann, A., Dimitracopoulos, C., Löwe, B. (eds.) CiE 2008. LNCS, vol. 5028, pp. 67–76. Springer, Heidelberg (2008). https://doi.org/10.1007/978-3-540-69407-6_7
8. Ben-Amram, A.M., Kristiansen, L.: On the edge of decidability in complexity analysis of loop programs. Int. J. Found. Comput. Sci. **23**(7), 1451–1464 (2012). https://doi.org/10.1142/S0129054112400588
9. Ben-Amram, A.M., Pineles, A.: Flowchart programs, regular expressions, and decidability of polynomial growth-rate. In: Hamilton, G., Lisitsa, A., Nemytykh, A.P. (eds.) Proceedings of the Fourth International Workshop on Verification and Program Transformation (VPT). EPTCS, vol. 216, pp. 24–49 (2016). https://doi.org/10.4204/EPTCS.216.2
10. Bojańczyk, M.: Factorization forests. In: Diekert, V., Nowotka, D. (eds.) DLT 2009. LNCS, vol. 5583, pp. 1–17. Springer, Heidelberg (2009). https://doi.org/10.1007/978-3-642-02737-6_1
11. Carbonneaux, Q., Hoffmann, J., Shao, Z.: Compositional certified resource bounds. In: Proceedings of the ACM SIGPLAN 2015 Conference on Programming Language Design and Implementation (PLDI). ACM (2015)

12. Colcombet, T., Daviaud, L., Zuleger, F.: Size-change abstraction and max-plus automata. In: Csuhaj-Varjú, E., Dietzfelbinger, M., Ésik, Z. (eds.) MFCS 2014. LNCS, vol. 8634, pp. 208–219. Springer, Heidelberg (2014). https://doi.org/10.1007/978-3-662-44522-8_18
13. Giesl, J., et al.: Analyzing program termination and complexity automatically with AProVE. J. Autom. Reasoning **58**(1), 3–31 (2017). https://doi.org/10.1007/s10817-016-9388-y
14. Hrushovski, E., Ouaknine, J., Pouly, A., Worrell, J.: Polynomial invariants for affine programs. In: Proceedings of the 33rd Annual ACM/IEEE Symposium on Logic in Computer Science, LICS 2018, pp. 530–539. ACM, New York (2018). https://doi.org/10.1145/3209108.3209142
15. Jones, N.D., Kristiansen, L.: A flow calculus of mwp-bounds for complexity analysis. ACM Trans. Comput. Logic **10**(4), 1–41 (2009). https://doi.org/10.1145/1555746.1555752
16. Kasai, T., Adachi, A.: A characterization of time complexity by simple loop programs. J. Comput. Syst. Sci. **20**(1), 1–17 (1980). https://doi.org/10.1016/0022-0000(80)90001-X
17. Kristiansen, L., Niggl, K.H.: On the computational complexity of imperative programming languages. Theor. Comput. Sci. **318**(1–2), 139–161 (2004). https://doi.org/10.1016/j.tcs.2003.10.016
18. Le Métayer, D.: ACE: an automatic complexity evaluator. ACM Trans. Program. Lang. Syst. **10**(2), 248–266 (1988). https://doi.org/10.1145/42190.42347
19. López-García, P., Darmawan, L., Klemen, M., Liqat, U., Bueno, F., Hermengildo, M.V.: Interval-based resource usage verification by translation into Horn clauses and an application to energy consumption. Theory Pract. Logic Program. **18**(2), 167–223 (2018)
20. Meyer, A.R., Ritchie, D.M.: The complexity of loop programs. In: Proceedings of the 22nd ACM National Conference, Washington, DC, pp. 465–469 (1967)
21. Müller-Olm, M., Seidl, H.: Computing polynomial program invariants. Inf. Process. Lett. **91**(5), 233–244 (2004). https://doi.org/10.1016/j.ipl.2004.05.004
22. Niggl, K.H., Wunderlich, H.: Certifying polynomial time and linear/polynomial space for imperative programs. SIAM J. Comput. **35**(5), 1122–1147 (2006). https://doi.org/10.1137/S0097539704445597
23. Podelski, A., Rybalchenko, A.: A complete method for the synthesis of linear ranking functions. In: Steffen, B., Levi, G. (eds.) VMCAI 2004. LNCS, vol. 2937, pp. 239–251. Springer, Heidelberg (2004). https://doi.org/10.1007/978-3-540-24622-0_20
24. Rosendahl, M.: Automatic complexity analysis. In: Proceedings of the Conference on Functional Programming Languages and Computer Architecture, FPCA 1989, pp. 144–156. ACM (1989). https://doi.org/10.1145/99370.99381
25. Simon, I.: Factorization forests of finite height. Theor. Comput. Sci. **72**(1), 65–94 (1990). https://doi.org/10.1016/0304-3975(90)90047-L
26. Sinn, M., Zuleger, F., Veith, H.: Complexity and resource bound analysis of imperative programs using difference constraints. J. Autom. Reasoning **59**(1), 3–45 (2017). https://doi.org/10.1007/s10817-016-9402-4
27. Wegbreit, B.: Mechanical program analysis. Commun. ACM **18**(9), 528–539 (1975). https://doi.org/10.1145/361002.361016
28. Zuleger, F.: Asymptotically precise ranking functions for deterministic size-change systems. In: Beklemishev, L.D., Musatov, D.V. (eds.) CSR 2015. LNCS, vol. 9139, pp. 426–442. Springer, Cham (2015). https://doi.org/10.1007/978-3-319-20297-6_27

13

A Dialectica-Like Interpretation of a Linear MSO on Infinite Words

Pierre Pradic[1,2] and Colin Riba[1(✉)]

[1] ENS de Lyon, Université de Lyon,
LIP, UMR 5668 CNRS ENS Lyon UCBL Inria, Lyon, France
colin.riba@ens-lyon.fr
[2] Faculty of Mathematics, Informatics and Mechanics,
University of Warsaw, Warsaw, Poland

Abstract. We devise a variant of Dialectica interpretation of intuitionistic linear logic for LMSO, a linear logic-based version MSO over infinite words. LMSO was known to be correct and complete w.r.t. Church's synthesis, thanks to an automata-based realizability model. Invoking Büchi-Landweber Theorem and building on a complete axiomatization of MSO on infinite words, our interpretation provides us with a syntactic approach, without any further construction of automata on infinite words. Via Dialectica, as linear negation directly corresponds to switching players in games, we furthermore obtain a complete logic: either a closed formula or its linear negation is provable. This completely axiomatizes the theory of the realizability model of LMSO. Besides, this shows that in principle, one can solve Church's synthesis for a given ∀∃-formula by only looking for proofs of either that formula or its linear negation.

Keywords: Linear logic · Dialectica interpretation · MSO on Infinite Words

1 Introduction

Monadic Second-Order Logic (MSO) over ω-words is a simple yet expressive language for reasoning on non-terminating systems which subsumes non-trivial logics used in verification such as LTL (see e.g. [2,30]). MSO on ω-words is decidable by Büchi's Theorem [6] (see e.g. [24,29]), and can be completely axiomatized as a subsystem of second-order Peano's arithmetic [28]. While MSO admits an effective translation to finite-state (Büchi) automata, it is a non-constructive logic, in the sense that it has true (*i.e.*provable) ∀∃-statements which can be witnessed by no continuous stream function.

On the other hand, Church's synthesis [8] can be seen as a decision problem for a strong form of constructivity in MSO. More precisely (see e.g. [12,32]),

Church's synthesis takes as input a $\forall\exists$-formula of MSO and asks whether it can be realized by a finite-state causal stream transducer. Church's synthesis is known to be decidable since Büchi-Landweber Theorem [7], which gives an effective solution to ω-regular games on finite graphs generated by $\forall\exists$-formulae. In traditional (theoretical) solutions to Church's synthesis, the game graphs are induced from deterministic (say parity) automata obtained by McNaughton's Theorem [19]. Despite its long history, Church's synthesis has not yet been amenable to tractable solutions for the full language of MSO (see e.g. [12]).

In recent works [25, 26], the authors suggested a Curry-Howard approach to Church's synthesis based on intuitionistic and linear variants of MSO. In particular, [26] proposed a system LMSO based on (intuitionistic) linear logic [13], in which via a translation $(-)^L : \mathsf{MSO} \to \mathsf{LMSO}$, the provable $\forall\exists(-)^L$-statements exactly correspond to the realizable instances of Church's synthesis. Realizer extraction for LMSO is done via an external realizability model based on alternating automata, which amounts to see every formula $\varphi(a)$ as a formula of the form $(\exists u)(\forall x)\varphi_{\mathcal{D}}(u, x, a)$, where $\varphi_{\mathcal{D}}$ represents a deterministic automaton.

In this paper, we use a variant of Gödel's "Dialectica" functional interpretation as a syntactic formulation of the automata-based realizability model of [26]. Dialectica associates to $\varphi(a)$ a formula $\varphi^D(a)$ of the form $(\exists u)(\forall x)\varphi_D(u, x, a)$. In usual versions formulated in higher-types arithmetic (see e.g. [1, 16]), the formula φ_D is quantifier-free, so that φ^D is a prenex form of φ. This prenex form is constructive, and a constructive proof of φ can be turned to a proof of φ^D with an explicit witness for $\exists u$. Even if Dialectica originally interprets intuitionistic arithmetic, it is structurally linear, and linear versions of Dialectica were formulated at the very beginning of linear logic [21–23] (see also [14, 27]).

We show that the automata-based realizability model of [26] can be obtained by a suitable modification of the usual linear Dialectica interpretation, in which the formula φ_D essentially represents a deterministic automaton on ω-words and is in general not quantifier-free, and whose realizers are exactly the finite-state accepting strategies in the model of [26]. In addition to provide a syntactic extraction procedure with internalized and automata-free correctness proof, this reformulation has a striking consequence, namely that there exists an extension $\mathsf{LMSO}(\mathfrak{C})$ of LMSO which is complete in the sense that for each closed formula φ, it either proves φ or its linear negation $\varphi \multimap \bot$. Since $\mathsf{LMSO}(\mathfrak{C})$ has realizers for all provable $\forall\exists(-)^L$-statements, its completeness contrasts with the classical setting, in which due to provable non-constructive statements, one can not decide Church's synthesis by only looking for proofs of $\forall\exists$-statements or their negations. Besides, $\mathsf{LMSO}(\mathfrak{C})$ has a linear choice axiom which is realizable in the sense of both $(-)^D$ and [26], but whose naive MSO counterpart is false.

The paper is organized as follows. We present our basic setting in Sect. 2, with a particular emphasis on particularities of (finite-state) causal functions to model strategies and realizers. Our variant of Dialectica and the corresponding linear system are discussed in Sect. 3, while Sect. 4 defines the systems LMSO and $\mathsf{LMSO}(\mathfrak{C})$ and shows the completeness of $\mathsf{LMSO}(\mathfrak{C})$.

2 Preliminaries

Alphabets (denoted Σ, Γ, etc) are finite non-empty sets of the form $\mathbf{2}^p$ for some $p \in \mathbb{N}$. We let $\mathbf{1} := \mathbf{2}^0$. Note that alphabets are closed under Cartesian products and set-theoretic function spaces. It follows that taking $[\![o]\!] := \mathbf{2}$, we have an alphabet $[\![\tau]\!]$ for each simple type $\tau \in \mathrm{ST}$, where

$$\sigma, \tau \in \mathrm{ST} \quad ::= \quad \mathbf{1} \quad | \quad o \quad | \quad \sigma \times \tau \quad | \quad \sigma \to \tau$$

We often write $(\tau)\sigma$ for the type $\sigma \to \tau$. Given an ω-word (or stream) $B \in \Sigma^\omega$ and $n \in \mathbb{N}$, we write $B{\upharpoonright}n$ for the finite word $B(0).\cdots.B(n-1) \in \Sigma^*$.

Church's Synthesis and Causal Functions. Church's synthesis consists in the automatic extraction of stream functions from input-output specifications (see e.g. [12,31]). These specifications are in general asked to be ω-regular, or equivalently definable in MSO over ω-words. In practice, proper subsets of MSO (and even of LTL) are assumed (see e.g. [5,11,12]). As an example, the relation

$$(\exists^\infty k)B(k) \;\Rightarrow\; (\exists^\infty k)C(k) \qquad \text{resp.} \qquad (\forall^\infty k)B(k) \;\Rightarrow\; (\exists^\infty k)C(k) \quad (1)$$

with input $B \in \mathbf{2}^\omega$ and output $C \in \mathbf{2}^\omega$ specifies functions $F : \mathbf{2}^\omega \to \mathbf{2}^\omega$ such that $F(B) \in \mathbf{2}^\omega \simeq \mathcal{P}(\mathbb{N})$ is infinite whenever $B \in \mathbf{2}^\omega \simeq \mathcal{P}(\mathbb{N})$ is infinite (resp. the complement of B is finite). One may also additionally require to respect the transitions of some automaton. For instance, following [31], in addition to either case of (1) one can ask $C \subseteq B$ and C not to contain two consecutive positions:

$$(\forall n)(C(n) \;\Rightarrow\; B(n)) \qquad \text{and} \qquad (\forall n)(C(n) \;\Rightarrow\; \neg C(n+1)) \qquad (2)$$

In any case, the realizers must be (finite-state) causal functions. A stream function $F : \Sigma^\omega \to \Gamma^\omega$ is causal (notation $F : \Sigma \to_{\mathbb{S}} \Gamma$) if it can produce a prefix of length n of its output from a prefix of length n of its input. Hence F is causal if it is induced by a map $f : \Sigma^+ \to \Gamma$ as follows:

$$F(B)(n) \quad = \quad f(B(0) \cdot \ldots \cdot B(n)) \qquad \text{(for all } B \in \Sigma^\omega \text{ and all } n \in \mathbb{N})$$

The finite-state (f.s.) causal functions are those induced by Mealy machines. A Mealy machine $\mathcal{M} : \Sigma \to \Gamma$ is a DFA over input alphabet Σ equipped with an output function $\lambda : Q_{\mathcal{M}} \times \Sigma \to \Gamma$ (where $Q_{\mathcal{M}}$ is the state set of $\mathcal{M}$). Writing $\partial^* : \Sigma^* \to Q_{\mathcal{M}}$ for the iteration of the transition function ∂ of $\mathcal{M}$ from its initial state, $\mathcal{M}$ induces a causal function via $(\bar{\mathsf{a}}.\mathsf{a} \in \Sigma^+) \;\mapsto\; (\lambda(\partial^*(\bar{\mathsf{a}}), \mathsf{a}) \in \Gamma)$.

Causal and f.s. causal functions form categories with finite products. Let $\mathbb{S}$ be the category whose objects are alphabets and whose maps from Σ to Γ are causal functions $F : \Sigma^\omega \to \Gamma^\omega$. Let $\mathbb{M}$ be the wide subcategory of $\mathbb{S}$ whose maps are finite-state causal functions.[1]

[1] A subcategory $\mathbb{D}$ of $\mathbb{C}$ is *wide* if $\mathbb{D}$ has the same objects as $\mathbb{C}$.

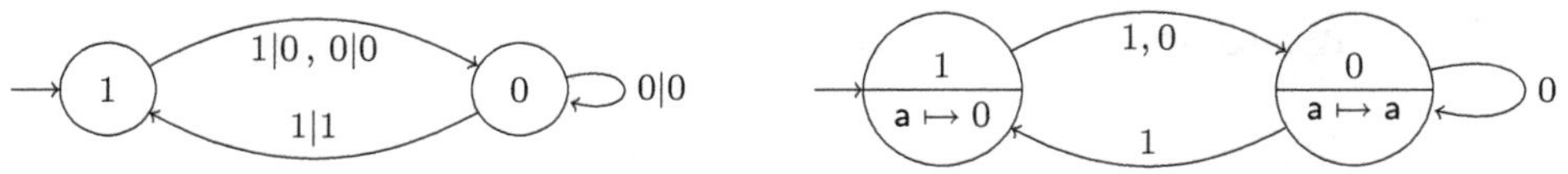

Fig. 1. A Mealy machine (left) and an equivalent eager (Moore) machine (right).

Example 1. (a) Usual functions $\Sigma \to \Gamma$ lift to (pointwise, one-state) maps $\Sigma \to_{\mathbb{M}} \Gamma$. For instance, the identity $\Sigma \to_{\mathbb{M}} \Sigma$ is induced by the Mealy machine with $\langle \partial, \lambda \rangle : (-, \mathsf{a}) \mapsto (-, \mathsf{a})$.
(b) Causal functions $\mathbf{1} \to_{\mathbb{S}} \Sigma$ correspond exactly to ω-words $B \in \Sigma^\omega$.
(c) The conjunction of (2) with either side of (1) is realized by the causal function $F : \mathbf{2} \to_{\mathbb{M}} \mathbf{2}$ induced by the machine $\mathcal{M} : \mathbf{2} \to \mathbf{2}$ displayed on Fig. 1 (left, where a transition $\mathsf{a}|\mathsf{b}$ outputs b from input a), taken from [31].

Proposition 1. *The Cartesian product of $\Sigma_1, \ldots, \Sigma_n$ (for $n \geq 0$) in $\mathbb{S}, \mathbb{M}$ is given by the product of sets $\Sigma_1 \times \cdots \times \Sigma_n$ (so that $\mathbf{1}$ is terminal).*

The Logic MSO(M). Our specification language $\mathsf{MSO}(\mathbf{M})$ is an extension of MSO on ω-words with one function symbol for each f.s. causal function. More precisely, $\mathsf{MSO}(\mathbf{M})$ is a many-sorted first-order logic, with one sort for each simple type $\tau \in \mathrm{ST}$, and with one function symbol of arity $(\sigma_1, \ldots, \sigma_n; \tau)$ for each map $[\![\sigma_1]\!] \times \cdots \times [\![\sigma_n]\!] \to_{\mathbb{M}} [\![\tau]\!]$. A term $\mathtt{t}$ of sort τ (notation $\mathtt{t}^\tau$) with free variables among $x_1^{\sigma_1}, \ldots, x_n^{\sigma_n}$ (we say that $\mathtt{t}$ is of arity $(\sigma_1, \ldots, \sigma_n; \tau)$) thus induces a map $[\![\mathtt{t}]\!] : [\![\sigma_1]\!] \times \cdots \times [\![\sigma_n]\!] \to_{\mathbb{M}} [\![\tau]\!]$. Given a valuation $x_i \mapsto B_i \in [\![\sigma_i]\!]^\omega \simeq \mathbb{S}[\mathbf{1}, [\![\sigma_i]\!]]$ for $i \in \{1, \ldots, n\}$, we then obtain an ω-word

$$[\![\mathtt{t}]\!] \circ \langle B_1, \ldots, B_n \rangle \quad \in \quad \mathbb{S}[\mathbf{1}, [\![\tau]\!]] \quad \simeq \quad [\![\tau]\!]^\omega$$

$\mathsf{MSO}(\mathbf{M})$ extends MSO with $\exists x^\tau$ and $\forall x^\tau$ ranging over $\mathbb{S}[\mathbf{1}, [\![\tau]\!]] \simeq [\![\tau]\!]^\omega$ and with sorted equalities $\mathtt{t}^\tau \doteq \mathtt{u}^\tau$ interpreted as equality over $\mathbb{S}[\mathbf{1}, [\![\tau]\!]] \simeq [\![\tau]\!]^\omega$. Write $\models \varphi$ when φ holds in this model, called the *standard* model. The full definition of $\mathsf{MSO}(\mathbf{M})$ is deferred to Sect. 4.1.

An instance of Church's synthesis problem is given by a closed formula $(\forall x^\sigma)(\exists u^\tau)\varphi(u, x)$. A positive solution (or realizer) of this instance is a term $\mathtt{t}(x)$ of arity $(\sigma; \tau)$ such that $(\forall x^\sigma)\varphi(\mathtt{t}(x), x)$ holds.

Proposition 1 implies that $\mathsf{MSO}(\mathbf{M})$ proves the following equations:

$$\pi_i(\langle \mathtt{t}_1, \ldots, \mathtt{t}_n \rangle) \doteq_{\sigma_i} \mathtt{t}_i \qquad \text{and} \qquad \mathtt{t} \doteq_{\sigma_1 \times \cdots \times \sigma_n} \langle \pi_1(\mathtt{t}), \ldots, \pi_n(\mathtt{t}) \rangle \tag{3}$$

Hence each formula $\varphi(a_1^{\sigma_1}, \ldots, a_n^{\sigma_n})$ can be seen as a formula $\varphi(a^{\sigma_1 \times \cdots \times \sigma_n})$.

Eager Functions. A causal function $\Sigma \to_{\mathbb{S}} \Gamma$ is eager if it can produce a prefix of length $n+1$ of its output from a prefix of length n of its input. More precisely, an eager $F : \Sigma \to_{\mathbb{S}} \Gamma$ is induced by a map $f : \Sigma^* \to \Gamma$ as

$$F(B)(n) \quad = \quad f(B(0) \cdot \ldots \cdot B(n-1)) \qquad \text{(for all } B \in \Sigma^\omega \text{ and all } n \in \mathbb{N}\text{)}$$

Finite-state eager functions are those induced by eager (Moore) machines (see also [11]). An eager machine $\mathcal{E} : \Sigma \to \Gamma$ is a Mealy machine $\Sigma \to \Gamma$ whose output function $\lambda : Q_{\mathcal{E}} \to \Gamma$ is does not depend on the current input letter. An eager $\mathcal{E} : \Sigma \to \Gamma$ induces an eager function via the map $(\bar{\mathsf{a}} \in \Sigma^*) \mapsto (\lambda_{\mathcal{E}}(\partial^*_{\mathcal{E}}(\bar{\mathsf{a}})) \in \Gamma)$.

We write $F : \Sigma \to_{\mathbb{E}} \Gamma$ when $F : \Sigma \to_{\mathbb{S}} \Gamma$ is eager and $F : \Sigma \to_{\mathbb{EM}} \Gamma$ when F is f.s. eager. All functions $F : \Sigma \to_{\mathbb{M}} \mathbf{1}$, and more generally, constants functions $F : \Sigma \to_{\mathbb{S}} \Gamma$ are eager. Note also that if $F : \Sigma \to_{\mathbb{S}} \Gamma$ is eager, then $F : \Sigma \to_{\mathbb{EM}} \Gamma$. On the other hand, if $F : \Sigma \to_{\mathbb{EM}} \Gamma$ is induced by an eager machine $\mathcal{E}$ then F is finite-state causal as being induced by the Mealy machine with same states and transitions as $\mathcal{E}$, but with output function $(q, \mathsf{a}) \mapsto \lambda_{\mathcal{E}}(q)$.

Eager functions do not form a category since the identity of $\mathbb{S}$ is not eager. On the other hand, eager functions are closed under composition with causal functions.

Proposition 2. *If F is eager and G, H are causal then $H \circ F \circ G$ is eager.*

Isolating eager functions allows a proper treatment of strategies in games and realizers w.r.t. the Dialectica interpretation. Since $\Sigma^+ \to \Gamma \simeq \Sigma^* \to \Gamma^\Sigma$, maps $\Sigma \to_{\mathbb{E}} \Gamma^\Sigma$ are in bijection with maps $\Sigma \to_{\mathbb{S}} \Gamma$. This easily extends to machines. Given a Mealy machine $\mathcal{M} : \Sigma \to \Gamma$, let $\boldsymbol{\Lambda}(\mathcal{M}) : \Sigma \to \Gamma^\Sigma$ be the eager machine defined as $\mathcal{M}$ but with output map taking $q \in Q_{\mathcal{M}}$ to $(\mathsf{a} \mapsto \lambda_{\mathcal{M}}(q, \mathsf{a})) \in \Gamma^\Sigma$.

Example 2. Recall the Mealy machine $\mathcal{M} : \mathbf{2} \to \mathbf{2}$ of Ex. 1.(c). Then $\boldsymbol{\Lambda}(\mathcal{M}) : \mathbf{2} \to \mathbf{2}^\mathbf{2}$ is the eager machine displayed in Fig. 1 (right, where the output is indicated within states).

Eager f.s. functions will often be used with the following notations. First, let $@$ be the pointwise lift to $\mathbb{M}$ of the usual application function $\Gamma^\Sigma \times \Sigma \to \Gamma$. We often write $(F)G$ for $@(F, G)$. Consider a Mealy machine $\mathcal{M} : \Sigma \to \Gamma$ and the induced eager machine $\boldsymbol{\Lambda}(\mathcal{M}) : \Sigma \to \Gamma^\Sigma$. We have

$$F_{\mathcal{M}}(B) \quad = \quad @(F_{\boldsymbol{\Lambda}(\mathcal{M})}(B), B) \qquad \text{(for all B} \in \Sigma^\omega)$$

Given $F : \Gamma \to_{\mathbb{E}} \Sigma^\Gamma$, we write $\mathbf{e}(F)$ for the causal $@(F(-), -) : \Gamma \to_{\mathbb{S}} \Sigma$. Given $F : \Gamma \to_{\mathbb{S}} \Sigma$, we write $\boldsymbol{\Lambda}(F)$ for the eager $\Gamma \to_{\mathbb{E}} \Sigma^\Gamma$ such that $F = \mathbf{e}(\boldsymbol{\Lambda}(F))$. We extend these notations to terms.

Eager functions admit fixpoints similar to those of contractive maps in the topos of tree (see e.g. [4, Thm. 2.4]).

Proposition 3. *For each $F : \Sigma \times \Gamma \to_{\mathbb{E}} \Sigma^\Gamma$ there is a* $\text{fix}(F) : \Gamma \to_{\mathbb{E}} \Sigma^\Gamma$ *s.t.*

$$\text{fix}(F)(C) \quad = \quad F\big(\mathbf{e}(\text{fix}(F))(C)\,,\, C\big) \qquad \text{(for all } C \in \Gamma^\omega)$$

If F is induced by the eager machine $\mathcal{E} : \Sigma \times \Gamma \to \Sigma^\Gamma$, then $\text{fix}(F)$ *is induced by the eager $\mathcal{H} : \Gamma \to \Sigma^\Gamma$ defined as $\mathcal{E}$ but with $\partial_{\mathcal{H}} : (q, \mathsf{b}) \mapsto \partial_{\mathcal{E}}\big(q,\, ((\lambda_{\mathcal{E}}(q))\mathsf{b}, \mathsf{b})\big)$.*

Games. Traditional solutions to Church's synthesis turn specifications to infinite two-player games with ω-regular winning conditions. Consider an $\mathsf{MSO}(\mathbf{M})$ formula $\varphi(u^\tau, x^\sigma)$ with no free variable other than u, x. We see this formula as defining a two-player infinite game $\mathcal{G}(\varphi)(u^\tau, x^\sigma)$ between the *Proponent* P ($\exists$loïse), playing moves in $[\![\tau]\!]$ and the *Opponent* O ($\forall$bélard), playing moves in $[\![\sigma]\!]$. The Proponent begins, and then the two players alternate, producing an infinite play of the form

$$\chi \quad := \quad \mathsf{u}_0\mathsf{x}_0 \cdots \mathsf{u}_n\mathsf{x}_n \cdots \quad \simeq \quad ((\mathsf{u}_k)_k, (\mathsf{x}_k)_k) \in [\![\tau]\!]^\omega \times [\![\sigma]\!]^\omega$$

The play χ is winning for P if $\varphi((\mathsf{u}_k)_k, (\mathsf{x})_k)$ holds. Otherwise χ is winning for O. Strategies for P resp. O in this game are functions

$$[\![\sigma]\!]^* \longrightarrow [\![\tau]\!] \qquad \text{resp.} \qquad [\![\tau]\!]^+ \longrightarrow [\![\sigma]\!] \;\simeq\; [\![\tau]\!]^* \longrightarrow [\![\sigma]\!]^{[\![\tau]\!]}$$

Hence finite-state strategies are represented by f.s. eager functions. In particular, a realizer of $(\forall x^\sigma)(\exists u^\tau)\varphi(u, x)$ in the sense of Church is a f.s. P-strategy in

$$\mathcal{G}\big(\varphi((u)x, x)\big)\big(u^{(\tau)\sigma}, x^\sigma\big)$$

Most approaches to Church's synthesis reduce to Büchi-Landweber Theorem [7], stating that games with ω-regular winning conditions are effectively determined, and that the winner always has a finite-state winning strategy. We will use Büchi-Landweber Theorem in following form. Note that an O-strategy in the game $\mathcal{G}(\varphi)(u^\tau, x^\sigma)$ is a P-strategy in the game $\mathcal{G}\big(\neg\varphi(u, (x)u)\big)\big(x^{(\sigma)\tau}, u^\tau\big)$.

Theorem 1 ([7]). *Let $\varphi(u^\tau, x^\sigma)$ be an $\mathsf{MSO}(\mathbf{M})$-formula with only u, x free. Then either there is an eager term $\mathtt{u}(x)$ of arity $(\sigma;\tau)$ such that $\models (\forall x)\varphi(\mathtt{u}(x), x)$ or there is an eager term $\mathtt{x}(u)$ of arity $(\tau;(\sigma)\tau)$ such that $\models (\forall u)\neg\varphi(u, \mathbf{e}(\mathtt{x})(u))$. It is decidable which case holds and the terms are computable from φ.*

Curry-Howard Approaches. Following the complete axiomatization of MSO on ω-words of [28] (see also [26]), one can axiomatize $\mathsf{MSO}(\mathbf{M})$ with a deduction system based on arithmetic (see Sect. 4.1). Consider an instance of Church's synthesis $(\forall x^\sigma)(\exists u^\tau)\varphi(u, x)$. Then we get from Theorem 1 the alternative

$$\vdash_{\mathsf{MSO}(\mathbf{M})} (\forall x)\varphi\big(\mathbf{e}(\mathtt{u})(x), x\big) \quad \text{or} \quad \vdash_{\mathsf{MSO}(\mathbf{M})} (\forall u)\neg\varphi\big((u)(\mathtt{x}(u)), \mathtt{x}(u)\big) \tag{4}$$

for an eager term $\mathtt{u}(x)$ or a causal term $\mathtt{x}(u)$. By enumerating proofs and machines, one thus gets a (naive) syntactic algorithm for Church's synthesis. But it seems however unlikely to obtain a complete classical system in which the provable $\forall\exists$-statements do correspond to the realizable instances of Church's synthesis, because $\mathsf{MSO}(\mathbf{M})$ has true but unrealizable $\forall\exists$-statements. Besides, note that

$$\begin{array}{rcl}
(\forall x^\sigma)\varphi\big(\mathbf{e}(\mathtt{u})(x), x\big) & \vdash_{\mathsf{MSO}(\mathbf{M})} & (\forall x^\sigma)(\exists u^\tau)\varphi(u, x) \\
(\forall u^{(\tau)\sigma})\neg\varphi\big((u)(\mathtt{x}(u)), \mathtt{x}(u)\big) & \vdash_{\mathsf{MSO}(\mathbf{M})} & (\forall u^{(\tau)\sigma})(\exists x^\sigma)\neg\varphi\big((u)x, x\big) \\
\neg(\forall x^\sigma)(\exists u^\tau)\varphi(u, x) & \vdash_{\mathsf{MSO}(\mathbf{M})} & (\forall u^{(\tau)\sigma})(\exists x^\sigma)\neg\varphi\big((u)x, x\big)
\end{array}$$

while it is possible both for realizable and unrealizable instances to have

$$\vdash_{\mathsf{MSO}(\mathbf{M})} \quad (\forall x^{\sigma})(\exists u^{\tau})\varphi(u,x) \quad \wedge \quad (\forall u^{(\tau)\sigma})(\exists x^{\sigma})\neg\varphi((u)x,\, x) \tag{5}$$

In previous works [25,26], the authors devised intuitionistic and linear variants of MSO on ω-words in which, thanks to automata-based polarity systems, proofs of suitably polarized existential statements correspond exactly to realizers for Church's synthesis. In particular, [26] proposed a system LMSO based on (intuitionistic) linear logic [13], such that via a translation $(-)^L : \mathsf{MSO} \to \mathsf{LMSO}$, provable $\forall\exists(-)^L$-statements exactly correspond to realizable instances of Church's synthesis, while (4) exactly corresponds to alternatives of the form

$$\vdash_{\mathsf{LMSO}} (\forall x^{\sigma})(\exists u^{\tau}) \left[\varphi((u)x,\, x)\right]^L \text{ or } \vdash_{\mathsf{LMSO}} (\forall u^{(\tau)\sigma})(\exists x^{\sigma}) \left[\neg\varphi((u)x,\, x)\right]^L \tag{6}$$

This paper goes further. We show that the automata-based realizability model of [26] can be obtained in a syntactic way, thanks to a (linear) Dialectica-like interpretation of a variant of LMSO, which turns a formula φ to a formula φ^D of the form $(\exists u)(\forall x)\varphi_D(u,x)$, where $\varphi_D(u,x)$ essentially represents a deterministic automaton. While the correctness of the extraction procedure of [25,26] relied on automata-theoretic techniques, we show here that it can be performed syntactically. Second, by extending LMSO with realizable axioms, we obtain a system $\mathsf{LMSO}(\mathfrak{C})$ in which, using an adaptation of the usual *Characterization Theorem* for Dialectica stating that $\varphi \multimapboth \varphi^D$ (see e.g. [16]), alternatives of the form (6) imply that for a closed φ,

$$\vdash_{\mathsf{LMSO}(\mathfrak{C})} \varphi \qquad \text{or} \qquad \vdash_{\mathsf{LMSO}(\mathfrak{C})} \varphi \multimap \bot$$

where $(-) \multimap \bot$ is a *linear* negation. We thus get a complete *linear* system with extraction of suitably polarized $\forall\exists$-statements. Such a system can of course not have a standard semantics, and indeed, $\mathsf{LMSO}(\mathfrak{C})$ has a functional choice axiom

$$(\forall x^{\sigma})(\exists y^{\tau})\varphi(x,y) \quad \multimap \quad (\exists f^{(\tau)\sigma})(\forall x^{\sigma})\varphi(x,(f)x) \tag{LAC}$$

which is realizable in the sense of both $(-)^D$ and [26], but whose translation to $\mathsf{MSO}(\mathbf{M})$ (which precludes (5)) is false in the standard model.

3 A Monadic Linear Dialectica-Like Interpretation

Gödel's "Dialectica" functional interpretation associates to $\varphi(a)$ a formula $\varphi^D(a)$ of the form $(\exists u^{\tau})(\forall x^{\sigma})\varphi_D(u,x,a)$. In usual versions formulated in higher-types arithmetic (see e.g. [1,16]), the formula φ_D is quantifier-free, so that φ^D is a prenex form of φ. This prenex form is constructive, and a constructive proof of φ can be turned to a proof of φ^D with an explicit (closed) witness for $\exists u$. We call such witnesses *realizers* of φ. Even if Dialectica originally interprets intuitionistic arithmetic, it is structurally linear: in general, realizers of contraction

$$\varphi(a) \quad \longrightarrow \quad \varphi(a) \wedge \varphi(a)$$

$$\frac{}{\varphi \vdash \varphi} \qquad \frac{\overline{\varphi} \vdash \gamma, \overline{\varphi}' \quad \overline{\psi}, \gamma \vdash \overline{\psi}'}{\overline{\varphi}, \overline{\psi} \vdash \overline{\varphi}', \overline{\psi}'} \qquad \frac{\overline{\varphi}, \varphi, \psi, \overline{\psi} \vdash \overline{\varphi}'}{\overline{\varphi}, \psi, \varphi, \overline{\psi} \vdash \overline{\varphi}'} \qquad \frac{\overline{\varphi} \vdash \overline{\varphi}', \varphi, \psi, \overline{\psi}'}{\overline{\varphi} \vdash \overline{\varphi}', \psi, \varphi, \overline{\psi}'}$$

$$\frac{\overline{\varphi} \vdash \overline{\psi}}{\overline{\varphi}, \mathbf{I} \vdash \overline{\psi}} \qquad \frac{}{\vdash \mathbf{I}} \qquad \frac{\overline{\varphi}, \varphi_0, \varphi_1 \vdash \overline{\varphi}'}{\overline{\varphi}, \varphi_0 \otimes \varphi_1 \vdash \overline{\varphi}'} \qquad \frac{\overline{\varphi} \vdash \varphi, \overline{\varphi}' \quad \overline{\psi} \vdash \psi, \overline{\psi}'}{\overline{\varphi}, \overline{\psi} \vdash \varphi \otimes \psi, \overline{\varphi}', \overline{\psi}'} \qquad \frac{\overline{\varphi}, \varphi \vdash \psi}{\overline{\varphi} \vdash \varphi \multimap \psi}$$

$$\frac{}{\bot \vdash} \qquad \frac{\overline{\varphi} \vdash \overline{\psi}}{\overline{\varphi} \vdash \bot, \overline{\psi}} \qquad \frac{\overline{\varphi}, \varphi \vdash \overline{\varphi}' \quad \overline{\psi}, \psi \vdash \overline{\psi}'}{\overline{\varphi}, \overline{\psi}, \varphi \parr \psi \vdash \overline{\varphi}', \overline{\psi}'} \qquad \frac{\overline{\varphi} \vdash \varphi_0, \varphi_1, \overline{\varphi}'}{\overline{\varphi} \vdash \varphi_0 \parr \varphi_1, \overline{\varphi}'} \qquad \frac{\overline{\varphi} \vdash \varphi, \overline{\varphi}' \quad \overline{\psi}, \psi \vdash \overline{\psi}'}{\overline{\varphi}, \overline{\psi}, \varphi \multimap \psi \vdash \overline{\varphi}', \overline{\psi}'}$$

$$\frac{\overline{\varphi}, \varphi \vdash \overline{\varphi}'}{\overline{\varphi}, (\exists z^\tau)\varphi \vdash \overline{\varphi}'} \qquad \frac{\overline{\varphi} \vdash \varphi[\mathtt{t}^\tau/x^\tau], \overline{\varphi}'}{\overline{\varphi} \vdash (\exists x^\tau)\varphi, \overline{\varphi}'} \qquad \frac{\overline{\varphi}, \varphi[\mathtt{t}^\tau/x^\tau] \vdash \overline{\varphi}'}{\overline{\varphi}, (\forall x^\tau)\varphi \vdash \overline{\varphi}'} \qquad \frac{\overline{\varphi} \vdash \varphi}{\overline{\varphi} \vdash (\forall z^\tau)\varphi}$$

Fig. 2. Deduction for MF (where z^τ is fresh).

only exist when the term language can decide $\varphi_D(u, x, a)$, which is possible in arithmetic but not in all settings. Besides, linear versions of Dialectica were formulated at the very beginning of linear logic [21–23] (see also [14, 27]).

In this paper, we use a variant of Dialectica as a syntactic formulation of the automata-based realizability model of [26]. The formula φ_D essentially represents a deterministic automaton on ω-words and is in general not quantifier-free. Moreover, we extract f.s. causal functions, while the category $\mathbb{M}$ is not closed. As a result, a realizer of φ is an *open* (eager) term $\mathtt{u}(x)$ of arity $(\sigma; \tau)$ satisfying $\varphi_D(\mathtt{u}(x), x)$. While it is possible to exhibit realizers for contraction on closed φ thanks to the Büchi-Landweber Theorem, this is generally not the case for open $\varphi(a)$. We therefore resort to working in a linear system, in which we obtain witnesses for $\forall\exists(-)^L$-statements (and thus for realizable instances of Church's synthesis), but not for all $\forall\exists$-statements.

Fix a set of atomic formulae At containing all $(\mathtt{t}^\tau \doteq \mathtt{u}^\tau)$, and a standard interpretation extending Sect. 2 for each $\alpha \in \mathrm{At}$.

3.1 The Multiplicative Fragment

Our linear system is based on *full intuitionistic linear logic* (see [15]). The formulae of the multiplicative fragment MF are given by the grammar:

$$\varphi, \psi \ ::= \ \mathbf{I} \mid \bot \mid \alpha \mid \varphi \multimap \psi \mid \varphi \otimes \psi \mid \varphi \parr \psi \mid (\exists x^\tau)\varphi \mid (\forall x^\tau)\varphi$$

(where $\alpha \in \mathrm{At}$). Deduction is given by the rules of Fig. 2 and the axioms

$$\frac{}{\vdash \mathtt{t}^\tau \doteq \mathtt{t}^\tau} \qquad \frac{}{\mathtt{t}^\tau \doteq \mathtt{u}^\tau,\ \varphi[\mathtt{t}^\tau/x^\tau] \vdash \varphi[\mathtt{u}^\tau/x^\tau]} \qquad \frac{[\![\mathtt{t}^\tau]\!] = [\![\mathtt{u}^\tau]\!]}{\vdash \mathtt{t}^\tau \doteq \mathtt{u}^\tau} \tag{7}$$

Each formula φ of MF can be mapped to a classical formula $\lfloor\varphi\rfloor$ (where $\mathbf{I}$, $\multimap$, $\otimes$, $\parr$ are replaced resp. by $\top, \to, \wedge, \vee$). Hence $\lfloor\varphi\rfloor$ holds whenever $\vdash \varphi$

The Dialectica interpretation of MF is the usual one rewritten with the connectives of MF, but for the disjunction $\parr$ that we treat similarly as $\otimes$. To each

$$
\begin{array}{rcll}
(\varphi \otimes \psi)^D(a) & := & \exists\langle u,v\rangle\forall\langle x,y\rangle.\ (\varphi\otimes\psi)_D(\langle u,v\rangle,\langle x,y\rangle,a) & := \\
 & & & \exists\langle u,v\rangle\forall\langle x,y\rangle.\ \varphi_D(u,x,a)\otimes\psi_D(v,y,a) \\
(\varphi \parr \psi)^D(a) & := & \exists\langle u,v\rangle\forall\langle x,y\rangle.\ (\varphi\parr\psi)_D(\langle u,v\rangle,\langle x,y\rangle,a) & := \\
 & & & \exists\langle u,v\rangle\forall\langle x,y\rangle.\ \varphi_D(u,x,a)\parr\psi_D(v,y,a) \\
(\varphi \multimap \psi)^D(a) & := & \exists\langle f,F\rangle\forall\langle u,y\rangle.\ (\varphi\multimap\psi)_D(\langle f,F\rangle,\langle u,y\rangle,a) & := \\
 & & & \exists\langle f,F\rangle\forall\langle u,y\rangle.\ \varphi_D(u,(F)uy,a)\multimap\psi_D((f)u,y,a) \\
(\exists w.\varphi)^D(a) & := & \exists\langle u,w\rangle\forall x.\ (\exists w.\varphi)_D(\langle u,w\rangle,x,a) & := \exists\langle u,w\rangle\forall x.\ \varphi_D(u,x,\langle a,w\rangle) \\
(\forall w.\varphi)^D(a) & := & \exists f\,\forall\langle x,w\rangle.\ (\forall w.\varphi)_D(f,\langle x,w\rangle,a) & := \exists f\,\forall\langle x,w\rangle.\ \varphi_D((f)w,x,\langle a,w\rangle)
\end{array}
$$

Fig. 3. The Dialectica Interpretation of MF (where types are leaved implicit).

formula $\varphi(a)$ with only a free, we associate a formula $\varphi^D(a)$ with only a free, as well as a formula φ_D with possibly other free variables. For atomic formulae we let $\varphi^D(a) := \varphi_D(a) := \varphi(a)$. The inductive cases are given on Fig. 3, where $\varphi^D(a) = (\exists u)(\forall x)\varphi_D(u,x,a)$ and $\psi^D(a) = (\exists v)(\forall y)\psi_D(v,y,a)$.

Dialectica is such that φ^D is equivalent to φ via possibly non-intuitionistic but constructive principles. The tricky connectives are implication and universal quantification. Similarly as in the intuitionistic case (see e.g. [1,16,33]), $(\varphi \multimap \psi)^D$ is prenex a form of $\varphi^D \multimap \psi^D$ obtained using (LAC) together with linear variants of the *Markov* and *Independence of premises* principles. In our case, the equivalence $\varphi \multimapboth \varphi^D$ also requires additional axioms for $\otimes$ and $\parr$. We give details for the full system in Sect. 3.3.

The soundness of $(-)^D$ goes as usual, excepted that we extract *open eager* terms: from a proof of $\varphi(a^\kappa)$ we extract a realizer of $(\forall a)\varphi(a)$, that is an open eager term $\mathtt{u}(x,a)$ s.t. $\vdash \varphi_D(@(\mathtt{u}(x,a),a),x,a)$. Composition of realizers (in part. required for the cut rule) is given by the fixpoints of Proposition 3. Note that a realizer of a closed φ is a finite-state winning P-strategy in $\mathcal{G}(\lfloor\varphi_D\rfloor)(u,x)$.

3.2 Polarized Exponentials

It is well-known that the structure of Dialectica is linear, as it makes problematic the interpretation of contraction:

$$\varphi(a) \quad\multimap\quad \varphi(a)\otimes\varphi(a) \qquad\text{and}\qquad \varphi(a)\parr\varphi(a) \quad\multimap\quad \varphi(a)$$

In our case, the Büchi-Landweber Theorem implies that all closed instances of contraction have realizers which are correct in the standard model. But this is in general not true for open instances.

Example 3. Realizers of $\varphi \multimap \varphi\otimes\varphi$ for a closed φ are given by eager terms $\mathtt{U}_1(u,x_1,x_2)$, $\mathtt{U}_2(u,x_1,x_2)$, $\mathtt{X}(u,x_1,x_2)$ which must represent P-strategies in the game $\mathcal{G}(\Phi)(\langle U_1,U_2,X\rangle,\langle u,x_1,x_2\rangle)$, where Φ is

$$\lfloor\varphi_D(u,(X)ux_1x_2)\rfloor \quad\longrightarrow\quad \lfloor\varphi_D((U_1)u,x_1)\rfloor \;\wedge\; \lfloor\varphi_D((U_2)u,x_2)\rfloor$$

By the Büchi-Landweber Theorem 1, either there is an eager term $\mathtt{U}(x)$ such that $\lfloor \varphi_D(\mathtt{U}(x), x) \rfloor$ holds, so that

$$\lfloor \varphi_D(u, x_1) \rfloor \quad \longrightarrow \quad \lfloor \varphi_D(\mathbf{e}(\mathtt{U})(x_1), x_1) \rfloor \;\wedge\; \lfloor \varphi_D(\mathbf{e}(\mathtt{U})(x_2), x_2) \rfloor$$

or there is an eager term $\mathtt{X}(u)$ such that $\neg \lfloor \varphi_D(u, \mathbf{e}(\mathtt{X})(u)) \rfloor$ holds, so that

$$\lfloor \varphi_D(u, \mathbf{e}(\mathtt{X})(u)) \rfloor \quad \longrightarrow \quad \lfloor \varphi_D(u, x_1) \rfloor \;\wedge\; \lfloor \varphi_D(u, x_2) \rfloor$$

Example 4. Consider the open formula $\varphi(a^o) := (\forall x^o)(\mathtt{t}(x, a) \doteq 0^\omega)$ where $[\![\mathtt{t}]\!](B, C) = 0^{n+1}1^\omega$ for the first $n \in \mathbb{N}$ with $C(n+1) = B(0)$ if such n exists, and such that $[\![\mathtt{t}]\!](B, C) = 0^\omega$ otherwise. The game induced by $((\forall a)(\varphi \multimap \varphi \otimes \varphi))_D$ is $\mathcal{G}(\Phi)(X, \langle x_1, x_1, a \rangle)$, where Φ is

$$\mathtt{t}((X)x_1x_2a, a) \doteq 0^\omega \quad \longrightarrow \quad \mathtt{t}(x_1, a) \doteq 0^\omega \;\wedge\; \mathtt{t}(x_2, a) \doteq 0^\omega$$

In this game, P begins by playing a function $\mathbf{2}^3 \to \mathbf{2}$, O replies in $\mathbf{2}^3$, and then P and O keep on alternatively playing moves of the expected type. A finite-state winning strategy for O is easy to find. Let P begin with the function X. Fix some $\mathsf{a} \in \mathbf{2}$ and let $i := \mathsf{X}(0, 1, \mathsf{a})$. O replies $(0, 1, \mathsf{a})$ to X. The further moves of P are irrelevant, and O keeps on playing $(-, -, 1 - i)$ (the values of x_1 and x_2 are irrelevant after the first round). This strategy ensures

$$\mathtt{t}((X)x_1x_2a, a) \doteq 0^\omega \quad \wedge \quad \neg(\mathtt{t}(x_1, a) \doteq 0^\omega \;\wedge\; \mathtt{t}(x_2, a) \doteq 0^\omega)$$

Hence we can not realize contraction while remaining correct w.r.t. the standard model. On the other hand, Dialectica induces polarities generalizing the usual polarities of linear logic (see e.g. [17]). Say that $\varphi(a)$ is *positive* (resp. *negative*) if $\varphi^D(a)$ is of the form $\varphi^D(a) = (\exists u^\tau)\varphi_D(u, -, a)$ (resp. $\varphi^D(a) = (\forall x^\sigma)\varphi_D(-, x, a)$). Quantifier-free formulae are thus both positive and negative.

Example 5. Polarized contraction

$$\varphi^+ \multimap \varphi^+ \otimes \varphi^+ \qquad \text{and} \qquad \psi^- \parr \psi^- \multimap \psi^- \qquad (\varphi^+ \text{ positive}, \psi^- \text{ negative})$$

gives realizers of all instances of itself. Indeed, with say $\varphi^D(a) = (\exists u)\varphi_D(u, -, a)$ and $\psi^D(a) = (\forall y)\psi_D(-, y, a)$, $\boldsymbol{\Lambda}(\pi_1)$ (for π_1 a $\mathbb{M}$-projection on suitable types) gives eager terms $\mathtt{U}(u, a)$ and $\mathtt{Y}(y, a)$ such that

$$\begin{array}{rcl} \varphi_D(u, -, a) & \multimap & \big(\varphi_D(\mathbf{e}(\mathtt{U})(u, a), -, a) \;\otimes\; \varphi_D(\mathbf{e}(\mathtt{U})(u, a), -, a)\big) \\ \text{and} \quad \big(\psi_D(-, \mathbf{e}(\mathtt{Y})(y, a), a) \;\parr\; \psi_D(-, \mathbf{e}(\mathtt{Y})(y, a), a)\big) & \multimap & \psi_D(-, y, a) \end{array}$$

We only have exponentials for polarized formulae. First, following the usual polarities of linear logic, we can let

$$\begin{array}{rclcl} (!(\varphi^+))^D(a) & := & (\exists u)(!(\varphi^+))_D(u, -, a) & := & (\exists u)!\varphi_D(u, -, a) \\ (?(\psi^-))^D(a) & := & (\forall y)(?(\psi^-))_D(-, y, a) & := & (\forall x)?\psi_D(-, y, a) \end{array} \tag{8}$$

$$\dfrac{\overline{\psi} \vdash \overline{\psi}'}{\overline{\psi}, !\varphi \vdash \overline{\psi}'} \qquad \dfrac{\overline{\psi}, !\varphi, !\varphi \vdash \overline{\psi}'}{\overline{\psi}, !\varphi \vdash \overline{\psi}'} \qquad \dfrac{\overline{\varphi}, \varphi \vdash \overline{\varphi}'}{\overline{\varphi}, !\varphi \vdash \overline{\varphi}'} \qquad \dfrac{!\overline{\varphi} \vdash \varphi, ?\overline{\psi}}{!\overline{\varphi} \vdash !\varphi, ?\overline{\psi}} \qquad \dfrac{\overline{\varphi}, !\varphi \vdash \psi, ?\overline{\psi}}{\overline{\varphi} \vdash !\varphi \multimap \psi, ?\overline{\psi}}$$

$$\dfrac{\overline{\psi} \vdash \overline{\psi}'}{\overline{\psi} \vdash ?\varphi, \overline{\psi}'} \qquad \dfrac{\overline{\psi} \vdash ?\varphi, ?\varphi, \overline{\psi}'}{\overline{\psi} \vdash ?\varphi, \overline{\psi}'} \qquad \dfrac{\overline{\varphi} \vdash \varphi, \overline{\psi}}{\overline{\varphi} \vdash ?\varphi, \overline{\psi}} \qquad \dfrac{!\overline{\varphi}, \varphi \vdash ?\overline{\psi}}{!\overline{\varphi}, ?\varphi \vdash ?\overline{\psi}} \qquad \dfrac{\overline{\varphi} \vdash \varphi, ?\overline{\psi}}{\overline{\varphi} \vdash (\forall z)\varphi, ?\overline{\psi}}$$

Fig. 4. Exponential rules of PF.

Hence $!\varphi$ is positive for a positive φ and $?\psi$ is negative for a negative ψ. The following exponential contraction axioms are then interpreted by themselves:

$$!(\varphi^+) \quad \multimap \quad !(\varphi^+) \otimes !(\varphi^+) \qquad \text{and} \qquad ?(\psi^-) \parr ?(\psi^-) \quad \multimap \quad ?(\psi^-)$$

Second, we can have exponentials $!(\psi^-)$ and $?(\varphi^+)$ with the automata-based reading of [26]. Positive formulae are seen as non-deterministic automata, and $?(-)$ on positive formulae is determinization on ω-words (McNaughton's Theorem [19]). Negative formulae are seen as universal automata, and $!(-)$ on negative formulae is co-determinization (an instance of the *Simulation Theorem* [10,20]). Formulae which are both positive and negative (notation $(-)^{\pm}$) correspond to deterministic automata, and are called *deterministic*. We let

$$\begin{array}{lllll} (!(\psi^-))^D(a) & := & (!(\psi^-))_D(-,-,a) & := & !(\forall x)\psi_D(-,x,a) \\ (?(\varphi^+))^D(a) & := & (?(\varphi^+))_D(-,-,a) & := & ?(\exists u)\varphi_D(u,-,a) \end{array} \tag{9}$$

So $!(\psi^-)$ and $?(\varphi^+)$ are always deterministic. The corresponding exponential contraction axioms are interpreted by themselves. This leads to the following polarized fragment PF (the deduction rules for exponentials are given on Fig. 4):

$$\begin{array}{lll} \varphi^{\pm}, \psi^{\pm} & ::= & \mathbf{I} \mid \bot \mid \alpha \mid !(\varphi^-) \mid ?(\varphi^+) \mid \varphi^{\pm} \otimes \psi^{\pm} \mid \varphi^{\pm} \parr \psi^{\pm} \mid \varphi^{\pm} \multimap \psi^{\pm} \\ \varphi^+, \psi^+ & ::= & \varphi^{\pm} \mid !(\varphi^+) \mid (\exists x^{\sigma})\varphi^+ \mid \varphi^+ \otimes \psi^+ \mid \varphi^+ \parr \psi^+ \mid \varphi^- \multimap \psi^+ \\ \varphi^-, \psi^- & ::= & \varphi^{\pm} \mid ?(\varphi^-) \mid (\forall x^{\sigma})\varphi^- \mid \varphi^- \otimes \psi^- \mid \varphi^- \parr \psi^- \mid \varphi^+ \multimap \psi^- \end{array}$$

3.3 The Full System

The formulae of the full system FS are given by the following grammar:

$$\varphi, \psi \ ::= \ \varphi^+ \mid \varphi^- \mid \varphi \multimap \psi \mid \varphi \otimes \psi \mid \varphi \parr \psi \mid (\exists x^{\tau})\varphi \mid (\forall x^{\tau})\varphi$$

Deduction in FS is given by Figs. 2, 4 and (7). We extend $\lfloor - \rfloor$ to FS with $\lfloor !\varphi \rfloor := \lfloor ?\varphi \rfloor := \lfloor \varphi \rfloor$. Hence $\lfloor \varphi \rfloor$ holds when $\vdash \varphi$ is derivable. The Dialectica interpretation of FS is given by Fig. 3 and (8), (9) (still taking $\varphi^D(a) := \varphi_D(a) := \varphi(a)$ for atoms). Note that $(-)^D$ preserves and reflects polarities.

Theorem 2 (Soundness). *Let φ be closed with $\varphi^D = (\exists u^{\tau})(\forall x^{\sigma})\varphi_D(u,x)$. From a proof of φ in* FS *one can extract an eager term* $\mathtt{u}(x)$ *such that* FS *proves* $(\forall x^{\sigma})\varphi_D(\mathtt{u}(x), x)$.

As usual, proving $\varphi \multimapboth \varphi^D$ requires extra axioms. Besides (LAC), we use the following (*linear*) *semi-intuitionistic principles* (LSIP), with polarities as shown:

$$\begin{array}{rcl} (\forall a)(\varphi^-(a) \otimes \psi^-) & \multimap & (\forall a)\varphi^-(a) \otimes \psi^- \\ (\forall a)(\varphi^-(a) \parr \psi^-) & \multimap & (\forall a)\varphi^-(a) \parr \psi^- \\ (\exists a)\varphi^-(a) \parr \psi & \multimap & (\exists a)(\varphi^-(a) \parr \psi) \\ (\psi^- \multimap (\exists a)\varphi^-(a)) & \multimap & (\exists a)(\psi^- \multimap \varphi^-(a)) \\ ((\forall a)\varphi^\pm(a) \multimap \psi^\pm) & \multimap & (\exists a)(\varphi^\pm(a) \multimap \psi^\pm) \end{array} \qquad (\mathsf{LSIP})$$

as well as the following *deterministic exponential* axioms (DEXP):

$$\delta \multimap\ !\delta \qquad \text{and} \qquad ?\delta \multimap \delta \qquad\qquad (\delta \text{ deterministic})$$

All these axioms but (LAC) are true in the standard model (via $\lfloor - \rfloor$). Moreover:

Proposition 4. *The axioms* (LAC) *and* (LSIP) *are realized in* FS. *The axioms* (DEXP) *are realized in* FS + (DEXP).

Theorem 3 (Characterization). *We have*

$$\begin{array}{rrcll} \vdash_{\mathsf{FS}+(\mathsf{LAC})+(\mathsf{LSIP})+(\mathsf{DEXP})} & \varphi(a) & \multimapboth & \varphi^D(a) & (\varphi\ \mathsf{FS}\text{-formula}) \\ \vdash_{\mathsf{FS}+(\mathsf{LSIP})+(\mathsf{DEXP})} & \varphi(a) & \multimapboth & \varphi^D(a) & (\varphi\ \mathsf{PF}\text{-formula}) \end{array}$$

Corollary 1 (Extraction). *Consider a closed formula* $\varphi := (\forall x^\sigma)(\exists u^\tau)\delta(u, x)$ *with* δ *deterministic. From a proof of* φ *in* FS + (LAC) + (LSIP) + (DEXP) *one can extract a term* $\mathtt{t}(x)$ *such that* $\models (\forall x^\sigma)\lfloor \delta(\mathtt{t}(x), x)\rfloor$.

Note that FS + (DEXP) proves $\delta \parr (\delta \multimap \bot)$ for all deterministic δ.

3.4 Translations of Classical Logic

There are many translations from classical to linear logic. Two canonical possibilities are the $(-)^T$ and $(-)^Q$-translation of [9] (see also [17,18]) targeting resp. negative and positive formulae. Both take classical sequents to linear sequents of the form $!(-) \vdash ?(-)$, which are provable in FS thanks to the PF rules

$$\frac{\overline{\varphi}, !\varphi \vdash \psi, ?\overline{\psi}}{\overline{\varphi} \vdash !\varphi \multimap \psi, ?\overline{\psi}} \qquad\qquad \frac{\overline{\varphi} \vdash \varphi, ?\overline{\psi}}{\overline{\varphi} \vdash (\forall z)\varphi, ?\overline{\psi}}$$

For the completeness of LMSO($\mathfrak{C}$) (Theorem 6, Sect. 4), we shall actually require a translation $(-)^L$ such that the linear equivalences (with polarities as displayed)

$$?\varphi^+ \multimapboth \lfloor \varphi^+ \rfloor^L \qquad\qquad \delta^\pm \multimapboth \lfloor \delta^\pm \rfloor^L \qquad\qquad !\psi^- \multimapboth \lfloor \psi^- \rfloor^L \qquad (10)$$

are provable possibly with extra axioms that we require to realize themselves. In part., (10) implies (DEXP), and $(-)^L$ should give deterministic formulae. While $(-)^T$ and $(-)^Q$ can be adapted accordingly, (10) induces axioms which make the resulting translations equivalent to the deterministic $(-)^L$-translation of [26]:

$$\bot^L := \bot \quad \top^L := \mathbf{I} \quad \alpha^L := \alpha \qquad (\varphi \vee \psi)^L := \varphi^L \parr \psi^L \qquad (\exists x^\sigma.\varphi)^L := ?(\exists x^\sigma)\varphi^L$$
$$(\varphi \to \psi)^L := \varphi^L \multimap \psi^L \qquad (\varphi \wedge \psi)^L := \varphi^L \otimes \psi^L \qquad (\forall x^\sigma.\varphi)^L := !(\forall x^\sigma)\varphi^L$$

Proposition 5. *The scheme (10) is equivalent in* FS *to* (DEXP)+(PEXP)*, where* (PEXP) *are the following* polarized exponential *axioms, with polarities as shown:*

$$\begin{array}{rclrcl} ?(\varphi^+) & \multimap & ?!(\varphi^+) & !?(\psi^-) & \multimap & !(\psi^-) \\ !(\varphi^-) \multimap ?(\psi^+) & \multimap & ?(\varphi^- \multimap \psi^+) & ?(\varphi^+) \multimap !(\psi^-) & \multimap & !(\varphi^+ \multimap \psi^-) \\ ?(\varphi^+) \otimes ?(\psi^+) & \multimap & ?(\varphi^+ \otimes \psi^+) & !(\varphi^- \otimes \psi^-) & \multimap & !(\varphi^-) \otimes !(\psi^-) \\ ?(\varphi^+) \parr ?(\psi^+) & \multimap & ?(\varphi^+ \parr \psi^+) & !(\varphi^- \parr \psi^-) & \multimap & !(\varphi^-) \parr !(\psi^-) \end{array}$$

Proposition 6. *If φ is provable in many-sorted classical logic with equality then* FS + (DEXP) *proves φ^L.*

Proposition 7. *The axioms* (PEXP) *are realized in* FS + (LSIP) + (DEXP) + (PEXP)*. Corollary 1 thus extends to* FS + (LAC) + (LSIP) + (DEXP) + (PEXP).

Note that φ^L is deterministic and that $\lfloor \varphi^L \rfloor = \varphi$.

4 Completeness

In Sect. 3 we devised a Dialectica-like $(-)^D$ providing a syntactic extraction procedure for $\forall\exists(-)^L$-statements. In this Section, building on an axiomatic treatment of MSO(**M**), we show that LMSO, an arithmetic extension of FS+(LSIP)+(DEXP)+(PEXP) adapted from [26], is correct and complete w.r.t. Church's synthesis, in the sense that the provable $\forall\exists(-)^L$-statements are exactly the realizable ones. We then turn to the main result of this paper, namely the completeness of LMSO($\mathfrak{C}$) := LMSO + (LAC). We fix the set of atomic formulae

$$\alpha \in \mathrm{At} \quad ::= \quad \mathtt{t}^\tau \doteq \mathtt{u}^\tau \mid \mathtt{t}^o \mathrel{\dot\subseteq} \mathtt{u}^o \mid \mathsf{E}(\mathtt{t}^o) \mid \mathsf{N}(\mathtt{t}^o) \mid \mathsf{S}(\mathtt{t}^o, \mathtt{u}^o) \mid \mathsf{0}(\mathtt{t}^o) \mid \mathtt{t}^o \mathrel{\dot\leq} \mathtt{u}^o$$

4.1 The Logic MSO(M)

MSO(**M**) is many-sorted first-order logic with atomic formulae $\alpha \in \mathrm{At}$. Its sorts and terms are those given in Sect. 2, and standard interpretation extends that of Sect. 2 as follows: $\dot\subseteq$ is set inclusion, E holds on B iff B is empty, N (resp. 0) holds on B iff B is a singleton $\{n\}$ (resp. the singleton $\{0\}$), and $\mathsf{S}(B, C)$ (resp. $B \mathrel{\dot\leq} C$) holds iff $B = \{n\}$ and $C = \{n+1\}$ for some $n \in \mathbb{N}$ (resp. $B = \{n\}$ and $C = \{m\}$ for some $n \leq m$). We write x^ι for variables x^o relativized to N, so that $(\exists x^\iota)\varphi$ and $(\forall x^\iota)\varphi$ stand resp. for $(\exists x^o)(\mathsf{N}(x) \wedge \varphi)$ and $(\forall x^o)(\mathsf{N}(x) \to \varphi)$. Moreover, $x^\iota \mathrel{\dot\in} \mathtt{t}$ stands for $x^\iota \mathrel{\dot\subseteq} \mathtt{t}$, so that $\mathtt{t}^o \mathrel{\dot\subseteq} \mathtt{u}^o$ is equivalent to $(\forall x^\iota)(x \mathrel{\dot\in} \mathtt{t} \to x \mathrel{\dot\in} \mathtt{u})$.

The logic MSO$^+$ [26] is MSO(**M**) restricted to the type o, hence with only terms for Mealy machines of sort $(\mathbf{2}, \ldots, \mathbf{2}; \mathbf{2})$. The MSO of [26] is the purely relational (term-free) restriction of MSO$^+$. Recall from [26, Prop. 2.6], that for

$$\frac{}{\mathsf{E}(\mathtt{t}) \vdash \mathtt{t} \mathrel{\dot\subseteq} \mathtt{u}} \qquad \frac{\overline{\varphi} \vdash \mathtt{t} \mathrel{\dot\subseteq} z, \overline{\varphi}'}{\overline{\varphi} \vdash \mathsf{E}(\mathtt{t}), \overline{\varphi}'} \qquad \frac{\overline{\varphi}, z \mathrel{\dot\subseteq} \mathtt{t} \vdash \mathsf{E}(z), z \doteq \mathtt{t}, \overline{\varphi}'}{\overline{\varphi} \vdash \mathsf{N}(\mathtt{t}), \mathsf{E}(\mathtt{t}), \overline{\varphi}'} \qquad \frac{\overline{\varphi}, \mathsf{N}(z), z \mathrel{\dot\subseteq} \mathtt{t} \vdash z \mathrel{\dot\subseteq} \mathtt{u}, \overline{\varphi}'}{\overline{\varphi} \vdash \mathtt{t} \mathrel{\dot\subseteq} \mathtt{u}, \overline{\varphi}'} \qquad \frac{}{\mathsf{N}(\mathtt{t}), \mathsf{E}(\mathtt{t}) \vdash}$$

$$\frac{}{\vdash \mathtt{t} \mathrel{\dot\subseteq} \mathtt{t}} \qquad \frac{}{\mathtt{t} \mathrel{\dot\subseteq} \mathtt{u}, \mathtt{u} \mathrel{\dot\subseteq} \mathtt{v} \vdash \mathtt{t} \mathrel{\dot\subseteq} \mathtt{v}} \qquad \frac{}{\mathtt{t} \mathrel{\dot\subseteq} \mathtt{u}, \mathtt{u} \mathrel{\dot\subseteq} \mathtt{t} \vdash \mathtt{t} \doteq \mathtt{u}} \qquad \frac{}{\mathsf{N}(\mathtt{t}), \mathtt{u} \mathrel{\dot\subseteq} \mathtt{t} \vdash \mathsf{E}(\mathtt{u}), \mathtt{u} \doteq \mathtt{t}} \qquad \frac{}{\mathsf{S}(\mathtt{t}, \mathtt{u}), \mathsf{0}(\mathtt{u}) \vdash}$$

$$\frac{}{\mathsf{N}(\mathtt{t}) \vdash \mathtt{t} \mathrel{\dot\leq} \mathtt{t}} \qquad \frac{}{\mathtt{t} \mathrel{\dot\leq} \mathtt{u}, \mathtt{u} \mathrel{\dot\leq} \mathtt{v} \vdash \mathtt{t} \mathrel{\dot\leq} \mathtt{v}} \qquad \frac{}{\mathtt{t} \mathrel{\dot\leq} \mathtt{u}, \mathtt{u} \mathrel{\dot\leq} \mathtt{t} \vdash \mathtt{t} \doteq \mathtt{u}} \qquad \frac{}{\mathsf{S}(\mathtt{t}, \mathtt{u}) \vdash \mathtt{t} \mathrel{\dot\leq} \mathtt{u}} \qquad \frac{}{\mathsf{0}(\mathtt{t}) \vdash \mathsf{N}(\mathtt{t})}$$

$$\frac{\overline{\varphi}, \mathsf{0}(z) \vdash \overline{\varphi}'}{\overline{\varphi} \vdash \overline{\varphi}'} \qquad \frac{}{\mathsf{S}(\mathtt{u}, \mathtt{v}), \mathtt{t} \mathrel{\dot\leq} \mathtt{v} \vdash \mathtt{t} \doteq \mathtt{v}, \mathtt{t} \mathrel{\dot\leq} \mathtt{u}} \qquad \frac{}{\mathtt{t} \mathrel{\dot\leq} \mathtt{u} \vdash \mathsf{N}(t)} \qquad \frac{}{\mathtt{t} \mathrel{\dot\leq} \mathtt{u} \vdash \mathsf{N}(u)} \qquad \frac{}{\mathsf{S}(\mathtt{t}, \mathtt{u}) \vdash \mathsf{N}(\mathtt{t})}$$

$$\frac{\overline{\varphi}, \mathsf{S}(\mathtt{t}, z) \vdash \overline{\varphi}'}{\overline{\varphi} \vdash \overline{\varphi}'} \qquad \frac{}{\mathsf{0}(\mathtt{t}), \mathsf{0}(\mathtt{u}) \vdash \mathtt{t} \doteq \mathtt{u}} \qquad \frac{}{\mathsf{S}(\mathtt{t}, \mathtt{u}), \mathsf{S}(\mathtt{t}, \mathtt{v}) \vdash \mathtt{u} \doteq \mathtt{v}} \qquad \frac{}{\mathsf{S}(\mathtt{u}, \mathtt{t}), \mathsf{S}(\mathtt{v}, \mathtt{t}) \vdash \mathtt{u} \doteq \mathtt{v}} \qquad \frac{}{\mathsf{S}(\mathtt{t}, \mathtt{u}) \vdash \mathsf{N}(\mathtt{u})}$$

Fig. 5. The Arithmetic Rules of $\mathsf{MSO}(\mathbf{M})$ and LMSO (with terms of sort o and z fresh).

each Mealy machine $\mathcal{M} : \mathbf{2}^p \to \mathbf{2}$, there is an MSO-formula $\delta_{\mathcal{M}}(\overline{X}, x)$ such that for all $n \in \mathbb{N}$ and all $\overline{B} \in (\mathbf{2}^\omega)^p$, we have $F_{\mathcal{M}}(\overline{B})(n) = 1$ iff $\delta_{\mathcal{M}}(\{n\}, \overline{B})$ holds.

The axioms of $\mathsf{MSO}(\mathbf{M})$ are the arithmetic rules of Fig. 5, the axioms (7) and the following, where $\mathcal{M} : \mathbf{2}^p \to \mathbf{2}$ and y, z, X are fresh.

$$\frac{}{\vdash (\forall \overline{X}^o)(\forall x^\iota)\left(x \mathrel{\dot\in} \mathtt{f}_{\mathcal{M}}(\overline{X}) \;\leftrightarrow\; \delta_{\mathcal{M}}(x, \overline{X})\right)} \qquad \frac{}{\vdash (\exists X^o)(\forall x^\iota)\left(x \mathrel{\dot\in} X \;\leftrightarrow\; \varphi\right)}$$

$$\frac{\overline{\varphi}, \mathsf{0}(z) \vdash \varphi[z/x], \overline{\varphi}' \qquad \overline{\varphi}, \mathsf{S}(y, z), \varphi[y/x] \vdash \varphi[z/x], \overline{\varphi}'}{\overline{\varphi} \vdash (\forall x^\iota)\varphi, \overline{\varphi}'}$$

The theory $\mathsf{MSO}(\mathbf{M})$ is complete. Thus provability in $\mathsf{MSO}(\mathbf{M})$ and validity in the standard model coincide. This extends [26, Thm. 2.11 (via [28])].

Theorem 4 (Completeness of $\mathsf{MSO}(\mathbf{M})$). *For closed $\mathsf{MSO}(\mathbf{M})$-formulae φ, we have $\models \varphi$ if and only if $\vdash_{\mathsf{MSO}(\mathbf{M})} \varphi$.*

4.2 The Logic LMSO

The system LMSO is $\mathsf{FS} + (\mathsf{LSIP}) + (\mathsf{DEXP}) + (\mathsf{PEXP})$ extended with Fig. 5 and

$$\frac{}{\vdash (\forall \overline{X}^o)(\forall x^\iota)\left(x \mathrel{\dot\in} \mathtt{f}_{\mathcal{M}}(\overline{X}) \;\multimapboth\; \delta^L_{\mathcal{M}}(x, \overline{X})\right)} \qquad \frac{}{\vdash ?(\exists X^o)!(\forall x^\iota)\left(x \mathrel{\dot\in} X \;\multimapboth\; \delta^{\pm}\right)}$$

$$\frac{!\overline{\varphi}, \mathsf{0}(z) \vdash \varphi^-[z/x], ?\overline{\varphi}' \qquad !\overline{\varphi}, \mathsf{S}(y, z), !\varphi^-[y/x] \vdash \varphi^-[z/x], ?\overline{\varphi}'}{!\overline{\varphi} \vdash (\forall x^\iota)\varphi^-, ?\overline{\varphi}'}$$

Let $\mathsf{LMSO}(\mathfrak{C}) := \mathsf{LMSO} + (\mathsf{LAC})$. Note that $\vdash_{\mathsf{MSO}(\mathbf{M})} \lfloor \varphi \rfloor$ whenever $\vdash_{\mathsf{LMSO}} \varphi$. Proposition 6 extends so that similarly as in [26] we have

Proposition 8. *If $\vdash_{\mathsf{MSO}(\mathbf{M})} \varphi$ then $\vdash_{\mathsf{LMSO}} \varphi^L$. In part., for a realizable instance of Church's synthesis $(\forall x^\sigma)(\exists u^\tau)\varphi(u, x)$, we have $\vdash_{\mathsf{LMSO}} (\forall x^\sigma)(\exists u^\tau)\varphi^L(u, x)$.*

Moreover, the soundness of $(-)^D$ extends to LMSO. It follows that $\mathsf{LMSO}(\mathfrak{C})$ is coherent and proves exactly the realizable $\forall\exists(-)^L$-statements.

Theorem 5 (Soundness). *Let φ be closed with $\varphi^D = (\exists u^\tau)(\forall x^\sigma)\varphi_D(u,x)$. From a proof of φ in* $\mathsf{LMSO}(\mathfrak{C})$ *one can extract an eager term* $\mathtt{u}(x)$ *such that* LMSO *proves* $(\forall x^\sigma)\varphi_D(\mathtt{u}(x),x)$.

Corollary 2 (Extraction). *Consider a closed formula $\varphi := (\forall x^\sigma)(\exists u^\tau)$ $\delta(u,x)$ with δ deterministic. From a proof of φ in* $\mathsf{LMSO}(\mathfrak{C})$ *one can extract a term* $\mathtt{t}(x)$ *such that* $\models (\forall x^\sigma)\lfloor\delta(\mathtt{t}(x),x)\rfloor$.

4.3 Completeness of $\mathsf{LMSO}(\mathfrak{C})$

The completeness of $\mathsf{LMSO}(\mathfrak{C})$ follows from a couple of important facts. First, $\mathsf{LMSO}(\mathfrak{C})$ proves the elimination of linear double negation, using (via Theorem 3) the same trick as in [26].

Lemma 1. *For all* LMSO*-formula φ, we have* $(\varphi \multimap \bot) \multimap \bot \vdash_{\mathsf{LMSO}(\mathfrak{C})} \varphi$.

Combining Lemma 1 with (LAC) gives classical linear choice.

Corollary 3. $(\forall f)(\exists x)\varphi(x,(f)x) \vdash_{\mathsf{LMSO}(\mathfrak{C})} (\exists x)(\forall y)\varphi(x,y)$.

The key to the completeness of $\mathsf{LMSO}(\mathfrak{C})$ is the following quantifier inversion.

Lemma 2. $(\forall x^\sigma)\varphi(\mathtt{t}^\tau(x),x) \vdash_{\mathsf{LMSO}(\mathfrak{C})} (\exists u^\tau)(\forall x^\sigma)\varphi(u,x)$, *where* $\mathtt{t}(x)$ *is eager.*

Lemma 2 follows (via Corollary 3) from the fixpoints on eager machines (Proposition 3). Fix an eager $\mathtt{t}^\tau(x^\sigma)$. Taking the fixpoint of $[\![(f)\mathtt{t}(x)]\!] : [\![\sigma]\!] \times [\![(\sigma)\tau]\!] \to_{\mathrm{EM}} [\![\sigma]\!]^{[\![(\sigma)\tau]\!]}$ gives a term $\mathtt{v}^\sigma(f^{(\sigma)\tau})$ such that $\mathtt{v}(f) \doteq @(f,\mathtt{t}(\mathtt{v}(f)))$. Then conclude with

$$
\begin{array}{rll}
(\forall x^\sigma)\varphi(\mathtt{t}(x),x) & \vdash_{\mathsf{LMSO}} & \varphi\big(\mathtt{t}(\mathtt{v}(f))\,,\,\mathtt{v}(f)\big) \\
& \vdash_{\mathsf{LMSO}} & \varphi\big(\mathtt{t}(\mathtt{v}(f))\,,\,@(f,\mathtt{t}(\mathtt{v}(f)))\big) \\
& \vdash_{\mathsf{LMSO}} & (\exists u^\tau)\varphi\big(u,(f)u\big) \\
& \vdash_{\mathsf{LMSO}} & (\forall f^{(\sigma)\tau})(\exists u^\tau)\varphi\big(u,(f)u\big) \\
& \vdash_{\mathsf{LMSO}(\mathfrak{C})} & (\exists u^\tau)(\forall x^\sigma)\varphi(u,x)
\end{array}
$$

Completeness of $\mathsf{LMSO}(\mathfrak{C})$ then follows via $(-)^D$, Proposition 5, completeness of $\mathsf{MSO}(\mathbf{M})$ and Büchi-Landweber Theorem 1. The idea is to lift a f.s. winning P-strat. in $\mathcal{G}(\lfloor\varphi_D(u,x)\rfloor)(u,x)$ to a realizer of $\varphi^D = (\exists u)(\forall x)\varphi_D(u,x)$ in $\mathsf{LMSO}(\mathfrak{C})$.

Theorem 6 (Completeness of $\mathsf{LMSO}(\mathfrak{C})$). *For each closed formula φ, either* $\vdash_{\mathsf{LMSO}(\mathfrak{C})} \varphi$ *or* $\vdash_{\mathsf{LMSO}(\mathfrak{C})} \varphi \multimap \bot$.

5 Conclusion

We provided a linear Dialectica-like interpretation of $\mathsf{LMSO}(\mathfrak{C})$, a linear variant of MSO on ω-words based on [26]. Our interpretation is correct and complete w.r.t. Church's synthesis, in the sense that it proves exactly the realizable $\forall\exists(-)^L$-statements. We thus obtain a syntactic extraction procedure with correctness proof internalized in $\mathsf{LMSO}(\mathfrak{C})$. The system $\mathsf{LMSO}(\mathfrak{C})$ is moreover complete in the sense that for every closed formula φ, it proves either φ or its linear negation. While completeness for a linear logic necessarily collapse some linear structure, the corresponding axioms (DEXP) and (PEXP) do respect the structural constraints allowing for realizer extraction from proofs. The completeness of $\mathsf{LMSO}(\mathfrak{C})$ contrasts with that of the classical system $\mathsf{MSO}(\mathbf{M})$, since the latter has provable unrealizable $\forall\exists$-statements. In particular, proof search in $\mathsf{LMSO}(\mathfrak{C})$ for $\forall\exists(-)^L$-formulae and their negation is correct and complete w.r.t. Church's synthesis. The design of the Dialectica interpretation also clarified the linear structure of LMSO, as it allowed us to decompose it starting from a system based on usual full intuitionistic linear logic (see e.g. [3] for recent references on the subject).

An outcome of witness extraction for $\mathsf{LMSO}(\mathfrak{C})$ is the realization of a simple version of the fan rule (in the usual sense of e.g. [16]). We plan to investigate monotone variants of Dialectica for our setting. Thanks to the compactness of Σ^ω, we expect this to allow extraction of uniform bounds, possibly with translations to stronger constructive logics than LMSO.

References

1. Avigad, J., Feferman, S.: Gödel's functional ("Dialectica") interpretation. In: Buss, S. (ed.) Handbook Proof Theory. Studies in Logic and the Foundations of Mathematics, vol. 137, pp. 337–405. Elsevier, Amsterdam (1998)
2. Baier, C., Katoen, J.P.: Principles of Model Checking. MIT Press, New York (2008)
3. Bellin, G., Heijltjes, W.: Proof nets for bi-intuitionistic linear logic. In: Kirchner, H. (ed.) FSCD. LIPIcs, vol. 108, pp. 10:1–10:18. Schloss Dagstuhl-Leibniz-Zentrum fuer Informatik, Dagstuhl, Germany (2018)
4. Birkedal, L., Møgelberg, R.E., Schwinghammer, J., Støvring, K.: First steps in synthetic guarded domain theory: step-indexing in the topos of trees. Logical Methods Comput. Sci. **8**(4), 1–45 (2012)
5. Bloem, R., Jobstmann, B., Piterman, N., Pnueli, A., Sa'ar, Y.: Synthesis of reactive (1) designs. J. Comput. Syst. Sci. **78**(3), 911–938 (2012)
6. Büchi, J.R.: On a decision method in restricted second-order arithmetic. In: Nagel, E., Suppes, P., Tarski, A. (eds.) Logic, Methodology and Philosophy of Science (Proc. 1960 Intern. Congr.), pp. 1–11. Stanford University Press, Stanford (1962)
7. Büchi, J.R., Landweber, L.H.: Solving sequential conditions by finite-state strategies. Transation Am. Math. Soc. **138**, 367–378 (1969)
8. Church, A.: Applications of recursive arithmetic to the problem of circuit synthesis. In: Summaries of the SISL. vol. 1, pp. 3–50. Cornell University, Ithaca (1957)
9. Danos, V., Joinet, J.B., Schellinx, H.: A new deconstructive logic: linear logic. J. Symb. Log. **62**(3), 755–807 (1997)

10. Emerson, E.A., Jutla, C.S.: Tree automata, mu-calculus and determinacy (extended abstract). In: FOCS. pp. 368–377. IEEE Computer Society (1991)
11. Filiot, E., Jin, N., Raskin, J.F.: Antichains and compositional algorithms for LTL synthesis. Form. Methods Syst. Des. **39**(3), 261–296 (2011)
12. Finkbeiner, B.: Synthesis of reactive systems. In: Esparza, J., Grumberg, O., Sickert, S. (eds.) Dependable Software Systems Engineering, NATO Science for Peace and Security Series, D: Information and Communication Security, vol. 45, pp. 72–98. IOS Press, Amsterdam (2016)
13. Girard, J.Y.: Linear logic. Theor. Comput. Sci. **50**, 1–102 (1987)
14. Hyland, J.M.E.: Proof theory in the abstract. Ann. Pure Appl. Logic **114**(1–3), 43–78 (2002)
15. Hyland, M., de Paiva, V.C.V.: Full intuitionistic linear logic (extended abstract). Ann. Pure Appl. Logic **64**(3), 273–291 (1993)
16. Kohlenbach, U.: Applied Proof Theory: Proof Interpretations and their Use in Mathematics. Springer Monographs in Mathematics. Springer, Heidelberg (2008). https://doi.org/10.1007/978-3-540-77533-1
17. Laurent, O., Regnier, L.: About translations of classical logic into polarized linear logic. In: Proceedings of LICS 2003, pp. 11–20. IEEE Computer Society Press (2003)
18. LLWiki: LLWiki (2008). http://llwiki.ens-lyon.fr/mediawiki/
19. McNaughton, R.: Testing and generating infinite sequences by a finite automaton. Inf. Control **9**(5), 521–530 (1966)
20. Muller, D.E., Schupp, P.E.: Simulating alternating tree automata by nondeterministic automata: new results and new proofs of theorems of Rabin, McNaughton and Safra. Theor. Comput. Sci. **141**(1&2), 69–107 (1995)
21. de Paiva, V.C.V.: The DIalectica categories. In: Proceedings of Categories in Computer Science and Logic, Boulder, CO, Contemporary Mathematics, vol. 92. American Mathematical Society (1987)
22. de Paiva, V.C.V.: A DIalectica-like model of linear logic. In: Pitt, D.H., Rydeheard, D.E., Dybjer, P., Pitts, A.M., Poigné, A. (eds.) Category Theory and Computer Science. LNCS, vol. 389, pp. 341–356. Springer, Heidelberg (1989). https://doi.org/10.1007/BFb0018360
23. de Paiva, V.C.V.: The DIalectica categories. Technical report 213, University of Cambridge Computer Laboratory, January 1991
24. Perrin, D., Pin, J.É.: Infinite Words: Automata, Semigroups, Logic and Games. Pure and Applied Mathematics. Elsevier (2004)
25. Pradic, P., Riba, C.: A Curry-Howard approach to Church's synthesis. In: Proceedings of FSCD 2017. LIPIcs, vol. 84, pp. 30:1–30:16. Schloss Dagstuhl - Leibniz-Zentrum fuer Informatik (2017)
26. Pradic, P., Riba, C.: LMSO: a Curry-Howard approach to Church's synthesis via linear logic. In: Proceedings of LICS 2018. ACM (2018)
27. Shirahata, M.: The DIalectica interpretation of first-order classical affine logic. Theory Appl. Categ. **17**(4), 49–79 (2006)
28. Siefkes, D.: Decidable Theories I: Büchi's Monadic Second Order Successor Arithmetic. LNM, vol. 120. Springer, Heidelberg (1970). https://doi.org/10.1007/BFb0061047
29. Thomas, W.: Automata on infinite objects. In: van Leeuwen, J. (ed.) Handbook of Theoretical Computer Science, vol. B: Formal Models and Semantics, pp. 133–192. Elsevier Science Publishers (1990)

30. Thomas, W.: Languages, automata, and logic. In: Rozenberg, G., Salomaa, A. (eds.) Handbook of Formal Languages, vol. III, pp. 389–455. Springer, Heidelberg (1997). https://doi.org/10.1007/978-3-642-59126-6_7
31. Thomas, W.: Solution of Church's problem: a tutorial. New Perspect. Games Interact. **5**, 23 (2008)
32. Thomas, W.: Facets of synthesis: revisiting Church's problem. In: de Alfaro, L. (ed.) FoSSaCS 2009. LNCS, vol. 5504, pp. 1–14. Springer, Heidelberg (2009). https://doi.org/10.1007/978-3-642-00596-1_1
33. Troelstra, A.: Metamathematical Investigation of Intuitionistic Arithmetic and Analysis. LNM, vol. 344. Springer, Heidelberg (1973). https://doi.org/10.1007/BFb0066739

Permissions

All chapters in this book were first published by Springer; hereby published with permission under the Creative Commons Attribution License or equivalent. Every chapter published in this book has been scrutinized by our experts. Their significance has been extensively debated. The topics covered herein carry significant findings which will fuel the growth of the discipline. They may even be implemented as practical applications or may be referred to as a beginning point for another development.

The contributors of this book come from diverse backgrounds, making this book a truly international effort. This book will bring forth new frontiers with its revolutionizing research information and detailed analysis of the nascent developments around the world.

We would like to thank all the contributing authors for lending their expertise to make the book truly unique. They have played a crucial role in the development of this book. Without their invaluable contributions this book wouldn't have been possible. They have made vital efforts to compile up to date information on the varied aspects of this subject to make this book a valuable addition to the collection of many professionals and students.

This book was conceptualized with the vision of imparting up-to-date information and advanced data in this field. To ensure the same, a matchless editorial board was set up. Every individual on the board went through rigorous rounds of assessment to prove their worth. After which they invested a large part of their time researching and compiling the most relevant data for our readers.

The editorial board has been involved in producing this book since its inception. They have spent rigorous hours researching and exploring the diverse topics which have resulted in the successful publishing of this book. They have passed on their knowledge of decades through this book. To expedite this challenging task, the publisher supported the team at every step. A small team of assistant editors was also appointed to further simplify the editing procedure and attain best results for the readers.

Apart from the editorial board, the designing team has also invested a significant amount of their time in understanding the subject and creating the most relevant covers. They scrutinized every image to scout for the most suitable representation of the subject and create an appropriate cover for the book.

The publishing team has been an ardent support to the editorial, designing and production team. Their endless efforts to recruit the best for this project, has resulted in the accomplishment of this book. They are a veteran in the field of academics and their pool of knowledge is as vast as their experience in printing. Their expertise and guidance has proved useful at every step. Their uncompromising quality standards have made this book an exceptional effort. Their encouragement from time to time has been an inspiration for everyone.

The publisher and the editorial board hope that this book will prove to be a valuable piece of knowledge for researchers, students, practitioners and scholars across the globe.

List of Contributors

Benedikt Bollig, Patricia Bouyer and Fabian Reiter
LSV, CNRS, ENS Paris-Saclay, Université Paris-Saclay, Cachan, France

Simon Castellan and Nobuko Yoshida
Imperial College London, London, UK

Michaël Cadilhac
University of Oxford, Oxford, UK

Guillermo A. Pérez
University of Antwerp, Antwerp, Belgium

Marie van den Bogaard
Université libre de Bruxelles, Brussels, Belgium

Sergueï Lenglet
Université de Lorraine, Nancy, France

Simone Barlocco and Clemens Kupke
University of Strathclyde, Glasgow, UK

Georg Zetzsche
Max Planck Institute for Software Systems (MPI-SWS), Kaiserslautern, Germany

Denis Kuperberg and Damien Pous
Univ Lyon, EnsL, UCBL, CNRS, LIP, 69342 Lyon Cedex 07, France

Pierre Pradic and Amina Doumane
Univ Lyon, EnsL, UCBL, CNRS, LIP, 69342 Lyon Cedex 07, France
Warsaw University, MIMUW, Warsaw, Poland

Luc Dartois
LACL-Université Paris-Est Créteil, Créteil, France

Emmanuel Filiot
Université Libre de Bruxelles, Brussels, Belgium

Jean-Marc Talbot
LIM-Aix-Marseille Université, Marseille, France

Jérémy Dubut
National Institute of Informatics, Tokyo, Japan
Japanese-French Laboratory for Informatics, Tokyo, Japan

Thomas Colcombet
CNRS, IRIF, Université Paris-Diderot, Paris, France

Nathanaël Fijalkow
CNRS, LaBRI, Université de Bordeaux, Bordeaux, France

Utkarsh Gupta, Preey Shah and S. Akshay
Department of CSE, IIT Bombay, Mumbai, India

Piotr Hofman
University of Warsaw, Warsaw, Poland

Amir M. Ben-Amram
School of Computer Science, Tel-Aviv Academic College, Tel Aviv, Israel

Geoff W. Hamilton
School of Computing, Dublin City University, Dublin 9, Ireland

Mario Alvarez-Picallo and C.-H. Luke Ong
University of Oxford, Oxford, UK

Pierre Pradic
ENS de Lyon, Université de Lyon, LIP, UMR 5668 CNRS ENS Lyon UCBL Inria, Lyon, France
Faculty of Mathematics, Informatics and Mechanics, University of Warsaw, Warsaw, Poland

Colin Riba
ENS de Lyon, Université de Lyon, LIP, UMR 5668 CNRS ENS Lyon UCBL Inria, Lyon, France

Index